# GET INTO MEDICAL SCHOOL

# 700 BMAT PRACTICE QUESTIONS

**Comprehensive tips, techniques & explanations**

**With contributions from official BMAT examiners and past BMAT candidates**

Lydia Campbell & Olivier Picard

Published by ISC Medical
97 Judd Street, London WC1H 9JG
Tel: 0845 226 9487

Second Edition (Reprinted 2018): ISBN: 978-1-905812-19-6
A catalogue record for this book is available from the British Library.

The information within this text is intended as a revision aid for the purpose of the BMAT only. Any information contained within the texts used in the essay section should not be regarded as views held by the authors of this book, but simply as text used in a question-setting context with the view of preparing students for a competitive test.

Printed in the United Kingdom by:
Optichrome, Maybury Road, Woking, GU21 5HX

# CONTENTS TABLE

# CONTRIBUTORS

We would like to thank profusely the many official BMAT examiners who have contributed directly and indirectly to the second edition of this book. Their wisdom and insight into the BMAT and its marking have been invaluable in helping us create one of the most comprehensive and insightful books available.

We would also like to thank all the past BMAT candidates whose feedback has helped us ensure that the questions reflect the level of the exam accurately and cover as much of the syllabus as possible.

# i  Purpose & structure of the BMAT

The BMAT is used by the following institutions:

**UK**
- University of Cambridge
- University of Oxford
- Imperial College London
- University College London
- Keele University
- Lancaster University
- Brighton & Sussex Medical School
- University of Leeds

**Netherlands**
- University of Twente
- Wageningen University
- Leiden University Medical Centre
- Eindhoven University of Technology

**Thailand**
- Mahidol University
- Thammasat University
- Srinakharinwirot University
- Khon Kaen University
- Chulalongkorn University

**Spain**
- Universidad de Navarra
- CEU Cardenal Herrera University

**Others**
- University of Malaya (Malaysia)
- University of Pécs (Hungary)
- Universities of Rjieka & Zagreb (Croatia)
- Lee Kong Chian School of Medicine (Singapore)

The BMAT is a two-hour exam and comprises three sections:

**1: Aptitude and Skills (60 minutes: 35 questions)**
Tests your problem-solving abilities (13 questions in 30 minutes), your ability to understand arguments (10 questions in 15 minutes) and your ability to analyse data, infer and deduce (12 questions in 15 minutes).

**2: Scientific Knowledge & Applications (30 minutes: 27 questions)**
Tests your knowledge and understanding of biology, physics, chemistry and mathematics, and ability to apply key principles to problems.

**3: Writing Task/Essay (30 minutes)**
Tests your ability to understand a question, argue and counter-argue and communicate your ideas clearly and effectively.

**How the BMAT is scored**

## Sections 1 and 2

For Section 1 and Section 2, the number of correct answers is added up and converted into a score on a scale from 1 to 9. The scale is designed in such a way that a typical candidate will score 5. As such, it changes slightly every year depending on the cohort's results.

As a rule of thumb, you can use the following conversion tables to get an approximate score:

| SECTION 1 | |
|---|---|
| **Correct answers (out of 35)** | **Score** |
| 3 or less | 1 |
| 6 | 2 |
| 8 | 3 |
| 12 | 4 |
| 17 | 5 |
| 21 | 6 |
| 25 | 7 |
| 29 | 8 |
| 31 or more | 9 |

| SECTION 2 | |
|---|---|
| **Correct answers (out of 27)** | **Score** |
| 0 or 1 | 1 |
| 3 | 2 |
| 5 | 3 |
| 8 | 4 |
| 11 | 5 |
| 14 | 6 |
| 18 | 7 |
| 21 | 8 |
| 23 or more | 9 |

The score for intermediate numbers of correct answers can be interpolated between each round score. Interestingly you will notice that, to score the maximum, you only need to answer 31 questions out of 35 for Section 1 and 23 questions out of 27 for Section 2.

Most candidates fit within the score range 4–7 for Section 1 and 4–6.5 for Section 2. A score greater than 7 would place you amongst the top candidates.

# Section 3

Section 3 is marked on a scale of 1 to 5 for the quality of the essay. Approximately 40% of candidates score 3.5 or more. Only 5% of candidates score 4.5 or 5.

An additional mark is also allocated for the quality of the English used in the essay. The Quality of English score for Section 3 is marked using a scale from A (good use of English) to E (rather weak English). There is also a special mark "X" for those who fall short of grade E. Approximately 60% of candidates achieve an A rating (the best) whilst 30% achieve a B rating. When universities want to incorporate the Quality of English score into the calculation of an overall mark, they tend to use the conversion scale: A=5, B=4, C=3, D=2, E=1 and X=0.

# How the BMAT score is used

All scores are communicated to the relevant institutions individually for each section. Each institution then allocates its own weighting to each of the sections in order to determine an overall score. For example, currently:

- Cambridge University does not have a university-wide policy and each college's Director of Studies sets his/her own criteria. Section 3 ranges from being highly important to not important, depending on which college you apply to, with some Directors of Studies allocating it a weighting as high as 50% with the balance being made up of A Level marks, interview performance and GCSE performance. Weightings are revisited every year to take account of the performance of the previous cohort. The original BMAT was tested on Cambridge medical students and showed that there was a correlation between BMAT scores and the Tripos exam results.

- Oxford University, in contrast, uses the BMAT score centrally and allocates weightings of 40% to Section 1, 40% to Section 2 and 20% to Section 3 (one-third of which is the Quality of English mark). In calculating the Section 3 score, Oxford uses double weighting for the "Quality of Content" score and single weighting for the "Quality of English" score. The total BMAT score is then combined with GCSE results using a

50:50 ratio. The overall mark is then used to decide who is invited for an interview.

- Imperial College requires a score of at least 50% in each of the BMAT sections (including the Quality of English in Section 3) in order to be invited to interview, though the cut-off mark can be higher depending on the rest of the cohort's results. Imperial College rejects 75% of applications based on the BMAT mark cut-offs. Successful candidates are then split into bands depending on their performance; the higher a candidate's mark is, the more likely and quickly he/she will be called for an interview.

- UCL looks at each section individually. The BMAT marks are incorporated into an overall weighting (including academics, personal statement and reference) to rank candidates for interviews. Applicants with higher BMAT scores tend to be interviewed first. At interview, the candidates' BMAT essays are often discussed.

- Brighton and Sussex Medical School scores the BMAT out of 28 (9 marks for Section 1, 9 for Section 2 and 5 marks for each element of Section 3). Almost all candidates invited for an interview have an overall score greater than 15. The average score of those who are invited for an interview is 17 (equivalent to scores of 4, 4 and 4A). BSMS rejects candidates if they score less than 3 in Sections 1 or 2, or have a Quality of English score of D or E in Section 3.

- The University of Leeds uses the total BMAT marks (10% weighting) alongside the personal statement (28%), predicted A2 grades (14%) and GCSE & AS level results (48%) to rank applicants. The top 30% of applicants are then invited to an interview. The total BMAT score is calculated as Section 1 + Section 2 + 50% of Section 3.

- Lancaster Medical School calculates the total BMAT score by combining the scores for Sections 1, 2 and 3. Section 1 and 2 is scored out of 9; and Section 3 is scored out of 5 (for quality of content). They do not use the quality of English score (A-E).

- Lee Kong Chian School of Medicine (Singapore) has a BMAT cut-off that is linked to the performance of the cohort. In general candidates who succeeded in gaining entry have performed above average (the bottom 10th percentile of successful entrants in 2015 was 4.9 for Section 1, 5.4 for Section 2 and 3.5 for Section 3).

# **iii** General tips & advice

## 1. Read the questions properly
Reading a question too quickly may lead you to provide an incorrect answer. The main issues you should watch out for are:

- The number of answers requested. Some questions may ask for two answers.

- The unit in which the answer has to be expressed. For example, is the volume requested in litres or pints?

- The variable that you are expected to calculate. In some exercises there may be several unknown variables. Make sure you understand what you are expected to calculate. For example, does the question ask for the age of the third child or the sum of all three children's ages?

## 2. Calculate intelligently
No calculator is allowed at the BMAT. You will need to calculate everything mentally or on paper. If a calculation looks as if it may take some time, look at the options offered to you and determine if you can get to the answer through logic (e.g. looking at the orders of magnitude) or using approximations.

## 3. Choose the most efficient approach
In some cases, it is quicker to calculate the answer and see which option it corresponds to. In other cases, it is best to try each of the options out and determine which one is the most appropriate. Through practice, you should gain a good understanding of which approach best suits which type of exercise.

## 4. Skip the difficult questions and come back to them later
Time is of the essence. Most candidates score under 7 in Sections 1 and 2, meaning that they only manage to answer 70–80% of questions correctly. If a question is difficult, skip it and attempt it later. It would be a shame to fail to answer easier questions that feature at the back of

the questions booklet because you spent a disproportionate amount of time on a hard question.

5. **Answer all questions and guess intelligently**
   The exam is not negatively marked (i.e. you are not penalised for giving incorrect answers). Therefore if you are stumped by a question, or are running out of time, you might as well guess the answer from the options available. You can optimise your chances of guessing correctly by using the following tips:

   • Eliminate first the options that you know to be incorrect.

   • Options that contain extreme qualifiers such as "all", "always" and "never" are more likely to be false than true.

   • An analysis of all available official specimen/sample questions shows that over 70–80% of correct Sections 1 and 2 answers are options B, C or D (out of 5 possible options, one would normally expect 60% to be the statistical average for options B, C and D if the answers were allocated randomly across the options). If all else fails, choose one of those options.

   • Look at the length of each option. Our analysis shows that, if an answer option is much longer or much shorter than the other options, it is more likely to be correct.

   • Look for repeated words or expressions. When writing questions, examiners tend to use similar phrases or keywords in their correct option as in the question stem.

6. **Write your answers legibly**
   Sections 1 and 2 are marked by a computer. Any answer that is not legible may be missed. For Section 3, legibility is not part of the marking scale; however, it goes without saying that if the examiner can't read your handwriting then parts of your arguments may be ignored during the marking process.

# Section 1

# Aptitude and Skills

# 376
## Practice Questions & Answers

# 1A Aptitude and Skills Introduction & Advice

## Format of Section 1 of the BMAT

Section 1 of the BMAT "Aptitude and Skills" consists of 35 questions, which you must answer within 60 minutes, giving you just under 2 minutes per question. The questions can be in a multiple-choice format (you are typically given four to six options to choose from) or in a short answer format, meaning that you must find the answer without being able to choose from a given list of options and enter it manually onto the answer sheet.

You will be asked three types of question:

### Problem solving questions
These questions test your ability to analyse, interpret and use data to solve specific problems. The information may be given to you in a text form or in the form of graphs and charts. The examiners will be testing:

- Whether you can distinguish between relevant and unnecessary information to solve a problem.
- Whether you can spot patterns and relationships between different sets of data.
- Whether you can combine data from different sources to identify a solution to a given problem.

### Data analysis and inference questions
This section of the paper tests your ability to analyse and interpret larger amounts of information. That information can be given in a text, graphical, tabular or other format. Each set of data is followed by up to six questions, which must be answered using the information provided.

### Understanding arguments questions
These questions test your ability to analyse, evaluate and interpret arguments. Most consist of a short piece of text (usually a few lines). You are

then given a list of statements from which you must choose the one that answers the question.

The question may be phrased as "What is the most logical conclusion from the text?" or "Which statement sets out the assumption needed to draw the conclusion presented on the last line?" etc.

Even though the BMAT examiners have a rough structure of the exam ("officially" dedicating 28% of the Section 1 exam to Understanding Arguments questions), in recent years the role of Understanding Arguments questions has crept up to occupy up to 40% of the total marks of the Section 1 paper itself since the 2008 syllabus update. We recommend that candidates spend a bit of time on these questions.

# Tips for Problem Solving questions and Data Analysis and Inference questions

These two sub-sections do not require particular knowledge other than basic mathematics and logic. Your biggest enemy, however, will be time and you therefore need to make sure that you work as efficiently as possible.

- Make sure that you practise percentages, speed calculations and time differences well as these are questions where you can easily waste time if you don't do the maths the right way round.

- Look carefully at the question before you embark on complex calculations. If a question looks like it will involve a lot of work, there may be a simpler approach that you can adopt, using logic.

- In some cases, it is easier to see which of the options would work instead of working out the answer using a formula.

- Don't assume that you can solve all problems in your head. Some will be easier to solve if you draw a diagram or write equations. If you can't find the answer straight away, start writing down what you are told mathematically.

# Tips for Understanding Arguments questions

This section has become prominent in Section 1 over the years and is probably one that candidates struggle with the most.

The purpose of this section is to test your ability to reason effectively. Most questions contain a piece of text, followed by a question and five possible answers. The piece of text is most often an argument presented from the author's perspective and you are then asked to choose a statement amongst the given options that either strengthens or weakens the argument made, or identify the flaw in the argument. The question may also ask you whether the text is based on some assumptions made by the author.

So for example:

**Text**
For the past four days, Jane has arrived late at work. This morning, as she was driving to work, she had a puncture in one of her tyres. Therefore she will be late for work today again.

You can see that the argument made above is less than perfect, in that the author is making a number of assumptions. For example, here the author is assuming that Jane lives so far away from work that she has no choice but to drive to her office. The author is also assuming that, because Jane has a flat tyre, she will opt for taking time off work to get it repaired instead of just dumping the car and sorting the problem out later. It is such imperfections in the logic (i.e. the conclusion reached by the author is not a guarantee) that lead to the BMAT questions. These are called inductive arguments.

**Strengthen / Weaken**

Based on this piece of text, the question may ask you to decide whether the following statements strengthen or weaken the argument presented.

*Statement: Jane has in fact arrived late for work not just for 4 days, but for the past 40 days.*

This still would not guarantee the conclusion that Jane will be late for work today, but it would make it more plausible, and therefore it strengthens the argument (whilst still not proving it).

*Statement: Jane has in fact had 4 flat tyres and her car is blocking the road.*

Again, it would not guarantee the conclusion that Jane will be late for work today because she might be able to sort the problem out before work starts, but it would make it more plausible and therefore it strengthens the argument (whilst still not proving it).

*Statement: Jane lives just 500 metres from work.*

This statement tells us that Jane may be able to walk to work and so it weakens the argument that she will be late for work.

IMPORTANT:
- It is crucial that you take the information given to you as true. For example, you cannot question the fact that Jane had a flat tyre (as the text says). So when you analyse the arguments, you can only consider how well the conclusion followed from the premise presented to you even if they don't make sense to you.

- Weakening the argument does not mean that it disproves it, but only that it makes the conclusion less likely to be true. Similarly, strengthening the argument does not mean that it proves it, but only that it makes the conclusion more likely to be true.

- The most common way to weaken an argument is to undermine an unstated assumption. In the example above we assumed that Jane could not get to work at all, but we are then told that she lives a short distance away.

**Assumptions**
Some questions ask you to determine which assumptions the author has made to reach the conclusion in question. For example, for the argument presented in the text above to make sense, we need to assume the following:

- That Jane's history of lateness will be repeated today.
- That there is not enough time to change a tyre before work starts.
- That Jane has no other means of transport by which to arrive at work on time.

15

When you are asked to determine which of five statements is an assumption made by the author, you must make sure that the assumption is absolutely necessary to the reach the conclusion set out in the text. If the option that you have selected would help but is not necessary, then it cannot be the correct answer. In other words, the assumption must be absolutely necessary to the argument to be valid.

Example:

**Text**
Ryan has been playing table tennis two hours a day for the past ten years. Therefore he will win the championship next month.

There are several assumptions made here:
- Ryan will live until the championship takes place.
- The championship will actually take place.
- Ryan is eligible to apply to play at the championship.
- Ryan will not fall ill during the championship.
- And so on.

All those are assumptions that it is necessary to make in order to conclude that he will win the championship. You can see that by using the "Negating" method, i.e. if you assume that a particular statement is false then you can conclude the argument is incorrect. In this case, if we assume that Ryan will die before the championship takes place then he won't be able to win it. If we assume that Ryan is not eligible to play, then he won't win it, etc.

The BMAT might, however, throw at you a number of statements that look like assumptions but are not. For example, consider the following:

*Statement: Ryan will wear his lucky bracelet during the championship.*

The wearing of the lucky bracelet might make him more confident and might influence the way he plays, thereby contributing to his success. But it is not a necessary thing that needs to happen in order for him to win (for example, he could win because all the others fall ill even if he is not wearing his lucky bracelet).

This is often where candidates get it wrong so you need to be vigilant.

# 1B Aptitude and Skills
# Problem Solving – 151 Questions

## Answers from page 225

**Q1.1**   The following tower is made up of cubes that are all identical. It is resting on a solid floor. Assuming no tiles can be suspended, how many sides of cubes are not in contact with any surface (i.e. are visible if you walk around the structure)?

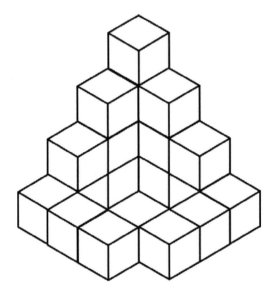

|   |   |
|---|---|
| **a.** | 47 |
| **b.** | 51 |
| **c.** | 53 |
| **d.** | 57 |
| **e.** | 59 |

**Q1.2**   If you cut shape A in two sections in a certain way, you can use the two new shapes created by the cut to make up all the other shapes except one. Which one?

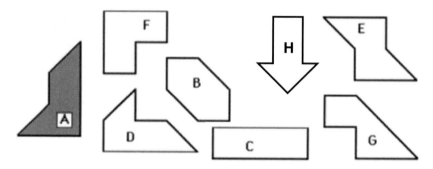

**Q1.3**   This wheel contains 19 circles, which you have decided to number from 1 through to 19, so that the numbers in every 3 circles on a straight line total 30. Which number should appear in the central circle?

    **a.**  8
    **b.**  10
    **c.**  11
    **d.**  12
    **e.**  13

**Q1.4**   Take every letter of the alphabet and number it according to its rank in the alphabet (A = 1, B = 2 ... Z = 26). For every string of letters, we calculate the 'product value' of that string by multiplying the values of all the letters in that string. So, for example, the product value of the string 'BDF' is 2 x 4 x 6 = 48. How many strings have a product value of 60 and do not contain the letter A?

    **a.**  23
    **b.**  27
    **c.**  32
    **d.**  37
    **e.**  41

**Q1.5**   A tap can fill an empty bathtub with water in 30 minutes, and the bathtub's sinkhole can empty a full tub in 40 minutes. The water flows at constant rates through both pipes regardless of the water level in the tub.

If both the tap and the sinkhole were left open, what fraction of the tub would be filled exactly 1 hour after water began to flow into the empty tub?

      a.   1/12
      b.   1/6
      c.   1/3
      d.   1/4
      e.   1/2

**Q1.6**   In normal circumstances, six similar ice cream making machines running simultaneously at a constant rate can complete a certain order in 8 hours. However, today, one of the machines is broken.

If only five of these machines run at that rate, how many more minutes will be required to complete the same order?

      a.   38
      b.   72
      c.   96
      d.   240
      e.   480

**Q1.7**   How many zeros are there at the end of the number 100! ?

      a.   21
      b.   22
      c.   23
      d.   24
      e.   25

**Q1.8** During a recent police investigation, a policeman was interviewing five local thieves to try to identify who stole an item from a local shop. Each thief always tells one lie and one truth. Below is a summary of their statements:

**Arnold:**
it wasn't Edward
it was Brian

**Brian:**
it wasn't Charles
it wasn't Edward

**Charles:**
it was Edward
it wasn't Arnold

**Derek:**
it was Charles
it was Brian

**Edward:**
it was Derek
it wasn't Arnold

Who stole the cake?

    **a.**   Arnold
    **b.**   Brian
    **c.**   Charles
    **d.**   Derek
    **e.**   Edward

**Q1.9** If you divide 68 by a certain number X then the remainder is 4. What is the sum of all the possible values of X?

    **a.**   118
    **b.**   120
    **c.**   124
    **d.**   126
    **e.**   127

**Q1.10** You have at your disposal six 6 x 6 squares. Each square contains opaque sections (represented in grey) and transparent sections (represented in white). You have been asked to select three squares which, when stacked together, form an opaque square. You are allowed to rotate the squares but they can't be turned over.

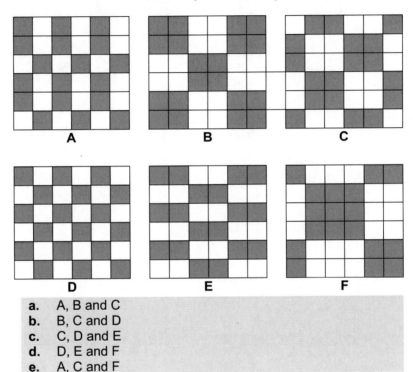

a. A, B and C
b. B, C and D
c. C, D and E
d. D, E and F
e. A, C and F

**Q1.11** A salesman drives from London to Birmingham. The first half of the distance, he drives at a constant speed of 80 mph. The second half he drives at a constant speed of 120 mph. What is his average speed for the total journey?

a. 90 mph
b. 93 mph
c. 96 mph
d. 100 mph
e. 106 mph

**Q1.12** Consider the following six shapes made up of grey building blocks:

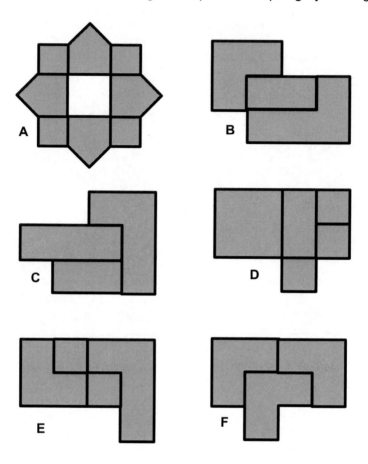

Within each shape except for one, all the blocks can be reassembled to make a square. Which shape is the exception?

a. A
b. B
c. C
d. D
e. E
f. F

**Q1.13** A motorist drives from A to B at a constant speed and then onto another destination. Arriving at point B, he calculates that if he increased his speed by 5 mph he would cover a further 70-mile distance in an hour. How many miles would he cover if he instead drove a further 2 hours at an average speed 10 mph faster than his original speed?

|    |     |
|----|-----|
| a. | 100 |
| b. | 120 |
| c. | 140 |
| d. | 150 |
| e. | 160 |

**Q1.14** Cars A and B started simultaneously from opposite ends of a straight 315-mile road and travelled towards each other without stopping until they passed each other at location X. The average speed of Car B was 15 mph higher than Car A's.

If Car B's average speed is a third higher than that of Car A, how many miles of the road had Car A travelled when the two cars passed each other?

|    |     |
|----|-----|
| a. | 100 |
| b. | 110 |
| c. | 135 |
| d. | 155 |
| e. | 175 |

**Q1.15** On the Medical Student Society committee, the number of females is one fewer than twice the number of males. Also, if one female was replaced by one male committee member then there would be an equal number of males and females on the committee. How many members are there on the committee in total?

|    |   |
|----|---|
| a. | 3 |
| b. | 4 |
| c. | 5 |
| d. | 6 |
| e. | 7 |
| f. | 8 |
| g. | 9 |

23

**Q1.16** Xavier, Ian and Ulrica are all playing a dice game starting with £600 each. At the end of each game, the two losers have to forfeit half their money to the winner.

If Ian wins game 1, Ulrica wins game 2 and Xavier wins game 3, how much money does Ian have at the end?

    **a.**   0
    **b.**   150
    **c.**   300
    **d.**   600
    **e.**   975

**Q1.17** A shop offers a loyalty discount card, which costs £232 per year and gives an 8% discount on all purchases.

How much will a shopper have to buy before his discount covers the cost of the loyalty card?

    **a.**   £232
    **b.**   £2,320
    **c.**   £2,900
    **d.**   £3,132
    **e.**   Cannot be determined

**Q1.18** A 22-carat gold ring is insured for £3,300, and the annual premium rate for the gold ring is £5 per carat.

If the annual premium and insured rates are the same over the years, after how many years would the total of the insurance premiums for those years first exceed the insured value of the gold ring?

    **a.**   20
    **b.**   30
    **c.**   31
    **d.**   32
    **e.**   35

**Q1.19** During the Alaskan crab fishing season, a shipment of 100,000 kg of Alaskan King Crab was purchased for £500,000 in total. On the day the crab shipment arrived, 50,000 kg were sold at a price per kilogram 20% higher than the purchase price per kilogram. The following day the rest was sold at a price per kilogram equal to 10% less than the price per kilogram sold for on the day before. What was the profit on this shipment of crabs?

    **a.**  £20,000
    **b.**  £50,000
    **c.**  £70,000
    **d.**  £72,727
    **e.**  £100,000

**Q1.20** A breakfast that contains 2 cups of Cornflake A and 100 ml of milk provides 400 calories. When the 2 cups of Cornflake A are substituted by 2 cups of Cornflake B, the total number of calories reduces to 300. If 1 cup of Cornflake A provides 1.5 times as many calories as 1 cup of Cornflake B, how many calories does each cup of Cornflake B contain?

    **a.**  100
    **b.**  200
    **c.**  300
    **d.**  400
    **e.**  1250

**Q1.21** Between 1 January 2005 and 1 January 2010, the number of employees of a company decreased by 300 every year.

If the number of employees on 1 January 2010 was 70% of the number on 1 January 2005, how many employees did the company have on 1 January 2010?

    **a.**  1500
    **b.**  2800
    **c.**  3500
    **d.**  4000
    **e.**  5000

**Q1.22** Three friends discuss their shopping experiences, comparing prices. All went shopping at the same supermarket on the same day. Maria bought 1 pint of milk, 1 loaf of bread and 2 tomatoes for a total of £3.50. Jenny bought 1 pint of milk and 3 tomatoes for a total of £3.00. Roberta bought a loaf of bread and 1 tomato for a total of £1.50.

How much does a loaf of bread cost?

    **a.** £0.5
    **b.** £0.75
    **c.** £1
    **d.** £1.25
    **e.** £1.5

**Q1.23** Richard had a GP appointment on a particular day. Exactly 60 hours before the appointment, it was a Monday. The appointment was between 1:00pm and 9:00pm. On what day of the week was the appointment?

    **a.** Monday
    **b.** Tuesday
    **c.** Wednesday
    **d.** Thursday
    **e.** Cannot be determined

**Q1.24** When driving to work, Richard always sets off at the same time to start work at 9am. One day, he drove from home to work at a speed averaging 40 miles per hour, and arrived 12 minutes late. The next day he left home at the same time, took the same route, averaging 48 miles per hour, and was 7 minutes late. What distance does he drive from home to work?

    **a.** 18.0 miles
    **b.** 20.0 miles
    **c.** 30.0 miles
    **d.** 37.5 miles
    **e.** 40.0 miles

**Q1.25** During a race on a straight line, Greyhound A starts running straight away at a speed of 20 m/s. Greyhound B is startled by the gunshot and only starts running after 10 seconds, but at a speed of 25 m/s.

Assuming both dogs run on the same racing line, at what distance from the starting line will Greyhound B catch up with Greyhound A?

    **a.**   250 m
    **b.**   375 m
    **c.**   500 m
    **d.**   750 m
    **e.**   1 km

**Q1.26** A player throws a pair of normal dice five times in a row. Every time, he records the product of the two numbers showing on each die (e.g. if one die has 4 and the other 5, he will record 20).

The score for the second roll is five more than the score for the first; the score for the third roll is six less than that of the second; the score for the fourth roll is eleven more than that of the third; and the score for the fifth roll is eight less than that of the fourth.

In what range is the score of the first throw contained?

    **a.**   0–7
    **b.**   8–15
    **c.**   16–23
    **d.**   24–30
    **e.**   31–36

**Q1.27** A digital 24-hour alarm clock currently shows the time 08:00. If the clock runs accurately for the next 11,995 hours, what hour will it indicate at the end of that time?

    **a.** 01:00
    **b.** 02:00
    **c.** 03:00
    **d.** 05:00
    **e.** 13:00
    **f.** 20:00

**Q1.28** An alarm clock currently shows the time 06:27. What time was it 2937 minutes earlier?

    **a.**   06:24
    **b.**   06:22
    **c.**   05:30
    **d.**   05:00
    **e.**   05:03

**Q1.29** Tim has an alarm clock, which is running fast. Every day, the alarm clock moves 1 minute faster than it should, but Tim never resets his alarm clock to the correct time.

His wife, Jane, has an alarm clock that runs slow and loses 2 minutes per day. She never resets her alarm clock either. Both alarm clocks display the time using a 12-hour display format and neither alarm clock has an am/pm indicator, meaning that 7pm will look exactly the same as 7am.

If both clocks currently show the same time, how many days will it be before they both show the same time again?

    **a.**   20 days
    **b.**   60 days
    **c.**   120 days
    **d.**   240 days
    **e.**   480 days

**Q1.30** An automated floor cleaner can clean an area of 4 metres by 25 metres in 24 minutes. How long would it take the automated floor cleaner to clean an area of 12 metres by 62.5 metres if it is working at the same constant rate?

    **a.**   1 hour
    **b.**   1.25 hours
    **c.**   2.5 hours
    **d.**   3 hours
    **e.**   7.5 hours

**Q1.31** At the train station, train A leaves the station every 120 minutes, train B leaves the station every 140 minutes and train C leaves the station every 150 minutes.

If, during a given day, the 3 trains leave at the exact same instant, how many minutes will pass before the 3 trains next leave the station simultaneously? (Assume the station runs constantly.)

    **a.** 525
    **b.** 1,050
    **c.** 2,100
    **d.** 3,700
    **e.** 4,200

**Q1.32** Three cars parked next to one another have left their warning lights on. Car A's lights blink every 0.8 seconds, car B's lights blink every 1.0 second, and car C's lights blink every 1.4 seconds. If, at a given time-point, the 3 sets of car lights blink at the exact same time, how many seconds will elapse before the 3 lights next blink simultaneously?

    **a.** 7
    **b.** 10
    **c.** 14
    **d.** 21
    **e.** 28

**Q1.33** A church has 3 bells. Bell A rings once every 24 minutes, bell B once every 30 minutes, and bell C once every 38 minutes. The 3 bells were last heard ringing together 1.5 hours ago. In how many hours will they next ring together?

    **a.** 28
    **b.** 31.5
    **c.** 34
    **d.** 36.5
    **e.** 38

**Q1.34** A Christmas tree has been decorated with a set of lights that contains two circuits. On each individual circuit, all the lights come on and go off at the same time, but the two circuits are out of sync.

Circuit 1: Lights are ON for 4 seconds and OFF for 9 seconds.
Circuit 2: Lights are ON for 7 seconds and OFF for 2 seconds.

Twenty seconds ago, both sets of lights came ON at exactly the same time. In how many seconds from now will both sets of lights go OFF at the same time?

    **a.**   15
    **b.**   17
    **c.**   19
    **d.**   21
    **e.**   23

**Q1.35** Consider the same Christmas tree as in Question 1.34 but with circuits following the following pattern:

Circuit 1: Lights are ON for 3 seconds and OFF for 5 seconds.
Circuit 2: Lights are ON for 2 seconds and OFF for 6 seconds.

Ten seconds ago, both sets of lights went ON at exactly the same time. In how many seconds from now will both sets of lights go OFF at the same time?

    **a.**   30
    **b.**   45
    **c.**   60
    **d.**   75
    **e.**   They will never go OFF at the same time

**Q1.36** A rugby team has won 40% of the 15 games it has already played. If the team were to win 75% of its remaining games, it would have won 60% of all its games. How many remaining games are there?

    **a.**   12
    **b.**   20
    **c.**   21
    **d.**   35
    **e.**   45

**Q1.37** A city has a sports centre, which cost £60m to build. The City Council provided £18m of the total funding. The amount of funding provided by private grants was half the amount provided by private endowments, and the amount provided by private endowments was one-third the amount provided by the City Council. The rest was made up of public donations. How much funding was provided by private grants and private endowments?

    **a.** £3m
    **b.** £5m
    **c.** £9m
    **d.** £12m
    **e.** £15m

**Q1.38** The Cambridge Journal of Hospital Medicine has 25,000 subscribers. 50 percent of the subscribers are consultants, 30 percent of whom are cardiologists. If 40 percent of the subscribers who are consultant cardiologists are specialising in interventional cardiology, how many of the journal's 25,000 subscribers are consultants specialising in interventional cardiology?

    **a.** 1,500
    **b.** 3,000
    **c.** 3,750
    **d.** 7,500
    **e.** 8,750

**Q1.39** Tom, a junior doctor who has just graduated, is paid £12 per hour for the first 42 hours he works in a week. Every hour worked on top of the first 42 hours is being paid at a rate of 1.5 times the regular hourly rate. His friend, who works in a different hospital, also gets paid £12 per hour, but does not get paid extra for hours above 42. How many hours will Tim's friend have to work in order to earn the same as Tim earns in a week of 52 hours?

    **a.** 57
    **b.** 64
    **c.** 67
    **d.** 70
    **e.** 78

**Q1.40** A washing up solution called Clean-Brite consists of 30% liquid X and 70% water. If 2 litres of water evaporate from 8 litres of the washing up solution and 2 litres of Clean-Brite are added to the remaining solution, what proportion of the new solution is liquid X?

    a.   30%
    b.   30.333%
    c.   37.5%
    d.   40%
    e.   60%

**Q1.41** 20% of medical syringes produced by a factory are defective. In quality control, 80% of the defective medical syringes are spotted and rejected but, unfortunately, 5% of the non-defective syringes are also rejected, by mistake. If all the syringes that are not rejected are then sold, what percentage of the syringes sold by the factory are defective?

    a.   4%
    b.   5%
    c.   6.25%
    d.   11%
    e.   16%

**Q1.42** Which of the following procedures is always equivalent to adding up 5 given numbers and then dividing the sum by 5?

  I. Multiplying the 5 numbers and then finding the 5th root of the product.
  II. Adding the 5 numbers, doubling the sum, and then moving the decimal point one place to the left.
  III. Ordering the 5 numbers numerically and then selecting the middle number.

    a.   I only
    b.   II only
    c.   III only
    d.   None of the above

**Q1.43** If X is the average (arithmetic mean) of 5 consecutive even integers, which of the following must be true?

I.   X is an even integer.
II.  X is an odd integer.
III. X is a multiple of 5.

a. I only
b. II only
c. III only
d. I and III only
e. None of the above

**Q1.44** The average (arithmetic mean) price of five houses on a given street is £600,000, with the least expensive house being worth £550,000.

What is the maximum possible value for the most expensive house?

a.   £650,000
b.   £675,000
c.   £750,000
d.   £800,000
e.   £850,000

**Q1.45** The average (arithmetic mean) of 10 numbers is X. If the numbers 20 and 48 are added to the list, the average (arithmetic mean) of these 12 numbers is also X.

What is the value of X?

a.   25
b.   32
c.   34
d.   38
e.   Cannot be determined from the data given

**Q1.46** Consider Z, an integer such that $12 < Z < 22$.

Which of the following is the only option that could possibly be the average (arithmetic mean) of 2, 8, 12, 17, 23 and Z?

a. 10.333
b. 12
c. 13.667
d. 14.667
e. 15.333

**Q1.47** Eight workers in a certain company have incomes that range from £24,000 to £100,000 and an average (arithmetic mean) income of £50,000.

If the worker with the highest income and the one with the lowest income are excluded, what is the average income for the remaining six workers?

a. £24,000
b. £36,000
c. £46,000
d. £58,000
e. £100,000

**Q1.48** On a certain island, 100 mice were caught, tagged and returned to their habitat.

A few days later 100 mice were caught again, of which 2 were found to have been tagged. Assuming the second sample is representative of the whole population, what is the approximate number of mice on the island?

a. 2,000
b. 2,400
c. 3,600
d. 4,000
e. 5,000

**Q1.49** A hospital has 500 healthcare workers, of which 15% are doctors. If 80 more workers are to be hired, how many of the new workers must be doctors to raise the total percentage of doctors to 20%?

> a. 16
> b. 25
> c. 29
> d. 41
> e. 57

**Q1.50** A cocktail is made up of gin, vodka and orange juice, and the ratio by volume is 2:20:100. The cocktail is to be altered so that, in relation to the original proportions, the ratio of gin to vodka is doubled, and the ratio of gin to orange juice is halved. If the altered cocktail contains 50 cm$^3$ of vodka, how many cubic centimetres of orange juice will it contain?

> a. 100
> b. 200
> c. 250
> d. 400
> e. 500
> f. 1,000

**Q1.51** A new brand of ketchup sauce is made up of 7 parts of tomato paste and 5 parts of hot sauce. If the tomato sauce and hot sauce can only be purchased in boxes of 500 ml, what is the smallest amount of ingredients that needs to be purchased in order to make 2 litres of the ketchup? (You do not need to use all the ingredients you buy.)

> a. 2 litres
> b. 2.5 litres
> c. 3 litres
> d. 3.5 litres
> e. 4 litres

**Q1.52** In the school council, the President is proposing to increase the number of break times during the school day, but also to shorten lunchtime to make up for it. This is put to the student body for a vote. When 1/6 of the votes have been counted, 1/4 are in favour of the resolution and 3/4 are against. What percentage of the remaining votes must be in favour of the resolution so that the total count will result in a vote of 3:1 in favour of the resolution?

a. 17%
b. 70.8%
c. 75%
d. 85%
e. 100%

**Q1.53** A paint mix is made by mixing red, orange, yellow and black in the ratio of 7:3:1:1. How many pints of orange paint are required to prepare 9 gallons of the paint blend? (1 gallon = 8 pints)

a. 18 pints
b. 9 pints
c. 7 pints
d. 3 pints
e. 1 pint

**Q1.54** A paint mix is made by mixing red, orange, yellow and black in the ratio of 7:3:1:1. The individual paints used within the mix cost the painter the following to buy:

- £3 per pint of red paint
- £4 per pint of orange and yellow paint
- £2 per pint of black paint.

If the painter sold the new paint mix at a price 50% over the total cost of the individual paints used to make up the mix, what would be the retail price of 8 pints of the new paint mix?

a. £13
b. £26
c. £39
d. £48
e. £58

**Q1.55** A school has 1,600 students. During an election for school council, 900 people voted for Jane, and the rest voted for Darren. If the voters indicated a preference for Jane over Darren in the ratio of 3:1, what was the percentage of students who took part in the vote?

    **a.**   56.25%
    **b.**   65 %
    **c.**   75%
    **d.**   80%
    **e.**   100%

**Q1.56** A cocktail contains 10% orange juice. The barman decides to replace a quarter of that cocktail with a mix that contains X% of orange juice. This results in a solution that has the same volume as the original cocktail but now contains 20% of orange juice. What is the percentage X of orange juice contained in the mix that was used as replacement for part of the original cocktail?

    **a.**   10%
    **b.**   20%
    **c.**   50%
    **d.**   80%
    **e.**   90%

**Q1.57** Rachel, David and Peter have red, brown and blonde hair, and are 13, 14 and 15 years old. We don't yet know the age and hair colour of each of the children, but we know that they all have different ages and a different hair colour. We also know that:

(1) The youngest child has blonde hair.
(2) David is older than Peter.
(3) David does not have red hair and Peter is not blonde.

How old is David?

    **a.**   11
    **b.**   12
    **c.**   13
    **d.**   14
    **e.**   15

**Q1.58** A year ago, Gary was twice as old as Ron is now. In four more years, Ron will be as old as Gary is now. How old is Gary now?

    **a.**  5
    **b.**  7
    **c.**  9
    **d.**  10
    **e.**  11

**Q1.59** A trader sells spices in units of 1 kg. He uses traditional balance scales with weights (i.e. not electronic). He has only 3 weights at his disposal and, using those weights only, he can sell any whole number of kilograms from 1 to 13. What weights does he have?

    **a.**  1 kg, 4 kg, 7 kg
    **b.**  1 kg, 2 kg, 10 kg
    **c.**  2 kg, 4 kg, 8 kg
    **d.**  1 kg, 3 kg, 9 kg
    **e.**  1 kg, 3 kg, 10 kg

**Q1.60** A farmer <u>always</u> plants his cabbage patch in a square configuration. The cabbages are planted in lines at regular intervals. This year, knowing that some of his cabbages inevitably get eaten by wild animals, he decided to plant additional cabbages. In total he planted 47 <u>additional</u> cabbages. How many cabbages did he plant last year?

    **a.**  23
    **b.**  49
    **c.**  225
    **d.**  484
    **e.**  529
    **f.**  576
    **g.**  729

**Q1.61** A number of people are stopped at random in the street. They are asked if they have two children and also if one is a boy born on a Friday. After a long search, we finally find someone who answers yes to both questions. What is the probability that this person has two boys? Assume an equal chance of giving birth to either sex and an equal chance of giving birth on any day.

    **a.**   27/196
    **b.**   25%
    **c.**   13/27
    **d.**   50%
    **e.**   62.5%

**Q1.62** Christine has a number of flowers. That number is less than 100.
    1.   If she puts them in groups of 2 she has 1 left over.
    2.   If she puts them in groups of 3 she has 1 left over.
    3.   If she puts them in groups of 4 she has 3 left over.
    4.   If she puts them in groups of 5 she has 1 left over.
    5.   If she puts them in groups of 6 she has 1 left over.
    6.   If she puts them in groups of 7 she has 0 left over.

In what range does the number of Christina's flowers lie?

    **a.**   51–60
    **b.**   61–70
    **c.**   71–80
    **d.**   81–90
    **e.**   91–100

**Q1.63** You have bought a rectangular bar of chocolate, which is made up of 10 x 6 individual squares. How many steps are required to break the bar into individual squares? You can only cut along the pre-made grooves, and you cannot make stacks to break more than one piece at a time.

    **a.**   14
    **b.**   30
    **c.**   54
    **d.**   59
    **e.**   60

**Q1.64** In the figure below, each of the digits 1 through to 8 is to be written in exactly one of the squares so that no two consecutive numbers will be next to each other in any direction, horizontally, vertically or diagonally. If 1, 2, 4 and 8 are to be written in the squares shown below, which digit will be written in the shaded square marked **d**?

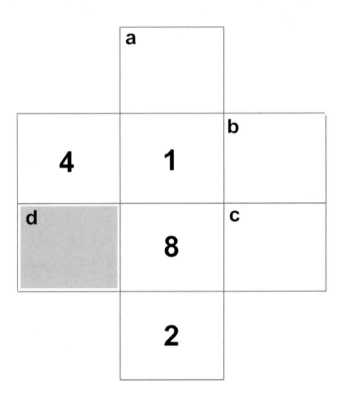

a.   3
b.   5
c.   6
d.   7
e.   9

**Q1.65** In a dancing competition, each performance is scored by 6 judges. The value of the performance is scored as follows:

- The highest and lowest scores are dropped.
- The total of the remaining 4 scores is multiplied by the degree of difficulty of the performance.

The total of the scores granted by the 6 judges for Richard's performance is 49.5. The sum of his highest judge score and lowest judge score for his performance was 16.5. The value of the performance was 99. What was the degree of difficulty of Richard's performance?

    **a.**   1
    **b.**   2
    **c.**   3
    **d.**   4
    **e.**   5

**Q1.66** In a school, the science book store-room has the following numbers of books:

- 50 books are on astronomy
- 65 books are on biology
- 90 books are on physics
- 50 books are on botany
- 110 books are on chemistry.

If the books are removed randomly from the storeroom, what is the minimum number of books that must be removed to ensure that at least 80 of the books removed are on the same subject?

    **a.**   80
    **b.**   159
    **c.**   166
    **d.**   285
    **e.**   324
    **f.**   365

**Q1.67** Consider the following process:

| | |
|---|---|
| Choose a 3-digit number: | 5 8 9 |
| Reverse the order: | 9 8 5 |

Add the two together       1 5 7 4

Find the largest 3-digit number that will give a total under 1000. Digits must be between 1 and 9, and can be used more than once. In what range does that number lie?

    a.    500–599
    b.    600–699
    c.    700–799
    d.    800–899
    e.    900–999

**Q1.68** Consider the following equation, where the square and circle represent a digit. Which digit is represented by the square?

$$2 \ \square \ 2$$
$$+ \ \square \ 2 \ \square$$
$$\overline{\bigcirc \ 2 \ 2 \ \bigcirc}$$

    a.    9
    b.    8
    c.    5
    d.    2
    e.    0

**Q1.69** In the following equation, each of the three shapes represents a different digit.

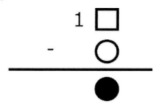

If □ is 1 lower than O, what is the value of ●?

    **a.**   2
    **b.**   3
    **c.**   4
    **d.**   7
    **e.**   9

**Q1.70** In a gold bullion store, the gold bricks are stacked up in a flat pyramid shape over a total of 6 rows. The number of bricks in a row is 1 less than the number of bricks in the row immediately below. If there are 105 gold bricks and 6 rows in total, how many bricks does the bottom row contain?

    **a.**   10
    **b.**   14
    **c.**   20
    **d.**   24
    **e.**   None of the above

**Q1.71** A computer shop sold 6 Computers X and 4 Laptops Y for a total of £21,000. If each Computer X was sold for 50% less than each Laptop Y, how much did each Computer X sell for?

    **a.**   £1,500
    **b.**   £2,400
    **c.**   £2,600
    **d.**   £3,000
    **e.**   £3,500

**Q1.72** A bouncing ball is being dropped from a given height. After being dropped, it bounces to a height that is equal to exactly 75% of the height from which it was dropped. As it bounces again, it bounces up to 75% of the height at which it was after the first bounce, and so on.

After how many bounces will the ball first bounce up to a height that is below 25% of the height from which it was originally dropped?

a. 3
b. 4
c. 5
d. 6
e. 7

**Q1.73** Consider the following T shape. If the shape's area is 324 cm², what is its perimeter (in cm)?

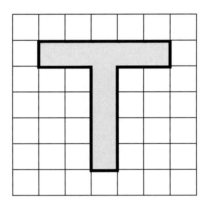

a. 112 cm
b. 114 cm
c. 116 cm
d. 118 cm
e. 120 cm

**Q1.74** 15 circles are arranged to form a rectangle measuring 3 x 5. A triangle is positioned on top of that pattern as shown below in such a way that its vertices are exactly in the centre of the 3 circles which contain them.

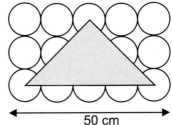

50 cm

What is the area of the shaded triangle (in cm$^2$)?

    **a.** 200 cm$^2$
    **b.** 300 cm$^2$
    **c.** 400 cm$^2$
    **d.** 500 cm$^2$
    **e.** 600 cm$^2$

**Q1.75** The volume of a box with a square base is 81 cm$^3$. If the height of the box is three times the width of the base, what is its height, in centimetres?

    **a.** 2
    **b.** 3
    **c.** 5
    **d.** 6
    **e.** 9

**Q1.76** A London hospital has 18 wards, each of which contains 10 bed cubicles. It plans to reconfigure 1/6 of the wards to have bigger bed cubicles, each one made from two old cubicles. How many bed cubicles will there be in the hospital after the restructuring?

    **a.** 15
    **b.** 90
    **c.** 150
    **d.** 165
    **e.** 180

**Q1.77** Prostate, lung, large bowel, bladder and stomach cancers are the top 5 diagnosed cancers in males and accounted for 73,100 cancer diagnoses last year. If X is the number of prostate cancer diagnoses, and Y is the number of cancers that appear elsewhere in the top 5 cancer diagnosis list, which of the following represents the ratio of the number of cancers that occur in the prostate to the number that did not occur in the prostate?

a. $\dfrac{X}{73,100 + Y}$

b. $\dfrac{X}{73,100}$

c. $\dfrac{X}{73,100 - Y}$

d. $\dfrac{X}{73,100 - X}$

e. $1 - \dfrac{X}{73,100 - Y}$

**Q1.78** Isobel has recently broken her mobile phone. She can either have her mobile phone repaired for £25, or she can trade it in, and receive £50 credit toward the purchase of a new mobile phone that retails for £105.

How much more expensive will it be for her to trade in her current broken mobile phone instead of getting it repaired?

a. 20%
b. 83%
c. 120%
d. 160%
e. 220%
f. 320%

**Q1.79** A doctor has signed up to a medical insurance plan that pays the following monthly disability benefit:

- 50% of the first £3,000 of monthly salary
- PLUS 30% of monthly salary between £3,000 & £5,000
- PLUS 20% of monthly salary in excess of £5,000.

What was the monthly salary of a doctor who receives £5,400 in disability benefits under this plan?

    **a.**  £6,500
    **b.**  £8,000
    **c.**  £15,000
    **d.**  £16,500
    **e.**  £21,500

**Q1.80** In the UK, for the tax years 2010/2011 and 2011/2012, income tax rates for people earning below £100,000 per annum were:

| Tax rate | Earnings range on which tax is charged | |
|---|---|---|
| | 2010 / 2011 | 2011 / 2012 |
| 0% | £0 – £6,475 | £0 – £7,475 |
| 20% | £6,475 – £43,875 | £7,475 – £42,875 |
| 40% | £43,875 – £100,000 | £42,875 – £100,000 |

John earned £70,000 in 2010/2011 and received a pay increase of 10% at the start of 2011/2012.

By how much did his tax bill increase in 2011/2012?

    **a.**  £400
    **b.**  £800
    **c.**  £1,200
    **d.**  £2,800
    **e.**  £3,200

**Q1.81** A school bus starts full with children. At each of its first 5 bus stops, it unloads exactly half of the children present in the bus. After the 4th stop, what proportion of the original busload of children is left on the bus?

    **a.**   1/4
    **b.**   1/8
    **c.**   1/16
    **d.**   12/16
    **e.**   15/16

**Q1.82** A group of 14 friends hired a bus to go from York to London for a stag weekend. The cost of the bus hire was shared equally amongst them.

If there had been 20 passengers sharing the cost, the cost per passenger would have been £5 lower. What was each friend's share of the cost of hiring the bus?

    **a.**   £16.67
    **b.**   £16
    **c.**   £15
    **d.**   £10
    **e.**   £6.67

**Q1.83** The rear wheels of a car cross a line 1 second after the front wheels have crossed the same line. If the wheels' axes of rotation are 5 metres apart, what is the speed of the car in kilometres per hour? (Assume the car has travelled in a straight line and at constant speed.)

    **a.**   1
    **b.**   5
    **c.**   18
    **d.**   300
    **e.**   None of the above

**Q1.84** A chef has a pot containing 150 black beans and 75 white beans. Next to the pot is a pile of black beans. He decides to play a game as follows:

- He takes two beans at random from the pot.

- If both beans are white, he discards them. He then takes one black bean from the pile and places it into the pot.

- If at least one of the beans is black, he places that bean on the pile and puts the other bean back in the pot, regardless of its colour.

What will be the colour of the last bean left in the pot?

a. Black
b. White
c. Could be either black or white
d. There will never be just one bean left in the pot.

**Q1.85** During the New Year sales, a shop is running a Buy-One-Get-One-For-£10 offer on clothes.

The set of clothes offered for £10 needs to be the same price or cheaper than the purchased item.

If, during the sale, a client buys 8 items which are priced at £60, £48, £67, £58, £43, £41, £56 and £39, what is the least amount the customer can expect to pay for the items?

a. £254
b. £241
c. £214
d. £181
e. £168

**Q1.86** A father gives pocket money to his 7 children in the following way:

- In week 1 he will give a total of £1. In week 2, he will give a total of £2 ... in week 25, he will give a total of £25 ... until week 50 when he will give a total of £50.

- The amount of money is distributed equally between the 7 children, but he only gives each of them a whole number of pounds. Any money left over is given to charity. For example, in week 4, the children would get no pocket money but £4 would be given to charity. In week 30, he would give £4 to each child (£4 x 7 = £28) and £2 to charity.

**Q1.86a** Over 50 weeks, how much has been given to charity?

    a.   £148
    b.   £150
    c.   £153
    d.   £158
    e.   £161

**Q1.86b** Over 50 weeks, how much has been given to each child?

    a.   £148
    b.   £150
    c.   £153
    d.   £158
    e.   £161

**Q1.87** A group of 5 boys can load 90 logs on to a bonfire in 18 minutes. A group of 2 adult men can move 120 logs in 30 minutes.

How long would it take 1 man and 3 boys to load 100 logs (to the nearest minute)?

    a.   15 minutes
    b.   17 minutes
    c.   20 minutes
    d.   22 minutes
    e.   24 minutes

**Q1.88** Jenny, a party organiser, is hosting a party. She can host it in her own house, which can host 50 people and where she would charge £5.00 for a ticket.

Alternatively, she can hold the party in a large club which can hold 100 and costs £250 per night to hire. The facilities at the nightclub are better, so she can charge £7.50 for a ticket there. There are no other expenses.

If she decides to use the nightclub venue, how many tickets would she need to sell to ensure that she makes more money than by using her own house?

    **a.**   55
    **b.**   56
    **c.**   65
    **d.**   66
    **e.**   67

**Q1.89** Phil's journey from his house to the hospital involves walking to the bus station and catching a bus to the hospital. The bus leaves the station at 20-minute intervals and the bus journey takes 15 minutes.

The hospital in which he works is a 10-minute walk from the bus stop where he gets off. If he arrives at the bus station at 8:15 am, he gets to the hospital at 8:50 am.

At what time will he get to the hospital if he arrives at the bus station at 9:00 am?

    **a.**   9.25 am
    **b.**   9.30 am
    **c.**   9.35 am
    **d.**   9.45 am
    **e.**   9.50 am

**Q1.90** On a die, the sum of the two numbers on opposite faces is 7. In the following stack of dice, what is the sum of the numbers found on the five faces that are in contact with another die or with the floor?

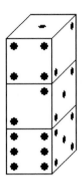

| a. | 12 |
| b. | 14 |
| c. | 18 |
| d. | 20 |
| e. | 21 |

**Q1.91** Consider the following four statements:

A. The number of false statements here is one.
B. The number of false statements here is two.
C. The number of false statements here is three.
D. The number of false statements here is four.

Which of these statements is true?

| a. | A |
| b. | B |
| c. | C |
| d. | D |
| e. | None is true. |

**Q1.92** Consider the following two wheels in their starting positions. Wheel A rotates clockwise and Wheel B rotates anticlockwise. We are told that, as Wheel A completes 1 rotation, Wheel B completes 4 rotations (drawing not to scale).

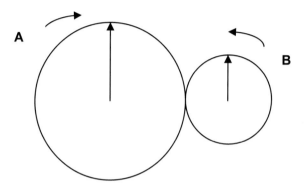

If the arrow on Wheel B is found pointing towards the left, how many possible positions are there for the arrow on Wheel A?

    **a.**   2
    **b.**   4
    **c.**   8
    **d.**   12
    **e.**   16

**Q1.93** Cougar – a taxi company – charges an initial flat rate for picking up a passenger (which is doubled if the pick-up is after 7 pm) plus a rate for each kilometre travelled.

In the morning, it costs David £7 to go to the hospital, which is 5 km away, and the 5 km return journey home at 8 pm costs £9. David then goes to the local nightclub at 11 pm, which costs him £6. What distance did he travel to the nightclub?

    **a.**   2 km
    **b.**   3.5 km
    **c.**   4 km
    **d.**   6 km
    **e.**   Cannot be determined from the information given

**Q1.94** The annual results of the Medical Society election are released for the 4 candidates. Tom received exactly two-fifths (2/5) of the votes cast, Roberta received 100 votes, Alice received 75 votes and Laura received exactly half as many votes as Roberta.

Who won the election and what was the winning margin?

    **a.** Roberta by 25 votes
    **b.** Roberta by 50 votes
    **c.** Tom by 25 votes
    **d.** Tom by 50 votes
    **e.** Tom by 65 votes

**Q1.95** Nurse Jackie is checking the ward's patients' blood pressure notes and it takes her 2 minutes 10 seconds to check the readings of all 10 patients sequentially. At the same time, Nurse John is taking the 10 patients' temperature via a tympanic thermometer placed in the ear and it takes him 1 minute and 45 seconds to get the readings.

The nurses will continually recheck and retake the readings of all the patients in the ward without stopping between 2 rounds (i.e. when they have reached the last patient, they start again with the first patient straight away).

Assuming that they start at the same time from the same patient, that they deal with patients in the same order on each round and that they work at a constant speed, how long would it take for the faster nurse to lap (i.e. catch up with) the slower nurse?

    **a.** 2 minutes 9 seconds
    **b.** 4 minutes 9 seconds
    **c.** 8 minutes 6 seconds
    **d.** 9 minutes 6 seconds
    **e.** 9 minutes 16 seconds

**Q1.96** Consider the following time data:

- Paris is 1 hour ahead of London
- New York is 5 hours behind London
- Los Angeles is 3 hours behind New York
- It takes 6 hours to fly from Paris to New York
- It takes 10 hours to fly from Los Angeles to Paris
- It takes 5 hours to fly from New York to Los Angeles.

I leave Paris at 9 am en route for New York. On arrival in New York, I wait 2 hours before being able to take my next plane to Los Angeles. Once in Los Angeles, I wait 4 hours before taking a plane back to Paris.

At what time will I land in Paris?

|    |       |
|----|-------|
| a. | 12 pm |
| b. | 3 pm  |
| c. | 6 pm  |
| d. | 9 pm  |
| e. | 9 am  |

**Q1.97** ITV's viewing share in 2008 was twice the viewing share of BBC2 in that year. Viewing share for BBC1 fell from 25% in 2006 to 22% in 2007. In the same period BBC2's share fell from 20% to 18% though it recovered to 25% the following year. This was 10% more than BBC1's share.

What was ITV's share in 2008?

|    |      |
|----|------|
| a. | 35%  |
| b. | 40%  |
| c. | 45%  |
| d. | 50%  |
| e. | 55%  |

**Q1.98** Three specific books may be purchased from an online bookshop but, instead of selling them individually, the bookshop sells them in packs of two as follows:
- Pack A: Book 1 + Book 2. Price = £27
- Pack B: Book 1 + Book 3. Price = £32
- Pack C: Book 2 + Book 3. Price = £29

What would be the cost of Book 3 if it were sold individually?

a. £13
b. £14
c. £15
d. £16
e. £17

**Q1.99** A teacher tells two of his students that he has two consecutive numbers between 1 and 10 (1 and 10 included) in mind. He tells Student 1 one number and Student 2 the second number. The following exchange takes place between the two students:

- First Student:  I do not know your number.
- Second Student:  Neither do I know your number.
- First Student:  Now I know your number.

Which of the following options is a possibility for the 2 numbers?

a. 1 and 2
b. 2 and 3
c. 3 and 4
d. 4 and 5
e. 5 and 6

**Q1.100** On a map drawn to scale 1:11,000, a street measures 9.091 cm. If on a different map, the same street measures 20 cm, what is the scale of that map?

a. 1:4,000
b. 1:5,000
c. 1:10,000
d. 1:20,000
e. 1:24,200

**Q1.101** A town has the shape of a square measuring 8 km by 8 km.

The town authorities decide to publish a booklet containing a map of the town, with each page showing a different rectangular area of the town measuring 20 cm by 10 cm.

All parts of the town are represented and there are no overlaps. If the map occupies 200 pages, what is the scale of the map?

   **a.**   1:2,000
   **b.**   1:4,000
   **c.**   1:8,000
   **d.**   1:16,000
   **e.**   1:16,000,000

**Q1.102** The postman meets Mary on her doorstep. They have the following conversation:

- Postman: I need to know how old your three kids are.
- Mary: The product of their ages is 36.
- Postman: I still don't know their ages.
- Mary: The sum of their ages is my house number.
- Postman: I still don't know their ages.
- Mary: The younger two are twins.
- Postman: Now I know their ages!

Based on this exchange, what is the age of the twins?

   **a.**   2
   **b.**   3
   **c.**   4
   **d.**   5
   **e.**   6

**Q1.103** A carpenter has made six objects as follows:

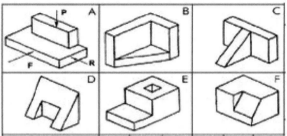

Once the objects were built, he drew their projections using a view from directions P, F and R, as shown on the diagram for A above. Those projections are shown below, numbered 1–18. However, it seems that Number 11 was accidentally deleted. Which of the six objects does it correspond to: A, B, C, D, E or F?

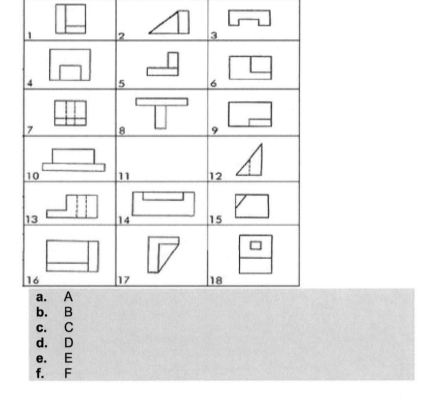

a. A
b. B
c. C
d. D
e. E
f. F

**Q1.104** In 2015, the months of March and November both started on a Sunday. However, every year there are two months that do not begin on the same day of the week as any other month. They are always the same two months and it does not matter whether it is a leap year or not. What are those two months?

    **a.**   May and June
    **b.**   June and October
    **c.**   January and May
    **d.**   April and September
    **e.**   January and December

**Q1.105** You are in possession of 9 coins, which all look identical. They all have the same weight except one, which is counterfeit and is lighter than all the others. You have, at your disposal, a balance scale as shown in the picture.

What is the minimum number of weighings you will need to make in order to <u>guarantee</u> that you will find the counterfeit coin?

    **a.**   1
    **b.**   2
    **c.**   4
    **d.**   6
    **e.**   8

**Q1.106** A woman has two children aged 5 and 2. We are told that at least one of them is a girl, though we don't know which one. Assuming that each pregnancy has a 50/50 chance of being a boy or a girl, what is the probability that the other child is a girl?

    **a.**   1/8
    **b.**   1/7
    **c.**   1/6
    **d.**   1/5
    **e.**   1/4
    **f.**   1/3
    **g.**   1/2

**Q1.107** Consider the following statements:

- If Amy went to the show then Bernard also went to the show.
- If Bernard went to the show then Carol also went to the show.

If Bernard did not go to the show, which of the following must be true?

1 – Amy went to the show.
2 – Carol did not go to the show.
3 – Amy did not go to the show.

| | |
|---|---|
| **a.** | 1 only |
| **b.** | 2 only |
| **c.** | 3 only |
| **d.** | 1 and 2 only |
| **e.** | 2 and 3 only |

**Q1.108** Consider the following statements:

Those who like bananas like avocados.
Those who like apples like oranges.
Those who like oranges don't like avocados.

If all those statements are true, which of the following statements must also be true?

1 – Those who like apples like avocados.
2 – Those who like bananas don't like oranges.
3 – Those who like avocados don't like apples.
4 – Those who like apples don't like bananas
5 – Those who like bananas like apples.

| | |
|---|---|
| **a.** | 1, 3 and 4 only |
| **b.** | 2, 3 and 5 only |
| **c.** | 1 and 4 only |
| **d.** | 2, 3 and 4 only |
| **e.** | 3, 4 and 5 only |

**Q1.109** You are facing three chests (A, B and C) filled with coins.

| Chest A | Chest B | Chest C |
|---------|---------|---------|
| 100 gold coins | 50 gold and 50 silver coins | 100 silver coins |

Each chest has a label attached to it, as shown above ("100 gold coins", "50 gold and 50 silver coins" and "100 silver coins"). Unfortunately, the labels previously fell off and someone replaced them on each chest in such a way that no label actually corresponds to the content of the chest onto which it has been placed.

You are allowed to pick one coin at random from any chest you want in order to help you identify which chest contains which coins.

Which chest should you take that coin from?

    **a.**   Chest A
    **b.**   Chest B
    **c.**   Chest C
    **d.**   This cannot be done by picking just one coin

**Q1.110** Jeremy, Anna, Mary, Robert and Carol are participating in a gift exchange. Everyone is required to bring exactly one gift and to leave with exactly one gift. No one is allowed to leave with the gift he or she brought. If we know that Robert went home with Anna's gift and Jeremy went home with Mary's gift, how many distinct ways are there to distribute the remaining gifts?

    **a.**   1
    **b.**   2
    **c.**   3
    **d.**   4
    **e.**   6

**Q1.111** A father wants to distribute his £60,000 savings to his six children aged 30, 32, 34, 36, 38 and 40, using the following principles:

- The older a child is, the more money he/she will get.
- Each child will receive a different amount.
- Each child will receive a minimum of £3,000.

What is the maximum amount that the child aged 36 can receive?

a. 16,997
b. 16,998
c. 16,999
d. 17,000
e. 17,001

**Q1.112** John is shaving in front of a mirror and sees that the hands of the analogue clock behind him indicate a particular time. However, he fails to account for the fact that he is looking at it via a mirror and therefore gets the time wrong.

John then immediately sets off for work and gets there 20 minutes later. Once at work, he glances at the clock and sees that the (real) time is actually 2.5 hours later than the wrong time he saw in the mirror earlier.

Assuming that all clocks are accurate, which one of the following times is a possible real time that his bathroom clock was showing when he was shaving?

a. 1:15
b. 3:05
c. 5:25
d. 6:35
e. 7:05

**Q1.113** Harry and Ahmed are two greengrocers with shops next to each other and are on very friendly terms. Harry sells apples at a price of 50 pence for two apples. Ahmed's apples are slightly smaller in size and therefore he sells them at a price of 50 pence for three apples. At one point, Ahmed needs to absent himself from the shop momentarily. He asks Harry to sell his apples for him. At that particular point, both Harry and Ahmed have exactly the same number of apples.

To make things simple, Harry puts all the apples from both shops into a big pile and sells them at a price of £1 for 5 apples. When Ahmed gets back, all the apples have been sold and they agree to split the money that Harry took: 50%/50%. When they look at how much money Harry took, the total taken seems to be £3.50 short of what they would have made if they had sold their apples separately. How much money has Harry lost through this deal?

    **a.**  £10.00
    **b.**  £10.25
    **c.**  £10.50
    **d.**  £10.75
    **e.**  £11.00

**Q1.114** A fast-food outlet sells chicken nuggets in boxes of either 6, 9 or 20 nuggets. With these boxes they can fulfil pretty much any order with any number of nuggets; for example, if a customer wants 50 nuggets, they can fulfil the order by providing one box of 20 nuggets and 5 boxes of 6 nuggets. Some orders, however, cannot be fulfilled.

For example, it is impossible to fulfil an order of 19 nuggets by using those three boxes. In which range is the <u>highest</u> order that <u>cannot</u> be fulfilled?

    **a.**  21–30 nuggets
    **b.**  31–40 nuggets
    **c.**  41–50 nuggets
    **d.**  51–60 nuggets
    **e.**  61–70 nuggets

**Q1.115** A shop owner is trying to display a batch of candles in a neat way. The owner finds that when she places them in groups of three there is always one left over. The same problem occurs when she places them in groups of 5, 7 or 9. The only way to have a perfect fit is to arrange them in groups of 11.

In what range is the number of candles that the owner is trying to display?

    **a.** 501–600
    **b.** 601–700
    **c.** 701–800
    **d.** 801–900
    **e.** 901–999

**Q1.116** You have four cards in front of you, as follows:

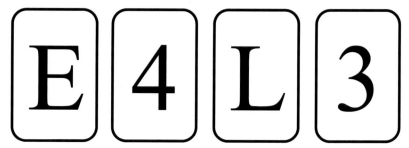

Each card has a letter on one side and a digit on the other side. You have been told that when there is a vowel on one side of a card then there is an even digit on the other side.

Which cards would it be sufficient to flip over to check whether this statement is true for this set of cards?

    **a.** E and L
    **b.** E and 3
    **c.** E and 4
    **d.** L and 3
    **e.** L and 4

**Q1.117** An opaque bag contains a snooker ball, which is known to be red. At this stage it does not contain anything else. From another bag, which contains 100 red and 100 yellow snooker balls, one ball is drawn at random and is placed into the opaque bag without anyone having a chance to see what colour it is.

The opaque bag now contains two balls: the original red ball and the ball that has just been placed into it, which has an equal chance of being red or yellow.

The opaque bag is shaken and a ball is drawn at random from it. That ball proves to be a red ball. What is the probability that the ball that remains in the opaque bag is also red?

    **a.**   1/4
    **b.**   1/3
    **c.**   1/2
    **d.**   2/3
    **e.**   3/4

**Q1.118** The figure on the right consists of one large circle containing seven smaller circles, all with the same radius.

There is a unique point of contact between each circle. What proportion of the large circle's area is not covered by a small circle (i.e. the grey area) to the nearest 1%?

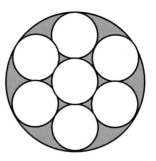

    **a.**   18%
    **b.**   22%
    **c.**   26%
    **d.**   33%
    **e.**   44%

**Q1.119** A hunter meets two shepherds. One of the shepherds has three loaves of bread; the other one has five loaves of bread. The three men agree to share the loaves equally between them. Once all the bread has been eaten, the hunter gives the shepherds eight coins as payment and tells them that they have to share those eight coins so that the money they each receive is proportionate to the amount of bread that they each gave him.

If each shepherd only ate his own bread, how should the shepherds split the eight coins?

    **a.**  8:0
    **b.**  7:1
    **c.**  6:2
    **d.**  5:3
    **e.**  4:4

**Q1.120** Amir and his wife went to a party attended by four other married couples. Some of the ten people had already met previously, and some had not. At the party, every person shook hands with every-one he or she had never met before. Once everyone had shaken hands, Amir asked everyone, including his wife, how many hands they shook. Everyone gave a different number.

How many hands did Amir's wife shake?

    **a.**  0
    **b.**  2
    **c.**  4
    **d.**  6
    **e.**  8

**Q1.121** Assume that the statement "All red shoes are made of leather" is always true. Which of the following is also true?

    **a.**  No blue shoe can be made of leather
    **b.**  Some red shoes can be made of plastic
    **c.**  All shoes made of leather must be red
    **d.**  No shoe made of plastic can be red
    **e.**  Some blue shoes are made of leather

**Q1.122** You have, in front of you, three boxes, each filled with a different type of coin. One of the boxes contains US Dollars, one of the boxes contains British Pounds and the third box contains Euros. You have labelled each box according to its content. However, the labels are not sticking very well and they all fall off. You then reattach the labels to the boxes at random without checking to see if they correspond to the correct box.

Having reattached the labels, you look inside the box marked "US Dollars" and see that it contains Euros. What is the probability that you labelled at least one box correctly?

    **a.**   0
    **b.**   1/3
    **c.**   1/2
    **d.**   2/3
    **e.**   1

**Q1.123** Cylinder A is filled with water to the top. It has a radius of 3 cm and a height of 10 cm. In Cylinder A, we now insert a rigid sphere with a radius of 3 cm. The sphere sinks to the bottom, making the water overflow. The water that overflowed is then recovered and placed into Cylinder B, which has a radius of 3 cm. What is the minimum value for the height H of Cylinder B in cm?

    **a.**   1 cm
    **b.**   2 cm
    **c.**   3 cm
    **d.**   4 cm
    **e.**   5 cm

**Q1.124** Out of 100 people in a group of tourists, 90 speak Italian, 80 speak Mandarin and 75 speak English. At least how many speak all three languages?

    **a.**   35
    **b.**   40
    **c.**   45
    **d.**   50
    **e.**   55

**Q1.125** A safe has a four-digit code. You have made four attempts. For each attempt shown below, you are told how many digits are in the correct position and how many digits are in an incorrect position. The information is as follows:

| 1 | 2 | 3 | 5 |
|---|---|---|---|
| 6 | 8 | 4 | 5 |
| 9 | 7 | 2 | 3 |
| 6 | 4 | 2 | 7 |
|   |   |   |   |

● ○

● ●

○

● ○ ○

● ● ● ●

● = 1 digit is in the correct place

○ = 1 digit is in the incorrect place

Which of these digits appears in position 4 in the code?

    a.  1
    b.  2
    c.  5
    d.  6
    e.  7

**Q1.126** A safe has four dials. If the digit in each triangle is linked in some way to the three digits at the corners of each triangle, what digit should be entered in fourth position?

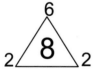 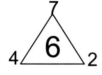  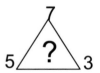

    a.  0
    b.  2
    c.  4
    d.  6
    e.  8

**Q1.127** A company has reserved five parking spaces for its top executives: CEO, President, Vice-President, Secretary and Treasurer. The car park spaces are lined up in that order. The top executives' names are Anna, Ben, Charlie, Davinder and Erin. They drive cars that are all of different colours: red, blue, purple, green and yellow. We know the following:

1. The car in the first space is red.
2. A blue car is parked between the red car and the green car.
3. The car in the last space is purple.
4. The secretary drives a yellow car.
5. Anna's car is parked next to Davinder's.
6. Erin drives a green car.
7. Ben's car is parked between Charlie's and Erin's.
8. Davinder's car is parked in the last space.

Who is the CEO?

    **a.**   Anna
    **b.**   Ben
    **c.**   Charlie
    **d.**   Davinder
    **e.**   Erin

**Q1.128** Pinocchio's nose doubles in size whenever he tells a lie but shortens by 1 cm whenever he tells the truth. This morning his nose measured 1 cm. It now measures 100 cm. What is the minimum number of times he has opened his mouth since this morning?

    **a.**   10
    **b.**   12
    **c.**   14
    **d.**   16
    **e.**   18

**Q1.129** Look at this pattern carefully. Which string of digits should appear in the final line?

2

12

1112

3112

132112

1113122112

311311222112

13211321322112

1113122113121113222112

?_____?

| | |
|---|---|
| a. | 31131122211311123113322112 |
| b. | 31222112233111111311211321 |
| c. | 12311211311111133221122213 |
| d. | 21111312222211122131121221 |
| e. | 13121213111311112311112211 |

**Q1.130** Cheryl, Sapna, Clara and Sameer all work in the same company. Some of them drive to work on their own and some of them share a car.

1. Cheryl and Sapna never share a car with anyone.
2. Clara only goes to work in the afternoon.
3. Sameer always shares a car with someone else when he goes to work in the morning.
4. Sapna is the only member of staff who goes home for lunch and therefore makes two return trips in one day.

Which of the following statements <u>must</u> be true?

| | |
|---|---|
| a. | A total of six return journeys are made each day. |
| b. | Clara makes more than two return journeys per day. |
| c. | There are at least five colleagues in this arrangement. |
| d. | Clara shares a car with Sameer. |
| e. | Sameer and Sapna share a car. |

**Q1.131** Five people live on the same side of a street. The houses are arranged as set out below and, for the purpose of this exercise, you should consider that they are being viewed as they are arranged, i.e. Number 10 is on the left of Number 12, etc.

1. Bertie is Annie's right-hand side direct neighbour.
2. Charlie lives next to Davey, who has Bertie directly on his left.
3. Eddie lives as far away from Charlie as he can.

Who lives at Number 10?

   **a.** Annie
   **b.** Bertie
   **c.** Charlie
   **d.** Davey
   **e.** Eddie

**Q1.132** Consider the following statements:
- All Italian speakers like pasta.
- All Greeks speak Italian.

Which of the following statements must be true?

1. People who don't like pasta cannot speak Italian.
2. People who don't like pasta cannot be Greek.
3. People who can't speak Italian cannot be Greek.
4. All Italian speakers are Greek.

   **a.** 1 and 2 only
   **b.** 2 and 3 only
   **c.** 1 and 3 only
   **d.** 1, 2 and 3 only
   **e.** 2, 3 and 4 only
   **f.** 1, 3 and 4 only
   **g.** All four statements

**Q1.133** A group of 30 students are deciding which language they would like to study. In that group:

- 16 students say they want to take French.
- 16 students want to take Spanish.
- 11 students want to take Latin.
- 5 students say they want to take both French and Latin and, of these, 3 want to take Spanish as well.
- 5 students want only Latin, and 8 want only Spanish.

How many students want to take French only?

    **a.**   4
    **b.**   6
    **c.**   7
    **d.**   8
    **e.**   11

**Q1.134** The following table shows the values allocated to each letter of the alphabet. Only 4 numerical values have been provided. For all the other letters, either no clue or a formula has been provided. All values are unique and range from 1 to 26.

| A | B | C | D | E | F | G | H | I | J |
|---|---|---|---|---|---|---|---|---|---|
| HxW | Q−T | >Y | T−L | | | I+J | F/N | E+N | K+T |
| | | | | 2 | | | | | |

| K | L | M | N | O | P | Q | R | S | T |
|---|---|---|---|---|---|---|---|---|---|
| | H−E | Q+E | | >Q | E+U | C−W | ExS | L+N | F−N |
| 4 | | | 6 | | | | | | |

| U | V | W | X | Y | Z |
|---|---|---|---|---|---|
| L+J | | <N | | G+L | >D |
| | | | 20 | | |

What is the value of W?

    **a.**   1
    **b.**   2
    **c.**   3
    **d.**   4
    **e.**   5

**Q1.135** You are given a 10x10x10 cube, made up of 1000 identical mini-cubes. If you remove the outermost layer, how many cubes will you have removed?

    **a.**   271
    **b.**   354
    **c.**   488
    **d.**   512
    **e.**   600

**Q1.136** Which of the following six logs are identical to this one?

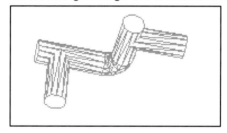

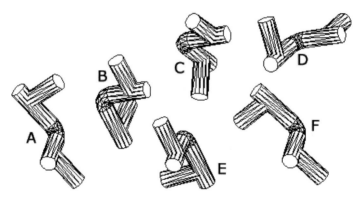

    **a.**   A and F
    **b.**   B and C
    **c.**   D and F
    **d.**   B and F
    **e.**   D and E

**Q1.137** Which of the contraptions are identical to this one?

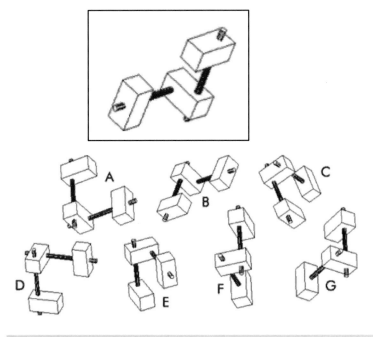

| | |
|---|---|
| **a.** | D, E and F |
| **b.** | A, E and G |
| **c.** | B, D and E |
| **d.** | B, C and E |
| **e.** | A, B and D |

**Q1.138** Find the smallest positive number that is divisible by 15 and consists only of ones and zeros (10, 11, 100, etc.). In what range does it lie?

| | |
|---|---|
| **a.** | 0–499 |
| **b.** | 500–999 |
| **c.** | 1,000–1,499 |
| **d.** | 1,500–1,999 |
| **e.** | 2,000–2,499 |

**Q1.139** There are four brothers in a family. The sum of the ages of each combination of three brothers is 30, 32, 32, and 35.

How old is the oldest brother?

a. 10
b. 11
c. 12
d. 13
e. 14

**Q1.140** Four children, Alcina, Bea, Catrina and Dimple, have 8 crayons in total.

There are two crayons of each of four colours: red, green, blue and yellow.

Each friend owns 2 of the 8 crayons, but none of them owns the same combination as the other three, and none of them has two crayons of the same colour.

- One of the friends has a yellow and a blue crayon.
- One of the friends has a blue and a green crayon.
- Alcina does not have a yellow crayon.
- Bea has a green crayon but not a red one.
- Catrina has a yellow crayon.
- Dimple has a blue crayon but not a green one.

Who owns a green and a red crayon?

a. Alcina
b. Bea
c. Catrina
d. Dimple
e. No one

**Q1.141** Amelie walks 20 metres to the east, turns right and walks another 15 metres in a straight line. She turns right again and walks another 40 metres in a straight line. What is the shortest distance between her start point and her end point?

    **a.**   20 metres
    **b.**   21 metres
    **c.**   23 metres
    **d.**   25 metres
    **e.**   27 metres

**Q1.142** A standard set of dominoes contains all the possible combinations of numbers from 0 to 6. There are 28 combinations in total, as shown on the picture below. If you choose two dominoes at random, what is the probability that these two dominoes match, i.e. that one of the ends of one of the dominoes matches at least one of the ends of the other?

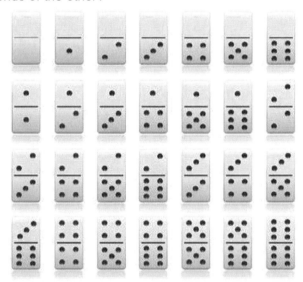

    **a.**   About 10%
    **b.**   About 20%
    **c.**   About 30%
    **d.**   About 40%
    **e.**   About 50%

**Q1.143** Mary enjoys baking but prefers to buy ready-made ready-rolled pastry to make her tartlets. The pastry sheets she buys are rolled out as a disc and, out of one, she can cut four round tartlet bases. Out of the leftover dough from three sheets, she can roll another sheet of similar dimensions, from which she can cut four more tartlet bases. And so on. If she has fewer than three leftover sheets, she makes no more cases.

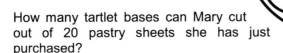

How many tartlet bases can Mary cut out of 20 pastry sheets she has just purchased?

a. 108
b. 112
c. 114
d. 116
e. 118

**Q1.144** Tom rolls two dice: one with his left hand and one with his right hand. If the right-hand die has an even number, then Tom rolls it again and again until he obtains an odd number. Once Tom has obtained an odd number with the right-hand die, then his score is calculated as follows:

- If the left-hand die has an odd number, then the overall score is zero.
- If the left-hand die has an even number, then the overall score is the sum of the two numbers.

What is the average score he will obtain after playing many times?

a. 3.0
b. 3.1
c. 3.2
d. 3.5
e. 3.8

**Q1.145** Subha has a rectangular kitchen measuring 230 cm x 440 cm. She has, at her disposal, an unlimited number of tiles of three possible dimensions: 5 cm x 5 cm, 10 cm x 10 cm and 15 cm x 15 cm.

What is the minimum number of tiles she will require to cover the floor surface without cutting any tile?

a.  373
b.  450
c.  522
d.  568
e.  632

**Q1.146** A straight fence is to be constructed from posts 6 inches wide and separated by lengths of chain 5 feet long. If the fence begins and ends with a post, which of the following could not be the length of the fence in feet? (12 inches = 1 foot)

a.  17
b.  28
c.  35
d.  39
e.  50

**Q1.147** The front wheels of a toy car have a circumference of 4 cm. The back wheels have a circumference of 7 cm. If the toy car travels in a straight line without slippage, how many centimetres will the toy car have travelled when the front wheels have made 12 more revolutions than the back wheels?

a.  16
b.  48
c.  64
d.  84
e.  112

**Q1.148** Consider six consecutive stations on a tube line and a specific train. Yesterday, on average, 32.5 passengers boarded at each of the six stations.

Given that, at each stop, beginning with the second, 3 fewer passengers boarded the train than at the previous stop, how many passengers boarded the tube train at its first station?

    **a.**   35
    **b.**   36
    **c.**   40
    **d.**   195
    **e.**   240

**Q1.149** A train travels from A to B in 4 hours. The train has an average speed of 48 kilometres per hour for the first 2 hours and an average speed of 41 kilometres per hour for the whole journey.

What was the train's average speed for the final 2 hours of the journey?

    **a.**   27 km/h
    **b.**   29 km/h
    **c.**   31 km/h
    **d.**   34 km/h
    **e.**   37 km/h

**Q1.150** David is given the task of painting numbers on the doors in a street of houses that is about to be demolished. There are fifty houses, to be numbered 1–50.

How many times does he need to paint the number 3?

    **a.**   12
    **b.**   13
    **c.**   14
    **d.**   15
    **e.**   16

# 1C Aptitude and Skills
Data Analysis/Inference - 153 Questions

## Answers from page 279

**1.151** The graph below is a cumulative plot of the length of a surgical waiting list for two types of operations in a district general hospital. The vertical axis shows the number of patients who have been waiting for less than the number of days on the horizontal axis.

The diamonds (top line) represent the length of the orthopaedic surgical waiting list and the squares (bottom line) represent the length of time spent on the cardiac surgical waiting list.

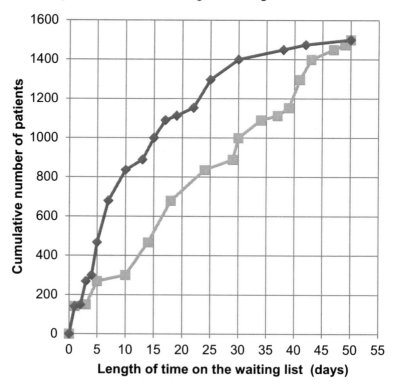

**Q1.151a** How many cardiac surgery patients waited for 10 days or more but less than 30 days?

   **a.** 300
   **b.** 500
   **c.** 700
   **d.** 900
   **e.** 1000

**Q1.151b** How many orthopaedic surgery patients waited for 15 days or more but less than 30 days?

   **a.** 400
   **b.** 700
   **c.** 1000
   **d.** 1200
   **e.** 1400

**Q1.152** The government is currently encouraging people to use energy-saving light bulbs. However, these are much more expensive than standard light bulbs, although they last a lot longer. The unit of electricity used by electricity suppliers is the kilowatt hour, i.e. 1000 watts running for one hour. Electricity costs 10p per kilowatt hour. We are given the following data about the two types of bulbs:

| | Energy-saving bulbs | Standard bulbs |
| --- | --- | --- |
| Price | £5.00 | £0.20 |
| Life | 10,000 hours | 2,000 hours |
| Wattage rating | 20 watts | 60 watts |

How much money will you save over 10,000 hours of usage by using an energy-saving bulb instead of a standard bulb?

   **a.** £35
   **b.** £36
   **c.** £40
   **d.** £41
   **e.** £46

**Q1.153** The table below shows the number of patients who experienced a post-operative infection, for different wards of the same hospital, in 2009 and 2010.

| Wards | 2009 | 2010 |
|-------|------|------|
| Coles | 58 | 62 |
| Jones | 38 | 42 |
| Patel | 35 | 40 |
| Smith | 34 | 40 |
| Taylor | 14 | 28 |
| **Total** | **179** | **212** |

**Q1.153a** Which of the following pie charts represents the contribution of each of the wards to the increase in infection between 2009 and 2010?

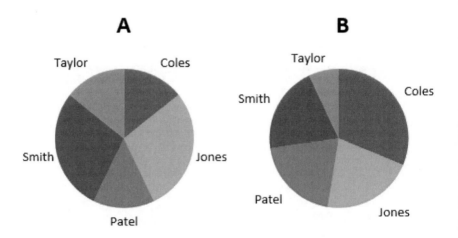

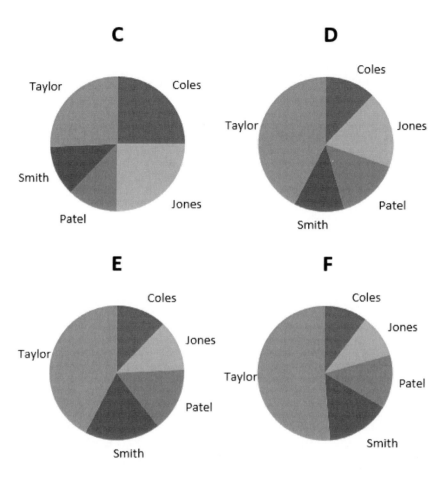

**Q1.153b** The manager who reported the figures in the table made a mistake. In fact, the number for the Coles ward in 2010 should have been 68 instead of 62. How will the area for the Taylor ward change as a consequence?

|    |                                    |
|----|------------------------------------|
| a. | It will be multiplied by 55/26     |
| b. | It will be multiplied by 31/34     |
| c. | It will be divided by 5/2          |
| d. | It will be divided by 13/11        |
| e. | It will be multiplied by 35/39     |

**Q1.154** The tables below enable nutritional requirements to be estimated for adults who are receiving treatment in hospitals.

| Step 1: Calculate Basic Metabolic Rate (BMR) |
|---|
| BMR (kcal) = 655 + (9.6 x weight in kg) + (1.8 x height in cm) − (4.7 x age in years) |

| Step 2: Calculate Harris Benedict Calorie Requirement (CR)<br>CR = BMR x Activity Factor x Stress Factor | |
|---|---|
| Status | Activity Factor |
| Sedentary (bed rest) | 1.2 |
| Light activity (sports 1–3 days/week) | 1.375 |
| Moderately active (sports 3–5 days/week) | 1.55 |
| Very active (hard exercise) | 1.725 |
| Status | Stress Factor |
| Burns (<10% body) | 1.2 |
| Minor Surgery | 1.3 |
| Respiratory Failure | 1.5 |
| Major Surgery | 1.5 |
| Major Sepsis | 1.6 |
| Burns (>50% body) | 2.0 |

| Step 3: Calculate Protein Requirement (g/day/kg of body weight) | | | |
|---|---|---|---|
| Status | | | |
| Normal | 0.8 | | |
| Elderly (>65 years) | 1.2 | | |
| Minor Surgery | 1.3 | | |
| Major Surgery | 1.5 | | |
| Burns | 1.6 | | |

| Step 4: Feed Formula | | |
|---|---|---|
| Formula | Calories (kcal/ml) | Protein (g/ml) |
| ProtoShake | 1 | 1 |
| ProtoShake XL | 31 | 1.5 |
| FortSure | 2 | 1 |
| FortSure Xtra | 21 | 1.5 |

**Q1.154a** What is the BMR (to the nearest kcal) of a healthy 30-year-old man weighing 90 kg and of height 1.8 m?

a. 1381 kcal
b. 1505 kcal
c. 1702 kcal
d. 1892 kcal
e. 1984 kcal

**Q1.154b** What is the calorie requirement (to the nearest kcal) of a 50-year-old man weighing 80 kg and of height 1.8 m, resting in bed after minor surgery?

a. 1512 kcal
b. 2108 kcal
c. 2359 kcal
d. 2505 kcal
e. 2945 kcal

**Q1.154c** What is the best feed formula for a 50-year-old man weighing 100 kg, of height 2 m, in bed rest after major surgery?

a. ProtoShake
b. ProtoShake XL
c. FortSure
d. FortSure Xtra

**Q1.154d** A nurse mixed 50 ml of ProtoShake and 50 ml of FortSure Xtra intending to make a 1250 kcal drink. Approximately what volume of ProtoShake XL is required to be added to the mix to reach the intended calorific goal?

a. 3 ml
b. 30 ml
c. 5 ml
d. 50 ml
e. 100 ml

**Q1.155** The Kaplan-Meier graph below plots the percentage of patients who incurred no post-operative complications in relation to the time elapsed since the operation, for obese (BMI >30) and non-obese (BMI <30) patients.

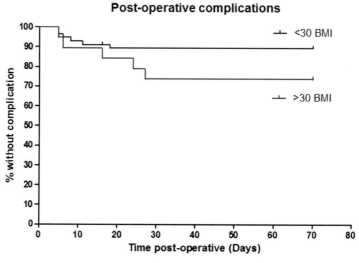

**Q1.155a** What percentage of obese patients has experienced a post-operative complication before day 50?

a. 10%
b. 28%
c. 72%
d. 75%
e. 90%

**Q1.155b** Assuming that the lines remain flat at the same level after 70 days and that a total of 840 patients (a quarter of whom were obese) never experienced any complications, approximately how many patients were included in the survey?

a. 1000
b. 2000
c. 3000
d. 5000
e. 7000

**Q1.156** Consider the following demographic and infrastructure information for three countries in South America.

|  | Brazil | Argentina | Peru |
|---|---|---|---|
| **Population (millions)** | 200 | 42 | 30 |
| **Urban:Rural population (%)** | 61:39 | 86:14 | 80:20 |
| **Internet (millions)** | 16 | 2 | 1 |

**Q1.156a** What is the approximate Urban:Rural population ratio when considering all three countries together?

   **a.** 62:38
   **b.** 67:33
   **c.** 70:30
   **d.** 75:25
   **e.** 80:20

**Q1.156b** If 75% of people living in urban areas and 20% of people living in rural areas have an internet connection in Brazil, what is the approximate Urban:Rural ratio for the people who <u>do not</u> have any internet connection in Brazil?

   **a.** 1:6
   **b.** 1:2
   **c.** 4:5
   **d.** 1:1
   **e.** 6:1

**Q1.156c** What percentage of the total rural population across all three countries lives in Peru?

   **a.** 6.1%
   **b.** 6.7%
   **c.** 11.2%
   **d.** 15.2%
   **e.** 27.4%

**Q1.157** Two factsheets are made available to you:

## CT Colonoscopy

A CT (computed tomography) colonoscopy investigation is a virtual examination of the lining of the bowel wall. Patients undergo helical CT scans and the results are analysed by specialists. It can diagnose the presence of bowel polyps or cancer.

False negative: Screened negative by CT colonoscopy investigation but a biopsy reveals polyps or cancer. In every 100 men screened, the average number screened negative but who actually have abnormalities is 6.

False positive: Screened positive by CT colonoscopy but a biopsy shows no bowel polyps or cancer. In every 100 men screened, the average number screened positive but who do not actually have any abnormalities is 16.

True positive: Screened positive by CT colonoscopy and with bowel polyp or cancer shown by biopsy. In every 100 men screened, the average number screened positive and with abnormalities is 14.

## Faecal Occult Blood test (FOBt)

The presence of blood in the stool can indicate bowel polyps or bowel cancer. Samples of stools are taken from separate bowel motions and are analysed for blood content. A normal FOBt does not exclude the presence of bowel abnormalities (false negative); neither does a positive FOBt confirm the presence of abnormalities (false positive).

2.5% of men will have a positive FOBt. Out of these, 10% will subsequently be found to have abnormalities and the remaining 90% will be shown to be false positives.

Of those with normal FOBt, 0.3% will later be found to have bowel abnormalities (false negatives).

**Q1.157a** If CT colonoscopy were to be used alone to diagnose bowel abnormalities, what would be the percentage of men screened positive?

    **a.**   8%
    **b.**   14%
    **c.**   16%
    **d.**   24%
    **e.**   30%

**Q1.157b** If the figures mentioned in the FOBt leaflet are to be trusted, in a screening group of 10,000 men, how many would you expect to actually have bowel abnormalities?

    **a.**   25
    **b.**   30
    **c.**   54
    **d.**   250
    **e.**   280
    **f.**   300
    **g.**   550

**Q1.157c** The NHS bowel cancer screening programme is investigating whether a 2-stage test procedure would increase accuracy. This screening programme seeks to use FOBt first. Any positive tests would then be referred for a CT colonoscopy.

If 10,000 men are screened in such a fashion, how many will have false positives on both tests (to the nearest whole number, assuming that both tests are independent of each other)?

    **a.**   1
    **b.**   4
    **c.**   36
    **d.**   74
    **e.**   93

**Q1.158** The table below shows the percentage of waste (weight) that was recycled during the years 2008 to 2011, per category, for a family.

|  | **2008** | **2009** | **2010** | **2011** |
|---|---|---|---|---|
| Paper | 75% | 80% | 96% | 50% |
| Glass | 40% | 50% | 55% | 50% |
| Plastic | 25% | 25% | 11% | 40% |
| Cardboard | 30% | 40% | 24% | 40% |

The following chart shows the representation of the waste that was recycled by the family during the year 2009, in kilograms:

**Waste recycled by the family in 2009 (in kg)**

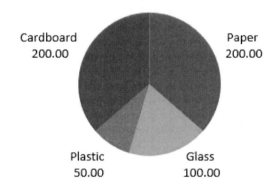

Cardboard 200.00

Paper 200.00

Plastic 50.00

Glass 100.00

The weight of waste recycled by the family in 2010 was 20% higher than in 2009 for cardboard and paper, and 10% higher than in 2009 for plastic and glass. What was the total weight of waste produced by the family in 2010?

    **a.**  550 kg
    **b.**  605 kg
    **c.**  1,150 kg
    **d.**  1,300 kg
    **e.**  1,800 kg
    **f.**  1,950 kg
    **g.**  2,200 kg

**Q1.159** Consider the following table showing the quality and efficiency scores achieved by a wide range of machines.

Given that the x-axis represents quality and the y-axis represents efficiency, which machine is represented by the white diamond on the chart?

| Machine | Quality | Efficiency | Machine | Quality | Efficiency |
|---------|---------|------------|---------|---------|------------|
| A | 25 | 12.5 | M | 13 | 10.3 |
| B | 20 | 15.4 | N | 12.5 | 12.5 |
| C | 15 | 11.3 | O | 11 | 12.5 |
| D | 30 | 12.5 | P | 14 | 12 |
| E | 12 | 12.5 | Q | 13.7 | 14 |
| G | 13 | 18.2 | R | 12 | 12 |
| H | 16 | 15.3 | S | 11.8 | 15 |
| I | 18 | 15.2 | T | 15 | 11 |
| J | 12 | 14.1 | U | 17.3 | 12 |
| K | 11 | 12.1 | V | 12 | 15 |
| L | 10 | 11.8 | W | 11.3 | 11.7 |

# Quality v. Efficiency

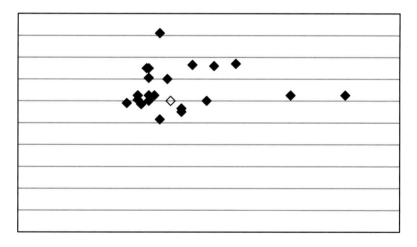

**Q1.160** ACE Petrochemicals had total production of crude oil products of 60 million barrels for last year, split as follows:

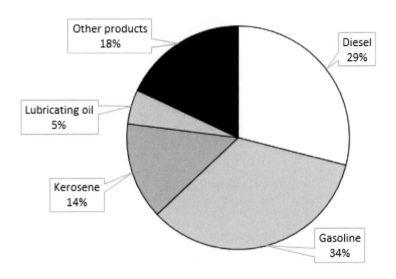

**Q1.160a** What was the total production of gasoline and kerosene combined (in barrels)?

    a.   285,000
    b.   480,000
    c.   26.4 million
    d.   28.8 million
    e.   48.0 million

**Q1.160b** If the total income generated by the sale of lubricating oil was £63 million last year, how much was the cost of a barrel of lubricating oil?

    a.   £16
    b.   £18
    c.   £21
    d.   £22
    e.   £24

**Q1.161** Staff distribution at HM Constructions Ltd – percentage of total staff in each role:

| Function | Year 1 | Year 2 | Year 3 | Year 4 | Year 5 |
|---|---|---|---|---|---|
| Marketing | 18 | 20 | 25 | 30 | 30 |
| Production | 40 | 39 | 30 | 30 | 32 |
| Finance | 9 | 8 | 5 | 4 | 3 |
| Distribution | 21 | 15 | 13 | 14 | 25 |
| Other | 12 | 18 | 27 | 22 | 10 |
| TOTAL | 100 | 100 | 100 | 100 | 100 |

**Q1.161a** In Year 3, 486 people were employed in areas other than Marketing, Production, Finance and Distribution. How many people were employed by HM Constructions Ltd in that year?

a. 1,700
b. 1,750
c. 1,800
d. 1,850
e. 1,950

**Q1.161b** Between which two years did the number of people employed in Marketing at HM Constructions change the most?

a. Year 1 and Year 2
b. Year 2 and Year 3
c. Year 3 and Year 4
d. Year 4 and Year 5
e. Cannot be determined

**Q1.161c** Assume that all employees present in Year 1 are still employed in the same role in Year 5 and no employee ever changes function. Consider the following statements:

I. There were at least 3 times more employees in Year 5 than in Year 1.
II. The total number of employees increased each year.
III. No new recruits joined the Finance department in any year.

Which of these statements can be deduced from the table?

a. I only   b. II only   c. III only   d. I and II   e. I and III

**Q1.162** A large corporation invested $168 million in several countries in 2015. Between 2015 and 2016 it increased or decreased the amount of dollars ($) invested in each country by a given percentage. The table below shows the distribution of the 2015 investment between countries, and the percentage by which each country's dollar investment increased between 2015 and 2016.

| Location | Distribution of 2015 investment between countries | Increase/decrease in $ investment between 2015 and 2016 |
| --- | --- | --- |
| USA | 50% | +20% |
| Japan | 20% | -50% |
| SE Asia | 10% | +20% |
| UK | 10% | ??? |
| Germany | 4% | -50% |
| Latin America | 4% | -25% |
| Middle East | 2% | +50% |
| | 100% | |

**Q1.162a** How much was invested in Japan in 2016?

a. $16.8 million
b. $33.6 million
c. $50.4 million
d. $88.3 million
e. $117.6 million

**Q1.162b** If the corporation's total investment in dollars was exactly the same in 2016 as it was in 2015, by what percentage did the UK investment increase or decrease?

a. +100%
b. +30%
c. +12%
d. +0%
e. -50%

**Q1.163** The following table shows the number of children born in 1994 and 1995, and the number of children who died under the age of 1 week in those two years, in five European countries.

| | Population in 1995 (thousands) | Births (thousands) | | Died under age of 1 week | |
|---|---|---|---|---|---|
| | | 1994 | 1995 | 1994 | 1995 |
| Ireland | 4,087 | 80.4 | 80.1 | 80 | 76 |
| France | 61,013 | 914 | 1,018 | 1,202 | 1,173 |
| Greece | 16,064 | 159 | 160 | 207 | 191 |
| Spain | 45,060 | 537 | 522 | 499 | 507 |
| Germany | 82,409 | 1,204 | 1,194 | 1,019 | 1,007 |

**Q1.163a** Which country had the highest birth rate (i.e. number of births per thousand inhabitants) in 1995?

    **a.** Ireland
    **b.** France
    **c.** Greece
    **d.** Spain
    **e.** Germany

**Q1.163b** An analyst wants to calculate the death rate for children born in 1995. This is calculated by following all children born in 1995 and counting those who died within 1 week of birth. The death rate is obtained by dividing the number of deaths by the number of births. Which of the following information is required in addition to the above table in order to be able to calculate that rate accurately?

    I.    The number of children born in the last week of 1994, who died in the first week of 1995 under the age of one week.
    II.    The number of children born in the last week of 1995, who died in the first week of 1996 under the age of one week.
    III.    The number of children born in the last week of 1994.

    **a.** No further information required
    **b.** I only
    **c.** II only
    **d.** III only
    **e.** I and II

**Q1.164** In 2015, OCE Industries had 50,000 employees, spread around the world as follows:

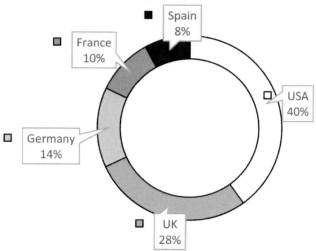

### Employee spread in 2015

On 31 December 2015, a number of employees were transferred from one country to another <u>within OCE Industries</u>, as shown in the table below:

| Country employees are transferring to: | Country employees are transferring from: | | | | |
|---|---|---|---|---|---|
| | France | Germany | UK | USA | Spain |
| France | | 200 | 180 | 1,000 | 200 |
| Germany | 150 | | 250 | 200 | 200 |
| UK | 200 | 100 | | 300 | 150 |
| USA | 50 | 100 | 100 | | 50 |
| Spain | 10 | 50 | 50 | 375 | |

In addition to internal transfers within OCE Industries, each country also recruited a number of new employees externally. The number of new employees recruited externally by OCE Industries on 31 December 2015 by each country was as follows:

| France | Germany | UK | USA | Spain |
|---|---|---|---|---|
| 1000 | 500 | 200 | 500 | X |

**Q1.164a** How many employees worked for OCE Industries in the USA in 2016?

    **a.**   18,000 employees
    **b.**   18,800 employees
    **c.**   18,925 employees
    **d.**   20,075 employees
    **e.**   20,800 employees

**Q1.164b** The number of employees recruited externally in Spain was not provided by the company (X in the table). However, we know that the Spanish subsidiary always increases its total number of employees by 10% each year. What is the value of X?

    **a.**   385
    **b.**   400
    **c.**   485
    **d.**   515
    **e.**   600

**Q1.164c** Which of the following charts best represents the proportion of employees who transferred internally <u>to</u> each country? (Note: the colours used for each country may be different to those used in the original chart.)

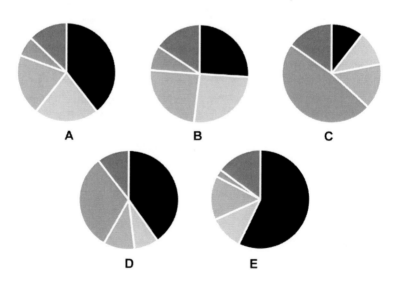

A             B             C

D             E

**Q1.165** The following table shows the costs of medications available from four separate pharmacies:

| | Rex (*) | Maxi (**) | Shoto | Bellar (***) |
|---|---|---|---|---|
| **100 ibuprofen tablets** | £25.00 | £24.00 | £30.00 | £36.50 |
| **50 paracetamol tablets** | £7.50 | £8.00 | £12.00 | £7.00 |
| **15 inhalers** | £1.80 | £2.00 | £2.00 | £2.10 |
| **5 aspirin tablets** | £4.70 | £4.65 | £5.20 | £4.50 |
| **20 insulin syringes** | £3.00 | £5.00 | £2.00 | £3.00 |

* Rex gives a 10% discount on orders over £100.
** Maxi gives away one packet of 20 insulin syringes with every 1,000 ibuprofen tablets bought.
*** Bellar has the following promotion: Buy one pack of 100 ibuprofen tablets and get a 25% discount on one pack of 50 paracetamol tablets.

**Q1.165a** A customer wishes to purchase 1,000 ibuprofen tablets, 200 paracetamol tablets and 100 insulin syringes. Which of the following options correctly ranks the four pharmacies from the cheapest to the most expensive for such a purchase?

   **a.**   Maxi < Rex < Bellar < Shoto
   **b.**   Rex < Shoto < Maxi < Bellar
   **c.**   Rex < Maxi < Shoto < Bellar
   **d.**   Maxi < Shoto < Bellar < Rex
   **e.**   Maxi < Rex < Shoto < Bellar

**Q1.165b** Shoto pharmacy is retailing a special pack containing 250 ibuprofen tablets and 250 paracetamol tablets for £120. What saving would a customer make by purchasing 4 such packs instead of the packs normally retailed by Shoto? (Assume Shoto cannot sell split packs)

   **a.**   11.1%
   **b.**   15.2%
   **c.**   17.5%
   **d.**   20.3%
   **e.**   20.8%

**Q1.166** A removal firm owns several trucks, which it hires out. For each truck, the maximum capacity (expressed as the number of large boxes it can carry) and the hire cost are shown in the table below. Each large box can contain four small boxes.

| Truck type | No. of large boxes | Truck hire cost |
|---|---|---|
| Toby truck | 15 | £150 |
| Tucker truck | 20 | £400 |
| Lensa truck | 10 | £95 |
| Tug truck | 1 | £25 |
| CB truck | 5 | £50 |
| Eastwind truck | 2 | £50 |

**Q1.166a** Which truck should be used to transport 12 small boxes with the least amount of empty space?

a. Toby truck
b. Tucker truck
c. Lensa truck
d. Tug truck
e. CB truck

**Q1.166b** The removal firm owns two of each type of truck. What is the smallest number of types of truck required to carry 76 small boxes without leaving any empty space?

a. 1
b. 2
c. 3
d. 4
e. 5

**Q1.166c** The firm has access to an unlimited number of each type of truck. A client wants to use the removal firm to transport 28 large boxes. What is the cheapest possible price he can pay?

a. £260
b. £285
c. £290
d. £300
e. £315

**Q1.167** The following graph shows the energy usage within a hospital:

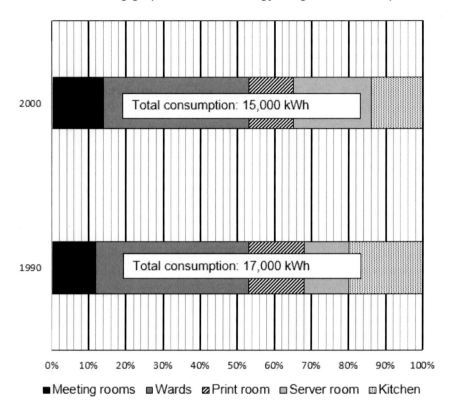

■ Meeting rooms ▦ Wards ▨ Print room ▢ Server room ▥ Kitchen

**Q1.167a** Between 1990 and 2000, what was the increase in energy use for the server room, meetings rooms and wards combined?

    **a.** 50 kWh
    **b.** 530 kWh
    **c.** 950 kWh
    **d.** 1,350 kWh
    **e.** 1,530 kWh

**Q1.167b** Between 1990 and 2000, which space experienced the smallest reduction in kWh used?

    **a.**  Meeting rooms
    **b.**  Wards
    **c.**  Print room
    **d.**  Server room
    **e.**  Kitchen

**Q1.167c** In 2010, a new wing was added to the hospital and it was decided that the energy consumption for that new wing would be represented by its own percentage block on the graph. In 2010, the total energy consumption was 18,000 kWh, with the energy consumed by the 'old' areas remaining the same in kWh as in the year 2000. Which of the following charts best represents the 2010 energy consumption?

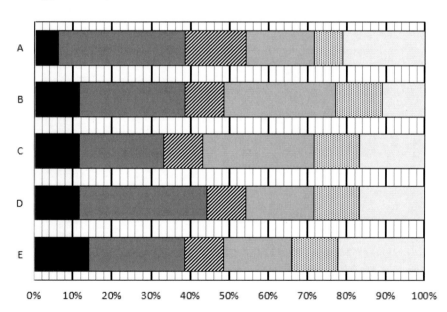

**Q1.168** The graph below shows the average daily number of hikers in Dirge National Park for four separate years. The number of children is assumed to be split 50% male, 50% female.

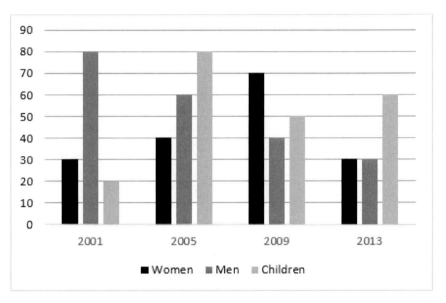

**Q1.168a** In which year was the average daily number of hikers the highest?

    a.    2001
    b.    2005
    c.    2009
    d.    2013
    e.    Cannot be deduced from the data

**Q1.168b** Which year had the highest number of male visitors (adults and children combined)?

    a.    2001 only
    b.    2005 only
    c.    2009 only
    d.    2013 only
    e.    More than two years qualify

**Q1.169** A London museum organises a special exhibition for which it sells tickets for specific entry times: 1pm, 2pm, 3pm, 4pm and 5pm.

Visitors can stay a maximum of two hours and can exit only at 2pm, 3pm, 4pm, 5pm or 6pm.

Today, 1,200 visitors went to the special exhibition. The number of visitors entering and exiting was recorded as follows:

|        | 1pm | 2pm | 3pm | 4pm | 5pm | 6pm |
|--------|-----|-----|-----|-----|-----|-----|
| Entry  | 210 | 240 | 360 | 270 | 120 |     |
| Exit   |     | 150 | 160 | 370 | 280 | 240 |

**Q1.169a** How many people stayed at the exhibition for only one hour?

    **a.** 150
    **b.** 350
    **c.** 525
    **d.** 750
    **e.** 900

**Q1.169b** We know that a group of tourists entered the exhibition. It is not known whether the group stayed one or two hours; however they all entered and left at the same time. What is the most accurate estimate of the size of that group?

    **a.** 60–100
    **b.** 60–230
    **c.** 120–150
    **d.** 120–360
    **e.** 150–240

**Q1.170** A school has four chemistry labs. In each lab are stored six different types of acid. The table below shows how many bottles of each acid are stored in each of the four labs:

| Acid | Lab 1 | Lab 2 | Lab 3 | Lab 4 | Total |
|---|---|---|---|---|---|
| Nitrous | 101 | 81 | 103 | 117 | 402 |
| Sulphuric | 68 | 98 | 111 | 107 | 384 |
| Nitric | 52 | 65 | 89 | 161 | 367 |
| Benzoic | 113 | 123 | 143 | 75 | 454 |
| Hydrochloric | 87 | 138 | 77 | 99 | 401 |
| Salicylic | 79 | 104 | 80 | 129 | 392 |
| **TOTAL** | **500** | **609** | **603** | **688** | **2400** |

The bottles in which those acids are stored come in a variety of sizes. One particular type of acid could be stored in bottles of different sizes. All we know is that the bottles of all labs considered together are split as follows:

| Size | S | M | L | XL | XXL |
|---|---|---|---|---|---|
| Proportion | 15% | 25% | 10% | 30% | 20% |

We also know that no more than 1% of the bottles stored in Lab 2 are of size XL. The same applies to Lab 3.

**Q1.170a** What is the minimum number of bottles of size XL that are stored in Lab 1, expressed as a percentage of the total number of bottles stored in Lab 1?

    **a.** 2%
    **b.** 3%
    **c.** 4%
    **d.** 5%
    **e.** 6%

**Q1.170b** If the number of XL bottles stored in Lab 4 is 3.5 times the number of XL bottles stored in Lab 1, how many XL bottles are stored in Lab 1?

    **a.** Between 155 and 157
    **b.** Between 158 and 160
    **c.** Between 161 and 163
    **d.** Between 164 and 167
    **e.** Between 168 and 170

**Q1.170c** Each of the following pie charts represents the allocation of a specific acid across the four labs. Which of the six acids is not represented by any chart?

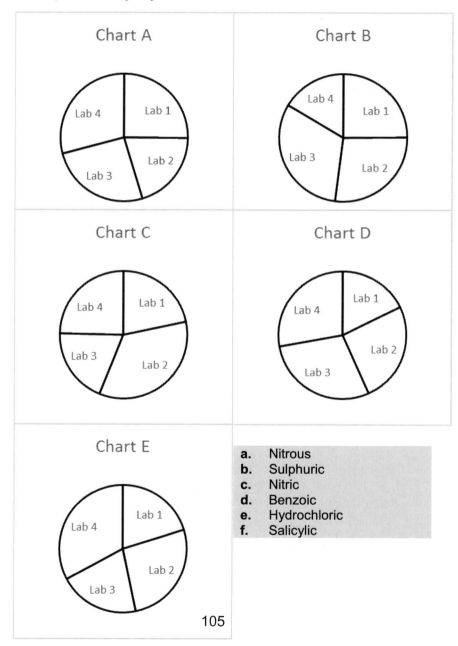

a. Nitrous
b. Sulphuric
c. Nitric
d. Benzoic
e. Hydrochloric
f. Salicylic

**Q1.171** The following graph shows the child vaccination uptake in four different countries in 2000 for three vaccines: smallpox (in black), polio (in dark grey) and MMR (in light grey).

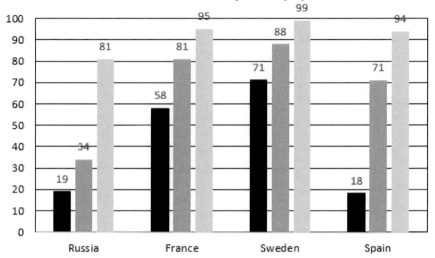

Child vaccination uptake (%) 2000

Which of the following statements are true?

I.      It is possible that no children were vaccinated for both smallpox and MMR in Russia, and for smallpox and polio in Spain.
II.     The minimum percentage of French children vaccinated for both smallpox and polio is 39%.
III.    The minimum percentage of Swedish children who received all three vaccines is 58%.

| | |
|---|---|
| **a.** | I only |
| **b.** | II only |
| **c.** | III only |
| **d.** | I and II |
| **e.** | I and III |
| **f.** | II and III |
| **g.** | All three statements |

**Q1.172** The following table shows financial information relating to the production and sale of cogs and springs by AM Ltd.

| Product | Total cost per unit | | | Sale price per unit | Profit per unit sold |
|---|---|---|---|---|---|
| | Manu-facture | Distribu-tion | Other | | |
| Cog M | £12.10 | £1.15 | £3.40 | £40.95 | £24.30 |
| Cog XL | £13.25 | £2.75 | £3.51 | £55.95 | £36.44 |
| Spring M | £20.20 | £2.30 | £4.20 | £72.00 | £45.30 |
| Spring XL | £25.40 | £3.50 | £7.60 | £121.00 | £84.50 |

The profit per unit sold is calculated as the sale price minus all the costs incurred per unit.

**Q1.172a** What is the minimum number of Cog XL units that need to be sold to make a higher profit than would be obtained by selling 150 units of Cog M?

a. 98
b. 99
c. 100
d. 101
e. 102

**Q1.172b** The company decides to halve the sale price of Spring XL units in the hope that it will increase its annual sales from 2,000 units to 4,000 units.

If it achieved that objective, what would be the impact on its annual profit?

a. A drop in profit of £169,000
b. A drop in profit of £96,000
c. A drop in profit of £73,000
d. An increase in profit of £73,000
e. An increase in profit of £96,000
f. An increase in profit of £169,000

**Q1.173** The following data relates to figures for a range of newspapers.

| Newspapers | Total number of paper version sold (millions) | | | Source of revenue (2007) | |
|---|---|---|---|---|---|
| | 2006 | 2007 | 2008 | Paper | Online |
| Spin Daily | 9.7 | 8.0 | 7.2 | 43% | 37% |
| The H Post | 8.3 | 8.0 | 7.2 | 45% | 47% |
| Carls News | 6.2 | 6.1 | 5.6 | 38% | 62% |
| The Voice | 2.8 | 4.0 | 3.8 | 25% | 75% |
| Daily Planet | 5.2 | 6.9 | 6.8 | 48% | 50% |

The column "Source of revenue" shows the percentage of the income generated by the newspapers for sales of paper copies and online subscriptions. Some newspapers may have income from additional sources, such as advertising, which is why the percentages for paper and online sales do not add up to 100%.

People buy either the paper version or the online version, but never both. When they buy the online version, they can only buy one day's online version of the newspaper at a time.

In 2007, the Spin Daily generated an income of £20 million from its paper and online sales combined. In the same year, The Voice generated an income of £4 million from paper copies. Online copies retail at the same price as paper copies.

**Q1.173a** By how much did the total number of paper versions of newspapers sold change between 2006 and 2008?

a. Up by 1.2 million
b. Up by 1.6 million
c. Down by 1.2 million
d. Down by 1.6 million
e. Down by 2.8 million

**Q1.173b** How much revenue was taken by The Voice from online copies in 2007?

a. £2 million
b. £4 million
c. £6 million
d. £8 million
e. £12 million

**Q1.173c** In 2008, the number of paper copies sold by The H Post was 10% lower than the 2007 number. However, at the same time, the paper saw the number of online copies sold increase by 20%. Overall the income generated was the same in 2007 as in 2008. The retail price of the paper and online versions remained the same during both years.

By what percentage did the income generated by other sources such as advertising increase or decrease?

   **a.**   A drop of 61%
   **b.**   A drop of 39%
   **c.**   No change
   **d.**   An increase of 61%
   **e.**   An increase of 39%
   **f.**   There is insufficient data to calculate it

**Q1.173d** Which of the following pie charts best illustrates the pro-portion of the combined revenue from advertising and other sources which was collected by each newspaper in 2007?

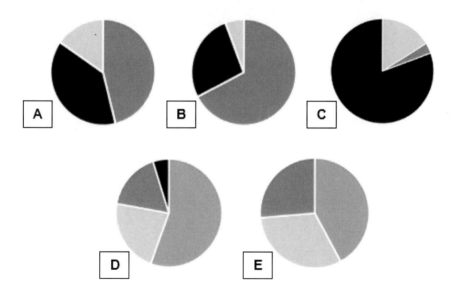

**Q1.174** A country has a population of 3,276,000 inhabitants, split between its different regions (A, B ... G) according to the following chart:

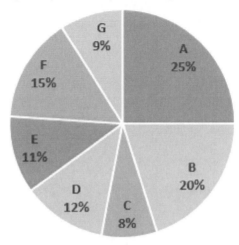

For each region the Male:Female and Literate:Illiterate ratios are as follows:

| Region | M:F Ratio | Literate:Illiterate Ratio |
|--------|-----------|---------------------------|
| A | 2:8 | 2:7 |
| B | 3:1 | 1:4 |
| C | 2:3 | 2:1 |
| D | 3:5 | 3:2 |
| E | 3:4 | 4:1 |
| F | 3:2 | 7:2 |
| G | 3:4 | 9:4 |

**Q1.174a** What is the number of men in region A?

- a. 163,800
- b. 180,215
- c. 204,750
- d. 208,550
- e. 209,850

**Q1.174b** What percentage of the whole country's population do the men living in regions B, D and F represent?

   a.  20%
   b.  22.5%
   c.  25%
   d.  26.5%
   e.  28.5%

**Q1.174c** If the Literate:Illiterate ratio within the male population of region C is 1:5, what is the Literate:Illiterate ratio for females in region C?

   a.  1:0
   b.  1:1
   c.  1:2
   d.  1:3
   e.  1:4

**Q1.174d** What is the ratio of females in region G over the females in region C?

   a.  2:1
   b.  5:4
   c.  9:8
   d.  13:12
   e.  15:14

**Q1.174e** This year, the population of region F is 10% higher than last year; and the population of region B is 12% higher than last year. What was the ratio of the population of region F over that of region B last year?

   a.  42:55
   b.  49:55
   c.  8:11
   d.  3:4
   e.  8:13

**Q1.175** The following chart shows the value of exports by three British companies over a period of seven years (the Y-axis shows the values in £millions).

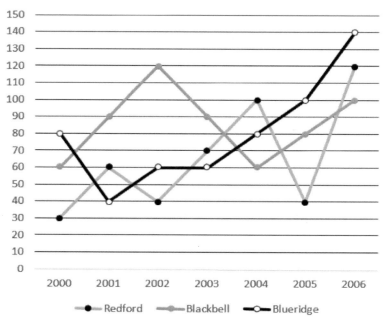

●—Redford  ●—Blackbell  ○—Blueridge

**Q1.175a** In which three years were the combined value of exports across all three companies the same?

    **a.** 2002, 2005 and 2006
    **b.** 2001, 2005 and 2006
    **c.** 2002, 2003 and 2005
    **d.** 2002, 2004 and 2006
    **e.** 2003, 2004 and 2006

**Q1.175b** By how much has the average value of exports across all three companies changed between 2004 and 2006?

    **a.** -50%
    **b.** -30%
    **c.** 0
    **d.** +30%
    **e.** +50%

**Q1.175c** Which of the following graphs is the most likely representation of the increase from the previous year in the average value of exports across all three companies, for the years 2001 to 2005?

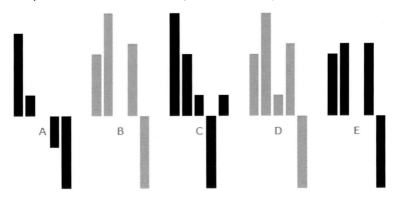

**Q1.175d** The following graph represents, for each year, the proportion of exports for each company in relation to the total value of exports across all three companies. However, the bar for one of the years has been incorrectly drawn. Which year?

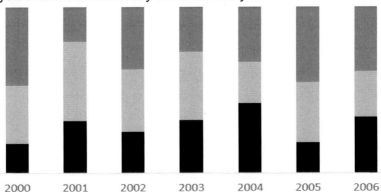

| | | | | | | | |
|---|---|---|---|---|---|---|---|
| 2000 | 2001 | 2002 | 2003 | 2004 | 2005 | 2006 | |

**a.** 2000
**b.** 2001
**c.** 2002
**d.** 2003
**e.** 2004
**f.** 2005
**g.** 2006

**Q1.176** To measure ingredients, bakers use what is called the "baker's percentage" method, where one "main" ingredient's weight is set at 100% and every other ingredient's weight is presented as a proportion of that main ingredient. They use a special set of scales on which they set the weight of their main ingredient as 100% and then they only have to worry about the percentage and not the actual weight anymore. For example, if a lay person's recipe calls for 150 g of flour and 75 g of butter, the baker's recipe will state 100% flour + 50% butter. The baker will place 150 g of flour on the scales and press the 100% calibration button. When it comes to measuring the butter, the baker will weigh the butter until the scales reach 50%. This stops him/her worrying about ratios.

A baker is preparing a sourdough starter to make some bread. Preparing the sourdough starter takes days and is done as follows:

### Day 1 – Prepare the initial dough

| Ingredient | Baker's % | Weight (g) |
|---|---|---|
| Wheat flour | 100% | 13.33 |
| Water | 50% | 6.67 |
| Total | 150% | 20.00 |

Let the mixture ferment in a jar. Note that the actual weight you need to use depends on the final amount of sour starter you want to produce. The weight of 20 g used here is only for illustration purposes. You can start with a higher amount if required.

### Days 2–7 (at least) – "Maintain-weight" feeding
Every day, throw away three-quarters of the sour starter, and add enough wheat flour and water in the same proportions as Day 1 (100%/50%) to maintain a total weight of 20 g throughout the whole culturing process. Do this every day until you are ready to make your bread, but at least until Day 7.

### Day 8 onwards, when ready to bake – "Increase-weight" feeding
Keep "maintain-weight" feeding until you are ready to bake. The day before you want to make your bread, increase the amount of sour starter. To do that, simply take the sour starter from the day before, do not discard any and add enough wheat flour and water in a 100%/50% ratio to quadruple the weight of the starter. Leave overnight and use the next day.

**Q1.176a** How much flour do I need to create a 300 g sourdough starter on Day 1?

- **a.** 50 g
- **b.** 100 g
- **c.** 150 g
- **d.** 200 g
- **e.** 250 g

**Q1.176b** At the start of Day 3, I have a starter that weighs 100 g and which I am about to feed. How much water do I need to add?

- **a.** 10 g
- **b.** 25 g
- **c.** 33 g
- **d.** 50 g
- **e.** 67 g

**Q1.176c** I have just fed my sourdough starter on Day 5, after which it weighs 600 g. How much flour have I used in total since the start of the process?

- **a.** 400 g
- **b.** 800 g
- **c.** 1.6 kg
- **d.** 1.8 kg
- **e.** 2.0 kg

**Q1.176d** I want to bake a loaf of bread on Day 9, made with 100 g of starter. How much starter do I need to prepare on Day 1?

- **a.** 5 g
- **b.** 25 g
- **c.** 50 g
- **d.** 75 g
- **e.** 100 g

**Q1.176e** Which column shows the baker's percentages for Day 2?

| | A | B | C | D | E |
|---|---|---|---|---|---|
| Wheat flour | 100% | 100% | 100% | 100% | 100% |
| Water | 50% | 100% | 50% | 75% | 25% |
| Starter | 25% | 100% | 50% | 25% | 25% |
| **Total** | **175%** | **300%** | **200%** | **200%** | **150%** |

115

**Q1.177** An estate agent's brochure lists a range of properties together with ratings for several features. Ratings range from 1 (poor) to 8 (good). Jane has a system to choose the properties in which she wants to invest. She first selects three properties that score the highest according to her most important criterion (interior, exterior, location or space). From those three properties, she dismisses the property that scores the lowest in her second most important criterion. And, out of the two properties left, she chooses the cheapest.

| Property | Interior | Exterior | Location | Space | Price |
|---|---|---|---|---|---|
| 67 Pontefract Lane | 8 | 6 | 2 | 6 | £390,000 |
| 83 Jason Creek | 6 | 3 | 3 | 4 | £301,000 |
| 23 Elwater Road | 1 | 5 | 6 | 5 | £250,000 |
| 8 Headway Park | 3 | 7 | 7 | 8 | £485,000 |
| 532 Scott Road | 4 | 8 | 4 | 3 | £350,000 |

**Q1.177a** What house will Jane buy if her criteria are: Most important: Location; Second most important: Interior?

    **a.**   67 Pontefract Lane
    **b.**   83 Jason Creek
    **c.**   23 Elwater Road
    **d.**   8 Headway Park
    **e.**   532 Scott Road

**Q1.177b** Jane has just bought 67 Pontefract Lane for £390,000. Her second most important criterion was Space. What was her most important criterion?

    **a.**   Interior
    **b.**   Exterior
    **c.**   Location
    **d.**   There is no solution to this problem
    **e.**   There are two possible solutions to this problem

**Q1.177c** If Jane picks two criteria at random to be her most important and second most important, what is the probability that she will end up purchasing the most expensive house?

    **a.**   0%
    **b.**   10%
    **c.**   20%
    **d.**   25%
    **e.**   30%

**Q1.178** The following table summarises sales made by different regional sales teams for a particular company:

| Region | Number of staff | Week 1 sales | | Week 2 sales | |
|---|---|---|---|---|---|
| | | Actual | Target | Actual | Target |
| North | 8 | 32 | 15 | 35 | 35 |
| East | 9 | 30 | 25 | 40 | 35 |
| South | 5 | 25 | 20 | 24 | 30 |
| West | 8 | 15 | 10 | 12 | 15 |
| London | 6 | 5 | 10 | 9 | 15 |
| Ireland | 4 | 15 | 10 | 24 | 12 |

**Q1.178a** How did the company perform across all regions?

| | Week 1 sales | Week 2 sales |
|---|---|---|
| a. | 22 over target | 2 over target |
| b. | 22 over target | 4 under target |
| c. | 32 over target | 2 under target |
| d. | 32 over target | 2 over target |
| e. | 32 under target | 2 under target |

**Q1.178b** Over the two weeks combined, which region achieved the highest sales per staff member?

a. North
b. East
c. South
d. West
e. London
f. Ireland

**Q1.178c** The company closed down one of the sales teams. If that had been done at the end of week 1, then the company would have overachieved by 5 sales across all remaining sales teams in week 2. Which team did it close down?

a. North
b. East
c. South
d. West
e. London
f. Ireland

117

**Q1.179** The following chart shows the number of research papers published by five prominent professors over a six-year period.

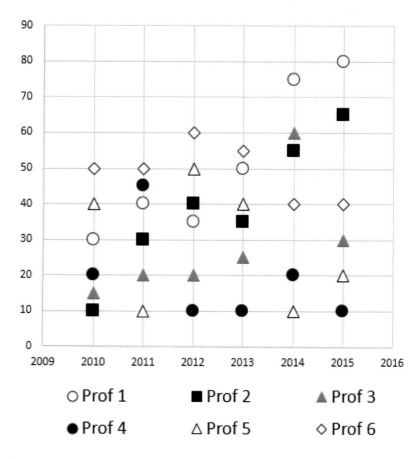

**Q1.179a** What is the total number of papers written by Prof 1 over the six years?

a. 300
b. 305
c. 310
d. 315
e. 320

**Q1.179b** Which professor has the average number of papers over the six years which is closest to 30 but with the average being above 30?

**a.** Prof 1
**b.** Prof 2
**c.** Prof 3
**d.** Prof 4
**e.** Prof 5
**f.** Prof 6

**Q1.179c** Which of the following graphs shows the proportion of publications for 2013 written by each professor?

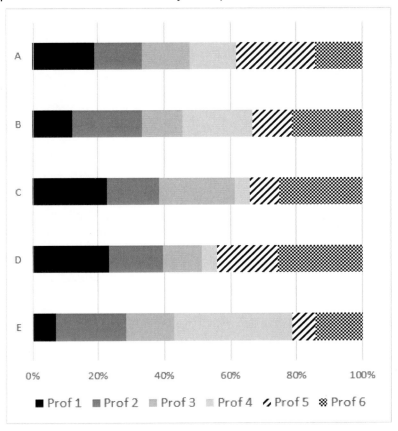

119

**Q1.180** The following table shows train journey times in the HH:MM format. There is only one possible direct route between towns, i.e. the journey from Town A to Town B has the same distance as the journey from Town B to Town A.

| Destination: | Brussels | Geneva | London | Luxem-bourg | Paris |
|---|---|---|---|---|---|
| **Departure station** | | | | | |
| **Brussels** | | X | 1:56 | X | 1:22 |
| **Geneva** | X | | 7:54 | X | 3:28 |
| **London** | 2:22 | 6:48 | | 5:45 | 2:25 |
| **Luxembourg** | X | X | 5:45 | | 2:16 |
| **Paris** | 1:20 | 3:33 | 2:15 | 2:39 | |

**Q1.180a** How much shorter than the Paris → Luxembourg journey is the Paris → London journey?

a.  5%
b.  10%
c.  15%
d.  20%
e.  25%

**Q1.180b** A man falls asleep on the train from London to Brussels. Once arrived at Brussels, the man fails to get off the train and, after the train has waited 35 minutes, it goes back towards London.

Once in London, the man has still not woken up and, after the train has waited 24 minutes, it goes back to Brussels, where the man eventually wakes up and disembarks.

How long was the man's trip in total?

a.  7:21
b.  7:39
c.  7:56
d.  8:05
e.  8:18

**Q1.180c** Consider the following trips:

- Max travels from Paris to London, stays in London for 4 hours and then travels to Luxembourg.
- David travels from London to Paris, stays in Paris for 4 hours and then travels to Luxembourg.
- Charles travels from London to Luxembourg, stays in Luxembourg for 4 hours and then travels to Paris.
- Tom travels from London to Paris, waits for 35 minutes and then travels back to London.

Which of the four travellers has the longest journey time?

| | |
|---|---|
| a. | Max |
| b. | David |
| c. | Charles |
| d. | Tom |
| e. | Max and Charles |


**Q1.180d** Consider the following trips:

- Tom travels from Paris to London, where he stays for 3 hours. He then travels to Luxembourg, where he stays for 1 hour before travelling back to Paris.
- Dick travels from London to Luxembourg, where he stays for 2 hours. He then travels to Paris, where he stays for 2 hours before travelling back to London.
- Harry travels from Luxembourg to Paris, where he stays for 1 hour. He then travels to London, where he stays for 3 hours before travelling back to Luxembourg.
- Max travels from Paris to London, where he stays for 2 hours. He then travels to Luxembourg, where he stays for 1 hour before travelling back to Paris.

Which of the four travellers has the fastest average speed?

| | |
|---|---|
| a. | Tom |
| b. | Dick |
| c. | Harry |
| d. | Max |
| e. | Cannot be determined using the data available |

**Q1.181** The results of a study into the impact of exercise on the risk of heart disease are shown below [BMI = Weight (kg)/Height$^2$ (m$^2$)]. The Y axis shows the relative risk of heart disease using inactive people as a control group (benchmark).

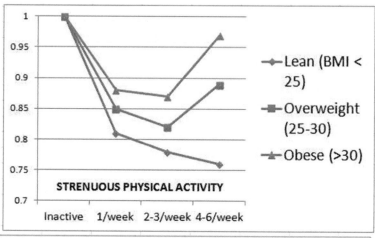

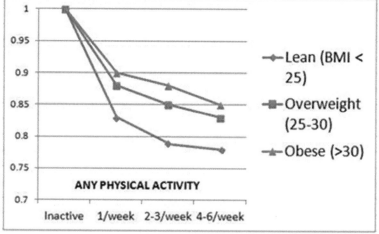

The study involved 1.1 million women from England and Scotland, who were enrolled in 1998 and reported how much physical activity they did at that time. They were then followed up for several years to determine if they suffered heart problems. 'Any physical activity' means a standard moderate amount.

**Q1.181a** Which of the following conclusions may be drawn from the graphs with regard to <u>obese</u> women?

    **a.**   They are likely to lose weight through exercise
    **b.**   They should avoid exercising more than 3 times a week
    **c.**   They should increase their level of exercise gradually
    **d.**   Those exercising strenuously once a week might as well exercise normally twice a week
    **e.**   The risk of heart disease for inactive obese women is the same as the risk for inactive lean people

**Q1.181b** Which of the following conclusions are true about <u>lean women who exercise 6 or fewer times a week</u>?

1.   The more they exercise, the lower their risk of heart disease, regardless of the intensity of the exercising.
2.   They can reduce their risk of heart disease by nearly 25% through exercising.
3.   The reduction in the risk of heart disease between 2-3/week and 4-6/week for lean women undertaking normal physical activity is lower than for obese women.

    **a.**   1 only
    **b.**   2 only
    **c.**   1 and 3 only
    **d.**   2 and 3 only
    **e.**   1, 2 and 3

**Q1.181c** To draw any conclusion from this study, a number of assumptions need to be made. Which of the following possible assumptions need to be made?

1.   People stuck to the same exercise regime throughout the observation period.
2.   The heavier someone is, the harder it is for them to exercise.
3.   People declared their true level of physical activity.

    **a.**   None
    **b.**   1 and 2 only
    **c.**   2 and 3 only
    **d.**   1 and 3 only
    **e.**   1, 2 and 3

**Q1.182** A study looked at the number of adults who received a recommendation by their family doctor to do more exercise. Data was collected from three years: 2005, 2010 and 2015, and covered six age ranges: 18–24, 25–44, 45–64, 65–74, 75–84 and over 85s. The following graphs show the percentage of adults whose doctor recommended they should exercise more.

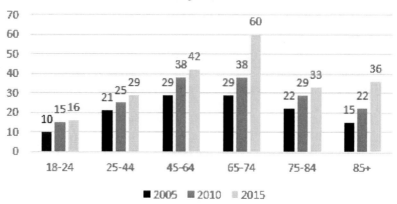

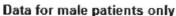

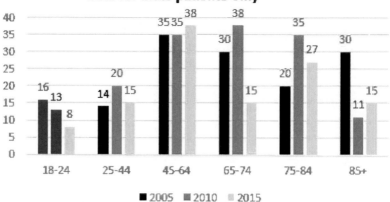

**Q1.182a** What proportion of <u>female patients aged 85 and over</u> were advised to do more exercise in 2015 if the male:female ratio for that age group was 2:3?

a.  27%
b.  38%
c.  50%
d.  51%
e.  53%

**Q1.182b** Which of the following conclusions may be drawn from the graphs with regard to <u>female patients aged 18-24</u>?

1.  In 2005, 4% were advised to do more exercise.
2.  In 2005, fewer than 10% were advised to do more exercise.
3.  The proportion advised to do more exercise was higher in 2015 than in 2010, and higher in 2010 than in 2005.

a.  2 only
b.  1 and 2 only
c.  2 and 3 only
d.  1, 2 and 3
e.  None

**Q1.182c** We are trying to estimate the proportion of the population aged 65–74 that was of male gender in 2015. What is the maximum possible value for that number?

a.  27%
b.  38%
c.  47%
d.  49%
e.  53%

**Q1.183** A City firm requires its graduate entrants to take a set of professional exams. We are told the following:

- There are 7 exams in total that need to be taken.
- Exams can only be taken once a year. Resits therefore must be taken the following year.
- Every graduate must sit one exam per year (and only one).
- Exams have to be taken in ascending order, e.g. Exam 2 can only be taken once Exam 1 has been passed.
- Failure to pass an exam after three attempts results in immediate dismissal from the firm.
- None left of their own accord during those years.

The firm recruited 25 graduates in one year. The table below shows how many graduates took each exam in the first eight years.

| Exam | Yr 1 | Yr 2 | Yr 3 | Yr 4 | Yr 5 | Yr 6 | Yr 7 | Yr 8 |
|------|------|------|------|------|------|------|------|------|
| 1 | 25 | 12 | 2 | | | | | |
| 2 | | 13 | 20 | 3 | | | | |
| 3 | | | 3 | 20 | 8 | | | |
| 4 | | | | 1 | 15 | 8 | | |
| 5 | | | | | 1 | 16 | 12 | |
| 6 | | | | | | 0 | 10 | 2 |
| 7 | | | | | | | 0 | 18 |

**Q1.183a** How many graduates were dismissed between Year 1 and Year 8?

    a.   1
    b.   3
    c.   5
    d.   7
    e.   9

**Q1.183b** How many graduates failed Exam 3 in Year 3?

    a.   0
    b.   1
    c.   2
    d.   3
    e.   Cannot be calculated

**Q1.183c** How many people failed Exam 1 at least once?

a. 2
b. 9
c. 12
d. 14
e. 17

**Q1.183d** What was the pass rate for Exam 2 in Year 2?

a. 3%
b. 13%
c. 23%
d. 33%
e. 43%

**Q1.183e** What was the pass rate for Exam 1 in Year 2?

a. 16.6%
b. 33.3%
c. 50%
d. 66.6%
e. 83.3%

**Q1.183f** What was the pass rate for Exam 2 in Year 4?

a. 0%
b. 33%
c. 66%
d. 100%
e. Cannot be calculated

**Q1.183g** What was the pass rate for Exam 2 in Year 3?

a. 50%
b. 65%
c. 75%
d. 85%
e. 90%

**Q1.184** The following diagram provides information about the number of people who attended a party and the types of dishes they ate.

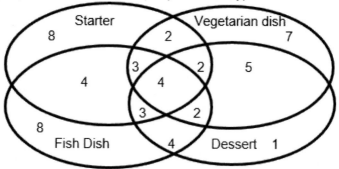

**Prices:**
Starter: £9
Dessert: £8

Main courses
Fish dish: £23
Vegetarian dish: £15

Special offers (each diner can benefit from only one offer)
A. Starter + 1 main course: 5% discount
B. Starter + 2 main courses: 10% discount
C. 1 main course + dessert: 5% discount
D. 2 main courses + dessert: 10% discount
E. Starter + 1 main course + dessert: 10% discount
F. Starter + 2 main courses + dessert: 15% discount
G. Starter + dessert: 5% discount

**Q1.184a** How many people ate at least two dishes?

   **a.** 20
   **b.** 29
   **c.** 36
   **d.** 43
   **e.** 51

**Q1.184b** How many people ate at least three dishes?

   **a.** 4
   **b.** 10
   **c.** 14
   **d.** 23
   **e.** 30

**Q1.184c** Assuming that diners always opt for the offer that gives them the biggest possible discount with regard to the food they eat, how many people benefited from Offer G?

    **a.**   0
    **b.**   1
    **c.**   2
    **d.**   3
    **e.**   4

**Q1.184d** How much was spent in total by diners opting for Offer D?

    **a.**   £82.80
    **b.**   £124.20
    **c.**   £248.40
    **d.**   £372.60
    **e.**   £414.00

**Q1.184e** If the people who ate only a starter joined forces with those who ate only one main course and a dessert so that all those involved could benefit from a discount, what is the <u>additional</u> amount that can be saved in total through that arrangement?

    **a.**   £10.80
    **b.**   £14.80
    **c.**   £18.00
    **d.**   £20.80
    **e.**   £28.80

**Q1.184f** If all diners decided to pool all their dishes together in order to obtain the best possible discount, how many of each type of discount would they obtain, based on what they ordered?

    **a.**   12 Type G + 7 Type B + 6 Type A
    **b.**   20 Type F + 5 Type D + 3 Type G
    **c.**   5 Type F + 12 Type B + 2 Type A
    **d.**   19 Type F + 6 Type E + 2 Type A
    **e.**   21 Type F + 4 Type B + 1 Type A

**Q1.185** The following table shows the production of alcoholic drinks in some European countries in million litres.

| Country | Population (thousands) | Wine | Spirits | Beer |
|---|---|---|---|---|
| France | 60013 | 53440 | 1751 | 17200 |
| Germany | 85000 | 9450 | 4057 | 93500 |
| Spain | 43060 | 320400 | 1866 | 30200 |
| Switzerland | 7500 | 1000 | 59 | 3600 |

**Q1.185a** If the Swiss population consume half of the wine produced in Switzerland, what is the average amount of Swiss wine consumed per person in Switzerland (to the nearest litre)?

a. 7 litres
b. 67 litres
c. 134 litres
d. 350 litres
e. 670 litres

**Q1.185b** What percentage of the beer produced across all four countries is produced in Germany?

a. 50%
b. 65%
c. 75%
d. 80%
e. 85%

**Q1.185c** Consumption of beer in Germany is on average 200 litres per person per year. They import 10% of their consumption from France and 10% of their consumption from Spain. The rest of their consumption is from local beer. Whatever is not consumed locally is exported. How much beer does Germany export each year?

a. 65,000 million litres
b. 69,900 million litres
c. 79,900 million litres
d. 92,140 million litres
e. 92,640 million litres

**Q1.186** The following graph represents the profits made by different sectors and different regions of the civil engineering firm Redford Ltd.

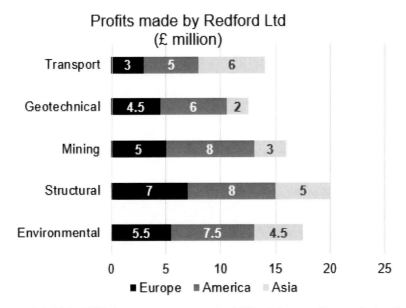

**Q1.186a** Which sector represents 25% of the profits made by the company overall?

| | |
|---|---|
| **a.** | Transport |
| **b.** | Geotechnical |
| **c.** | Mining |
| **d.** | Structural |
| **e.** | Environmental |

**Q1.186b** If the profit to turnover ratio for European contracts was 2:5, what was the turnover for the Geotechnical division in Europe?

| | |
|---|---|
| **a.** | £11.2 million |
| **b.** | £11.25 million |
| **c.** | £11.3 million |
| **d.** | £11.35 million |
| **e.** | £11.4 million |

**Q1.187** The following table information relates to the share prices and dividends paid for several companies.

Dividends are normally paid out once the company's accounts have been finalised and the profits have been accurately calculated. However, when a company has a good idea of the level of profit it is expecting to make before its annual accounts are finalised, it may pay out an interim dividend beforehand and then pay the balance (called 'final dividend') once the annual accounts have been finalised. The total annual dividend paid is therefore equal to the sum of the interim dividend and the final dividend.

Dividends are expressed as an amount payable per share.

| Share Prices | | | | |
|---|---|---|---|---|
| Company | Today's price (£ per share) | % change from yesterday | Maximum price (£) Last 12 months | Minimum price (£) Last 12 months |
| Amos plc | 1111 | +1% | 1325 | 850 |
| Bravo plc | 201 | +0.5% | 220 | 111 |
| Chiara plc | 1710 | -10% | 1965 | 1250 |
| Dross plc | 495 | -1% | 725 | 460 |
| Eliad plc | 2525 | +1% | 2630 | 2200 |

The minimum and maximum prices show the lowest and highest price reached by the shares in the last 12 months.

**Dividend paid per share this year (£)**

| | Amos | Bravo | Chiara | Dross | Eliad |
|---|---|---|---|---|---|
| Interim | 0.9 | 0.4 | 0.3 | 0.1 | 0.5 |
| Final | 1.9 | 1.2 | 1.2 | 0.4 | 1.1 |

**Q1.187a** Which company had the largest difference between the highest and lowest price over the last 12 months?

a. Amos plc
b. Bravo plc
c. Chiara plc
d. Dross plc
e. Eliad plc

**Q1.187b** What was yesterday's cost difference between 100 shares in Eliad plc and 50 shares in Chiara plc?

  a.   £155,000
  b.   £155,950
  c.   £157,260
  d.   £163,000
  e.   £167,000

**Q1.187c** What was the annual dividend paid to the holder of 1500 shares in Bravo plc?

  a.   £600
  b.   £1,000
  c.   £1,800
  d.   £2,400
  e.   £2,600

**Q1.187d** Yesterday a Spanish investor sold 10 shares in each company and received a total of 74,400 euros. What was the exchange rate at the time?

  a.   £1 = 1.25 euros
  b.   £1 = 1.20 euros
  c.   £1 = 1.15 euros
  d.   £1 = 1.05 euros
  e.   £1 = 1.02 euros

**Q1.187e** An investor is bragging that he invested in shares of one of the companies in the past 12 months and that, when he sold them, he had more than doubled his money. Which company had he invested in?

  a.   Amos plc
  b.   Bravo plc
  c.   Chiara plc
  d.   Dross plc
  e.   Eliad plc
  f.   None. He is lying

**Q1.188** The huge success of artists such as One Direction and Adele means that the UK music industry accounted for 17.1% of the global music market in 2015 – its highest ever share. Adele was the driving force, selling 17.4 million copies of her third album, "25", released on 19 November 2015, in just six weeks. But despite the industry's impressive market share, total revenues for UK albums fell by 1% to £688m.

The BPI, which represents the British music industry, laid the blame with advertising-funded sites like YouTube and Daily Motion, saying the industry made more money from vinyl sales last year than it did from music video streaming. In its annual yearbook, a guide to the UK recorded music industry, the BPI said YouTube and other ad-funded video streaming websites paid out a "meagre" £24.4m in 2015. This was despite fans streaming almost 27 billion music videos – an 88% increase from 2014. That was narrowly eclipsed by the £25.1m earned from the sale of 2.1 million vinyl LPs in 2015. Audio streams on subscription services like Apple Music, Spotify and Deezer surpassed both. The BPI says that between 2014 and 2015 it saw an 82% increase in audio streams, to 27bn individual songs, accounting for a 69% rise in income to £146.1m. (1 billion (bn) = 1,000 million.)

**Q1.188a** Approximately how much did the music industry make for each sale of a vinyl LP in 2015?

    a.   £10
    b.   £11
    c.   £12
    d.   £13
    e.   £14

**Q1.188b** How many albums were sold worldwide in 2015?

    a.   98 million
    b.   100 million
    c.   102 million
    d.   104 million
    e.   Cannot be determined

**Q1.188c** How many copies of her new album did Adele sell in 2015?

    **a.**   17.4 million
    **b.**   19 million
    **c.**   21 million
    **d.**   21.2 million
    **e.**   Cannot be determined

**Q1.188d** In 2015, how many times did a video have to be streamed to generate approximately the same revenue as streaming an audio file?

    **a.**   3
    **b.**   5
    **c.**   6
    **d.**   8
    **e.**   10

**Q1.188e** If a vinyl album contains on average 10 songs and is listened to by customers on average 20 times, in 2015 approximately how much did the industry lose or gain per customer if a vinyl album was audio streamed instead of being purchased (to the nearest pound)?

    **a.**   Loss of £11
    **b.**   Loss of £6
    **c.**   Loss of £2
    **d.**   Gain of £2
    **e.**   Gain of £6
    **f.**   Gain of £11

**Q1.188f** What was the income per audio stream in 2014?

    **a.**   0.4 pence
    **b.**   0.6 pence
    **c.**   0.8 pence
    **d.**   1.0 pence
    **e.**   1.2 pence

**Q1.189** The following chart represents the journey of a commuter going to work in the morning. He sets off from home at 7am and arrives at work at 9am. During his journey, he uses a mix of walking and bus rides. He cannot walk at a speed of more than 6 km/h.

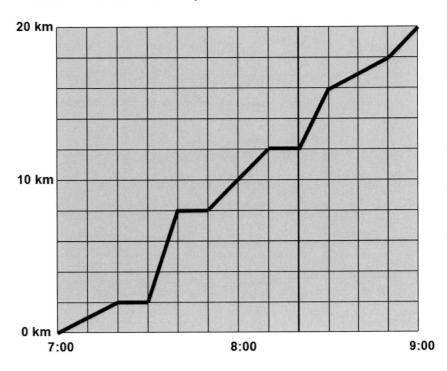

**Q1.189a** What is his average speed across the whole journey?

a. 5 km/h
b. 10 km/h
c. 12.75 km/h
d. 15.3 km/h
e. 20 km/h

**Q1.189b** What is the maximum distance that he could have walked during this journey?

    **a.**  1 km
    **b.**  2 km
    **c.**  3 km
    **d.**  4 km
    **e.**  8 km

**Q1.189c** Between 7:30 and 8:10 he needs to use two buses, which are very crowded. He has the option of taking one single bus, which drives along exactly the same route as the other two buses combined; however, he would need to wait 10 more minutes for it. How fast would that new bus need to drive to enable the commuter to arrive <u>just on time</u> to catch the same bus he normally takes next?

    **a.**  5 km/h
    **b.**  10 km/h
    **c.**  12.5 km/h
    **d.**  15 km/h
    **e.**  17.5 km/h

**Q1.189d** Between 8:20 and 9:00, the commuter uses one single bus. Due to varying levels of traffic, that bus's speed varies along the route, which is reflected on the graph by three different portions with different angles. If that bus arrived 10 minutes later than expected to pick up its passengers but then drove twice as fast as it normally drives for the duration of the journey, at what time would the commuter arrive at work?

    **a.**  8:50
    **b.**  8:55
    **c.**  9:00
    **d.**  9:05
    **e.**  9:10

**Q1.190** Mr Travis, an avid skier, wants to travel from his home to Zermatt in Switzerland for his annual winter holiday. He has a choice between two departure airports, Manchester or Birmingham, to take a plane to Geneva, from which he then needs to take either a train or a bus to reach his destination. His options are as follows:

| Journey | Distance | Cost | Time |
|---|---|---|---|
| **Car journey to the airport** | | | |
| Home – Manchester Airport | 90 miles | 40p/mile | 1:30 |
| Home – Birmingham Airport | 40 miles | 40p/mile | 0:50 |
| **Flights to Geneva** | | | |
| From Manchester Airport | 770 miles | £145 | 1:25 |
| From Birmingham Airport | 680 miles | £155 | 1:15 |
| **Airport to Zermatt transfer** | | | |
| By taxi | 150 miles | £150 | 2:50 |
| By train | 150 miles | £120 | 2:10 |

Flight/transfer costs/times are the same for the return journey, e.g. a flight from Geneva to Birmingham lasts 1:15 and costs £155.

**Car park fees:**
- £30 per day
- 1–7 days: £95
- 8–14 days: £160

The combination of fees giving the cheapest price is used, e.g. for a stay of 8 days, the cheapest combination is 1–7 days (£95) + an additional day (£30), giving a total of £125.

A day is defined as 0:00 – 24:00 or partial period. Leaving the car on Monday at 8am and picking it up on Wednesday at 2pm would count as 3 days.

**Q1.190a** Mr Travis is being driven to Manchester airport by his brother. No parking is necessary. What is the cost per minute of the journey for the brother?

a. 20p
b. 30p
c. 40p
d. 50p
e. 60p

**Q1.190b** What is the full cost of a return journey through Birmingham, using the train for the Swiss leg of the journey, for someone who leaves on a Monday and comes back on the Friday of the same week, knowing that this person is driving their own car and are parking it at the airport?

a. £566
b. £582
c. £677
d. £732
e. £772

**Q1.190c** Mr Travis travels to the airport 2 hours before the flight departs and, once in Geneva, his transfer vehicle leaves 20 minutes after he has landed. His journey lasts 7 hours and 15 minutes. How did he travel?

a. Through Birmingham airport with taxi in Switzerland
b. Through Birmingham airport with train in Switzerland
c. Through Manchester airport with taxi in Switzerland
d. Through Manchester airport with train in Switzerland

**Q1.190d** What is the maximum saving that Mr Travis can make when parking at the airport for 9 days?

a. £100
b. £105
c. £110
d. £115
e. £120

**Q1.190e** If Mr Travis moved to a new house which is also 90 miles away from Manchester airport, how far would he need to live from Birmingham so that the combined cost of travelling to the airport and flight are the same regardless of which airport he uses?

a. 25 miles
b. 65 miles
c. 90 miles
d. 115 miles
e. 135 miles

**Q1.191** The following table summarises the percentage of insurance claims for each cause of claim, for 2005 and 2009.

| Cause of claim | 2009 (% of total number of claims) | 2005 (% of total number of claims) |
|---|---|---|
| Flooding | 27 | 32 |
| Fire | 48 | 41 |
| Theft | 9 | 8 |
| Gas leak | 2 | 1 |
| Leaking roof | 12 | 15 |
| Other | 2 | 3 |
| TOTAL | 100 | 100 |

The total number of claims in 2005 was 915. The number of claims increased by 20% between 2005 and 2009.

**Q1.191a** If the total number of claims increased by 20% between 2005 and 2009, how many claims were made for theft in 2009?

a.  82
b.  88
c.  92
d.  99
e.  104

**Q1.191b** By what percentage did the number of claims for leaking roofs increase or decrease between 2005 and 2009?

a.  A decrease of 4%
b.  A decrease of 3%
c.  A decrease of 2%
d.  A decrease of 1%
e.  No change
f.  An increase of 1%
g.  An increase of 2%
h.  An increase of 3%
i.  An increase of 4%

**Q1.191c** By what percentage should the total number of claims have increased between 2005 and 2009 for the number of claims due to flooding to be equal in both years?

a.  15.5%
b.  17%
c.  18.5%
d.  20%
e.  21.5%

**Q1.191d** An audit revealed that, in 2009, 298 claims classified as caused by fire were in fact due to other causes, as follows:

| | |
|---|---|
| **Flooding** | 5 |
| **Theft** | 2 |
| **Gas leak** | 220 |
| **Leaking roof** | 66 |
| **Other** | 5 |
| **TOTAL** | **298** |

What percentage of total claims was actually caused by gas leaks?

a.  16%
b.  18%
c.  20%
d.  22%
e.  24%

**Q1.191e** In 2005, the figures recorded failed to include another category called "Accidental damage", which accounted for 135 claims on top of those shown. What percentage of total claims did claims caused by leaking roofs actually represent in 2005?

a.  11%
b.  12%
c.  13%
d.  14%
e.  15%

**Q1.192** The table below summarises the total population in five different countries in 2015 and the number of people in each population who suffered a stroke in that year.

|  | Population (million) | No. of strokes |
|---|---|---|
| **Albania** | 2.8 | 4000 |
| **Denmark** | 5.6 | 4000 |
| **Greece** | 10.8 | 7000 |
| **Ireland** | 4.6 | 5000 |
| **Serbia** | 7.2 | 11000 |

Research carried out into the survival of people who suffered a stroke shows that more than 50% of them will live at least another five years after a stroke. The following table shows the percentage of people who have had a stroke who are expected to survive until 1 week, 1 year and 5 years after their stroke. The data is not mutually inclusive in that, for example, those who survived for 5 years are also included in the number for those who survived 1 week.

**Stroke survival rates as a percentage of people who had a stroke:**

|  | 5 years | 1 year | 1 week |
|---|---|---|---|
| **Albania** | 54 | 78 | 89 |
| **Denmark** | 72 | 91 | 85 |
| **Greece** | 74 | 84 | 91 |
| **Ireland** | 62 | 87 | 92 |
| **Serbia** | 62 | 81 | 86 |

**Q1.192a** The figure for post-stroke 1-week survival for one of the countries is incorrect. Which country?

a. Albania
b. Denmark
c. Greece
d. Ireland
e. Serbia

**Q1.192b** What proportion of the combined population of those five countries had a stroke in 2015?

    **a.**   1 per thousand
    **b.**   5 per thousand
    **c.**   1%
    **d.**   1.5%
    **e.**   2%

**Q1.192c** How many people from Ireland who had a stroke in 2015 are expected to die between 1 week and 5 years?

    **a.**   1,500
    **b.**   2,600
    **c.**   3,100
    **d.**   4,600
    **e.**   5,100

**Q1.192d** Which country has the best 4-year survival rate for those who have succeeded in surviving for a year?

    **a.**   Albania
    **b.**   Denmark
    **c.**   Greece
    **d.**   Ireland
    **e.**   Serbia

**Q1.192e** If we assume that the graph showing the number of deaths between year 1 and year 5 shows a straight line for each country, which country is expected to have the best 4-year post-stroke survival rate?

    **a.**   Albania
    **b.**   Denmark
    **c.**   Greece
    **d.**   Ireland
    **e.**   Serbia

**Q1.193** A company categorises employees according to four grades. Grade 1 is the lowest and Grade 4 the highest. Entry into the company at Grade 1 is possible for anyone who has the required qualifications and is successful at the interview process. Promotions from one grade to the next are organised as follows:

### Promotion from Grade 3 to Grade 4
- The employee must be at least 38 years old and must have worked at Grade 3 for at least two years.
- The employee must have good references from at least three people who have worked at Grade 4 for at least two years.
- New entrants to the organisation at this level can be considered depending on the requirements of the organisation.

### Promotion from Grade 2 to Grade 3
- The employee must be over the age of 35 and must have worked at Grade 2 for at least three years.
- The employee must have two or three recommendations from senior people working at Grade 4.
- New entrants to the organisation cannot be taken at Grade 3.

### Promotion from Grade 1 to Grade 2
- An employee is automatically promoted if he/she has spent five years at Grade 1 AND there are no adverse reports about him/her AND the employee is at least 35 years old. The age restriction can be lifted if the employee has obtained two or three strong references from members of the promotion committee.
- Promotions can also be granted at any age on a discretionary basis provided the employee has spent more than two years at Grade 1.
- New entrants to the organisation cannot normally be taken at Grade 2, although exceptions can be made if there is no internal candidate suitable for promotion.

**Q1.193a** Andrew wants to join the company, having never worked there before. At which grade can he not enter the company?

a. Grade 1
b. Grade 2
c. Grade 3
d. Grade 4

**Q1.193b** What is the minimum number of years in which someone who joins the company at age 24 will be able to reach Grade 4, assuming that they are in continuous employment (i.e. they do not leave the company and rejoin it later)?

a.   5 years
b.   7 years
c.   9 years
d.   12 years
e.   14 years

**Q1.193c** What is the minimum age at which an employee must join the company at Grade 1 in order to enjoy the fastest possible career progression to Grade 4?

a.   29
b.   30
c.   31
d.   32
e.   33

**Q1.193d** Which of the following statements are incorrect?

1. An employee with no or bad recommendations can never be promoted to a higher grade.
2. No one below the age of 35 can be promoted.
3. If an employee is Grade 3 then he must have at least five years of service with the company.

a.   None of them
b.   1 only
c.   2 only
d.   3 only
e.   1 and 2 only
f.   1 and 3 only
g.   2 and 3 only
h.   All of them

**Q1.194** This table shows the unemployment situation in a number of European countries in 2016 (workforce = people of working age):

| Countries | Total population of country (millions) | Unemployed (thousands) | | Unemployed as proportion of the workforce of each gender | |
|---|---|---|---|---|---|
| | | Men | Women | Men | Women |
| France | 61.8 | 1100 | 1300 | 8% | 10% |
| Italy | 60.0 | 1000 | 1000 | 5% | 10% |
| Spain | 44.5 | 900 | 1100 | 7% | 12% |
| UK | 61.3 | 800 | 600 | 3% | 1% |

**Q1.194a** What was the total size of the workforce in Italy in 2016?

    **a.**   2 million
    **b.**   20 million
    **c.**   30 million
    **d.**   40 million
    **e.**   58 million

**Q1.194b** How many more women than men were unemployed across all four countries in 2016?

    **a.**   90,000
    **b.**   130,000
    **c.**   189,000
    **d.**   200,000
    **e.**   250,000

**Q1.194c** Which of these statements are true for the workforce?

1. In France, women are 2% more likely to be unemployed than men.
2. In Italy, women are twice as likely to be unemployed as men.
3. The figures for the UK are not correct.

    **a.**   1 only
    **b.**   2 only
    **c.**   3 only
    **d.**   1 and 2 only
    **e.**   1 and 3 only
    f.   2 and 3 only

**Q1.195** A recruitment firm has summarised data obtained from a recent survey as follows. The firm aims to recruit people who have a university degree and over three years' experience. Each black circle represents 10 people.

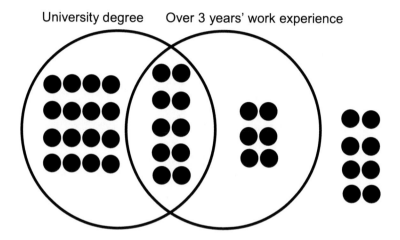

**University degree**     **Over 3 years' work experience**

**Q1.195a** What is the probability that if we select one person at random he/she will not be recruited by the recruitment firm?

| | |
|---|---|
| a. | 15% |
| b. | 20% |
| c. | 25% |
| d. | 40% |
| e. | 75% |

**Q1.195b** What is the probability that a person selected at random has less than three years' work experience and has no university degree?

| | |
|---|---|
| a. | 15% |
| b. | 20% |
| c. | 25% |
| d. | 40% |
| e. | 75% |

147

**Q1.196** Consider carefully the meaning of the following information:

A large number of shoppers were interested in purchasing a kitchen utensil recommended by a famous TV chef through the only online retailer that stocked it: Kitchen Online. The TV programme was broadcast late on Sunday evening and shoppers flocked to Kitchen Online's website on Monday to purchase the item in question. However, Kitchen Online had no stock as it did not expect any demand whatsoever for that utensil.

For each of the first three days of the week (Monday, Tuesday, Wednesday), the chart graph below shows the subsequent behaviour of all the Monday shoppers, with some of them giving up on finding the item altogether, some of them coming back on a different day to see if it had become available and others purchasing a different utensil of the same kind but at an average price that was 25% more expensive than the recommended item.

**Behaviour of Monday shoppers on Monday, Tuesday and Wednesday**

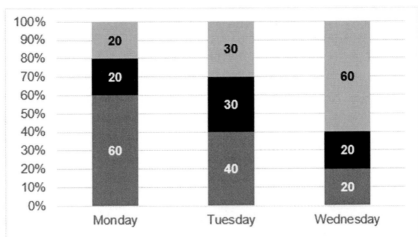

■ Purchased a different item and did not revisit the site that week.

■ Did not make a purchase but revisited the site the next day.

■ Did not make a purchase and did not revisit the site that week.

**Q1.196a** If 1,000 people accessed the site on Monday, how many of them did not purchase anything on Monday?

   **a.**   200
   **b.**   400
   **c.**   500
   **d.**   600
   **e.**   800

**Q1.196b** What proportion of Monday shoppers bought an item from the site on Tuesday?

   **a.**   4%
   **b.**   6%
   **c.**   10%
   **d.**   15%
   **e.**   20%

**Q1.196c** What proportion of Monday shoppers visited the site on Thursday?

   **a.**   0%
   **b.**   1.2%
   **c.**   2.6%
   **d.**   3.9%
   **e.**   Cannot be determined

**Q1.196d** What proportion of shoppers who visit the site on Thursday need to purchase a substitute item so that the retailer overall takes as much money from the sales made between Monday and Thursday as he would have taken if everyone had purchased the original recommended item on Monday?

   **a.**   10%
   **b.**   30%
   **c.**   50%
   **d.**   70%
   **e.**   It is not possible as it would need to be over 100%

**Q1.197** The table below presents, for various countries, the percentage of the population that visited different places of cultural interest last year.

| Country | Library | Zoo | Museum | Theatre |
|---------|---------|-----|--------|---------|
| UK | 15 | 30 | 5 | 2 |
| Italy | 25 | 28 | 7 | 4 |
| Spain | 35 | 8 | 20 | 10 |
| France | 35 | 37 | 30 | 18 |
| Austria | 41 | 51 | 13 | 19 |
| Portugal | 48 | 41 | 20 | 12 |
| Malta | 65 | 48 | 27 | 26 |

**Q1.197a** What is the minimum percentage of Maltese people who visited both a library and a zoo?

a. 13%
b. 24%
c. 29%
d. 34%
e. 41%

**Q1.197b** Which of the following statements, if true, would help explain the information presented in the table?

1. The proportion of the Italian population that lives close to either a museum or a theatre is greater than in the UK.

2. Out of all the countries listed, Spain has the fewest zoos per capita.

3. Entry to museums is free in the UK.

a. 1 only
b. 2 only
c. 3 only
d. 1 and 2 only
e. 1 and 3 only
f. 1, 2 and 3

**Q1.198** A teacher gives a maths exercise to his students, as follows:

> Last year, a local bookshop was retailing a rare book at the full price of P. At the start of this year, it increased the price of the book by A%. Shortly after that, the bookshop had a sale and Josie bought the book at a discount of B% of the current full price and she was surprised to see that B was greater than A. How much money did Josie save by buying the book this year during the sale instead of last year?

However, some students complained that the text did not contain enough information to be able to solve the problem. Which of the two following possible pieces of information would be sufficient to help the students solve the problem?

1.  P = £25
2.  B − A = 5

a.  1 only
b.  2 only
c.  1 and 2 together
d.  Either 1 or 2 (i.e. Option a. and Option b. are both correct)
e.  1 and 2 together are not sufficient. More data is needed.

**Q1.199** A teacher is giving a maths exercise to his students, as follows:

> A pet store sells only dogs and cats. If the ratio of dogs to cats is 3:2, how many dogs are in the pet store?

However, some students complained that the text did not contain enough information to be able to solve the problem. Which of the two following possible pieces of information would be sufficient to help the students solve the problem?

1.  If 3 cats were added, there would be more cats than dogs.
2.  If 5 cats and 3 dogs were added, there would be more cats than dogs.

a.  1 only
b.  2 only
c.  1 and 2 together
d.  Either 1 or 2 (i.e. Option a. and Option b. are both correct)
e.  1 and 2 together are not sufficient. More data is needed.

**Q1.200** Memo to all staff:

As you all know we currently employ three bloggers (John, Paul and Nazia) to promote our company on the web and it will continue to be our policy to publish at least four new blog articles every week. However, to promote even more excitement, we have now also recruited the services of a well-known freelance writer, Ahmed, who will contribute at least one blog article per week. The first of his articles was published on 15 February. Also, to make sure that people stick around on our site and visit other pages after reading our articles (which we call making the site 'stickier'), we have now started to add links to related posts under each blog article and on other pages of the website. The results of these enhancements can be seen in the following tables:

**10 highest ranking site pages by total views (15 – 28 February)**

| Page view rank | Site section (contributor) | % of website's total page views |
|---|---|---|
| 1 | Home page | 25 |
| 2 | Blog (Ahmed) | 10 |
| 3 | Blog (Ahmed) | 9 |
| 4 | Blog (Paul) | 8 |
| 5 | Blog (Ahmed) | 7 |
| 6 | Blog (Paul) | 6 |
| 7 | Blog (John) | 5 |
| 8 | Blog (Nazia) | 4 |
| 9 | Blog (Nazia) | 3 |
| 10 | Blog (John) | 1 |

**Page Views, Site Visits and Blog Posts**
(Weekly Totals for February)

| Week No. | Page views | Site visits | Number of blog articles posted | | | |
|---|---|---|---|---|---|---|
| | | | Paul | Nazia | John | Ahmed |
| 1 | 300,000 | 150,000 | 3 | 0 | 1 | n/a |
| 2 | 340,000 | 160,000 | 3 | 1 | 0 | n/a |
| 3 | 350,000 | 180,000 | 1 | 0 | 2 | 1 |
| 4 | 400,000 | 220,000 | 0 | 2 | 0 | 2 |

**Note: This is not a leap year**

152

**Q1.200a** How many page views did the front page of the website receive during the last two weeks of February?

a. 132,500
b. 187,500
c. 220,000
d. 335,000
e. 750,000

**Q1.200b** Which of the following statements can be concluded from the information provided?

1. Ahmed was the most popular blogger in February when looking at the total monthly page views.

2. At least five of the nine blog articles viewed most often during the second half of the month were posted during those two weeks.

3. The site was stickier during the second half of the month than during the first half.

a. 1 only
b. 2 only
c. 3 only
d. 1 and 2 only
e. 1 and 3 only
f. 1, 2 and 3
g. None of them

## Aptitude and Skills
## Understanding Arguments - 72 Questions

## Answers from page 326

**Q1.201** The cost of manufacturing vacuum cleaners in China is 10% less than the cost of manufacturing them in India.

Even after transportation fees and tariff charges are added, it is still cheaper to import vacuum cleaners from China into India than to produce them in India.

Which of the following statements can be deduced from the text?

a. Labour costs in China are 10% below those in India.

b. Importing vacuum cleaners from China to India will lead to the suppression of 10% of manufacturing jobs in India.

c. The tariff charge imposed on a vacuum cleaner imported from China into India is at most 10% of the manufacturing cost in India.

d. The tariff charge imposed on a vacuum cleaner imported from China into India is at most 10% of the manufacturing cost in China.

e. The transport cost for a vacuum cleaner imported from China into India is more than 10% of the manufacturing cost in China.

**Q1.202** A scientist is testing a home pregnancy test which has recently become available on the market: BluePreg. A positive result indicates the woman is pregnant.

Before giving the test kit to his patients, the scientist carried out accurate pregnancy testing on all of them and selected 200 patients: 100 who were confirmed not to be pregnant and 100 who were confirmed to be pregnant.

His results are as follows:

- Out of the 100 confirmed non-pregnant women who took the BluePreg test, 10 tested positive.

- Out of 100 confirmed pregnant women who took the test, 99 tested positive.

Therefore if we give the BluePreg test to a group of random women, the vast majority of those who test positive will be pregnant.

---

Which of the following statements best describes the flaw in the argument?

a. It does not take into consideration the test's margin of error.

b. It assumes that the test's accuracy is not affected by other factors.

c. It ignores the fact that women who do not test positive may be pregnant.

d. It presupposes the number of pregnant women in the random sample.

e. It suggests that non-pregnant women are more likely to test positive than pregnant women are.

**Q1.203** Some councils have expressed concerns at the amount of rubbish that is being collected weekly from homes. One proposal to deal with this issue is to charge households according to the weight of the rubbish they throw away.

As the bin is being loaded onto the bin lorry, that bin will be weighed. The weight will be recorded and each month each household will be charged for each kilogram of rubbish they placed in their bin.

This will force residents to reduce the amount of rubbish they throw away and will also ensure a better protection of the environment by limiting the amount of rubbish that is being taken to landfill sites and by protecting our remaining forests.

---

Which of the following statements is an assumption made in drawing this conclusion?

a. The fee will not affect the purchasing power of households in any significant way, even if they fail to reduce the amount of rubbish they throw away.

b. Households will reduce the amount of rubbish they throw away by purchasing fewer products.

c. The charge will not push residents to dump their rubbish in surrounding forests.

d. Residents are concerned about the environment.

e. Residents could use landfill sites in surrounding counties.

**Q1.204** Measuring productivity in the service industry is tricky. Consider hospitals for example. Health bosses tell us all the time that a hospital is more productive because it is increasing the number of patients being seen in outpatient clinics, or because the number of patients seen in A&E within the four-hour target is higher, or because the number of operations being postponed or cancelled is lower.

But is this really the truth? What if, at the same time as all those wonderful things happen, doctors are making more mistakes or are being ruder to patients?

Which of the following statements is the author doubting the most when he raises the above objection?

**a.** Individual doctors are representative of service workers in general.

**b.** Outpatient clinics, emergencies and surgery are the primary activities in hospitals.

**c.** Productivity should be measured on groups of individuals and not on single individuals.

**d.** The quality of the service rendered can be ignored when measuring productivity.

**e.** The A&E four-hour target is relevant to measuring the productivity of a hospital.

**Q1.205** Cuts in the budgets of most universities over the past 5 years have resulted in staffing shortages for language courses. The shortage of language lecturers is most likely caused by the fact that in recent years their salaries have become lower than the salaries of colleagues who teach other subjects. In addition, unlike their colleagues, they have not experienced any improvements in working conditions, which must have led to disgruntlement.

Which of the following statements, if true, would best support the claims made in the text above?

a.  A survey of students shows that they are reluctant to apply to language courses because the lecturer-to-student ratio is much lower than it used to be.

b.  A survey of language lecturers currently employed shows that, despite a large number of resignations, all are happy with their working conditions and salary.

c.  Most language lecturers who resign from their posts end up taking employment in the private sector at a level of salary that is 30% higher than what they earned in their university and where they are looked after by employers.

d.  For the past 5 years, a survey of language students has shown that most are put off applying to lecturer posts because, in the private sector, they can earn as much as a maths lecturer.

e.  All lecturers leaving their job attended an exit interview to explore their motives. Last year 20% of language lecturers interviewed said they were leaving because of worsening of working conditions and 30% said they were leaving because of poor pay conditions.

**Q1.206** Hypochondriacs, plagued with abnormal anxiety over their health, often visit their GP complaining of vague symptoms. They often exaggerate each of their symptoms and link them, however superficially, to an illness that they may have read about on the internet or other media.

Medical TV dramas often make hypochondriacs think that they, too, suffer from conditions similar to those described within the programme and make them extremely anxious. This is not helped by the fact that the information shown on TV is dramatised and can sometimes be inaccurate.

---

What conclusion can be inferred from this paragraph?

**a.** Hypochondriacs are wasting GPs' time, to the detriment of other patients.

**b.** The proportion of hypochondriacs watching medical dramas is greater than in the "normal" population.

**c.** The distortion of reality present in medical dramas can exacerbate the anxiety experienced by hypochondriacs.

**d.** Removing inaccuracies from medical dramas will lead to a substantial reduction in the fear experienced by hypochondriacs.

**e.** Hypochondria is an illness that is acquired through experience.

**Q1.207** The prevalence of heart disease in society is such that all employers can expect to have amongst their employees a non-negligible number of employees who suffer from one form or another of it, even if not all of those are actually aware that they are suffering from it. If left untreated, heart disease can lead to a heart attack.

A number of studies undertaken over the years show that approximately 70% of people who have suffered a heart attack are allowed to return to work, as long as they don't undertake strenuous activities.

Whenever possible, employers should therefore ensure that returning employees are given lighter duties when their work previously involved heavy physical activity. Those who worked in a high pressure environment where they were exposed to stress should also be given less stressful work.

---

Which of the following statements can be deduced from the text?

a. Stress and hard physical work can bring on a heart attack.

b. The majority of people who suffered a heart attack returned to work.

c. Heart disease may affect employees in any business.

d. Employees involved in heavy physical work tend to stress easily.

e. The risk of heart disease is greater amongst older employees.

**Q1.208** Although some people think that radiation emitted by airport security body scanners may damage the organs of users, no conclusive evidence has been found of adverse effects on health in the short term. Internet rumours circulate that wearing a special foil-lined vest can protect the user from the effects of radiation. However, it was found that, with the foil-lined vest on, the reduction in the level of radiation reaching the organs was "negligible to small", depending on whether the customer followed the exact instructions on how to wear the vest correctly.

Which one of the following can be drawn as a conclusion from the above passage?

a. The use of body scanners is unlikely to have adverse effects on health.

b. Consumers who wear the vest will be protected against radiation.

c. The special vest protects the body by reflecting the radiation away from the body.

d. During a scan, some organs receive different levels of radiation than others.

e. Using the foil-lined vest correctly reduces the level of radiation reaching the organs of a user in the body scanner.

**Q1.209** Breakfast clubs are becoming increasingly popular in primary schools in the UK. Studies show that eating a healthy breakfast improves children's ability to learn, and improves attendance and behaviour at school.

However, it is not the remit of the school to provide something that should be the responsibility of the parents. In addition, the cost of providing a breakfast club in the current financial climate is such that it takes money away from other more important educational resources such as the purchase of new textbooks. In the long run, children benefit more when primary schools focus on the services they traditionally provide and the parents do what they are supposed to do.

---

Which of the following can be deduced from the text?

**a.** Most parents don't provide breakfast for their children.

**b.** Studies about schools and breakfast clubs are inconclusive, and more evidence is needed to determine whether school breakfasts are healthier than home breakfasts.

**c.** Breakfasts eaten at home are usually unhealthy.

**d.** The cost of school textbooks is increasing.

**e.** It costs more to a school to provide a healthy breakfast than it would cost the parents.

**Q1.210** Some political groups want to make burning the British flag a criminal offence. They believe that the UK has become lenient on extremist demonstrators, who aim to stir up hatred and deepen divisions amongst society. They also argue that people have fought and died for the flag and that citizens ought to respect that. However, most UK citizens who have served in the army did not fight for the flag; they fought for what the flag represented. One of the values the flag represents is freedom of expression, which includes the right for a citizen to exercise disapproval with the government by burning the flag in protest.

**Q1.210a** Which of the following best expresses the main conclusion of the above argument?

   **a.** Those who served in the army care about flag burning.

   **b.** Flag burning almost never happens except during rare demonstrations, so criminalising it is a waste of time.

   **c.** Flag burning will be a major issue in the next election.

   **d.** To make flag burning illegal is to criminalise what the flag represents.

   **e.** Burning the British flag should be illegal.

**Q1.210b** Which of the following, if true, would seriously weaken the above argument?

   **a.** The world's relevant authorities do not consider a physical action as being freedom of expression.

   **b.** People who burn the flag usually commit other violent crimes as well.

   **c.** The British Military Colours (Queen's Colours and Regimental Colours) are draped on the dirty ground when part of the Royal salute or as part of Remembrance Sunday.

   **d.** Most law-abiding citizens of all backgrounds are against flag burning.

**Q1.211** The proportion of smokers amongst low-income individuals is twice as high as in high-income individuals. On average, low-income smokers consume twice as many cigarettes per day as high-income smokers.

What conclusion can be drawn from the above paragraph?

a. The number of cigarettes smoked by all low-income smokers over a day is four times the number of cigarettes smoked by all high-income smokers on the same day.

b. There are more low-income smokers than high-income smokers.

c. People who smoke earn on average less than those who don't smoke.

d. Low-income smokers are less aware of the unhealthy nature of smoking than high-income earners.

e. Low-income earners have more stressful jobs than high income earners.

f. The majority of people dying of lung cancer have low incomes.

g. None of the above.

**Q1.212** Over the last six years, most students who originate from Bailey city have preferred to study for their audiology degree in neighbouring Helina city rather than in their home town. However, a recent change in policy in Helina city is expected to lead to an increase in the level of fees that Helina city colleges charge for audiology courses; as a result, the fees charged by Helina city colleges will be almost at the same level as those charged by colleges in Bailey city. Therefore, inevitably, the audiology colleges in Bailey city will see a surge in the number of students enrolling with them to pursue their audiology degrees.

Which of the following is an assumption on which the argument depends?

**a.** The lecturers at the audiology colleges in Helina city are generally considered far superior to those at the audiology colleges in Bailey city.

**b.** Bailey city does not have good quality audiology colleges.

**c.** The low fees charged by the audiology colleges at Helina city are the primary reason why students from Bailey city move to these colleges.

**d.** Students who study at the audiology colleges in Bailey city do not perform better than those who study at the audiology colleges in Helina city.

**e.** Helina city has fewer audiology colleges than Bailey city.

**Q1.213** Last year, New York's best-selling book was a biography of Lenin, a revolutionary philosopher who masterminded the Bolshevik take-over of power in Russia in 1917, and was the architect and first head of the USSR. The book states that Lenin was both very wise and very poor. A book reviewer stated that the book must be incorrect, because a man possessing such wisdom would surely find a way to avoid poverty.

---

Which of the following would be the best response to expose the flaw in the reviewer's argument?

**a.** Rich people are usually wise people.

**b.** Lenin would not have endured an attempted assassination if he had not been influential.

**c.** Conceptions of wealth vary over time. What is now considered poor would have been very wealthy in Lenin's time.

**d.** Many people who are regarded as wise care more about their principles than about their economic status.

**e.** Although Lenin was not wealthy, he had many wealthy friends who willingly took care of him.

**Q1.214** Leonardo da Vinci started painting the Mona Lisa after 1503 and completed it before 1506. He cannot have started painting it earlier than 1503 because one of the buildings appearing in the background of the painting was not built until that year. He cannot have painted any of it after 1506 because he used a pigment that was no longer produced after 1506.

---

Which of the following statements, if true, would strengthen the author's argument?

1. Most of the painting required use of the abandoned pigment.

2. No stock of the abandoned pigment existed after 1506.

3. The building was one of the first things he painted.

   **a.**  None of them.

   **b.**  1 and 2 only.

   **c.**  2 and 3 only.

   **d.**  1 and 3 only.

   **e.**  All of them.

**Q1.215** Many Londoners believe that extremely cold winters are always followed by extremely high temperatures in the following summer. But this is totally unfounded. Indeed, although the three London winters with the lowest average temperature were followed by summers with extremely high average temperatures, the two warmest London winters were also followed by summers in which average temperatures were extremely high.

---

Which of the following statements best explains where the author has gone wrong in his logic?

a.  The fact that cows are mammals does not mean that cats are not mammals too.

b.  If we are told that all cats and cows are mammals then we cannot conclude that cats are cows.

c.  If we know that all cats are mammals then we can't conclude that an animal which is not a cat is not a mammal.

d.  Just choosing one or two examples of years where the Londoners' belief may be incorrect is not sufficient to disprove it.

e.  The author is not looking at the level of winter temperatures following high summer temperatures.

**Q1.216** Large corporations use several strategies to minimise their tax payments without doing anything explicitly illegal. One such strategy involves the use of subsidiary companies in different countries cross-charging each other for goods or services "sold" within the group. These intra-company transactions aim to minimise profits in high-tax countries and maximise them in low-tax ones.

---

Which of the following strategies is most effective to get the maximum benefit from this tax reduction technique?

a. Make a subsidiary located in a high-tax rate country buy services from a subsidiary located in a low-tax country at a high price.

b. Make a subsidiary located in a high-tax rate country buy services from a subsidiary located in a low-tax country at a low price.

c. Make a subsidiary located in a low-tax rate country buy services from a subsidiary located in a high-tax country at a high price.

d. Make a subsidiary located in a low-tax rate country buy services from a subsidiary located in a high-tax country at a low price.

e. Get any subsidiary to charge a subsidiary located in a high-tax rate country inflated prices for services.

**Q1.217** Some species of Arctic birds are threatened by recent sharp increases in the population of snow rabbits, which breed in the Arctic and are displacing various Arctic birds by disrupting their nests. Snow rabbit is a popular quarry for hunters in the southern regions where they winter. The duration of the hunting season is set by law; that law allows the hunting season to end prematurely if and when hunting has reduced the population of snow rabbits by 5%. Clearly, dropping this restriction would allow the Arctic bird species to recover.

---

Which of the following, if true, most seriously undermines the argument?

a. Hunting limits for snow rabbits were imposed many years ago in response to a sharp decline in the population of snow rabbits.

b. It has been many years since the hunting cap on snow rabbits has led to the hunting season for snow rabbits being closed earlier than the scheduled date.

c. The number of snow rabbits taken by hunters each year has grown every year for several years.

d. As their population has increased, snow rabbits have recolonised wintering grounds that they had not used for several seasons.

e. In the snow rabbits' winter habitats, the rabbit faces no significant natural predator.

**Q1.218** The average age and racing experience of Formula 1 drivers has increased each year between 1965 and 1980. One reason is that drivers during that period had a longer life expectancy than their predecessors. Safety features introduced on Formula 1 cars in 1965 reduced the impact of crashes of the kind that formerly took drivers' lives and were primarily responsible for the increase in the average age of Formula 1 drivers.

---

Which of the following, if true, would be most likely to be part of the evidence used to show that the safety features that were installed on the cars were responsible for the increase in the average age of drivers in Formula 1?

**a.** The major crashes that took place between 1965 and 1980 mostly involved young drivers.

**b.** Major accidents on high-speed racetracks occurred at about the same rate between 1965 and 1980 as they did before 1965.

**c.** The average age of drivers attempting to qualify for Formula 1 decreased slightly between 1965 and 1980.

**d.** Between 1965 and 1980 the rate of major accidents on Formula 1 racetracks was the same as on general UK roads.

**e.** Other safety features, involving changes to the shape of the racetrack and to the materials used to make the drivers' uniforms, were adopted in Formula 1 between 1965 and 1980.

**Q1.219** Researchers have noticed that people whose blood contains abnormally low levels of potassium usually have intestinal polyps. In order to reduce the risk of polyps, the researchers recommend a diet high in potassium-rich foods such as dairy products and green, leafy vegetables.

---

Which of the following, if true, most strongly suggests that following the researchers' recommendation would <u>not</u> be effective?

    **a.** Dairy products contain compounds that are difficult for many people to digest.

    **b.** Intestinal polyps sometimes disappear without treatment.

    **c.** Intestinal polyps cause a change in body chemistry that results in greater secretion of potassium.

    **d.** Fresh vegetables are not always available in all seasons.

    **e.** Low levels of potassium can sometimes be remedied with vitamin pills.

**Q1.220** Drinking unhygienic tap water always results in cases of stomach infection or food poisoning. Richard is currently suffering from food poisoning, so he must have drunk unhygienic tap water in the last few days.

---

Which of the following is an assumption on which the argument depends?

a.  In most cases, drinking unhygienic tap water leads to food poisoning and not a stomach infection.

b.  Richard has a strong immune system and has never experienced food poisoning from any source before.

c.  Richard can make out the difference between hygienic and unhygienic food.

d.  Drinking unhygienic tap water is the only way to get food poisoning.

e.  Unhygienic tap water contains harmful bacteria and other pathogens that lead to food poisoning.

**Q1.221** To encourage UK citizens to save more for their long-term needs, the Chancellor of the Exchequer has decided to implement a plan that allows investors to save up to £4,000 per year in special accounts without paying tax on the interest earned unless withdrawals are made before the investor reaches the age of 60.

The interest rate granted will be in line with the rates paid by high-street banks on savings accounts before deduction of tax.

Withdrawal of money from these accounts prior to aged 60 would result in the investors having to pay tax on all the interest accumulated up to the time of withdrawal. So someone who withdraws his/her money before the age of 60 will, in effect, earn no more than they would have using a normal high-street bank account.

---

Which of the following, if true, most strongly supports the prediction that the plan will have its intended effect?

a. Most UK citizens have little disposable income.

b. Focus group research has shown that many people are likely to use the new savings plans to help their children buy a house when they are still young.

c. Most UK citizens who are not members of a company's pension scheme are discouraged to save for their retirement because the high-street banks' savings accounts offer poor interest rates.

d. In the ten years prior to implementation of the plan, UK citizens deposited an increasingly smaller percentage of their annual income in long-term savings accounts.

e. Many UK citizens have substantial savings sitting in normal high-street bank savings accounts earning little or no interest.

**Q1.222** My gardener says that dried grass clippings mixed into the garden soil will gradually decompose, enriching beneficial soil bacteria, resulting in a better-than-average plant growth on anything that is planted in it.

However, he advises that mixing fresh grass clippings into garden soil usually causes poorer-than-average plant growth.

---

Which one of the following, if true, most helps to explain the difference in plant growth described above?

a. Beneficial bacteria thrive better in a wet environment.

b. Some dried grass clippings retain nutrients originally derived from commercial lawn fertilisers, and thus provide additional enrichment to the soil.

c. Fresh grass clippings mixed into soil decompose rapidly, generating high levels of heat that kill beneficial soil bacteria.

d. When a mix of fresh and dried grass clippings is mixed into garden soil, plant growth often decreases.

e. The number of beneficial soil bacteria increases whenever any kind of plant material is mixed into garden soil.

**Q1.223** A recent survey shows that 60% of people living in the UK are too busy to sit down properly to eat their lunch.

Such behaviour is unhealthy. It makes you fat (and we have all heard about the recent obesity epidemics!); and not paying attention to what we eat and taking our time to digest it means that we never really feel satisfied when we have finished. Also, if we eat whilst performing other tasks, we tend to lose track of what we have ingested and we tend to eat a lot more than we should.

---

Which of the following statements could be used to support the author's point of view?

**a.** Several studies have revealed that people who are overweight tend to eat more quickly than those who are not.

**b.** Studies have shown that multitasking does not increase productivity because we waste a lot of time switching from one task to the other.

**c.** The majority of professionals who eat lunch at their desk whilst working are overweight.

**d.** A large majority of workers who only focus on one task at a time and take proper lunch breaks are overweight.

**e.** Studies have shown that the majority of overweight people eat in front of the television.

**Q1.224** In the UK the current fuel duty is 58 pence per litre for petrol and 32 pence per litre for liquefied petroleum gas (LPG).

An increase in the fuel duty by an additional 1 penny per litre would raise £1 billion per year at current consumption rates.

A tax of 59 pence per litre would therefore raise £59 billion per year; it seems a perfect way to deal with the country's £59 billion budget deficit.

This duty increase would lead to a drop in demand, which would be beneficial to the environment and would keep our country from being too dependent on foreign oil producers.

---

Which one of the following most clearly identifies an error in the author's reasoning?

a. He contradicts himself.

b. He assumes that people care about the environment.

c. He uses incorrect or misleading data.

d. The author mistakes an effect for a cause.

e. He would need to know the split in consumption between petrol and LPG use to draw an accurate conclusion.

**Q1.225** Press release: Ten years ago, the Perez Hotel's entrance areas were carpeted with Durasin carpet while the entrance areas of the nearby Oaxaca Hotel were carpeted with our competitor's most durable carpet.

Today, after a decade in which the two hotels have had similar amounts of foot traffic, the Oaxaca Hotel is having to replace the worn-out carpets near its entrances, whereas the Perez Hotel's Durasin carpets have years of wear left in them.

---

Which of the following, if true, most seriously weakens the force of the advertisement's evidence for concluding that the Durasin carpet is more durable than the carpet of its competitor?

a. The Perez Hotel has five different entrances, which are used equally by all customers, whereas the other hotel has only two.

b. The carpet of the Perez Hotel's lobby is not the most durable carpet that Durasin manufactures.

c. The Oaxaca Hotel has a popular restaurant that can be reached from outside without walking through the hotel.

d. The carpet that is being used to replace carpeting near the Oaxaca Hotel's entrances is not Durasin carpet.

e. A third hotel located near the other two has not replaced the Durasin carpet in its lobby for more than 15 years.

**Q1.226** Integrated hands-free capability for mobile phones in cars has become increasingly popular because it allows people to make or receive business calls while driving.

As an additional benefit, motorists can quickly call for help in the event of an accident or breakdown.

Nevertheless, car integrated hands-free sets should be prohibited because their use causes hazardous driving.

---

Which of the following statements best summarises the author's argument?

**a.** The increasing popularity of integrated hands-free sets is due primarily to the fact that they permit motorists to call for help in the event of an accident.

**b.** The reason why the use of integrated hands-free sets causes hazardous driving is that, while dialling calls, drivers cannot keep both hands on the wheel.

**c.** The advantages afforded by integrated hands-free sets do not outweigh the risks of hazardous driving created by them.

**d.** In order to receive calls, drivers must momentarily take their eyes off the road, and this practice is hazardous.

**e.** The ability to use integrated hands-free sets to call for help is a more important advantage than the ability to use these phones to engage in business calls.

**Q1.227** Editor's note to writers: Articles published in the *Gardening Times* Magazine often spur sales of the plants they describe, particularly amongst people new to gardening. Accordingly, we will no longer publish articles or accept advertisements praising the beauty of rare wild flowers.

Most such plants sold to gardeners have been difficult to propagate under cultivation, so plant sellers often collect them from the wild with the view to sell them on. Our new policy is part of our efforts to halt this yearly plundering of our native plant populations.

---

Which of the following, if true, provides the best indication that the editorial policy will have a very limited effect?

   **a.** When people who are new to gardening buy plants, they often fail to take adequate care of the plants that they buy and become discouraged from buying those varieties again.

   **b.** A survey of readers shows that 95% of them regularly access online resources which deal with rare wild flowers.

   **c.** The demand for rare wild flowers rarely exceeds the number of such plants that can be collected in the wild by plant sellers.

   **d.** The propagation of rare wild flowers often depends on the plants' interaction with other organisms in their environment, such as plants that create suitable soil conditions or insects and birds that disperse seeds.

   **e.** Revenues from sales of plants collected in the wild are supporting the discovery of new low-cost techniques enabling rare wild flowers to be readily propagated in nurseries.

**Q1.228** In the book *Hospitals Abroad,* the author claims that European hospitals are designed with more complexity than American hospitals.

This claim is justified by a thorough comparison of 25 popular European hospitals and 25 popular American hospitals. In this comparison, all the American hospitals had a simpler design than the European ones.

---

Which of the following criticisms is the author most likely to attract with regard to his argument?

a. The hospitals reviewed by the book are likely to have been carefully selected to suit the argument.

b. Hospitals can be judged by other merits besides design.

c. Other books written by the same author show that he has a strong bias against European healthcare.

d. American hospitals may be better designed but their health system is failing a large part of the population.

e. Americans and Europeans have a different perspective on aesthetics.

**Q1.229** Insurance companies believe that the installation of a burglar alarm in a home makes it less vulnerable and therefore they charge lower insurance premiums to home owners who install an alarm system.

However, statistics clearly show that homes equipped with burglar alarms are actually, on average, burgled more often than homes where no alarm has been installed.

---

Which of the following statements, if true, would most help reconcile the insurance companies' belief with the statistics mentioned?

   **a.**  Burglar alarms can easily be disabled by burglars.

   **b.**  Burglar alarms are often ignored by neighbours and the police as they generate a high volume of false alarm calls.

   **c.**  A burglar alarm is only a deterrent if a box containing a flashing blue light is on display at the front of the house, but few home owners install those since they affect the character of their house.

   **d.**  Burglar alarms tend to be installed in burglary-prone areas.

   **e.**  The presence of a burglar alarm tends to reassure home owners that they are safe.

**Q1.230** A prominent doctor declared in one of his publications the following:

"Proxyform does seem to be an effective treatment. But we can't continue using Proxyform to treat this disease just because people feel that it is better to give a treatment of some form rather than give nothing.

"We should also bear in mind that Proxyform can have serious side effects and is also very expensive for the NHS to buy from pharmaceuticals."

---

Which of the following statements best paraphrases the point made by the physician?

a. The most effective drugs are often the most expensive ones.

b. Proxyform is the most effective treatment available for this disease.

c. Proxyform is more effective than a placebo.

d. Effectiveness is not the only criterion that should be considered when deciding whether to use Proxyform.

e. Proxyform is the most expensive treatment available for this disease.

**Q1.231** The study recruited 128 adults, who were divided into two distinct groups: those with high violence consumption (HVC) and those with low violence consumption (LVC), based on the number of hours of violent TV programmes that the adults watched every day.

The results showed that a significantly larger percentage of the HVC group than of the LVC group demonstrated a high level of aggression.

Consequently, we believe that watching too many violent TV programmes causes higher aggression levels.

---

Which of the following statements, if true, most seriously weakens the conclusion drawn by the author?

   **a.** Some of the programmes watched by adults in the HVC group had lower levels of aggression than some of the programmes watched by others in the same group.

   **b.** Some adults in the LVC group only watched programmes that had no violence at all.

   **c.** Some adults restricted the number of hours they spent watching TV for fear of being accused of watching too many violent programmes.

   **d.** Some adults watched live TV programmes whereas other viewers watched pre-recorded TV programmes.

   **e.** A different study shows that adults who watch no TV and behave aggressively towards others tend to choose programmes that contain a high level of violence when they are given the chance to watch TV.

**Q1.232** The medical school's hockey team has two distinct possible team formations: the "Angels" and the "Devils". The manager of the team chooses whichever formation is most appropriate depending on the strength of the opposite team but once a particular formation has been chosen for a match, it is used throughout the whole match.

Last season, the Angels formation was responsible for 60% of all the points scored across both teams and it was used for 54% of the total game time played. In every match where the Angels formation was used, the team scored their first point in the first minute of the game.

The Devils formation was responsible for the remainder of the points and the time played, but the first point was always scored in the second half of each game in which it was used.

---

If the above statements are true, which of the following statements must be true?

1. The Devils formation was used when facing stronger opponents than when the Angels formation was used.
2. In matches where the Devils formation was used, fewer points per minute were scored than when playing with the Angels formation.
3. If, for each match, we ignore the period of time before the first point was scored and only take account of the time from the moment the first point was scored, more points per minute were scored when using the Devils formation than when using the Angels formation.

a. None of the statements are true.
b. 1 only.
c. 2 only.
d. 3 only.
e. 1 and 2 only.
f. 2 and 3 only.
g. 1 and 3 only.
h. All statements are true.

**Q1.233** Recruitment of women in Intelligence Agencies

UK intelligence agencies say they are recruiting more female staff – and are targeting middle-aged and "mid-career" women for jobs. MI6 and GCHQ advertised on the Mumsnet website for the first time this year, and MI5 has raised its target for women employees to 46% by 2021. Flexible working and the importance of "high emotional intelligence" are also being stressed in recruitment. The agencies were responding to calls from MPs to recruit more women. Parliament's Intelligence and Security Committee reported in March 2015 that 37% of intelligence agency staff were women and women only make up 19% of senior civil servants in the agencies.

One year on, the government says that it and the agencies – internal security service MI5, external spy agency MI6 and the government listening post GCHQ – "agree wholeheartedly" with the need for "diversity" in agency staff. It says action has been taken since the report was published to "increase their focus" on "all aspects of diversity", including recruiting more women. Recruitment targets, "diversity champions", events such as a recent "Women in Cyber" event and more career support for female officers are part of efforts to employ more women and encourage talented existing women to apply for promotion.

They also say they are doing more to "promote a flexible working culture" for men and women with childcare commitments and to allow women returning from maternity leave to take up their old jobs – including in intelligence roles. The three agencies also said they were always looking for "new and innovative ways to recruit those with the right skills, mindset and diversity of approach".

MI5 had already used Mumsnet as well as local newspapers to target women "not currently in work" while the other two agencies did so for the first time this year. GCHQ has also removed a requirement of a 2:1 university degree from its "fast-stream" recruitment to encourage women who had followed a "non-traditional graduate route". The government said the initiatives were having an effect as MI5 had recently been placed in the Times Top 50 employers for women and had increased its number of new female employees by 5% to 46% of new recruits. GCHQ had seen applications from women rise to 40%. MI6 had increased its female recruitment targets for 2016/17 (after seeing a 4% drop in women) – to 41% of new recruits. The government also said career support for female staff was having a "real impact" with increased numbers of women applying for senior roles in MI5.

**Q1.233a** Which of the following could be deduced from the text to be a reason for the lack of recruitment of women in the past?

> **a.** Most women had degrees below grade 2:1.
>
> **b.** Women felt the skills required were more 'male-type' skills.
>
> **c.** Women felt that promotion to senior levels was limited.
>
> **d.** The agencies' ways of working were not flexible enough.
>
> **e.** In the old days, the work did not require much emotional intelligence.

**Q1.233b** Which of the following statements can be deduced from the text?

**1.** Before 2016, MI6's recruitment target for women was 45% of new recruits.

**2.** Before 2016, the recruitment target for women for MI5 was lower than for MI6.

**3.** Of all agencies, GCHQ has the lowest recruitment target for women.

> **a.** None of them.
>
> **b.** 1 and 2 only.
>
> **c.** 2 and 3 only.
>
> **d.** 1 and 3 only.
>
> **e.** All of them.

**Q1.234** The new bridge that was opened this year has greatly alleviated traffic congestion in the city centre and has saved commuters time.

Unfortunately, this year's harsh frost has caused the bridge's surface to deteriorate, creating numerous potholes; consequently, the city has seen a substantial increase in the number of accidents caused by people swerving to avoid those potholes.

There is real fear amongst the population that if the bridge is not resurfaced before next winter it will be totally unusable next year. Therefore, the bridge must be closed temporarily to allow the repairs to take place.

It is estimated that the work could take as long as three weeks.

Which of the following, if true, would most seriously weaken the argument above?

a. Closing the bridge will lead to congestion in the city centre.

b. Closing the bridge will increase journey times.

c. The local council has reallocated part of the road maintenance budget to the public transport budget.

d. A report commissioned by the local council observed that swerving could be avoided by reducing traffic on the bridge to one lane instead of the two lanes that are currently being used. This could safely be done as an interim measure for a few months.

e. Repairing the bridge will require use of very durable material, which is expensive.

**Q1.235** Bronchodilators are a type of medication that make breathing easier by relaxing the muscles in the lungs and widening the airways. They are often used to treat long-term conditions where the airways may become narrow and inflamed, such as asthma and chronic obstructive pulmonary disease (COPD).

Over the past few years, most doctors have opted to move away from bronchodilator therapy for all but the mildest asthmatics. Combined sales of all bronchodilators rose slowly until 1995, when they peaked. They still currently account for just roughly 50% of the 10 million asthma-related prescriptions written by doctors in the UK.

Instead, doctors are now increasingly prescribing anti-inflammatory therapy in the form of inhalers containing steroids. In the same period leading to 1995, prescriptions of inhaled steroids doubled but they still only account for roughly 10% of asthma-related prescriptions.

Article from *The Best Medical Journal*, 1998

Which of the following statements can be deduced from the text?

**a.** Inhalers are only effective in cases of mild asthma.

**b.** Use of bronchodilators has been increasing since 1995.

**c.** There are 10 million asthma sufferers in the UK.

**d.** Bronchodilators do not come in the form of inhalers.

**e.** Bronchodilators are the single most prescribed treatment for asthma.

**Q1.236** In a bid to increase readership numbers, *Abacus* magazine is considering changing the style of the articles it publishes.

A survey of young adult readers commissioned by the magazine shows that young adults have increasingly found old-style articles uninteresting and hard to read, and have started to lose the incentive to read and therefore to purchase the magazine.

To increase its popularity with young adults and increase its number of subscribers, *Abacus* magazine plans to recruit writers who can write in a less journalistic and more fun fashion.

---

Which of the following statements would most reinforce the case for *Abacus* magazine to recruit new writers?

a. Changing the style of writing will not have an immediate impact on subscription rates.

b. Some young adults enjoy articles written in a journalistic style.

c. Switching to a new style of writing may cause older readers to cancel their subscriptions.

d. Some young adults do not like articles written in a more fun fashion.

e. *Abacus* has lost 50% of its readers spread equally across all ages to a rival magazine written in a more fun fashion.

f. The majority of readers who subscribe to the magazine are young adults.

**Q1.237** Numerous ancient Indian cities have been discovered in the Uttarakhand peninsula in recent decades. The ruins lack any evidence of destruction by invading forces, internal revolts or disease, and appear simply to have been abandoned.

Some archaeologists have theorised that the cities were abandoned due to a severe drought known to have occurred in the region between 800 and 1000 AD.

---

Which of the following, if true, most strongly supports the archaeologists' theory?

a. There is ample archaeological evidence of Indian peasant revolts and city-state warfare existing but such events could never result in the permanent abandonment of cities.

b. No monumental inscriptions created after 900 AD have been found in these cities but inscriptions dating before that time have been found in abundance.

c. Studies of Uttarakhand lake sediment cores provide conclusive evidence that there are only four factors that might cause Indian cities to be abandoned between 800 and 1000 AD: invading forces, internal revolts, disease and weather.

d. Climatic studies have documented cycles of intermittent drought in the Uttarakhand peninsula dating from the present to at least 7,000 years ago.

e. The Indian city, Kasha, was continuously inhabited from 500–1550 AD.

**Q1.238** A wave of incidents of unusual acts of violence, from murder to acts of self-destruction, plagued the small medieval town for a period of five years, nearly wiping out the population.

At the same time, several studies have shown there was an unusual shift in the area's weather pattern. Rainfall was so heavy and continuous that the wheat crop probably fell prey to the ergot fungus. When eaten, grain thus affected can cause ergotism: a disease associated with hallucinations and other disturbing psychological side effects.

In the end, we can conclude that the violence was most likely the result of freakish weather conditions.

---

Which of the following choices best describes the flaw in the reasoning above?

a. It is entirely based upon a series of plausible suppositions rather than upon any evidence.

b. No clear distinction is drawn between cause and effect.

c. Explanations of historical events cannot be convincing when too great a role is assigned to chance or the irrational.

d. The author makes no distinction between coincidence and causality.

e. Crucial terms such as "unusual acts of violence" are not adequately defined in regard to the specific historical event.

**Q1.239** A conversation takes place between two friends:

Arnie: The contribution of commercial airlines to carbon dioxide emissions in a given period of time is greater than the carbon dioxide emitted by the whole of Africa in the same period. So reducing the number of commercial flights would help reduce carbon dioxide emissions and therefore global warming.

Clara: Interesting. And did you know that the contribution of one single London–New York flight produces more pollution than one year's worth of car travel for a typical UK resident?

---

What purpose does Clara's statement serve?

a. Weaken Arnie's argument by suggesting an alternative solution.

b. Add more weight to Arnie's argument that the number of flights should be reduced.

c. Question Arnie's understanding of the immediacy of the global warming issue.

d. Reinforce Arnie's assertion that commercial airlines are major contributors to increased carbon dioxide levels.

e. Question the assertion that high levels of carbon dioxide are the cause of global warming.

**Q1.240** Alphatech plc has recently been named as one of the worst sexual discrimination offenders, with only 1 woman sitting on the board (out of 20 directors) and only 6 women being appointed at middle-managerial level (out of a total of 50 middle managers).

A member of the trade union representing employees at the company said: "It is disgusting that, in this day and age, women find that they are being refused prominent positions within the company simply because they have the 'wrong' gender."

---

What evidence should Alphatech present to best defend itself against the accusation?

    **a.** That, at the same level of hierarchy, men and women have the same level of qualification.

    **b.** That men and women doing a similar job are paid the same.

    **c.** That only 10% of applicants are women.

    **d.** That the job involves a high degree of stress and requires a degree of flexibility that married women or women with children find difficult to accept.

    **e.** That all job applicants who were rejected had fewer qualifications than those who were given a job.

**Q1.241** The government has recently proposed that prisoners released from jail after a long period of time should be granted a monetary allowance on which they could live until they can find a job. This would reduce the likelihood that they might reoffend.

A large section of the public is violently opposed to this move as they see it as a reward for criminal activity.

---

What is the most plausible criticism that the government could make towards the protestors?

   **a.** That they feel crime prevention is not an important matter.

   **b.** That they only aim to punish and not prevent.

   **c.** That they are too materialistic.

   **d.** That they value emotions before justice.

   **e.** That they would think differently if one of their family members was about to be released from jail.

**Q1.242** People are affected by different foods in different ways. For example, some people get a migraine after drinking coffee whilst others don't. This is because they are more sensitive to caffeine than others.

Many people who suffer from migraines have reported that they ate chocolate approximately four hours before the onset of the migraine. People who are prone to migraines should, therefore, avoid eating chocolate.

---

Which of the following statements, if true, would weaken the argument made the most?

**a.** Chocolate contains caffeine.

**b.** Migraines start well before the person can feel it. Those who develop a migraine tend to crave sweet foods before they can feel the migraine.

**c.** Some people develop migraines without ever eating any chocolate.

**d.** People who eat chocolate tend to have coffee with it.

**e.** 50% of people who develop a migraine after eating chocolate also develop a migraine after eating Parmesan cheese.

**Q1.243** Company Press Release

Our company is keen to address some of the severe criticisms it has received lately from various members of the public and from unsavoury bloggers, who claimed that many studies have demonstrated that artificial substances such as colourants, preservatives, flavour enhancers and other food additives can have harmful effects and that there was therefore a risk that our own food may put our clients at risk.

Let me reassure you: our own food does not contain any artificial substances – we only use natural ingredients and so you can be confident that our food is totally safe to eat.

---

Which of the following statements, if true, would weaken the point made by this food manufacturer?

a. Many foods that don't contain preservatives are perfectly harmless.

b. Many artificial substances are not harmful.

c. Food additives are essential in ensuring good flavour.

d. Some natural substances used in food can be harmful.

e. People value health over flavour.

**Q1.244** A fruit known as amla in certain parts of Asia is an excellent source of vitamin C. A small quantity of the fruit grated and added to salads provides almost all the daily requirement of this vitamin. However, the fruit is very sour.

A new process designed to remove most of the sour taste will make the fruit acceptable to American tastes. We are therefore starting to grow this fruit for sale in the United States.

---

The argument above assumes all of the following statements except which one?

**a.** Apart from its sourness, there is no other objection to eating this fruit.

**b.** A market exists for a new source of vitamin C.

**c.** The fruit can only be used in salads.

**d.** The new process does not remove a significant part of the vitamin content.

**e.** Americans generally won't eat sour foods.

**Q1.245** At a known Homo sapiens campsite dating from 10,000 BC, archaeologists have unearthed part of an object that looks like an incomplete flute. The flute fragment only contains four holes, which are at a distance from one another such that one could play four of the seven musical notes contained in the diatonic musical scale we use nowadays (which was only really fully adopted by us in the 16th century). It has therefore been suggested that the diatonic scale was in fact developed by our Homo sapiens ancestors well before we started using it.

---

Which of the following statements, if true, most supports this belief?

a. The flute seems to be made from a bear's femur bone, which would have been long enough to make the flute capable of playing a complete diatonic scale of seven notes.

b. No instrument capable of playing part or all of the diatonic scale has ever been found before this one was found.

c. Flutes are the simplest instrument capable of playing the diatonic scale.

d. The flute seems to be made of bear bone and was found near skeletons of bears.

e. No other musical instrument except this one has ever been found in a Homo sapiens campsite.

**Q1.246** Over the course of my career I have travelled around the world and have had the opportunity to compare and contrast the quality of the various hotels in which I have stayed. In this book, I have decided to show you, the reader and seasoned traveller, how hotels rank in terms of comfort, look and feel in the UK.

One thing that particularly struck me in the course of my travels around the UK this year is the difference in style between hotels built before 1940 and those built after 1940. Based on all the hotels I can honestly say that, overall, the quality of the wooden frames in pre-1940 hotels tends to be superior to the quality of the wooden frames found in hotels built after 1940. Nearly all hotels built pre-1940 had good quality frames, which is not something I can say about the more recent buildings.

There is absolutely no doubt that those who built hotels before 1940 worked with more precision, care and ability than those who built hotels after 1940.

---

Which of the following statements, if true, most seriously weakens the travel writer's argument?

a. World War II led to a shortage of carpenters but an increasing need to repair buildings and work at a faster speed.

b. The higher the quality of the wooden frames, the less likely they are to fall into disrepair and the less likely the building is to be demolished or abandoned.

c. Hotels built after 1940 were bigger than those built previously.

d. Apprenticeships available to carpenters before 1940 were on average one year longer than those granted after 1940.

e. The quality of materials used was roughly the same pre- and post-1940.

**Q1.247** The project to build the HS2 (High Speed 2) train line is now going ahead. This will reduce journey times by 35 minutes between London and Birmingham, 1 hour between London and Manchester and 50 minutes between London and Leeds.

But all this comes at a huge cost. When one considers that the project will cost over £50 billion for the train line and then £10 billion for the trains and that one could buy a brand new plane for something like £50 million, one wonders why the government did not simply try to develop air travel instead. Planes go just as fast and can go anywhere. Trains are fixed to a track and do not allow us to go everywhere we want in the way that a car, a bus or a plane does.

---

Which of the following statements, if true, most seriously weakens the author's argument?

a.  Cars and buses are far slower than trains.

b.  Planes use air corridors, which are similar to train tracks and can only link one airport to another, with airports not being as conveniently located as train stations.

c.  Trains could run without drivers whereas planes could not.

d.  The number of stations that can accommodate high-speed trains is limited.

e.  People rarely consider using trains for long distances and would rather fly.

**Q1.248** At a local town hall meeting on the topic of crime and security, the following exchange takes place:

Mrs Khan: The number of robberies has increased every year for the past 15 years. I appreciate robberies are not serious crimes but still it shows that the police are useless at doing their job and I blame you for cutting their budget and forcing them to focus only on major crimes instead of the crimes that concern people like me on a daily basis.

Councillor: They may not be classified as serious crimes but it does not mean we are not taking them seriously. In your reasoning, however, you are not taking account of the fact that the number of people living in the area has increased every year for the past 15 years. If you actually calculate the percentage of burglaries as a percentage of the population, you will see that this has gone down every year over that period. So the police are doing an excellent job.

---

Which of the following statements, if true, most weakens the councillor's argument?

a. The rate of burglaries is higher amongst the elderly and lower amongst younger people.

b. Better insurance policies mean that people are now more likely to report burglaries than they would have been 15 years ago.

c. The number of police officers has steadily increased over the past 15 years.

d. The local police station has been closed and people who wish to report a non-serious crime need to travel 5 miles along a busy road to reach the next available police station.

e. The rate for serious crimes has steadily decreased over the past 15 years.

**Q1.249** To estimate changes in lobster populations, marine biologists have installed a number of traps in strategic locations. Every year, commercial fishermen go out to sea and lay traps. At the end of the fishing season, a figure called the Lobster Per Trap (LPT) figure is recorded, calculated as the average number of lobsters that fishermen have caught per trap. The current LPT is the same as it was 15 years ago and so marine biologists conclude that today's lobster population is the same as it was 15 years ago.

---

Which of the following statements, if true, most weakens the argument?

a. In the past 10 years the LPT has halved.

b. For the past 5 years, commercial fishermen have been using sonar equipment enabling them to locate lobsters with great accuracy.

c. A fungal infection nearly drove the lobster population to extinction 5 years ago.

d. The number of traps laid by commercial fishermen has remained relatively constant in the past 15 years.

e. Demand for lobsters has dropped in the past 15 years.

**Q1.250** A new local fitness centre, Moving It, recently launched a marketing campaign aiming specifically at enticing members currently enrolled at other local fitness clubs to give up their current membership and join Moving It instead. Part of their strategy is to offer a range of free extras such as free locker rental, free health checks and two free personal trainer sessions. As a result of that campaign, the management of Moving It claims that the campaign has been a huge success since it has already increased membership by 100 people, i.e. an increase of 20% in membership levels in the first two weeks of the campaign.

---

Which of the following pieces of information would be most useful to support the fact that the marketing campaign has been a success?

1. The number of people who have just joined Moving It in the past two weeks having never visited any other local fitness club before.

2. The percentage of members of rival clubs who left those clubs since the marketing campaign began.

3. The number of members of other fitness clubs who left their club in the past two weeks and joined Moving it.

**a.** 1 only.

**b.** 2 only.

**c.** 3 only.

**d.** 1 or 3.

**e.** 1 and 3.

**f.** 1 or 2 or 3.

**Q1.251** A recent research study presented at a scientific conference showed that those treated with the drug atorvastatin, which is a well-known cholesterol-reducing drug, have 30% fewer non-fatal heart attacks and 30% fewer deaths from coronary heart disease than those who do not take the drug.

Therefore we can conclude that lowering cholesterol levels helps reduce the risk of heart disease.

---

The flaw in this argument is that:

a. It neglects the possibility that atorvastatin may have severe side effects.

b. It fails to consider that atorvastatin may reduce the risk of heart disease but not as a consequence of its lowering cholesterol levels.

c. It relies on past findings, rather than drawing its principal conclusion from the data found in the specific study cited.

d. It draws a conclusion regarding the effects of lowering cholesterol levels on heart disease, when in fact the conclusion should focus on the relation between atorvastatin and cholesterol levels.

e. It fails to consider the percentage of the general population that might be taking atorvastatin.

**Q1.252** The London Tube is getting increasingly crowded and the difficulties that passengers experience on exiting their carriage often lead to significant delays.

The number of passengers is expected to increase by 25% in the next ten years, but Transport for London (TfL) only has plans to increase the capacity of the network over the same period by adding 8% more capacity.

A representative from TfL said: "We predict that this 8% increase in capacity will be sufficient to guarantee that there is no increase in the delays incurred by passengers as a result of overcrowding."

---

Which of the following statements, if true, would provide the strongest justification for the comment made by the TfL representative?

a. TfL can increase the number of train trips without incurring any additional operational costs.

b. By creating clever rotas, TfL can achieve the 8% increase in train trips without the need to purchase any more carriages.

c. Most commuters who use the Tube don't have any alternative mode of public transport that meets their needs adequately.

d. Most of the projected increase in the number of passengers is expected to occur at off-peak times when hardly anyone uses the Tube.

e. TfL also plans to increase the number of bus trips by 5% on routes that connect to Tube stations.

**Q1.253** One apple contains more calories than one orange.

One pear contains more calories than one mango.

Therefore one apple contains more calories than one mango.

---

All of the statements below would contribute individually to making the above paragraph logical except one. Which one?

a. The number of calories is the same in one apple as in one pear.

b. There are more calories in one pear than in one apple.

c. The number of calories in one orange is the same as in one pear.

d. There are more calories in one orange than in one mango.

e. There are more calories in one orange than in one pear.

**Q1.254** One of the theories that circulates is that birds may be more intelligent than once thought and even, possibly, on a par with apes. For example, it has been long known that the corvids – a group that includes crows, ravens, rooks, jackdaws, jays and magpies – use tools that may at least rival, and even surpass, those that primates such as chimpanzees make.

Professor Richmond, of the University of California, feels that the fact that birds have brains smaller than a golf ball is not actually the point and that what one needs to look at is how that compares to body size. Both primates and corvids have brains that are far larger than one would anticipate for the size of their body.

---

What conclusion can be drawn from the above passage?

a.   Corvids are the most intelligent of all birds.

b.   Intelligence is measured through the ability to create tools.

c.   Relative brain size is a better indicator of intelligence than absolute brain size.

d.   Body size is a useful indicator of intelligence.

e.   Animals with larger brains tend to be intelligent.

**Q1.255** Ten per cent of the world's population is left-handed and, as such, left-handed people can be considered a minority. Some people argue that there are grounds to consider that left-handed people, by not being in a majority, are therefore not "normal" and should be deemed disabled. That means they should be entitled to receive a disability allowance.

Which of the following statements, if true, weakens this argument?

a. Most left-handed people were actually forced to write with their right hand when they went to school.

b. Most tools in life are designed for right-handed people.

c. Left-handed people are more likely to suffer from depression and allergies.

d. Left-handed people tend to have more serious car accidents than right-handed people.

e. The percentage of high achievers in science, sport, theatre and music who are left-handed is well over 10%.

**Q1.256** People who work in fast food outlets always moan that "it's like a factory in there". But maybe they have a point. Let's look at the evidence:

- Both essentially deal with mass production.
- Both entail jobs that are very routine and boring.
- Both are based on protocols and automatic behaviours.
- Both involve paying low wages.
- Both have workers who risk getting the sack if they complain about their working conditions.

---

Which of the following statements best expresses the conclusion of this argument?

**a.** People who work in boring jobs are underpaid.

**b.** Mass production leads to poor working conditions.

**c.** Factories and fast food outlets employ people from the same social classes.

**d.** Physical working conditions in factories and food outlets are the same.

**e.** None of the above.

**Q1.257** With resources such as Wikipedia, blogs and social media, people have been able to regain control of their health. Most view formal medical advice as too complicated and contradictory and accessing information through those other sources is far easier. In recent years, we have seen massive improvements in the health and well-being of the population and so clearly people are better off continuing to inform themselves through whatever means at their disposal rather than following formal medical advice.

---

Which of the following statements, if true, weakens the argument?

a. Medical advances are complex to explain to patients.

b. It is quicker to go on the internet than to get an appointment with a doctor.

c. Health is an individual issue and individuals tend to be more aware of what is good for them.

d. The health improvements noted by surveys are in medical fields where online sources match medical advice.

e. Some websites can be more informative than an average doctor.

**Q1.258** Consider the following statements:

1. There are at least as many taxis as there are buses.
2. There are not more taxis than there are buses.
3. There are fewer taxis than there are buses.
4. There are not more buses than there are taxis.

---

Which of the two above statements are equivalent?

a. 1 and 3.

b. 1 and 4.

c. 2 and 3.

d. 2 and 4.

e. 3 and 4.

**Q1.259** Nearly two-thirds of the world's population speaks at least two languages, and some people see that as a new phenomenon.

I agree that many people indeed speak Arabic or Spanish around the world and English is pretty much the most commonly spoken language. But, in the 17$^{th}$ century French and Italian were pretty common in the world of commerce. In the 19$^{th}$ century French was the official diplomatic language. And, in the 15$^{th}$ century, Latin was the main language for education, religion and commerce in the Western world, despite the fact that quite obviously no one spoke Latin at home.

---

Which of the following statements best summarises the conclusion of this text?

**a.** The vast majority of multilingual people speak English.

**b.** English will one day be superseded by another language.

**c.** Speaking another language to improve one's chances in life is not a new consideration.

**d.** Most travellers are multilingual.

**e.** The popularity of English is caused by social media.

**Q1.260** I once went on holiday to Northumberland to visit a nature reserve where puffins can be found in substantial numbers. I was shocked to see that a nearby restaurant had opted to put puffin on its menu. I am not sure if they are a protected species but, if they aren't, then they should be. Anyway, I felt like having an argument so I went into the restaurant to confront the owner. Her argument was that puffins were a very lean meat, it was available locally and so had very low carbon footprint and it was a healthy meat. But that is total rubbish; it is quite obviously a cheap way of drumming up business and a massive publicity stunt.

---

Which of the following statements best highlights the flaw in this argument?

a. It assumes that puffins are protected.

b. It assumes that puffins are sustainable.

c. It attacks the owner's motives rather than the reasons.

d. It assumes that puffins don't have natural predators.

e. It assumes that puffins do not damage the environment.

**Q1.261** There will always be people who will refuse, at all cost, to use public transport and will insist on driving. A survey commissioned by the Transport minister shows that 75% of Londoners who take the car would opt to travel by train or bus instead if the system was more reliable. So it seems to me that it would make sense to free up some cash to invest in public transport nationwide as soon as possible.

---

Which of the following statements best highlights the flaw in this argument?

a. The survey does not identify whether the investment should be in buses or trains.

b. The statistic quoted is not representative of the whole population.

c. It ignores the reasons that the remaining 25% may have to continue using their car.

d. It does not specify what improvements would be necessary.

e. It does not take account of people who do not drive.

**Q1.262** The internet is full of amazing facts. Did you know that 25% of chief executives of companies in the FTSE 100 are called David, 20% are called Paul and 15% are called Kevin?

So, if you ever want your boy to head up a company, you should call him David, Paul or Kevin.

---

Which of the following statements best highlights the flaw in this argument?

a.  It fails to consider the other possible names.

b.  It confuses a correlation with a cause.

c.  It jumps to conclusion without evidence.

d.  It confuses a necessary condition with a sufficient one.

e.  It generalises from anecdotal evidence.

**Q1.263** Some people have suggested that medical degrees should be shortened from 5 years to 4 years. But many teachers are complaining that they waste the first year taking students up to a common level of biology knowledge that used to be taught at high school in the past. When you consider that, by the end of the second year, only 10% of students have reached the level of knowledge that students attained 30 years ago, it is quite unbelievable. So, there is no way that we can cope with 4-year degrees in medicine.

---

Which of the following statements is an assumption of the argument in the passage above?

a. School exams are easier now than they used to be.

b. 4-year degrees will be a condensed version of the same content as 5-year degrees.

c. Medicine is more competitive now than 30 years ago.

d. Medical students prefer shorter degrees.

e. Biology is more important to the study of medicine now than it was 30 years ago.

**Q1.264** Who hasn't been shocked by pictures of rotting teeth, tumours or other disgusting body parts that are displayed on cigarettes packets in various countries around the world?

Much research has been conducted on smoking cessation and many experts agree that showing shocking pictures is a cost effective deterrent.

So it is about time all countries used this tactic to encourage smoking cessation.

---

Which of the following statements, if true, most weakens the argument?

**a.** Smokers have a shorter than average life expectancy.

**b.** Governments are benefitting from taxes on tobacco products.

**c.** In countries where such images are displayed, tobacco is highly taxed and there is a ban on tobacco advertising.

**d.** Pictures are a proven way of arousing emotions.

**e.** More people are now smoking less harmful e-cigarettes.

**Q1.265** Rent controls are often put in place through legislation to limit rent increases to a defined percentage per year or to cap the amount a landlord/owner can charge. However, owners of apartment buildings argue that rent control should be abolished. Although they acknowledge that, in the short term, they would increase the rents they charge, owners argue that, in the long term, the rent increases would benefit everyone.

Indeed, higher profits would lead to increased apartment construction. Increased apartment construction would then lead to a greater supply of apartments that can be let; and in turn this would lead to lower rents as potential tenants would have a greater selection of apartments to choose from.

Thus, abolishing rent control would, ultimately, reduce prices.

---

Which of the following is an assumption made by the author?

a. Current residents of rent-controlled apartments would be able to find new apartments once their rents increased.

b. The fundamental responsibility of any society is to house its citizens.

c. Only current apartment owners would profit significantly from market deregulation.

d. New apartment construction will generate a great number of jobs.

e. The increase in the number of apartments available would exceed the number of new potential tenants.

**Q1.266** In many pre-schools, children tend to get colds before their resistance develops, and the colds become much less frequent over time.

It is clear that a child's immune system requires them to get several colds before it is fully activated and able to effectively deal with colds.

---

Which of the following, if true, most seriously weakens this theory?

a. Children commonly spread viruses and bacteria in a small closed environment.

b. The use of vitamin C increases resistance to the common cold and decreases its frequency.

c. Parents stock up on cold medicine after a child is ill that alleviates the symptoms of a cold.

d. There are many strains of the cold virus (new ones are, in fact, found every year), and children develop resistance to individual strains.

e. White blood cells fight infection and their production levels are stimulated by high infection levels.

**Q1.267** Although Locke has been hailed as a giant figure in European intellectual history, his ideas were largely borrowed from his predecessors, who are now unfairly neglected by historians.

Furthermore, Locke never wrote a truly great book; his most widely known works are muddy in style, awkwardly constructed and often self-contradictory.

---

Which of the following statements best expresses the author's conclusion?

a. Locke made use of ideas without acknowledging his predecessors as the sources of those ideas.

b. Current historians are re-evaluating Locke's work in the light of present-day knowledge.

c. Locke's contributions to the development of European thought have been greatly exaggerated.

d. Historians should re-examine Locke's place in European intellectual history.

e. Although Locke's ideas were important, his way of expressing them in writing was sadly inadequate.

**Q1.268** Every house that has a view onto the park has a large bay window; those bay windows are painted either white or brown.

---

If this statement is true, which of the following statements must also be true?

1. If a house does not have a large bay window then it does not have a view onto the park.

2. If a house has a white bay window then it has a view onto the park.

3. If a house does not have a view onto the park, then it does not have a large bay window.

4. If a house does not have a view onto the park, then it has a large bay window but that bay window can be of a different colour than white or brown.

   **a.** None of the statements can be true.

   **b.** 1 only.

   **c.** 2 only.

   **d.** 3 only.

   **e.** 4 only.

   **f.** 1 and 2 only.

   **g.** 1 and 4 only.

   **h.** 2 and 3 only.

   **i.** 1, 2 and 4 only.

**Q1.269** Mr Randolph is a manager at a local factory with an excellent reputation for quality and reliability. His motto is "If it is not broken, don't fix it".

---

Which of the following actions is he least likely to take?

a.   Agree to trade union demands for better storage of dangerous equipment in the interest of safety, as several workers reported they nearly got injured when some of the equipment fell off the storage units.

b.   Respond to the difficulty in recruiting and retaining women workers by setting up a crèche in a spare room at the factory.

c.   Set up a programme of preventive maintenance for major pieces of machinery recently ordered and delivered.

d.   Order the replacement of windows that were broken by a tree, which fell down during a recent violent storm.

e.   Replace the quality control manager following several complaints about defective goods in recent shipments from the factory.

**Q1.270** The life expectancy of people living below the poverty line in the United States is seven years shorter than the national average. A public health advocate argues that this is due to the fact that the poor cannot afford preventative medical care and often live in substandard housing where harmful substances such as lead paint and asbestos are common. An expansion of health insurance services to those below the poverty line is an ultimately more cost-efficient way of raising life expectancy, because preventative care will forestall many expensive emergency treatments.

---

Which of the following, if true, accurately identifies the most significant flaw in the public health advocate's argument that health insurance services for those below the poverty line should be expanded?

a. The public health advocate does not provide sufficient information about the amount of money that will be saved by preventing emergency medical treatments.

b. The expansion of health insurance services to those below the poverty line will not address health problems caused by substandard housing.

c. Many healthcare providers are especially concerned with treating complications caused by exposure to lead paint and asbestos.

d. Census results do not clearly indicate what percentage of the population falls below the poverty line.

e. Lead paint and asbestos, though they cause medical problems, have not been conclusively proven to shorten life expectancy.

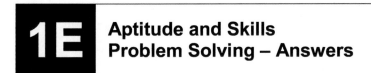

## 1E Aptitude and Skills Problem Solving – Answers

**Q1.1 – e: 59**

The number of sides for the cubes that we can see from this point of view is as shown on the diagram (total: 53).

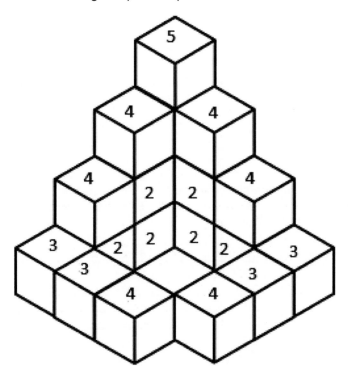

However, below the top cube, there are also 3 more cubes that are not shown on the picture, which will form the back corner. Each of those cubes will have 2 apparent sides. So the grand total is 53 + 3 x 2 = 59 sides.

## Q1.2 – Shape H

All the other shapes can be made using the same two sub-shapes derived from Shape A as follows:

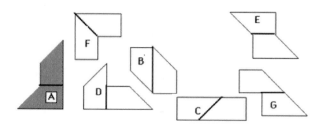

## Q1.3 – b: 10

In the range 1–19, we can pair numbers so that they add up to 20:
1 + 19 = 20, 2 + 18 = 20, …, 9 + 11 = 20. Therefore the number 10 has to appear in the middle.

## Q1.4 – e: 41

First you need to list the different ways in which 60 can be calculated as a product of other numbers. Once you have done that, you will obtain the equivalent letters and will be able to calculate the number of strings that can be made from those letters.

| Product | Letters | Number of strings |
|---|---|---|
| 2 × 2 × 15 | b, b, o | 3 x 2 / 2 = 3 |
| 2 × 2 × 3 × 5 | b, b, c, e | 4 x 3 x 2 / 2 = 12 |
| 2 × 5 × 6 | b, e, f | 3 x 2 = 6 |
| 2 × 3 × 10 | b, c, j | 3 x 2 = 6 |
| 3 × 20 | c, t | 2 |
| 3 × 4 × 5 | c, d, e | 3 x 2 = 6 |
| 4 × 15 | d, o | 2 |
| 5 × 12 | e, l | 2 |
| 6 × 10 | f, j | 2 |
| **TOTAL** | | **41** |

**Q1.5 – e: 1/2**
Let's call X the volume of the tub.

The tub can be completely filled in 30 minutes via the tap; this means that in 1 hour the tap can deliver 2X amount of water.

The tub can be completely emptied in 40 minutes via the sinkhole. This means that in 1 hour the sinkhole can drain 60/40 X, i.e. 1.5X of water.

If, in 1 hour, the tap can deliver 2X worth of water, but the sinkhole can drain 1.5X, then after 1 hour only 0.5X would remain, i.e. 1/2.


**Q1.6 – c: 96**
The 8 hours that the broken machine should have been working will need to be spent instead by the other machines as extra time. Divided between five machines, this takes an additional 8/5 = 1.6 hours (running concurrently), which is equivalent to 96 minutes.


**Q1.7 – d: 24**
Zeros will be present each time a multiple of 10 is created. This will happen whenever a 2 is multiplied by a 5.

Looking at the prime factors for all numbers between 1 and 100, there will be 50 even numbers, accounting for at least 50 '2's. There will be many more in reality because for example 12 = 3 x 2 x 2 and 16 = 2 x 2 x 2 x 2; but at least 50.

The number of 5s will be far lower. There will be a minimum of 20 (one for each multiple of 5) but 25 (5x5), 50 (2x5x5), 75 (3x5x5) and 100 (4x5x5) will account for an extra 4 '5's. Hence there are 24 '5's in total.

Therefore, there are 24 zeros in 100!


**Q1.8 – c: Charles**
If each suspect tells one lie then, based on Brian's statements, the answer is either Charles or Edward. If we look at Derek's statement, the answer is either Charles or Brian. The common factor is Charles.

**Q1.9 – b: 120**
If 68 / X leaves a remainder of 4 then that number has to be a divisor of 64. Possible values of X are therefore: 1, 2, 4, 8, 16, 32, 64.

However, any divisor leaving a reminder of 4 cannot be equal to or lower than 4 since no divisor can leave a remainder which is equal to or greater than itself.

Hence the sum is: 8 + 16 + 32 + 64 = 120.


**Q1.10 – b: B, C and D**
This exercise would be too hard to do in a reasonable amount of time if you were not given any options as there are many possible permutations. You should therefore limit yourself to testing the options given rather than working the answer from scratch. Here B and D can be used as they are but C needs to be rotated 90 degrees.

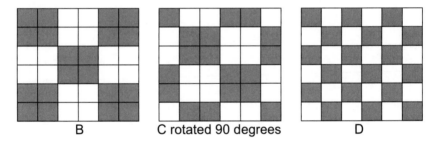

B          C rotated 90 degrees          D


**Q1.11 – c: 96 mph**
It is tempting to answer 100 mph but that is not the correct answer. Let's call J the length of his journey in miles.

The first half of his journey will take $(J/2)/80 = J/160$. The second half of this journey will take $(J/2)/120 = J/240$. Therefore the average speed over the whole journey will be $J / (J/160 + J/240) = 1 / (1/160 + 1/240)$.

This is equal to $1 / (3/480 + 2/480) = 480 / 5 = 96$ mph.

## Q1.12 – f: F

All shapes can be reconfigured to make a square, as shown below, except Shape F.

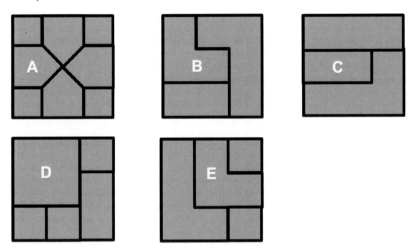

## Q1.13 – d: 150

The question gives that if the motorist was to drive for an hour longer and at 5 mph faster he would travel 70 miles further. That means that his speed would be 70 mph. His average speed between A and B was therefore 65 mph.

The distance covered at a speed of 65 + 10 = 75 mph during a 2-hour drive would therefore be 150 miles.

## Q1.14 – c: 135

We know that Car B's average speed was 15 mph higher than Car A's and we are told that it is also a third higher than Car A's average speed. Therefore 15 mph is one-third of Car A's speed, meaning that Car A's speed is 3 x 15 = 45 mph.

We can now calculate the distance X travelled by Car A until the two cars meet. The time taken to get from starting point to meeting point will be the same for both Car A and Car B. We can therefore combine the two speed/time equations:

Time = (X/45) = (315 − X)/60 and therefore 60X = 45(315) − 45X.
This gives: 105X = 45 x 315, i.e. X = 45 x 315 / 105 = 45 x 3 = 135 miles.


### Q1.15 – f: 8

Calling M the number of males and F the number of females we have:
F = 2M − 1.

Also, since replacing a female with a male would lead to an equivalent number of people of both genders on the committee, we can write:
M + 1 = F − 1, i.e. F = M + 2.

By combining both equations, we get: M + 2 = 2M − 1. Thus M = 3 and so F = 5. The total number of members on the committee is therefore 8.


### Q1.16 – c: 300

At the start of the game, everyone has £600. At the end of game 1, Ian is the winner. He will therefore keep his £600 and will win £300 from each of the other two players, making his total pot 600 + 2 x 300 = £1,200.

As he loses game 2, he will forfeit 1/2 of his pot, leaving him with £600. He will then lose 1/2 of that amount at the end of game 3, which he also loses, leaving him with £300.


### Q1.17 – c: £2,900

The loyalty card is worthwhile when the savings made on purchases outweigh the cost of the card. We therefore simply need to calculate at which point 8% of the purchases will equal £232. This will be when the client has spent 232 / 0.08 = £2,900.


### Q1.18 – c: 31

The ring's insured value is given at £3,300. The premium is 22 carats x £5/carat = £110. Thus at 3300 / 110 = 30 years the insurance premiums would equal the cost of the insured ring, and so only after 31 years would the total insurance premiums exceed the insured value of the ring.

**Q1.19 – c: £70,000**
The cost of the Alaskan King Crabs is £500,000/100,000 kg = £5/kg.

50,000 kg were sold at 20% above cost, i.e. £6/kg, thus at a profit of £1/kg. The profit on that sale was therefore £50,000.

The remaining 50,000 kg were sold for 10% less than the price per kilogram the day before, i.e. at 90% x £6 = £5.40, thus at a profit of £0.40/kg. This led to a profit of 0.40 x 50,000 = £20,000.

The total profit was therefore £70,000.


**Q1.20 – a: 100**
We can write out the breakfasts as equations and solve for each:

100 ml milk + 2 cups A = 400 calories
100 ml milk + 2 cups B = 300 calories
Therefore 2A – 2B = 100

Since we are told that A = 1.5B in terms of calories, we can substitute that into the equation and find for B: 2 (1.5 B) – 2B = 100. Therefore B = 100 calories per cup.


**Q1.21 – c: 3500**
There are 5 years between 1 January 2005 and 1 January 2010, during which the company will have lost 5 x 300 = 1500 employees. Since the company is left with 70% of the original number of employees, then the 1500 lost employees will account for 30% of the original 1 January 2005 workforce. The number of employees on 1 January 2005 was therefore 1500 / 0.3 = 5,000. The number of employees on 1 January 2010 was therefore 5,000 – 1,500 = 3,500.


**Q1.22 – c: £1**
If we set:

- M = pint of milk
- B = loaf of bread
- T = 1 tomato

we can write the following three equations:

(1) M + B + 2T = 3.5
(2) M + 3T = 3
(3) B + T = 1.5

If we add Equation 2 and Equation 3 together we get:
M + B + 4T = 4.5.

We know that M + B + 2T = 3.5 (Equation 1).
Subtracting one equation from the other, we can conclude that:
2T = 4.5 – 3.5; hence 2T = 1. Therefore T = 0.5.

From Equation 3 we can then deduce that B = 1.5 – 0.5 = 1.


### Q1.23 – c: Wednesday
60 hours is essentially 2 x 24 hours + 12 hours. The day Monday covers the time period 0 to 23:59. Adding 48 hours to the range Monday (0 to 23:59) gives Wednesday (0 to 23:59). Adding a further 12 hours gives the range Wednesday 12pm (noon) to Thursday 12pm (noon). Since we know that his appointment was between 1pm and 9pm then the day must have been a Wednesday.


### Q1.24 – b: 20.0 miles
If we call T the time it normally takes him to get to work (in minutes), we have the following:

Distance to work = 40(T+12) / 60 = 48(T+7) / 60
This gives 40T + (40 x 12) = 48T + (48 x 7)
Therefore 8T = 144, i.e. T = 18 minutes
Thus distance = 40(18 + 12) / 60 = 20 miles.


### Q1.25 – e: 1 km
If X is the distance between the starting line and the point where Greyhound B catches up with Greyhound A, and T the time elapsed between the start of the race and the time Greyhound B catches up with Greyhound A, we have:

Greyhound A: X = 20T
Greyhound B: X = 25(T − 10) since he will cover the distance in 10s less.

Therefore 20T = 25(T − 10), i.e. 5T = 250, i.e. T = 50s.

Thus X = 20 x 50 = 1000 m, i.e. 1 km.


**Q1.26 – b: 8–15**
If we call X the product of the two dice in the first throw, the products for all the throws will be:
- Throw 1: X
- Throw 2: X + 5
- Throw 3: X + 5 − 6 = X − 1
- Throw 4: (X − 1) + 11 = X + 10
- Throw 5: (X + 10) − 8 = X + 2

Since each die is numbered 1–6, we deduce that the product has to be between 1 and 36. From Throw 3 we can conclude that X cannot be equal to 1. From Throw 4, we can deduce that X must be equal to or lower than 26.

The quickest way to get to the answer is to try different values of X between 2 and 26, checking that each of the values obtained in the 5 throws can be obtained by multiplying 2 numbers that are between 1 and 6.

X = 2. Does not work as Throw 2 would be 7. Not possible.
X = 3. Does not work as Throw 4 would be 13. Not possible.
X = 4. Does not work as Throw 4 would be 14. Not possible.
X = 5. Does not work as Throw 5 would be 7. Not possible.
X = 6. Does not work as Throw 2 would be 11. Not possible.
X = 7. Is not a possible product for 2 dice.
X = 8. Does not work as Throw 2 would be 13. Not possible.
X = 9. Does not work as Throw 4 would be 19. Not possible.
X = 10. Works as it would give:
- Throw 1 = 10 (2 x 5)
- Throw 2 = 15 (3 x 5)
- Throw 3 = 9 (3 x 3)
- Throw 4 = 20 (4 x 5)
- Throw 5 = 12 (3 x 4 or 6 x 2)

If you check all remaining values, you will see that no other value satisfies the criteria as there is always one throw that requires a number greater than 6. Therefore the answer is the range 8–15.

### Q1.27 – c: 03:00
11,995 is equal to 12000 hours minus 5 hours. A period of 12000 hours is equivalent to 500 periods of 24 hours, which can be discounted as the clock will show the same time of 08:00 every time a 24-hour period is completed. We are therefore left with 5 hours, which we need to deduct, giving a time of 03:00.

### Q1.28 – c: 05:30
2937 minutes is 3000 minutes – 63 minutes, which we can express as:

- 50 hours minus 63 minutes, or
- 49 hours minus 3 minutes, or
- 48 hours plus 57 minutes.

We therefore simply need to deduct 57 minutes from 6:27, giving 05:30.

### Q1.29 – d: 240 days
The easiest way to visualise the problem is to ignore the normal passage of time and to see the relative speed of convergence of the two times. If we take 12:00 as the starting point:

On Day 0, Tim's clock will show 12:00 and Jane's 12:00 too.
On Day 1, Tim's clock will show 12:01 and Jane's 11:58.
On Day 2, Tim's clock will show 12:02 and Jane's 11:56.

The difference increases by 3 minutes every day until all 12 hours (i.e. 720 minutes) that separate them have been used up. Therefore it will take 720 / 3 = 240 days.

### Q1.30 – d: 3 hours
4 m x 25 m = 100 m$^2$.
12 m x 62.5 m = 750 m$^2$, i.e. 7.5 times larger.

234

24 minutes is 2/5 of an hour.
Therefore it would take 2/5 x 7.5 = 15 / 5 = 3 hours.

## Q1.31 – e: 4,200

Essentially this question is asking for the lowest common multiple (LCM), i.e. the smallest number that is a multiple of all the numbers present. One way to do this would be to write out all the multiples of the numbers together (i.e. for Train A: 120, 240, 360, 480, 560, etc.) and then circle the one that matches all 3. However, this could prove very time-consuming.

Another way to find the LCM is to use prime factorisation. All numbers can be written as products of prime numbers as follows:

Train A: $120 = 2 \times 2 \times 2 \times 3 \times 5 = 2^3 \times 3 \times 5$
Train B: $140 = 2 \times 2 \times 5 \times 7 = 2^2 \times 5 \times 7$
Train C: $150 = 2 \times 3 \times 5 \times 5 = 2 \times 3 \times 5^2$

The lowest common multiple is the product of the highest power in each prime factor category together. Out of all the prime categories: 2, 3, 5, and 7, the highest powers from each category are $2^3$, 3, $5^2$, and 7.

The LCM is therefore $2^3 \times 3 \times 5^2 \times 7 = 4200$ minutes.

## Q1.32 – e: 28

The easiest way to solve the problem is to use the lowest common multiple (LCM) method, turning all the seconds into integers (multiply by 10) to make prime factorisation easier, and then reversing this once we find the LCM (by dividing by 10).

Car A: $8 = 2^3$
Car B: $10 = 2 \times 5$
Car C: $14 = 2 \times 7$

Thus the highest primes from each category would be: $2^3 \times 5 \times 7 = 280$.
The LCM is 280. Divide by a factor of 10 = 28 seconds.

**Q1.33 – d: 36.5**
The prime factors are:

Bell A: 24 = $2^3$ x 3
Bell B: 30 = 2 x 3 x 5
Bell C: 38 = 2 x 19

Thus the highest primes from each category would be: $2^3$ x 3 x 5 x 19 = 2280. It would therefore take 2280 minutes, i.e. 38 hours, before all 3 bells ring at the same time again, measured from the time they were last ringing together.

Since we are told that it last happened 1.5 hours ago, then the answer is 36.5 hours.


**Q1.34 – e: 23**
The main problem with this question is that we are told when the lights last came ON but are asked when they will next go OFF. If we had been given the time when they last went OFF at the same time, it would have been a simple case of using the LCM method with frequencies 13 and 9 seconds. In this case, we have no choice but to adopt a manual method, as follows below.

If we take as point 0 the time when they both came ON at the same time, then the times at which they would switch OFF are:

Circuit 1: 4 (first time off), 17, 30, 43, 56, 69, and so on every 13 seconds
Circuit 2: 7 (first time off), 16, 25, 34, 43, and so on every 9 seconds

The first time they go OFF at the same time is therefore after 43 seconds. Since this takes a starting point that was 20 seconds ago, then the lights will actually next go OFF at the same time in 23 seconds' time.


**Q1.35 – e: They will never go OFF at the same time**
Both sets of lights have a cycle of 8 seconds.

We can map out the times at which each circuit will go OFF as follows (using the time when they both went ON simultaneously as Point 0):

Circuit 1: 3, 11, 19, and so on every 8 seconds
Circuit 2: 2, 10, 18, and so on every 8 seconds

You can see that they will always go OFF 1 second apart. They will, however, always switch ON at the same time.

## Q1.36 – b: 20
Let's call Z the number of games remaining.

We can write an equation setting out the number of games won:
$(0.4 \times 15) + (0.75 \times Z) = 0.6 (Z + 15)$
$6 + 0.75Z = 0.6Z + 9$
$0.15Z = 3$
$Z = 20$

## Q1.37 – c: £9m
Take:
- Private Grants = PG
- Private Endowments = PE
- City Council = CC.

The amount provided by CC was £18m, therefore PE = 1/3 x 18 = £6m. We are also told that PG = 0.5 x PE. Therefore PG = £3m.

Total = 3 + 6 = £9m.

## Q1.38 – a: 1,500
We start with 25,000 subscribers. Out of those, we know that 50% are consultants (i.e. 12,500). Out of those, 30% are consultant cardiologists (so 3,750), of which 40% are interventional cardiologists (so 1,500).

## Q1.39 – a: 57
Since they both earn the same rate, this can be resolved without calculating the actual payments made. Both will earn the same for the first 42 hours. During the 10 hours of overtime, Tim will receive 1.5 times the normal rate, i.e. the equivalent of 15 hours' pay at normal rate. Therefore the total number of hours his friend will need to work is 42 + 15 = 57.

**Q1.40 – c: 37.5%**
The original 8 litres would contain 2.4 litres of liquid X (30%) and 5.6 litres of water.

Once 2 litres of water have evaporated we are left with 2.4 litres of liquid X and 3.6 litres of water.

Adding 2 litres of Clean-Brite will add 0.6 litres of liquid X and 1.4 litres of water, giving a total of 3 litres of liquid X and 5 litres of water.

The final solution will therefore consist of 3/8 of liquid X, i.e. 37.5%.

**Q1.41 – b: 5%**
Take a sample of 100 syringes. Out of that sample, 80 would be good and 20 would be defective.

Out of the 80 good syringes, 5% (i.e. 4) would be mistakenly rejected, leaving us with just 76 to be sold.

Out of the 20 defective syringes, 80% (i.e. 16) would be spotted and rejected, meaning that 4 would slip through the net and would end up being sold.

Therefore, the following syringes would be sold:

- 76 good syringes
- 4 defective syringes.

The proportion of defective syringes amongst those sold would therefore be 4 / 80 = 5%.

**Q1.42 – b: II only**
We are trying to find the mean. Option I does not do that. Option III gives the median (the middle number). Option II, at first glance, seems rather arbitrary, but does actually give you the mean. By moving the decimal point by 1 place to the left, we are effectively dividing the sum by 10. Therefore, by doubling the whole sum and then moving the decimal point 1 place to the left, we are effectively dividing it by 5.

**Q1.43 – a: I only**
Imagine that the first (even) integer in the string is called N. The next even integer would be N + 2, etc. The mean of the 5 integers would thus be:

$$X = \frac{N + (N+2) + (N+4) + (N+6) + (N+8)}{5} = N + 4$$

Since N is an even integer, then X must also be an even integer. This means that I is true and that II is false. With regard to III, the equation X = N+4 does not imply that X should be a multiple of 5, though it is not impossible. Since the question asks which of the options MUST be true then III is not a correct answer.

**Q1.44 – d: £800,000**
The average of the five prices is £600,000; therefore the sum of all five house prices is £3,000,000.

If the cheapest house is £550,000, then the maximum price that a house could fetch can be calculated by setting the price of four of the houses at £550,000, with the last house having to make up the shortfall. The price of the last house would then be: 3,000,000 – 4 x 550,000, i.e. £800,000.

**Q1.45 – c: 34**
The average of the original 10 numbers can be written as:

$$\frac{\text{sum of 10 numbers}}{10} = X = \frac{\text{sum of 10 numbers} + 68}{12}$$

Thus 10X = sum of 10 numbers, and 12X = sum of 10 numbers + 68.

Therefore 10X = 12X – 68, thus X = 34. Note that this is also the average of the two numbers being added.

**Q1.46 – c: 13.6**
The sum of 2, 8, 12, 17 and 23 is 62. So factoring in the possible values of Z we can write this as: $(12 + 62) = 74 < \text{Sum} < (22 + 62) = 84$

The average would be the sum of the numbers divided by 6:
Therefore: $74 / 6 < \text{Average} < 84 / 6$

Thus the average is between 12.33 and 14. The only possible option is therefore c: 13.667 (which, if you have decided to calculate all possible averages, corresponds to Z=20).

**Q1.47 – c: £46,000**
The equation can be written as follows:
(24,000 + (salaries of 6 workers) + 100,000) / 8 = 50,000. Therefore the total salaries of the 6 workers is: 8 x 50,000 – 124,000, i.e. £276,000. This gives an average of £46,000.

**Q1.48 – e: 5,000**
2 out of 100 mice were found to be tagged when the second sample was taken. This means that an estimated 2% of the mice population would be tagged. Since we know that there are 100 tagged mice in total, then the population is equal to 100 / 0.02 = 5,000.

**Q1.49 – d: 41**
The number of doctors currently employed is 500 x 0.15 = 75. Adding 80 workers would take the total number of employees to 580, of which we want 20% (i.e. 116) to be doctors. The increase needed is: 116 – 75 = 41.

**Q1.50 – f: 1,000**
The original ratios are:
- gin to vodka: 2:20
- gin to orange juice: 2:100

We are therefore looking for the following new ratios:
- gin to vodka: double, i.e. 4:20 (which we can express as 1:5)
- gin to orange juice: half, i.e. 1:100

The new ratio is therefore 1:5:100. A cocktail containing 50 cm$^3$ of vodka would therefore contain 100 / 5 x 50 = 1,000 cm$^3$ of orange juice.

**Q1.51 – b: 2.5 litres**
The tomato sauce to hot sauce ratio is 7:5. Therefore, to make 1 litre of ketchup we need:

$$\frac{7}{12} \text{ litre tomato sauce} + \frac{5}{12} \text{ litre hot sauce}$$

To make 2 litres of hot sauce we need:

$$\frac{14}{12} \text{ litre tomato sauce} + \frac{10}{12} \text{ litre hot sauce}$$

This corresponds to 1.167 litres of tomato sauce and 0.833 litres of hot sauce. Since we can only buy ingredients in boxes of 500 ml, we will be required to purchase 1.5 litres of tomato sauce and 1 litre of hot sauce. This gives a total volume of 2.5 litres.


**Q1.52 – d: 85%**
Working directly with percentages can be confusing; an easy way round that is to work with a convenient number.

Consider a voting population of 600. We know that 1/6 of the votes, i.e. 100 votes, have been counted and that 1/4 (i.e. 25) were in favour and 3/4 (i.e. 75) were against.

We are looking for an overall 3:1 victory, i.e. 450 votes in favour versus 150 against. To achieve this we need a total of 450 – 25 = 425 votes to be in favour out of the 500 votes that remain to be counted. This is equivalent to 425 / 500 = 85% of the remaining votes.


**Q1.53 – a: 18 pints**
9 gallons is equivalent to 72 pints. This will require 3 / 12 x 72 = 18 pints of orange paint.


**Q1.54 – c: £39**
Making 8 pints of the paint mix will cost:
8 x (7 / 12 x £3 + 3 / 12 x £4 + 1 / 12 x £4 + 1 / 12 x £2)
= 8 / 12 x (21 + 12 + 4 + 2)

241

= 2 / 3 x £39 = £26.

The retail price will therefore be £26 x 1.5 = £39.

## Q1.55 – c: 75%
We know that 3 times more people voted for Jane than for Darren. If 900 people voted for Jane then only 300 voted for Darren. In total there were therefore 1,200 voters, out of a possible 1,600, i.e. a 75% turnout.

## Q1.56 – c: 50%
If we assume that the original cocktail has a volume of 100 ml, then it would contain 10 ml of orange juice. By taking out 1/4 (i.e. 25 ml) of the cocktail, we are also removing 2.5 ml of orange juice, leaving 7.5 ml in the glass.

We now need to add 25 ml of the new mix. We know that, once this has been done, we will end up with 20% of orange juice overall, i.e. 20 ml of orange juice out of the total 100 ml. We already have 7.5 ml of orange juice in the glass so we need an additional 12.5 ml of orange juice to make it up to 20 ml. This constitutes 50% of the 25 ml of the new mix that we are adding.

## Q1.57 – e: 15
If the youngest has blonde hair (1) and David is older than Peter (2) then David can't have blonde hair.

We know from (3) that David does not have red hair and therefore he must have brown hair.

Peter does not have blonde hair (3) and can't have brown hair since we determined this was David, therefore Peter has red hair.

We then deduce that Rachel has blonde hair: the only hair colour still unallocated.
From (1) we now know that, since she is blonde, Rachel is the youngest and is therefore 13. From (2) we deduce that Peter is 14 and David 15.

## Q1.58 – b: 7

If we call G and R Gary's and Ron's ages now, we can write the following equations: G – 1 = 2R and R + 4 = G.

Substituting G in the first equation gives R + 4 – 1 = 2R, i.e. R = 3. Therefore G = 7.

## Q1.59 – d: 1 kg, 3 kg, 9 kg

We must first understand how the weighing process works. If the spices are on the right-hand side of the scales, they can be weighed by placing weights on the left-hand side until equilibrium is reached. It is also possible to place one or more weight on top of the spices on the right-hand side, in which case the weight of the spices will be equal to the total weights on the left minus the weights on the right.

All three weights must add up to at least 13 kg otherwise he would not be able to weigh 13 kg. This excludes option a, which only adds up to 12.

Under option b (1, 2, 10), we can achieve the following weights:
- 1, with weight 1 on the left
- 2, with weight 2 on the left
- 3, with weights 1 and 2 on the left

Thereafter the only weights we can achieve are:
- 10 – 1 – 2 (i.e. 10 on the left and 1 + 2 on the spices) = 7
- 10 – 2 (i.e. 10 on the left and 2 on the spices) = 8
- 10 – 1 (i.e. 10 on the left and 1 on the spices) = 9
- 10 (on the left by itself)
- 10 + 1 = 11
- 10 + 2 = 12
- 10 + 1 + 2 = 13

Option b therefore leaves a gap between 3 and 7.

Option c (2 kg, 4 kg, 8 kg) only allows the trader to weigh even numbers of kilograms.

Option e (1 kg, 3 kg, 10 kg) allows the following:
- 1
- 3 – 1 = 2

243

- 3
- 1 + 3 = 4
- 10 – 1 – 3 = 6
- 10 – 3 = 7
- 10 + 1 – 3 = 8
- 10 – 1 = 9
- 10
- 10 + 1 = 11
- 10 + 1 – 3 = 12
- 10 + 3 = 13

It does not allow the trader to weigh 5 kg.

Option d, however, allows all weights between 1 and 13 to be achieved, as follows:

- 1
- 3 – 1 = 2
- 3
- 3 + 1 = 4
- 9 – 1 – 3 = 5
- 9 – 3 = 6
- 9 – 3 + 1 = 7
- 9 – 1 = 8
- 9
- 9 + 1 = 10
- 9 + 3 – 1 = 11
- 9 + 3 = 12
- 9 + 3 + 1 =13

This process looks long-winded but in reality you can calculate all of it in your head quickly, without the need to write anything down. You just need to be systematic. If you ran out of time and needed to guess, you could easily eliminate Option a and Option c and choose amongst the remaining three options.


**Q1.60 – e: 529**
The solution is slightly easier to work out if you draw a diagram to set out the nature of the problem. The key here is the fact that the field is always

square and so any cabbages added this year will need to fit around last year's square field to make it a new, bigger, square as follows:

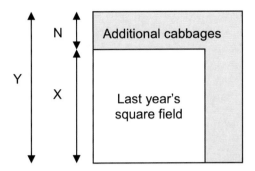

Let's call X the number of cabbages along one edge last year and let's call Y the number of cabbages along one edge of the new field this year. The number of cabbages in the field last year was $X^2$ and this year is $Y^2$. We therefore have the equation $Y^2 - X^2 = 47$.

Let's call N the additional number of cabbages that we need along one edge this year. We have $Y = X + N$.

Substituting Y in the first equation gives us:

$(X + N)^2 - X^2 = 47$

Therefore: $X^2 + 2XN + N^2 - X^2 = 47$, i.e. $2XN + N^2 = 47$ or $X = (47 - N^2)/2N$

This is an equation with 2 unknowns but there are other parameters we need to consider:

- X and N must both be integers since they represent a number of cabbages.
- X and N are both positive; therefore $N < 7$ (otherwise $N^2$ would exceed 47).

Taking $N = 1$ gives $2X = 46$, i.e. $X = 23$.
Taking $N = 2$ gives $X = 43/4$. Not an integer.
Taking $N = 3$ gives $X = 38/6$. Not an integer.
Taking $N = 4$ gives $X = 31/8$. Not an integer.
Taking $N = 5$ gives $X = 22/10$. Not an integer.

Taking N = 6 gives X = 11/12. Not an integer.

Therefore the number of cabbages planted last year is $23^2 = 529$.

**Q1.61 – c: 13/27**

We are looking at a population that consists of parents who have two children including one boy born on a Friday. We then need to identify which proportion of that group has the second child who is also a boy.

The easiest way to approach the question is to draw a diagram setting out the different possibilities:

| | | | First child | | | | | | | | | | | | | |
|---|---|---|---|---|---|---|---|---|---|---|---|---|---|---|---|---|
| | | | b | b | b | b | b | b | b | g | g | g | g | g | g | g |
| | | | M | T | W | T | F | S | S | M | T | W | T | F | S | S |
| Second child | b | M | bb | bb | bb | bb | bb | bb | bb | gb | gb | gb | gb | gb | gb | gb |
| | b | T | bb | bb | bb | bb | bb | bb | bb | gb | gb | gb | gb | gb | gb | gb |
| | b | W | bb | bb | bb | bb | bb | bb | bb | gb | gb | gb | gb | gb | gb | gb |
| | b | T | bb | bb | bb | bb | bb | bb | bb | gb | gb | gb | gb | gb | gb | gb |
| | b | F | bb | bb | bb | bb | bb | bb | bb | gb | gb | gb | gb | gb | gb | gb |
| | b | S | bb | bb | bb | bb | bb | bb | bb | gb | gb | gb | gb | gb | gb | gb |
| | b | S | bb | bb | bb | bb | bb | bb | bb | gb | gb | gb | gb | gb | gb | gb |
| | g | M | bg | bg | bg | bg | bg | bg | bg | gg | gg | gg | gg | gg | gg | gg |
| | g | T | bg | bg | bg | bg | bg | bg | bg | gg | gg | gg | gg | gg | gg | gg |
| | g | W | bg | bg | bg | bg | bg | bg | bg | gg | gg | gg | gg | gg | gg | gg |
| | g | T | bg | bg | bg | bg | bg | bg | bg | gg | gg | gg | gg | gg | gg | gg |
| | g | F | bg | bg | bg | bg | bg | bg | bg | gg | gg | gg | gg | gg | gg | gg |
| | g | S | bg | bg | bg | bg | bg | bg | bg | gg | gg | gg | gg | gg | gg | gg |
| | g | S | bg | bg | bg | bg | bg | bg | bg | gg | gg | gg | gg | gg | gg | gg |

There are 27 possible situations where a family with two children will have at least one boy born on a Friday (highlighted in grey). Out of those, 13 will have two boys. The probability is therefore 13/27.

**Q1.62 – e: 91–100**

We know from (6) that the number of flowers is divisible by 7.
We also know from (1) that the number of flowers is odd.

The only possibilities can therefore be: 7, 21, 35, 49, 63, 77 and 91. According to (4), dividing the number by 5 leaves a remainder of 1. Therefore the number must end with a 1 or a 6. This leaves us with 21 or 91 only.

Since, according to (2), the number is not divisible by 3, then only 91 is suitable, which is in the 91–100 range.

Check on (3): 91 / 4 = 22 with a remainder of 3. Okay.
Check on (5): 91 / 6 = 15 with a remainder of 1. Okay.

**Q1.63 – d: 59**
When you break a piece of chocolate into two pieces, you are merely increasing the total number of pieces by 1. For example, we start with one big piece, which then becomes 2 smaller pieces. When you break one of the two pieces in half, you are left with 2 pieces from the first half + the second half, so 3 pieces, etc. If we want to end up with 6 x 10 = 60 pieces we therefore need to break the chocolate tablet in 59 separate steps.

**Q1.64 – c: 6**
Because the number 8 touches boxes **b**, **c** and **d**, number 7 can only be placed in box **a**. That leaves only 3, 5, and 6 to be placed.

Number 3 cannot be placed in box **d** since it would touch the 4, or in box **c** since it would touch the 2 diagonally. Number 3 can therefore only be placed in box **b**.

Number 5 can only be placed in **c** since it cannot be next to number 4. The shaded box **d** must therefore contain number 6.

**Q1.65 – c: 3**
The middle 4 scores add up to 49.5 – 16.5 = 33. The value of the performance is 99; therefore the level of difficulty is 3.

**Q1.66 – e: 324**
The key to the question is in the fact that you want to <u>ensure</u> that 80 of the books are on the same subject. There are only two subjects with more than 80 books: physics and chemistry. To make sure that you are guaranteed to

have 80 books from the same topic, you must look at the worst case scenario:

- The most unlucky person in the world would inadvertently remove all the books that are not on physics or chemistry, i.e. 50 books on astronomy, 65 on biology and 50 on botany (total = 165). Therefore withdrawing 165 books would not in any way guarantee that you have taken out 80 books from either physics or chemistry.

- Once you have taken out all the 165 books that are not on either chemistry or physics, the second worst-case scenario would be if you took out 79 books on each of physics and chemistry (so another 158). If that were the case then you would just need to take out one extra book to make it to 80.

The number of books that you need to remove in order to guarantee that 80 will be on the same subject is therefore 165 + 158 + 1 = 324.

### Q1.67 – d: 800–899

All digits must be between 1 and 9. Both the main number and its reverse have 3 digits, which means that the main number cannot be over 900 otherwise, when added to its reverse number, it would come to a total greater than 1000.

We can therefore start by allocating the first position to the digit 8, meaning that the last position has to be for the digit 1 (if it was anything other than 1, we would go over 1000 when adding the two up). The number, therefore, looks like 8X1.

After that, it is pretty much a case of trial and error:
811 + 118 = 929
821 + 128 = 949
831 + 138 = 969
841 + 148 = 989
851 + 158 = 1009.

Therefore the largest number is 841, which is in the range 800–899.

**Q1.68 – a: 9**

In the tens column, the implication is that $\square$ + 2 = 2 or 12 (with 1 being potentially carried forward from the units column).

The only way this can be true is if $\square$ represents 0 or 9. By substituting in 0 as a square into the equation, we see that it does not satisfy the circle representation. However, if we assume that the square represents 9, then we can see that the circle then represents 1.

**Q1.69 – e: 9**

You can get to the result intuitively or by following this approach:

The equation can be written as $(10 + \square) - O = \bullet$.

We know that $\square = O - 1$, therefore $\bullet = 10 - 1 = 9$.

**Q1.70 – c: 20**

Let N be the number of bricks in the bottom row.

Since the row above has 1 brick less than the bottom row, it will contain N – 1 bricks, and the row above that will contain N – 2 bricks, etc.

We know that in total there are 105 bricks in this gold bullion stack, with each row having one brick less than the row below; thus we can write the equation as:

N + (N – 1) + (N – 2) + (N – 3) + (N – 4) + (N – 5) = 105.

Hence 6N – 15 = 105, i.e. N = 20.

**Q1.71 – a: £1,500**

Writing the question as an equation, we get: 6X + 4Y = 21000. Since X = 0.5Y we can substitute this into the original equation to solve for Y.

6(0.5Y) + 4Y = 21000.
Y = 21000 / 7 = 3000, thus X = 1500.

**Q1.72 – c: 5**
The answer is N where $0.75^N < 0.25$. The main problem here is that you do not have the luxury of a calculator and multiplying by 0.75 manually can take some time. The best approach is to use fractions, multiply iteratively by 3/4 and compare the top and bottom figures, stopping when the top figure is below one quarter of the bottom figure.

| Bounce | 1 | 2 | 3 | 4 | 5 |
|---|---|---|---|---|---|
| Top (x3) | 3 | 9 | 27 | 81 | 243 |
| Bottom (x4) | 4 | 16 | 64 | 256 | 1024 |

243 is lower than 1/4 of 1024 and therefore 5 is the correct answer.

**Q1.73 – e: 120 cm**
The T shape is made up of 9 squares. Therefore the area of each square is 324 / 9 = 36. This means that one side of each square measures 6 cm. The perimeter contains 20 sides and therefore measures 6 x 20 = 120 cm.

**Q1.74 – c: 400 cm$^2$**
The diameter of a circle is 50 / 5 = 10 cm. The base of the triangle spans 3 full circles and 2 half circles, i.e. a total of 4 diameters, i.e. 40 cm.

Similarly, the height of the triangle spans the equivalent of 2 diameters, i.e. 20 cm. The area of the triangle is therefore 40 x 20 / 2 = 400 cm$^2$.

**Q1.75 – e: 9**
The volume of the box can be calculated as L x W x H.
We know that the base is a square and therefore L = W.
We also know that the height is three times the width and therefore H = 3W.
This gives us the equation: W x W x 3W = 81.
Thus $W^3 = 27$ and W = 3. The height is therefore H = 3W = 9 cm.

**Q1.76 – d: 165**
The number of wards being remodelled will be 1/6 x 18 = 3. Following the remodelling, those 3 wards will have 10 / 2 = 5 cubicles each. The total number of cubicles will therefore be 15 x 10 + 3 x 5 = 165.

## Q1.77 – d: X / (73,100 – X)

The number of cancers occurring in the prostate is X.
The number of cancers occurring elsewhere is defined as Y but can also be taken as 73,100 – X. Therefore the answer is X / (73,100 – X).

## Q1.78 – c: 120%

Isobel's new mobile phone will cost her (with trade-in) 105 – 50 = £55. The cost of repairing the old mobile phone is £25. Therefore the additional cost expressed as a percentage of the repair cost is: (55 – 25) / 25 = 1.2, i.e. 120%.

## Q1.79 – e: £21,500

An individual earning £3,000 would receive 50% of £3,000 = £1,500.
An individual earning £5,000 would receive:
- £1,500 for the first tranche of salary
- 30% of (£5,000 – £3,000) = £600
- i.e. a total of £1,500 + £600 = £2,100

Since the doctor receives more than £2,100, he must be earning over £5,000. If we call S his salary, then the benefit payable on the salary above £5,000 can be written as follows:

20% (S – 5000) = 5400 – 2100, i.e. S = 3300 / 0.2 + 5000 = £21,500.

## Q1.80 – d: £2,800

This is a typical example of a question where calculating everything could take a long time and would likely lead to many calculation errors. In this example, the easiest approach is to compare how the figures have changed from one year to the next.

Looking at the 20% range, the bottom figure (£6,475) went up by £1000 and the top figure (£43,875) went down by £1,000 Therefore the amount of income falling under the 20% tax rate has decreased by £2,000, leading to a saving of 20% x £2,000 = £400.

Looking at the 40% range, the bottom figure (£43,875) has decreased by £1,000, and John's salary has increased by 10% of £70,000 = £7,000. Therefore the income falling under the 40% tax rate has increased by £8,000, leading to additional tax of £3,200.

The total additional tax paid by John is therefore £3,200 – £400 = £2,800.

**Q1.81 – c: 1/16**
After the first stop, only 1/2 of the children will remain.
After the second stop, 1/2 x 1/2 = 1/4 of the children will remain.
After the third stop, 1/2 x 1/4 = 1/8 of the children will remain.
After the fourth stop, 1/2 x 1/8 = 1/16 will remain.

**Q1.82 – a: £16.67**
If we call X the cost per passenger when split between 14 passengers, we can write the equation: 14X = 20(X – 5). Therefore 6X = 100 and X = 16.67.

**Q1.83 – c: 18**
The speed of the car is 5 metres per second. To express this in km/h we need to multiply this by 3600 (convert to hours) / 1000 (convert to km). This gives: 5 x 3.6 = 18.

**Q1.84 – b: White**
First let's have a look at option d (i.e. there will never be just one bean left in the pot):

- If both beans taken out are white, they are both discarded (meaning that we lose two beans from the pot), but we then put one bean from the pile into the pot. Therefore, overall, we lose one bean.

- If at least one of the beans is black, then one bean is taken out and one is put back into the pot. Therefore we also lose one bean.

Consequently, we are losing one bean at each turn and the pot will eventually be depleted. Therefore option d is incorrect.

Secondly, let's have a look at the depletion of the white beans. The only possible way in which white beans can be taken out is two by two. Indeed if two white beans are picked up together they are both discarded, whereas if a white bean is picked up with a black bean, the black bean is discarded but the white bean is put back into the pot. Since the number of white beans is 75, this means that there will always be an odd number of white beans in the pot.

Consequently, once we are down to just two beans left in the pot, there has to be one white bean and one black bean. When they both get picked up, the black bean is discarded and the white bean is put back in the pot, making it the last one.

## Q1.85 – a: £254
In order to make the maximum saving, the client will need to ensure that the items with the highest possible price tags are sold for £10. The item costing the most is £67, and will not qualify as it won't be the cheaper of two items. Therefore the best saving can be done by purchasing the second most expensive item with it, i.e. £60.

Using this approach, all you need to do is pair up the prices in decreasing order of price: £67 & £60, £58 & £56, £48 & £43, £41 & 39.

The lowest cost is therefore £67 + £58 + £48 + £41 + 4 x £10 = £254.

## Q1.86a – a: £148
In a week that is divisible by 7, everything will be distributed to the children and therefore nothing will go to charity. The week after, charity will receive 1, the week after that it will receive 2, then 3, then 4, then 5, then 6. At that point it will fall back down to zero again. Over a cycle of 7 weeks, charity will therefore receive 1 + 2 + 3 + 4 + 5 + 6 = £21.

Over 50 weeks, there are 7 cycles of 7 weeks + week 50 where £1 will be given to charity. Therefore the amount given to charity can be calculated as: 7 x 21 + 1 = £148.

## Q1.86b – e: £161
The children get the following each:
- Week 1 to 6: 0
- Week 7 to 13: £1 per week, i.e. £7
- Week 14 to 20: £2 per week, i.e. £14
- Week 21 to 27: £3 per week, i.e. £21
- Week 28 to 34: £4 per week, i.e. £28
- Week 35 to 41: £5 per week, i.e. £35
- Week 42 to 48: £6 per week, i.e. £42
- Weeks 49 and 50: £7 per week, i.e. £14

Total = £161

**Q1.87 – c: 20 minutes**
The boys can load the logs at a rate of 90 / 18 = 5 logs per minute, i.e. 1 log per boy per minute.

The men can load the logs at a rate of 120 / 30 = 4 logs per minute, i.e. 2 logs per man per minute.

Therefore 1 man and 3 boys will have a load rate of 2 + 3 = 5 logs/min. 100 logs will therefore take 20 minutes to load.

**Q1.88 – e: 67**
Hosting the party at home will bring a profit of 50 x £5 = £250 (there are no expenses to take into account).

In order to make more profit by using the nightclub, she needs to make a profit of at least £250 after recouping the additional cost of £250 to hire the venue. Ticket sales must therefore exceed £500.

500 / 7.5 = 66.66, i.e. she needs to sell 67 tickets.


**Q1.89 – b: 9:30 am**
From the moment the bus leaves the bus station to the time he arrives at the hospital, Phil has travelled 15 + 10 = 25 minutes. If he gets to the hospital at 8:50 then, working backwards, we can deduce that the bus left 25 minutes earlier, i.e. at 8:25. Since there are buses every 20 minutes, then the next bus must be at 8:45 and the following bus at 9:05.

Arriving at 9 am at the bus station means that he will catch the 9:05 bus. After a 25-minute journey he will arrive at the hospital at 9:30.


**Q1.90 – d: 20**
For the top die, the hidden face must contain a 6 since the opposite face is showing a 1. For the other two dice, we cannot see the numbers but we know that they add up to 7. Therefore the sum is 7 + 7 + 6 = 20.

**Q1.91 – c: C**
Since all statements are saying that the number of false statements is a different number and are therefore mutually exclusive, then only one statement can be true. Therefore three statements are false and C is the correct statement.

**Q1.92 – b: 4**
Whenever Wheel B does a revolution, Wheel A rotates by a quarter. Therefore there are 4 possible positions for the arrow on Wheel A. The 4 possible positions for Wheel A are 1/16th to the right of each vertical and horizontal.

**Q1.93 – a: 2 km**
Let's call P the normal pick-up rate (and therefore 2P the pick-up rate after 7 pm). Let's call K the rate per kilometre. We have:
- (1): $P + 5K = 7$
- (2): $2P + 5K = 9$

By doing (2) – (1), we can deduce that P = 2. Therefore K = 1.

At 11 pm, the pick-up rate will be 2 x £2 = £4. Therefore out of the £6 fare paid to go to the nightclub, only £2 will be in respect of the distance. At a rate of £1 per kilometre, this gives a distance of 2 km.

**Q1.94 – d: Tom by 50 votes**
We can summarise the information in equation form:

Tom = 2/5 X (where X is the total number of votes cast)
Roberta = 100 votes
Alice = 75 votes
Laura = 1/2 of Roberta's, i.e. 50 votes.

Therefore: X = 2/5 X + 100 + 75 + 50. Hence X = 2/5 X + 225.
This gives 3/5 X = 225 and X = 375.
Thus Tom received 150 votes, i.e. 50 more than the next candidate.

**Q1.95 – d: 9 minutes 6 seconds**
Let's call T the time at which the faster nurse (John) will catch up with the slower nurse (Jackie).

John takes 1 min 45 s, i.e. 105 s to do a round.

Jackie's performance is 130 s per round.

At point T, John will have done one more round than Jackie. Therefore, if we call N the number of rounds that Jackie will have done, we can write:

130N = 105(N + 1) i.e. N = 105 / 25 = 4.2.

This will be achieved in 4.2 x 130 = 546 seconds, i.e. 9.1 minutes. Therefore the time is 9 minutes 6 seconds.

**Q1.96 – a: 12 pm**
Since we know the Paris departure time and are being asked to calculate the arrival time back in Paris, there is no need to worry about time differences. We can simply add up the various travelling and waiting times:
6 + 2 + 5 + 4 + 10 = 27 hours, i.e. 24 hours + 3 hours. Therefore I will arrive at 9 am + 3 hours = 12 pm.

**Q1.97 – d: 50%**
The text says that BBC2's share was 20% in 2006, 18% in 2007, and 25% in 2008. Since ITV's share for 2008 was twice BBC2's share then the answer is 50%.

**Q1.98 – e: £17**
Let's call B1, B2 and B3 the three different prices.
We have:
  (1) B1 + B2 = 27
  (2) B1 + B3 = 32
  (3) B2 + B3 = 29.

If we do (1) + (2) – (3), we get 2B1 = 30. Therefore B1 = 15.
From (2) we then get B3 = 32 – 15 = £17.

**Q1.99 – b: 2 and 3**
Because the numbers are consecutive, if either of the students knew that their own number was 1, then they would automatically know that the other

256

one's number was 2. There would be no need for the exchange to take place. Therefore option a can be discounted.

If Student 1 knew about number 3, then he would not know what the other student had. The other student, who would hold number 2 or number 4 would not know either what the other one had. After the exchange Student 1 would still be none the wiser. Therefore Student 1 cannot be holding number 3. The same reasoning applies to numbers 4, 5, and 6.

The only possibility for Student 1 to know the missing number, once Student 2 has admitted he didn't know either, is if he holds number 2.

Indeed if he holds number 2, he will know that the other student must be holding number 1 or number 3. If the other student holds number 1 then he will say that he knows the missing number, but if he holds number 3 then he will say that he doesn't know.

The same logic applies to numbers 8 and 9, but they are not possible options.

## Q1.100 – b: 1:5,000
The actual length of the street is 9.091 x 11,000 i.e. 100,000 cm. On a map where its length is represented by a 20 cm street, the scale would be 20:100,000 = 1:5,000.

## Q1.101 – b: 1:4,000
The area of the town is 8 x 8 = 64 $km^2$ or 64,000,000 $m^2$.
The area of the map is 200 pages x 20 x 10 = 40,000 $cm^2$ or 4 $m^2$.
This gives a ratio of 4:64,000,000 = 1:16,000,000.

However this is the ratio for the area, which is squared and therefore the scale for simple distances will be the square root, i.e. 1:4,000.

Another way to calculate the same result is as follows:
The area occupied by the map is 20 x 10 x 200 = 40,000 $cm^2$. Therefore since the town is square when the map is reconstituted flat it measures 200 cm x 200 cm, i.e. 2 m x 2 m. The real-size town measures 8 km x 8 km, therefore the scale is 2:8,000 = 1:4,000.

**Q1.102 – a: 2**
36 can be divided by 1, 2, 3, 4, 6, 9, 12, 18 and 36.
The different options are therefore:

- 1, 1 and 36 (Total 38)
- 1, 2 and 18 (Total 21)
- 1, 3 and 12 (Total 16)
- 1, 4 and 9 (Total 14)
- 1, 6 and 6 (Total 13)
- 2, 2 and 9 (Total 13)
- 2, 3 and 6 (Total 11)
- 3, 3 and 4 (Total 10)

Since the postman is aware of Mary's house number, the only options where he might have a doubt would be the two which add up to 13. Since we know that the younger two are twins, we can exclude 1, 6, 6 and the answer is therefore 2, 2 and 9.


**Q1.103 – c: C**
Unless you have a good eye, you may need to go through each object and view to get to the answer. The objects and views can be matched as follows:

|   | A | B | C | D | E | F |
|---|---|---|---|---|---|---|
| P | 14 | 17 | 8 | 3 | 18 | 9 |
| F | 10 | 1 | Missing | 4 | 7 | 6 |
| R | 5 | 16 | 2 | 12 | 13 | 15 |

The missing item (no. 11) should look like this:


**Q1.104 – a: May and June**
Two months will start on the same day if the number of days between the 1st of each month is a multiple of 7. Consider the following table:

| Jan | Feb | Mar | Apr | May | Jun | Jul | Aug | Sep | Oct | Nov | Dec |
|---|---|---|---|---|---|---|---|---|---|---|---|
| 31 | 28/29 | 31 | 30 | 31 | 30 | 31 | 31 | 30 | 31 | 30 | 31 |

- We know that March and November are not part of the answer because they are given in the text of the question.

- In non-leap years, since February has 28 days, it will start on the same day as March.

- 91 is a multiple of 7, therefore any month which starts a sequence of 30-31-30 will start on the same day as the month that is three months later. Hence April and July start on the same day. And September and December start on the same day.

- There are also 91 days between 1 January and 1 April on leap years.

- Between 1 January and 1 October, there are 31 + 28 + 31 + 30 + 31 + 30 + 31 + 31 + 30 = 273 days (= 39 x 7). Therefore January and October start on the same day in non-leap years.

Therefore the two months that never start on the same day as other months are May and June.

**Q1.105 – b: 2**
Divide the coins into three groups: A, B and C. Weigh A against B. If the scales tilt then the counterfeit coin is in whichever group (A or B) is the lightest. If the scales remain level then the counterfeit coin is in group C. Either way you will know in which group of 3 coins the counterfeit coin is.

Weigh one of the three coins from the suspect group against any of the other two in that group. Using the same principle as above, you will have identified the counterfeit coin at the second weighing.

**Q1.106 – f: 1/3**
This question contains a trap because one would instinctively go for a 50% chance when this is not the case at all. The reason is that, out of the two children whose ages we are given, we do not know which one is actually a girl. Knowing that one of the children is a girl, the possibilities are as follows:

| Child 1 | Girl | Boy | Girl |
| Child 2 | Boy | Girl | Girl |

The probability that the woman has two girls is therefore 1/3.
Note that if we had been told which of the children was a girl in the first instance then the answer would have indeed been 1/2.

### Q1.107 – c: 3 only

In all such exercises, you need to use the following logic rule:
If A → B then (non-A) → (non-B).
The first statement tells us: (Amy went) → (Bernard went). From this we can deduce that (Bernard did not go) → (Amy did not go).

The second statement tells us that (Bernard went) → (Carol went). From this we can deduce that (Carol did not go) → (Bernard did not go).
Hence if Bernard did not go then the only thing we can conclude is that Amy did not go either, i.e. statement 3.

Note: The fact that Carol would go if Bernard went to the show does not mean that she wouldn't go on her own. This would be different if the statement said: "Carol would only go to the show if Bernard went too."

### Q1.108 – d: 2,3 and 4 only

From the three main statements we have the following relationships:

**Like bananas → Like avocados**, from which we can deduce:
**Don't like avocados → Don't like bananas**.

**Like apples → Like oranges**, from which we can deduce:
**Don't like oranges → Don't like apples**.

**Like oranges → Don't like avocados**, from which we can deduce:
**Like avocados → Don't like oranges**.

Using those six statements we can now solve the exercise:

*Statement 1: Those who like apples like avocados.*
We know that:
- Like apples → Like oranges.
- Like oranges → Don't like avocados.

So this statement is actually false.

*Statement 2: Those who like bananas don't like oranges.*
We know that:
- Like bananas → Like avocados.
- Like avocados → Don't like oranges.

Therefore we can conclude that Like bananas → Don't like oranges.
This statement is therefore true.

*Statement 3: Those who like avocados don't like apples.*
We know that:
- Like avocados → Don't like oranges.
- Don't like oranges → Don't like apples.

Therefore we can conclude that Like avocados → Don't like apples.
This statement is therefore true.

*Statement 4: Those who like apples don't like bananas.*
We know that:
- Like apples → Like oranges.
- Like oranges → Don't like avocados.
- Don't like avocados → Don't like bananas.

Therefore we can conclude that: Like apples → Don't like bananas.
This statement is therefore true.

*Statement 5: Those who like bananas like apples.*
We know that:
- Like bananas → Like avocados.
- Like avocados → Don't like oranges.
- Don't like oranges → Don't like apples.

This statement is therefore false.

**1.109 – b: Chest B**
Chest A is labelled "100 gold coins". Since this is incorrect, it either contains 100% silver or 50% gold + 50% silver. Therefore if you pick a coin from Chest A, that coin could be either silver or gold. If the coin is gold then you will know that Chest A contains 50 gold and 50 silver coins (since it cannot contain 100 gold coins) but, if that coin is silver, you will not know what Chest A contains.

The same reasoning applies to Chest C. Therefore you should pick the coin from Chest B. If the coin from Chest B is gold then you will know that Chest B contains 100 gold coins. And, similarly, if the coin is silver then you will know that Chest B contains 100 silver coins.

If you know that Chest B contains 100 gold coins then Chest C cannot contain 100 gold coins and nor can it contain 100 silver coins since we know its label is incorrect. Therefore Chest C will contain the 50/50 mix. The same reasoning applies if Chest B contains 100 silver coins instead of gold.

## Q1.110 – d: 4

The easiest way to solve this problem is to draw a table. We know:

| Guest | Person whose gift they took | | | | |
|---|---|---|---|---|---|
| | Jeremy | Anna | Mary | Robert | Carol |
| Jeremy | | | YES | | |
| Anna | | | | | |
| Mary | | | | | |
| Robert | | YES | | | |
| Carol | | | | | |

It is easier to organise the discussion around Carol as there are only two possibilities (whereas there are three for Anna and Mary).

If Carol took Jeremy's gift, then the table becomes as follows:

| Guest | Person whose gift they took | | | | |
|---|---|---|---|---|---|
| | Jeremy | Anna | Mary | Robert | Carol |
| Jeremy | | | YES | | |
| Anna | | | | | |
| Mary | | | | | |
| Robert | | YES | | | |
| Carol | YES | | | | |

This then leaves two possibilities: Anna took Robert's or Carol's gift.

If, instead, Carol took Robert's gift then we would have a similar table, except that Anna would have had a choice between Carol's and Jeremy's gift.

Therefore in total there are four distinct ways to distribute the remaining gifts.

## Q1.111 – b: 16,998

The maximum amount can only be given to the third child if the others receive as little as possible. As far as children 4, 5 and 6 are concerned, this can only happen if they receive £3,000, £3,001 and £3,002 respectively, since they must receive at least £3000 and they must each receive a different amount.

So their total will be £9,003, leaving 60,000 – 9,003 = £50,997 to distribute. Child 3 will receive as much as he/she can if what he/she receives is close to what the top two are receiving. If we divide 50,997 by 3, we obtain 16,999. Therefore, Child 1 will receive £17,000, Child 2 will receive £16,999 and Child 3 will receive 16,998.

### Q1.112 – e: 7:05
If the journey took 20 minutes, then the actual time was only 2h30 – 20 minutes = 2h10 (= 130 minutes) wrong compared to the reflection.

Since the time is read in reflection then John will have seen the symmetry of the real time in relation to the vertical axis 12 o'clock – 6 o'clock. Therefore we must consider half of the difference (65 minutes) and add it either to 6 o'clock or to 12 o'clock to give 7:05 or 1:05.

### Q1.113 – c: £10.50
50% of the large pile of apples is made of Harry's apples costing 1/4 of a pound and 50% of that pile is made of Ahmed's apples at 1/6 of a pound. The average price is therefore (1/4 + 1/6) / 2 = (3/12 + 2/12) / 2 = 5/24. However, Harry is selling the apples at a cost of £1 for five and therefore 20 pence each (= 1/5 of a pound). That means that each apple is sold at a loss of 5/24 – 1/5 = (5 x 5 – 1 x 24) / (24 x 5) = 1/120 pounds.

If the shortage overall is £3.50 then it means that there were 3.5 x 120 = 420 apples in the large pile. At a cost of 1/5 of a pound each, this means that Harry took a total of 420 x 1/5 = £84, and each greengrocer should receive £42 (half each).

However, if Harry had sold his 210 apples himself at a price of 50p for two apples, he would have made 0.50 x (210 / 2) = £52.50. Hence he is £10.50 short.

### Q1.114 – c: 41–50 nuggets
It is clear that if the order consists of a number of nuggets which is divisible by 3 (except for 3 itself) then that order can be fulfilled by using a combination of boxes of 6 and 9 nuggets. So, for example, an order of 33 nuggets can be fulfilled by 3 boxes of 9 + one box of 6. In fact, only orders that are divisible by 3 can be fulfilled with boxes of 6 or 9.

If the number ordered is not divisible by 3, then if one deducts 20 from the order number, that order might then be divisible by 3. For example, 53 is not divisible by 3, but 53 – 20 = 33. Therefore such an order could be fulfilled by a combination of all boxes.

If, however, once 20 has been deducted, the number is still not divisible by 3, then deducting a further 20 will make it divisible by 3. For example, 58 is not divisible by 3, and nor is 58 – 20 = 38. However, 38 – 20 = 18 is divisible by 3. So an order of 58 nuggets would be fulfilled as 2 x 20 + 3 x 6.

But this works only if there is scope to deduct two lots of 20 nuggets from the nuggets order. That means that all orders above (but excluding) 3 + 2 x 20 can be fulfilled because all you need to do is give out one or two boxes of 20 to get back to a multiple of 3. Therefore the highest order that cannot be fulfilled has 3 + 40 = 43 nuggets.

Check:
44 nuggets = 1 x 20 + 4 x 6
45 nuggets = 5 x 9
46 nuggets = 2 x 20 + 6
47 nuggets = 1 x 20 + 3 x 9
48 nuggets = 8 x 6
49 nuggets = 2 x 20 + 9
And so on. After that, just add a box of 6 to the above.

**Q1.115 – e: 901–999.**
Take C = number of candles. If there is one candle left over when they are arranged in groups of 3, 5, 7 or 9 then it means that C – 1 is divisible by 3, 5, 7 and 9.

So we are looking for a value N that satisfies C – 1 = 5 x 7 x 9 x N,
i.e. C = 315N + 1. (Note: no need to include the 3 since 9 is divisible by 3).

We also know that C is divisible by 11.
All we now need to do is try various values for N:

N = 1 → C = 316 – not divisible by 11
N = 2 → C = 631 – not divisible by 11
N = 3 → C = 946 (which is 11 x 86)

**Q1.116 – b: E and 3**
The statement is that a vowel always has an even digit behind it.

- If you turn E (which is a vowel) and there is an even digit behind then this will confirm the statement. If it is an odd digit then it will prove the statement wrong.

- If you turn 4 (which is an even number) then whatever the letter is, the card will always satisfy the statement. Indeed, if the letter is a vowel then it will reinforce the statement, but if it's a consonant then it won't matter. Just because we are told that there is an even number behind a vowel it doesn't mean that there can't be an even number behind a consonant. So turning 4 will be pointless.

- If you turn L (a consonant) then the same issue will arise. Whether the number behind L is odd or even does not matter as the statement does not place any conditions on the number that features at the back of consonants.

- Turning 3 will be useful. Indeed, if the letter at the back of 3 happens to be a vowel then it will prove the statement right. But if it is a consonant then it will prove the statement wrong.

**Q1.117 – d: 2/3**
With the two balls in the opaque bag, there are two possible configurations and for each configuration there are two possible ways of drawing a ball. Hence a total of four possible outcomes:

- Red ball added; original red ball drawn.
- Red ball added; newly added red ball drawn.
- Yellow ball added; original red ball drawn.
- Yellow ball added; newly added yellow ball drawn.

Once a red ball has been drawn out of the bag, then we are left with only three possible outcomes (the last one can be discounted now since it involves drawing a yellow ball). Out of those three, two of them have a red ball remaining and one of them has a yellow ball remaining. Hence the probability that the remaining ball is red is 2/3.

**Q1.118 – b: 22%**

If we call R the radius of a small circle, then the radius of the large circle is 3R.

The area of a small circle is: $\pi R^2$. The area of the large circle is: $\pi(3R)^2$. Therefore the ratio of all the small circles over the large circle is:

$[7 \times \pi R^2] / [\pi(3R)^2] = 7/9$.

Hence the area not included within a small circle is 2/9 = 22.2%.


**Q1.119 – b: 7:1**

There are eight loaves of bread in total. Each man will eat 8/3 = 2 + 2/3 loaves of bread.

This means one shepherd will have given 5 – (2+2/3) = 2 + 1/3 loaves to the hunter; and the other one will have given 3 – (2+2/3) = 1/3 of a loaf to the hunter. This represents a 7:1 ratio.


**Q1.120 – c: 4**

Amir will have asked 9 people how many hands they had shaken. No one will shake their own hand or their wife/husband's hand, therefore the maximum number of hands that anyone can shake is eight. That means that Amir obtained the answers: 0, 1, 2, 3, 4, 5, 6, 7 and 8.

The person who shook 8 hands, shook hands with all other persons (who therefore each shook at least 1 hand), except with his or her partner. Therefore, the partner of the person who shook 8 hands must be the person who shook 0 hands.

The person who shook 7 hands, shook hands with all other persons (who therefore each shook at least 2 hands), except with his or her partner and the person who shook 0 hands. Therefore, the partner of the person who shook 7 hands must be the person who shook 1 hand.

The person who shook 6 hands, shook hands with all other persons (who therefore each shook at least 3 hands), except with his or her partner and the persons who shook 1 and 0 hands. Therefore, the partner of the person who shook 6 hands must be the person who shook 2 hands.

The person who shook 5 hands, shook hands with all other persons (who therefore each shook at least 4 hands), except with his or her partner and the persons who shook 2, 1, and 0 hands. Therefore, the partner of the person who shook 5 hands must be the person who shook 3 hands.

The only person left is the one who shook 4 hands, which must be Amir's wife.

**Q1.121 – d: No shoe made of plastic can be red**
In logic, if A implies B then the relationship non-B implies non-A also applies. Here we have "Red Shoe" implies "Leather".

Therefore "Non-Leather" implies "Non-Red Shoe", i.e. if a shoe is not made of leather then it cannot be red, which is option d.

**Q1.122 – c: 1/2**
If the box labelled "US Dollars" contains Euros, then there are only two possible outcomes:

| Label | US Dollars | Euros | British Pounds |
|---|---|---|---|
| Content 1 | Euros | US Dollars | British Pounds |
| Content 2 | Euros | British Pounds | US Dollars |

Only one of these outcomes has one box labelled correctly. Therefore the probability is 1/2.

**Q1.123 – d: 4 cm**
Note that, for the purpose of calculating the volume of water that overflowed, the volume of Cylinder 1 is irrelevant. All that matters is the volume of the sphere, which is: $4/3 \times \pi \times 3^3 = 36\pi$.

The volume of cylinder B is: $\pi \times 3^2 \times H = 9 \times \pi \times H$.
H is at its minimum when $36\pi = 9 \times \pi \times H$. Hence H = 4 cm.

**Q1.124 – c: 45**
We know that 10 tourists do not speak Italian, 20 do not speak Mandarin and 25 do not speak English. To calculate the minimum number of people

who can speak all three languages, we must assume that those people who cannot speak one language are all different. So the minimum number of people who speak all three languages is 100 – 10 – 20 – 25 = 45.

### Q1.125 – a: 1
Only one digit in Line 3 is correct. Consider the digit "2", which is the most common on the board. If digit "2" belongs to the code, then digits 9, 7 and 3 cannot belong to the code. Therefore in Line 4, where we know there are three correct digits, then "6", "4" and "2" must belong to the code.

From Line 2, we know that if "6" and "4" belong to the code then they are in positions 1 and 3. So the code looks like this: 6 __ 4 __, where one of the blanks is the digit 2.

We also know from Line 2 that, if "6" and "4" belong to the code, then "5" and "8" cannot belong to the code. Since we have already identified that 3 cannot belong to the code either (see first paragraph) then, based on Line 1, 1 and 2 must belong to the code. And since the first place of the code is occupied by the digit "6" then, in Line 1, "1" is in the wrong place and "2" in the right place.

The correct code is therefore 6241 and "1" is the fourth digit.

### Q1.126 – d: 6
The digit in the centre is calculated as:
(top digit – left-hand digit) x right-hand digit. So, for example, the second triangle's calculation is (7 – 4) x 2 = 6.
Therefore the last triangle's inside digit is (7 – 5) x 3 = 6.

### Q1.127 – c: Charlie
The CEO is parked in the first space and therefore has a red car (1). So:
- It cannot be Erin since she drives a green car (6).
- It cannot be Davinder since he is parked in the last space (8).
- It cannot be Anna since she is parked next to Davinder (5) and therefore is in the penultimate space.
- It cannot be Ben since he is parked between two other cars (7).

Hence it must be Charlie.

**Q1.128 – a: 10**
To find the answer we need to work backwards from 100 down to 1. To ensure he opens his mouth as little as possible we need to maximise the number of times he lies.

We need to end up with 100 cm. We can achieve that by doing 50 x 2, i.e. finish with a lie. To get to 50, we can do 25 x 2, i.e. another lie. We cannot halve 25 so the only possibility is to add 1 (to simulate the fact he told the truth), hence we move up to 25 + 1 = 26.

26 / 2 = 13
13 + 1 = 14
14 / 2 = 7
7 + 1 = 8
8 / 2 = 4
4 / 2 = 2
2 / 2 = 1

Hence he has opened his mouth 10 times: Lie (1→2), Lie (2→4), Lie (4→8), Truth (8→7), Lie (7→14), Truth (14→13), Lie (13→26), Truth (26→25), Lie (25→50), Lie (50→100).

**Q1.129 – a: 31131122211311123113322112**
Each line describes the content of the line above.
So, if in the first line there is 'one 2' then we write 12.

In the second line we now have one 1 and one 2. So we write 11 and 12. We now have three 1s and one 2. So we write 31 and 12, etc.

Looking at the penultimate line:

| 111 | 3 | 1 | 22 | 11 | 3 | 1 | 2 | 111 | 3 | 222 | 11 | 2 |
|-----|---|---|----|----|----|----|----|-----|----|-----|----|----|
| 3x1 | 1x3 | 1x1 | 2x2 | 2x1 | 1x3 | 1x1 | 1x2 | 3x1 | 1x3 | 3x2 | 2x1 | 1x2 |

Hence the last line should be 31131122211311123113322112.

**Q1.130 – c: There are at least five colleagues in this arrangement**
We know that Sameer always shares a car with someone else when he goes to work in the morning (3). This cannot be Cheryl or Sapna since we

know they never share a car with anyone (1). It cannot be Clara either, since we know she only goes to work in the afternoon (2). Therefore it has to be with another colleague who is not named here.

Looking at the other options:

- a: Cheryl and Sapna possibly make only one journey each; we certainly cannot conclude they do more since they never share a car with anyone (2 trips). We are told that Sapna makes two trips (2 trips – see statement 4), which only leaves Sameer who possibly makes only one trip (1 trip). So all we can conclude is that there are at least five trips.

- b: We know that Clara only goes to work in the afternoon. There is no reason to suspect she makes more than one trip. And if she does, then we can't deduce that from the text.

- d: Nothing indicates Clara shares a car with Sameer since we know she goes to work in the afternoon and that he shares a car in the morning with someone else. So, if they shared a car, that would only be possible if Sameer went home at lunchtime, but nothing indicates this is the case.

- e: Sapna never shares a car so Option e has to be wrong.

**Q1.131 – e: Eddie**
Statement 2 tells us that Bertie, Davey and Charlie live in that order on the street.

Statement 1 indicates that Annie lives on Bertie's left-hand side. Hence Annie, Bertie, Davey and Charlie live in that order on the street.

Statement 3 says that Eddie lives as far away from Charlie as he can and so Eddie, Annie, Bertie, Davey and Charlie live in that order.

Hence Eddie lives at number 10.

**Q1.132 – d: 1, 2 and 3 only**
If all Greeks speak Italian and all Italian speakers like pasta then we can deduce that all Greeks like pasta.

If all Greeks speak Italian then it follows that, if someone cannot speak Italian, they cannot be Greek. Hence Statement 3 is true.

If those who speak Italian like pasta, then it follows that, if someone does not like pasta, they can't be an Italian speaker. So Statement 1 is true.

If all Greeks like pasta (which we deduced earlier), then it follows that, if someone does not like pasta, they cannot be Greek. So Statement 2 is true.

However, the fact that all Greeks speak Italian does not imply that all Italians speak Greek. Hence Statement 4 cannot be proven.


**Q1.133 – c: 7**
This is probably best solved using Venn diagrams.

The first three statements allow us to write the following:

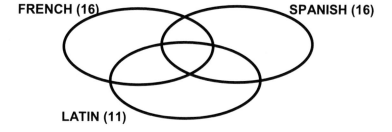

FRENCH (16)       SPANISH (16)

LATIN (11)

We know that 5 students want only Latin and 8 students want only Spanish. Therefore we can write:

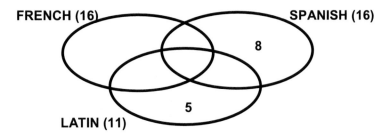

We are also told that 5 students want to take both French and Latin and that, out of those, 3 also want to take Spanish. So we can write:

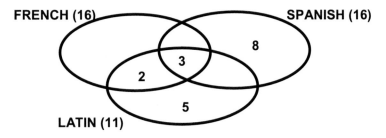

Therefore:
- The number of people taking Spanish and Latin only is 11–3–2–5 = 1.
- The number of people taking Spanish and French only is 16–3–8–1= 4.
- The number of people taking French only is 16–3–2–4 = 7.

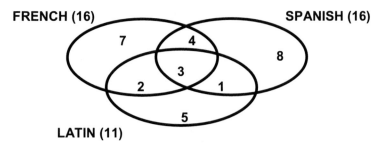

## Q1.134 – e: 5

At the start, the only values known are E=2, K=4, N=6 and X=20.

The only value we can calculate straight away is I = E+N = 8, but that doesn't lead anywhere for the moment.

What we do know, however, is that H = F / N, which means that F is divisible by 6. The only possibilities are:
- F cannot equal 6 as this value is already taken by N.
- F = 12 would mean that H = 2 but that is already taken by E.
- F = 18 would mean that H = 3. That is a possible value.
- F = 24 would mean that H = 4, which is already taken by K.

Since F cannot exceed 26, then it means that F = 18 and H = 3. We can then deduce that:

- T = F – N = 18 – 6 = 12
- J = K + T = 4 + 12 = 16
- G = I + J = 8 + 16 = 24
- L = H – E = 3 – 2 = 1
- D = T – L = 12 – 1 = 11

We also know that W<N. And since N = 6 and all values below 6 have already been allocated to letters except 5, then W = 5.

## Q1.135 – c: 488

If you remove the outermost layer of a 10x10x10 cube then you are left with an 8x8x8 cube, which contains 8x8x8 = 512 mini-cubes. This means 1000 – 512 = 488 mini-cubes have been removed.

## Q1.136 – d: B and F

## Q1.137 – c: B, D and E

## Q1.138 – c: 1,000–1,499

If the number is divisible by 15 then it must be divisible by 5. Since only 1s and 0s are allowed then it must end with a 0.

Being divisible by 15 also means it must be divisible by 3 and, therefore, that the sum of its digits must be divisible by 3. Hence there must be three 1s.

Bearing in mind that the number cannot start with a 0, the smallest number that satisfies all those conditions is 1110, which is in the 1,000–1,499 range.

### Q1.139 – d:13
Each brother is included in three of the four totals we are given. Therefore if we add those totals up and divide the result by 3, we will get the sum of all four ages: (30 + 32 + 32 + 35) / 3 = 129 / 3 = 43.
The smallest total (30) is the sum of the ages of the three youngest brothers. Therefore the age of the oldest brother is 43 – 30 = 13.

### Q1.140 – a: Alcina
The first task is to identify which combinations of crayons the friends have. We know that one has Yellow + Blue and another one has Blue + Green. Since there are two crayons of each colour and we have already allocated the two blue crayons, the two remaining combinations are made up of 1 x Yellow, 1 x Green and 2 x Red. The only possible allocation is Red + Yellow and Red + Green.

We can then draw a table using the information we know (0 means no):

|       | Alcina | Bea | Catrina | Dimple |
|-------|--------|-----|---------|--------|
| Y + B | 0      | 0   | 0       | YES    |
| B + G | 0      | YES | 0       | 0      |
| Y + R | 0      | 0   | YES     | 0      |
| G + R |        | 0   | 0       | 0      |

From that table we can then see that the person who owns a green and a red crayon is Alcina.

**Q1.141 – d: 25 metres**
Amelie's journey was as follows:

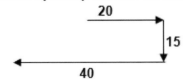

Therefore the distance D between her starting and end points can be represented as follows:

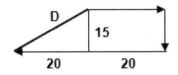

And so: $D^2 = 20^2 + 15^2 = 400 + 225 = 625$. Hence D = 25 metres.


**Q1.142 – d: About 40%.**
In total there are $(28 \times 27) / 2 = 378$ possible pairings of dominoes.
The 7 doubles (i.e. those who have twice the same number) can be matched to 6 other dominoes, i.e. $7 \times 6 = 42$ matches in total.

If we now ignore the doubles, the remaining 21 dominoes can each be matched to 10 other dominoes. For example, the domino [6-1] can be matched to [0-6], [2-6], [3-6], [4-6] and [5-6] as well as [1-0], [1-2], [1-3], [1-4] and [1-5]. Hence a total of $21 \times 10 / 2 = 105$ matches.

So the probability of two dominoes matching is $(105 + 42) / 378 = 38.9\%$ i.e. about 40%.


**Q1.143 – d: 116**
To start with, she can cut 4 tartlet bases per sheet, making it $20 \times 4 = 80$.

She can then take 18 of the 20 leftover sheets to make 6 new sheets (which means that, for the moment, there are 2 leftover sheets which remain unused). Out of those 6 sheets, she can cut 24 tartlet bases.

She can then take the 6 leftover sheets to make 2 new sheets, out of which she can cut 8 tartlet bases.

She can then take the 2 leftover sheets she has just created, and add to them one of the 2 leftover sheets she set aside at the beginning, to make a total of 3 leftover sheets, out of which she can create one new sheet. From that new sheet she can cut 4 more tartlet bases.

So, in total, she can cut 80 + 24 + 8 + 4 = 116 tartlet bases.

**Q1.144 – d: 3.5**
The possible scores are:

- 0 (if the left-hand die is odd)
- 3 (2+1)
- 5 (2+3 or 4+1)
- 7 (2+5, 4+3, 6+1)
- 9 (4+5, 6+3)
- 11 (6+5)

The probability of obtaining a score of 0 is ½ since it will happen every time the left-hand die has an odd number regardless of the number showing on the right-hand die. The average score is therefore:

0.5 x 0 + 0.5 x (1x3 + 2x5 + 3x7 + 2x9 + 1x11) / 9 = 3.5.

**Q1.145 – c: 522**
We have 230 = 15 x 15 + 5
And 440 = 29 x 15 + 5. So we could cover most of the surface with 29 x 15 = 435 tiles measuring 15 x 15.

We would then be left with a strip of 5 cm around two sides of the kitchen, which could be covered by: 230 / 5 + 440 / 5 − 1 (double counting corner tile), i.e. 133 tiles. This would give a total of 435 + 133 = 568 tiles.

However, covering an area with 5x5 tiles means using a lot of small tiles, which end up making a large number (it takes four 5x5 tiles to cover the same area as one 10x10 tile). It may be more beneficial leaving a larger gap of 20 cm around the room, which could be covered by 10x10 cm tiles.

This would give the following calculation:
230 = 14 x 15 + 20
440 = 28 x 15 + 20

This would require 14 x 28 = 392 of the 15x15 tiles.
We would then need to tile the 20 cm strip around two of the sides with 10x10 tiles. This would be done using:

2 x 230/10 + 2 x 440/10 – 4 (not double counting the corner 20x20 area) = 130 tiles. Hence a total of 392 + 130 = 522, i.e. 46 tiles less.


**Q1.146 – c: 35**
A fence will be made up of a number of post + chain combinations, plus a final post at the end of it.

**(Post + Chain) in series**          **+ Final Post**

Each post + chain combination measures 6 inches (i.e. 0.5 ft) + 5 ft, i.e. a total of 5.5 ft. The final post accounts for just 0.5 ft.

So the length of a fence will be 5.5 x N + 0.5, where N is the number of post + chain combinations. Hence we are looking for a number that, once we have deducted 0.5, is NOT divisible by 5.5. Looking at the options available:

Option a: 17 – 0.5 = 16.5, which is 3 x 5.5.
Option b: 28 – 0.5 = 27.5, which is 5 x 5.5.
Option c: 35 – 0.5 = 34.5, which is not divisible by 5.5. You can stop here.

To check the others:
Option d: 39 – 0.5 = 38.5, which is 7 x 5.5.
Option e: 50 – 0.5 = 49.5, which is 9 x 5.5.


**Q1.147 – e: 112**
The distance travelled by the perimeter of each wheel must be the same. If we call N the number of revolutions done by the back wheels, we can write the distance as follows:

For the front wheels: (N+12) x 4 cm
For the back wheels: N x 7 cm.

We have 7N = 4(N+12).
Therefore 3N = 48 and N =16.

The distance travelled is therefore 16 x 7 = 112 cm.


### Q1.148 – c: 40
The total number of passengers is 32.5 x 6 = 195. The tube train stops at six stations, with each stop resulting in 3 fewer passengers boarding it than the station preceding it.

If we call X the number of people getting on at the first station, the total number of people getting on to the train can be written as follows:
X + (X–3) + (X–6) + (X–9) + (X–12) + (X–15) = 195.
This gives 6X – 45 = 195 and therefore X = 40.


### Q1.149 – d: 34 km/h
The distance between A and B is 41 x 4 = 164 km.
The distance travelled during the first 2 hours is 48 x 2 = 96 km.
Therefore the distance covered in the final 2 hours is 164 – 96 = 68, making it an average speed of 34 km/h.


### Q1.150 – d: 15
In the 0s, 10s, 20s, and 40s there will be only one number in each that contains the digit 3 (3, 13, 23 and 43). In the 30s, all ten numbers will contain the digit 3 but 33 will contain two, so there will be eleven occurrences. The total number of occurrences is therefore 4 + 11 = 15.

**Aptitude and Skills**
**Data Analysis/Inference – Answers**

**Q1.151a – c: 700**
The number of patients who have waited between 10 and 30 days can be calculated as:

• The number of people who waited less than 30 days: 1000
minus
• The number of people who waited less than 10 days: 300

which gives 700.

**Q1.151b – a: 400**
Using a similar approach to 1.151a, the answer is 1400 – 1000 = 400.

**Q1.152 – b: £36**
First we need to work out how much electricity both types of bulbs use during 10,000 hours:
    • Energy-saving light bulbs use 20 watts. Over 10,000 hours, this results in 200,000 watt hours (i.e. 200 kilowatt hours). Since each kilowatt hour costs 10p, the electricity used by energy-saving light bulbs costs 200 x 10p = £20.
    • Standard light bulbs – at 60 watts for 10,000 hours, we get 600,000 watt hours (i.e. 600 kilowatt hours) at a cost of £60.

Factoring in the base cost of the bulbs themselves: an energy-saving light bulb lasts the full 10,000 hours and costs £5. Standard light bulbs require replacing every 2,000 hours; we therefore need 5 bulbs for 10,000 hours of use at a cost of £1 for 5 bulbs.

The resulting costs are therefore £61 for standard bulbs and £25 for energy-saving bulbs, giving a saving of £36.

279

**Q1.153a – Chart E**
The increase in infection is calculated as the difference between the 2010 and 2009 figures.

| Wards | 2009 | 2010 | In-crease |
|-------|------|------|-----------|
| Coles | 58 | 62 | 4 |
| Jones | 38 | 42 | 4 |
| Patel | 35 | 40 | 5 |
| Smith | 34 | 40 | 6 |
| Taylor | 14 | 28 | 14 |
| **Total** | **179** | **212** | **33** |

We are therefore looking for a chart where Taylor's sector is just under half of the total area and where the sector occupied by Smith is 50% larger than that occupied by Coles and Jones (who must occupy the same area size).

Chart A: Taylor is too small.
Chart B: Taylor is too small. (This is the graph for the year 2010.)
Chart C: Taylor, Coles and Jones are of equal size.
Chart D: Jones is larger than Coles and Patel.
Chart F: Taylor is over 50% of the graph.

**Q1.153b – d: It will be divided by 13/11**
If the 2010 number for Coles becomes 68 then the increase will be 10 instead of 4. All the other increases will remain at the same level but the total will rise from 33 to 39. The portion allocated to Taylor will therefore reduce from 14/33 to 14/39. The ratio is therefore (14/39) / (14/33) = 33/39 = 11/13. Multiplying by 11/13 is the same as dividing by 13/11.

**Q1.154a – c: 1702 kcal**
BMR (kcal) = 655 + (9.6 x weight in kilos) + (1.8 x height in cm) – (4.7 x age in years). This gives: BMR = 655 + (9.6x90) + (1.8x180) – (4.7x30). Therefore BMR = 1702. Instead of calculating everything, you may want to use an approximation such as: 655 + 10x90 + 2x180 – 5x30 = 1765. The closest answer would be 1702.

**Q1.154b – c: 2359 kcal**
Calorie requirement (CR) = BMR x 1.2 (bed rest) x 1.3 (minor surgery)
CR = [655 + (9.6 x 80) + (1.8 x 180) – (4.7 x 50)] x 1.2 x 1.3
CR = 1512 x 1.2 x 1.3 = 2359


**Q1.154c – b: ProtoShake XL**
First we need to work out the calorie requirement then the protein requirements. We can then compare the appropriate ratio.

Calorie requirement (CR) = BMR x 1.2 (bed rest) x 1.5 (major surgery)
CR = [655 + (9.6 x 100) + (1.8 x 200) – (4.7 x 50)] x 1.2 x 1.5 = 3132

Protein requirements (PR) = 1.5 x 100 = 150 g/day
Looking at the Step 4 table, 100 ml of ProtoShake XL would provide 3100 kcal and 150 g of protein, which is close to the requirements we calculated.


**Q1.154d – c: 5 ml**
First we need to work out the number of calories in 50 ml ProtoShake (PS) and 50 ml FortSure Xtra (FSX).

50 ml ProtoShake gives 50 x 1 = 50 kcal
50 ml FortSure Xtra gives 50 x 21 = 1050 kcal
Therefore PS + FSX = 1100 kcal

To reach a total of 1250 kcal, we therefore require 150 kcal from ProtoShake XL. ProtoShake XL's calorific value is 31 kcal/ml, thus we require approximately 5 ml of ProtoShake XL to make up the calorific difference.


**Q1.155a – b: 28%**
The Kaplan-Meier curve estimates event function from timed data.

A plot of the curve may show horizontal steps of declining magnitude with "clicks", which represent an individual event, i.e. in this case each "click" and subsequent decline in plot represents a patient who has experienced post-operative complications. BMI represents body mass index and a figure >30 represents obesity. The graph clearly shows that obese patients experience more post-operative complications than non-obese patients.

We can see that on the line for BMI >30, on day 50, around 72% of obese patients are without post-operative surgical complications; conversely it means that 28% of patients have experienced complications before then.


**Q1.155b – a: 1000**
The number of patients who did not experience any complications was 840. We know that a quarter of patients were obese and therefore this can be split into 210 obese patients and 630 non-obese patients.

The graph tells us that approximately 70% of obese patients and 90% of non-obese patients did not experience any complication. Therefore the total number of patients is 210/0.7 + 630/0.9 = 300 + 700 = 1000.


**Q1.156a – b: 67:33**
The number of people living in urban areas in all three countries is:
61% x 200 + 86% x 42 + 80% x 30 = 122 + 36.12 + 24 = 182.12 out of a total population of 272, which represents 67%. The ratio is therefore 67:33.


**Q1.156b – b: 1:2**
The percentage of the population that does not have internet is:

Urban areas: 25% x 61 = 15.25
Rural areas: 80% x 39 = 31.2.

The ratio is therefore 15.25 : 31.2 i.e. approximately 1:2.


**Q1.156c – b: 6.7%**
The rural population across all three countries is:
39% x 200 + 14% x 42 + 20% x 30 = 78 + 5.88 + 6 = 89.88.
Peru therefore represents 6 / 89.88 (think of it as 6 / 90) = 6.7%.


**Q1.157a – e: 30%**
The number of men with a screening test which shows a positive result is equal to the sum of the false positives (16) and the true positives (14), i.e. 30.

**Q1.157b – c: 54**

We know that 2.5% of FOBt will result in a positive test, of which 10% will actually have bowel abnormalities confirmed. This corresponds to a correct detection rate of 0.25% of bowel abnormalities across the population.

In addition, 0.3% of those with a normal FOBt (i.e. the remaining 97.5%) will have the disease but will have tested negative. This is equivalent to 0.3% x 97.5% = 0.29%.

The percentage of the population with actual bowel abnormalities would therefore be (0.25% + 0.29%) x 10,000 = 54.

**Q1.157c – c: 36**

We first need to work out the number of people with false positive results with FOBt. In a 10,000 sample size we expect a 2.5% total positive rate, i.e. 250 people. The false positive rate is 90% for FOBt, thus out of 250 people we expect 225 of them to be false positive.

We know that the rate of false positives in a CT scan is 16%; since the two tests are independent, the number of false positives amongst the 225 who were false positives after the FOBt is 0.16 x 225 = 36.

**Q1.158 – f: 1,950 kg**

The table gives the percentage of waste recycled in each year. Therefore if we know how much of each category was recycled in 2010, we can work out the total amount of waste in that year.

The amount recycled for each category in 2010 was:
- Cardboard: 200 x 1.2 = 240
- Paper: 200 x 1.2 = 240
- Plastic: 50 x 1.1 = 55
- Glass: 100 x 1.1 = 110

The total amount of waste is therefore:
240/0.24 + 240/0.96 + 55/0.11 + 110/0.55
= 1000 + 250 + 500 + 200
= 1950 kg.

### Q1.159 – Machine P
One of the fastest ways to answer the question is to spot that the white diamond is the 9th dot along the x-axis when counting from the right. All you therefore need to do is to eliminate the 8 machines with the highest quality score. The next highest will then be Machine P.


### Q1.160a – d: 28.8 million
Gasoline and kerosene represent 34 + 14 = 48% of the total production. i.e. 0.48 x 60 = 28.8 million barrels.


### Q1.160b – c: £21
The number of lubricating oil barrels produced was: 5% x 60 = 3 million. Therefore the cost per barrel was 63 / 3 = 21.


### Q1.161a – c: 1,800
The percentage in the "Other" category in Year 3 is 27%. 486 / 0.27 = 1,800.


### Q1.161b – e: Cannot be determined
The table only gives the percentage of the total staff working in each role for each year. Without knowing the total number of employees in each year, we are unable to calculate the number of employees working in Marketing and therefore the increase from one year to the next.


### Q1.161c – a: I only
We can see that 9% of employees worked in Finance in Year 1. That number becomes 3% in Year 5. If we assume that the total number of employees in Year 1 was 100, then 9 of them would have been working in Finance. We know from the text of the question that those 9 people are still there in Year 5. So, for them to represent only 3% of the total number of staff, there would need to be at least 300 people employed in total in Year 5.

It is possible that some people may have joined the Finance team after Year 1; but if that were the case, this would push the total number of employees over 3 times the Year 1 level. So, in total, at the very least there were 3 times more people in Year 5 than in Year 1.

Statement II: Within each category the percentages will vary depending on the relative movement of staff. So for example, if a percentage increases, it could be because more people were recruited into that category, or because another category lost people. All we know (from the fact that all Year 1 employees are still employed in Year 5 in the same function) is that the number of employees in any year is greater than the number of employees in Year 1, but we cannot conclude whether there is an increase every single year. It could be, for example, that there was a huge increase in Year 2 and then the numbers have been falling ever since.

Statement III: The fact that the percentage decreases only indicates that the number of people in Finance has not increased by as much as in the other categories put together. It does not help to conclude anything with regard to lack of recruitment in Finance.

**Q1.162a – a: $16.8 million**
168 x 20% x (1 – 0.5) = 33.6 x 0.5 = $16.8 million

**Q1.162b – d: +0%**
If the total investment is the same then we can apply the $ increase/decrease to the percentage of the split for each country. The new percentages for 2016 should also add up to 100% of $168 million.

| Location | Split of 2015 investment between countries | Increase/decrease in $ investment between 2015 and 2016 | New proportion |
|---|---|---|---|
| USA | 50% | +20% | 60% |
| Japan | 20% | -50% | 10% |
| S.E Asia | 10% | +20% | 12% |
| UK | 10% | ??? | ?? |
| Germany | 4% | -50% | 2% |
| Latin America | 4% | -25% | 3% |
| Middle East | 2% | +50% | 3% |
| | 100% | | |

The sum of the known percentages is 60 + 10 + 12 + 2 + 3 + 3 = 90; therefore the UK's percentage for 2016 is 100 – 90 = 10. Hence the investment has neither increased nor decreased between 2015 and 2016.

**Q1.163a – a: Ireland**
This is best worked out using approximations if you don't want to waste too much time on it. Here we are simply dividing the approximate number of births in 1995 (in thousands) by the approximate population in 1995 (in millions) to obtain the birth rate.

Ireland: 80 / 4 = 20
France: 1000 / 60 = 17
Greece: 160 / 16 = 10
Spain: 520 / 45 = 12
Germany: 1200 / 80 = 15

This is enough to get a picture and, in this case, establish that Ireland is the country with the highest birth rate. If the top two countries had been close, we would have done a more accurate calculation for those thereafter.

**Q1.163b – e: I and II**
The calculation requires knowledge of the number of children born in 1995, which we are given.

It also requires knowledge of the number of those children who died within 1 week. In his calculation, the analyst uses the number of children who died within 1 week in 1995. However, this causes issues because:

- Some children born in the last week of 1994 who died within 1 week of birth in the first few days of 1995 will be included in that figure. For example, a child born on 30 December 1994 who died after 4 days will be registered as a 1995 death. So, such children should be excluded from the figure that appears in the column showing the number of deaths in 1995. This is given by (I).

- Similarly, some children born in the last week of 1995 might have died in the first week of January 1996. Those need to be added to the death rate for children born in 1995 figure. This is given by (II).

Hence both I and II are required.

**Q1.164a – c: 18,925 employees**
In 2015, there were 40% x 50,000 = 20,000 employees.

The number of employees who transferred from the USA to another country was 1000 + 200 + 300 + 375 = 1875.

The number of employees who transferred from another country to the USA was 50 + 100 + 100 + 50 = 300.

In addition, the USA recruited 500 people externally. The number of USA employees in 2016 was therefore: 20000 – 1875 + 300 + 500 = 18,925.


**Q1.164b – d: 515**
Transfers into Spain = 10 + 50 + 50 + 375 = 485.
Transfers out of Spain = 200 + 200 + 150 + 50 = 600.

The number of employees in 2015 was 8% x 50,000 = 4000. An increase of 10% would therefore require 400 additional employees. The internal transfers led to a loss of 600 – 485 = 115 employees. Spain therefore needs 400 + 115 = 515 employees to end up with an increase of 10% to the final number.


**Q1.164c – Chart A**
The data can be summarised as follows:

| France | | 200 | 180 | 1000 | 200 | **1580** |
|---|---|---|---|---|---|---|
| Germany | 150 | | 250 | 200 | 200 | **800** |
| UK | 200 | 100 | | 300 | 150 | **750** |
| USA | 50 | 100 | 100 | | 50 | **300** |
| Spain | 10 | 50 | 50 | 375 | | **485** |
| TOTAL | | | | | | **3915** |

The pie chart we need therefore has a large area, two medium areas and two smaller areas. This is best represented by Chart A. Looking at the other options:

- Chart B shows that three countries have similar numbers, which is not true.
- Chart C shows that one country has nearly half the numbers, which is not true.

287

- Chart D shows that the countries with the two highest numbers have roughly the same number of people, which is not true.
- Chart E shows that one country has over half the total number, which is not true.

### Q1.165a – c: Rex < Maxi < Shoto < Bellar

For Rex: 90% x (10 x 25 + 4 x 7.50 + 5 x 3) = 90% x 295 = £265.50.

For Maxi:
- 1000 ibuprofen tablets: 10 x 24 = £240
- Insulin syringes: 20 given for free + 4 x 5 = £20
- Paracetamol: 4 x 8 = 32
- Total: 240 + 20 + 32 = £292.

Similarly:

For Shoto: 10 x 30 + 4 x 12 + 5 x 2 = £358.

For Bellar: 10 x 36.50 + 0.75 x 4 x 7 + 5 x 3 = 365 + 21 + 15 = £401.

So they rank as follows: Rex < Maxi < Shoto < Bellar

### Q1.165b – a: 11.1%

Buying 1,000 ibuprofen tablets and 1,000 paracetamol tablets from Shoto via the bulk package deal costs £120 x 4 = £480.

Buying them via their usual pricing structure would cost:
10 x 30 + 20 x 12 = £540. The discount is therefore 540 – 480 = £60.

60 is 1/9th of 540, thus the discount is 11.1%.

### Q1.166a – e: CB truck

Carrying 12 small boxes will require 12 / 4 = 3 large boxes. The truck large enough to carry 3 large boxes with a minimum amount of empty space is the CB truck (capacity of 5 large boxes).

**Q1.166b – b: 2**

76 small boxes would make up 76 / 4 = 19 large boxes. This can be achieved with one Toby truck (capacity: 15) and two Eastwind trucks (capacity: 2 each, total: 4). This will therefore require three trucks but only two types.

Note that it would actually be possible to use two Lensa trucks only (and thus only one type of truck), but this would have a total capacity of 20, which would leave space empty.

**Q1.166c – b: £285**

Note that, for this question, the customer is looking for the cheapest deal. There is no mention of the fact that space has to be optimised.

Looking at the table we can deduce a number of things:

- We can eliminate the use of the Toby truck because it would cost £150 to carry 15 boxes, whereas it would be cheaper to use a combination of Lensa truck (£95) + CB truck (£50), which adds up to £145.

- We can also eliminate the Tucker truck because it costs £400 to carry 20 boxes whereas two Lensa trucks would only cost 2 x 95 = £190 to carry the same number of boxes.

- Since the CB and the Eastwind trucks have the same cost but the CB truck has a higher capacity then we can also eliminate the use of the Eastwind truck as it would make no difference to the final cost.

We are now left with three types of truck:

| Truck type | No. of large boxes | Truck hire cost |
|---|---|---|
| Lensa truck | 10 | £95 |
| Tug truck | 1 | £25 |
| CB truck | 5 | £50 |

- The Tug truck costs half as much as the CB truck but carries only 1 box instead of 5. So as soon as we need more than one Tug truck, then we might as well use the CB truck instead as it has a higher capacity for the same or a cheaper price. If we used the Tug truck to carry 1 box then we would still need to find transport for 27 boxes using the other trucks. But since the other trucks offer spare capacity there is no need to use the Tug truck.

This leaves us with the Lensa and the CB trucks. It is cheaper to use one Lensa truck than it is to use two CB trucks. So we would only want to use the CB truck if only one was needed. In this case, three Lensa trucks would be sufficient to cope with the demand without the need to use a CB truck. If CB trucks were used, we would need to use more than one and it would not be cheaper.

Therefore the cheapest option is to use three Lensa trucks at a cost of: 3 x £95 = £285.

**Q1.167a – a: 50 kWh**
For this question, there are shortcuts you can take:
   (i)      Add up the relevant percentages and then apply the total to the total kWh consumption.
   (ii)     In the graph, meeting rooms and wards are next to each other. You can therefore read the total of those two simply by looking at the end of the wards bar.

For 2000:
   •   Meeting rooms + wards = 53%
   •   Server room = 21%
   •   Total = (53% + 21%, i.e. 74%) of 15,000 = 11,100

For 1990:
   •   Meeting rooms + wards = 53%
   •   Server room = 12%
   •   Total = (53% + 12%, i.e. 65%) of 17,000 = 11,050

The difference is therefore 11,100 – 11,050 = 50 kWh.

**Q1.167b – c: Print room**
We are looking for the smallest reduction in consumption. The total consumption went down from 17,000 kWh to 15,000 kWh. Therefore any area that has seen a decrease in its percentage or less than a 12% increase (15 / 17 = 0.88, i.e. a decrease of 12% which needs to be compensated for) would have experienced a decrease in its consumption. This rules out the

server room, whose percentage has nearly doubled and thus will have experienced a substantial increase in consumption.

We can also rule out the kitchen area because it has experienced a large decrease in its percentage (20% down to 14%), and therefore the loss of consumption in the kitchen will be far greater than that experienced by other areas whose percentage has remained roughly stable. This leaves us with just three areas to consider:

- Meeting rooms: 14% x 15000 – 12% x 17000 = 2100 – 2040 = 60 (so a small <u>increase</u>)
- Wards: 39% x 15000 – 41% x 17000 = 5850 – 6970 = -1,120
- Print room: 12% x 15000 – 15% x 17000 = 1800 – 2550 = -750

**Q1.167c – Chart D**
We know that the new wing area represents 18,000 – 15,000 = 3,000 kWh out of 18,000, i.e. 1/6th (= 16.7%). Only Charts C and D show such percentage.

We are told that the consumption in kWh for the 'old' areas remains the same in 2010 as in 2000. Therefore, if we add the new wing into the equation, it means that all the percentages for the old areas should have reduced (since the same number of kWh is now compared to a larger consumption). We can see that, in Chart C, the 2010 percentage for the server room is nearly 30% compared to 20% in 2000. Therefore Chart C can be excluded.

This leaves Chart D as the answer.

**Q1.168a - b: 2005**
Since the daily average for each category will have been calculated using the same denominator (i.e. 365 since all years are non-leap years), it is possible to add the individual averages together within each year.

2001: 30+80+20=130
**2005: 40+60+80=180**
2009: 70+40+50=160
2013: 30+30+60=120

**Q1.168b – b: 2005 only**
Again, since the denominator is constant at 365 in the calculation of the average, we can obtain the desired result simply by looking at the average numbers.

2001: 80 + ½ x 20 = 90
**2005: 60 + ½ x 80 = 100**
2009: 40 + ½ x 50 = 65
2013: 30 + ½ x 60 = 60

**Q1.169a – d: 750**
The simplest way to deal with this question is to draw up a table of entry and exit movements using the fact that those who left at 2pm must have entered at 1pm and that visitors can only stay a maximum of 2 hours.

So:
• If 210 people arrived at 1pm and 150 of them left at 2pm, then the remaining 60 will have left at 3pm, since the maximum stay is 2 hours.
• We know from the table that 160 people left at 3pm. From the previous point we know that 60 of them came from the 1pm entry batch, and therefore 100 of them will come from the 2pm entry batch.
• And so on. The remaining numbers cascade in exactly the same manner from then on as follows:

| 1pm | 2pm | 3pm | 4pm | 5pm | 6pm |
|------|------|------|------|------|------|
| +210 | -150 | - 60 | | | |
| | +240 | -100 | -140 | | |
| | | +360 | -230 | -130 | |
| | | | +270 | -150 | -120 |
| | | | | +120 | -120 |

The total number of people who stayed for only one hour is therefore the sum of all the second numbers on each line: 150 + 100 + 230 + 150 + 120 = 750.

**Q1.169b – b: 60–230**
The range we are looking for is basically the minimum and the maximum negative number from the table above. The group size was therefore between 60 and 230.

**Q1.170a – c: 4%**
The total number of XL bottles is 30% x 2400 = 720.

We know that there can be up to 1% x 609 = 6 XL bottles in Lab 2 and similarly 6 XL bottles in Lab 3, i.e. a total of 12 XL bottles.

If we assume that all bottles in Lab 4 are of XL size (which is possible since 688 < 720) then, at most, up to 12 + 688 = 700 XL bottles can be found in Labs 2, 3 and 4. This means that Lab 1 must contain at least 720 – 700 = 20 XL bottles. This represents 20 / 500 = 4% of all Lab 1 bottles.


**Q1.170b – b: Between 158 and 160**
If we call X the number of XL bottles stored in Lab 1, and Y the number of XL bottles stored in Labs 2 and 3 (which can be anything between 0 and 12), then we have: X + Y + 3.5X = 720. Therefore 4.5X + Y = 720.

If Y = 0 then 4.5X = 720, i.e. X = 160
If Y = 12 then 4.5X = 720 – 12 = 708, i.e. X = 708 / 4.5 = 157.333
Hence the number of XL bottles in Lab 1 is between 158 and 160.


**Q1.170c – c: Nitric**
There are several ways of dealing with this question. One would be to calculate all the percentages and see which graph is the best fit, but that could take some time. An easier way is to spot patterns. For example:

- Charts A and B show that Lab 1 represents approximately 25% of the total. Looking at the table, we can see this is the case for Nitrous and Benzoic acids.

- Chart C shows that Lab 4 represents approximately 25% of the total. Looking at the table, this happens only for the Hydrochloric acid.

- Looking at the data for Sulphuric acid, we can see that this is the only acid for which the Lab 3 and Lab 4 figures are roughly the same. We can see that this is the case in Chart D.

- Looking at the data we can see that the figures for Lab 1 and Lab 3 for the Salicylic acid are similar. This is also the case in Chart E.

Therefore the acid that is not represented is the Nitric acid. As a check, we can see that the figures for Nitric acid increased from Lab 1 to Lab 4: $52 < 65 < 89 < 161$. We would therefore expect a chart showing increasingly larger sections. None of the charts show that pattern.

### Q1.171 – g: All three statements

The calculation of minimum percentages requires looking at the smallest overlaps between the bars.

*Statement I: It is possible that no children were vaccinated for both smallpox and MMR in Russia, and for smallpox and polio in Spain.*

In Russia, if 19% of children were vaccinated for smallpox and 81% for MMR, then since the two numbers add up to 100% it is entirely possible that no child received both vaccines. Similarly, in Spain, if 18% were vaccinated for smallpox and 71% for polio, since it adds up to less than 100%, those may be entirely different children.

*Statement II: The minimum percentage of French children vaccinated for both smallpox and polio is 39%.*

The smallest possible overlap between the two can be visually represented as follows:

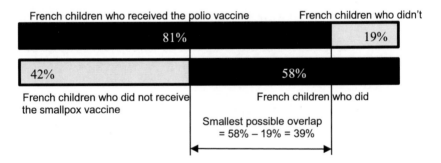

*Statement III: The minimum percentage of Swedish children who received all three vaccines is 58%.*

The same principle as above can be applied when dealing with three overlaps. All you need to do is take the first two and get a result for them. Then apply that result to the third one.

So:
- Smallest overlap for smallpox and polio in Sweden = 88 – (100 – 71) = 88 – 29 = 59%.

- Smallest overlap between the 59% calculated above and the 99% MMR vaccination rate = 59 – (100 – 99) = 58%.

Therefore all three statements are correct.


**Q1.172a – d: 101**
The profit for one unit of Cog M is £24.30 and the profit for one unit of Cog XL is £36.44. If we sold 100 units of Cog XL, the profit would be £3,644, compared to a profit of 150 x £24.30 = £3,645 for Cog M. Therefore we need to sell 101 Cog XL units to make a higher profit than by selling 150 Cog M units.


**Q1.172b – c: A drop in profit of £73,000**
Halving the price will mean that it will make a profit of £60.50 less per item sold, reducing it from £84.50 to £24 per item.

The movement in profit will therefore be:
4000 x 24 – 2000 x 84.50 = 96,000 – 169,000 = -73,000, so a drop in profit of £73,000.


**Q1.173a – d: Down by 1.6 million**
The total readership for 2006 for all five papers was:
9.7 + 8.3 + 6.2 + 2.8 + 5.2 = 32.2.

For 2008 it was 7.2 + 7.2 + 5.6 + 3.8 + 6.8 = 30.6. Hence it was down by 32.2 – 30.6 = 1.6 million.


**Q1.173b – e: £12 million**
We know that 25% of The Voice's income was generated by paper sales in 2007 and that those sales amounted to £4 million. The revenue from online sales was 75% of the total revenue, which is three times the revenue from paper sales. Hence the total revenue from online sales amounted to 3 x £4 million = £12 million.

**Q1.173c – a: A drop of 61%**
We know that, in 2007, 45% of the income was generated by paper copies and 47% by online copies. This leaves 100 – 45 – 47 = 8% generated by other sales. If the retail price and the total income have not changed then we can work directly with the percentages.

A drop of 10% in the number of paper copies sold means a drop in 10% in the revenue (since the retail price has not changed). The percentage of income represented by paper sales in 2008 was therefore 90%x45= 40.5%.

An increase of 20% in the number of online purchasers means an increase of 20% in the revenue (since the retail price has not changed). The percentage of income represented by online sales in 2008 was 47 x 1.2 = 56.4%.

Therefore a total of 40.5% + 56.4% = 96.9% of revenue came from sales of paper and online versions, meaning that only 3.1% of revenue needed to come from advertising or other sources.

This represents a change of 3.1 / 8 = 0.39, i.e. a drop of 61%.


**Q1.173d – Chart B**
The revenue from advertising and other sources in 2007 was as follows:

Spin Daily: (1 – 0.43 – 0.37) x 8 = 20% x 8 = 1.6
The H Post: (1 – 0.45 – 0.47) x 8 = 8% x 8 = 0.64
Carls News: 0 since sales from paper and online add up to 100%
The Voice: 0 since sales from paper and online add up to 100%
Daily Planet: (1 – 0.48 – 0.50) x 6.9 = 2% x 6.9 = 0.138

So we are looking for a chart with 3 parts (which excludes D), where the largest part represents approximately 1.6 / (1.6 + 0.64 + 0.138) = 1.6 / 2.378 = 0.67 = roughly 2/3. The only possibility is Chart B.


**Q1.174a – a: 163,800**
The male/female ratio is 2:8 therefore 2/10$^{th}$ of the population of region A is male. Region A accounts for 25% of the national population. Therefore the number of men in region A = 0.20 x 0.25 x 3,276,000 = 5% of 3,276,000, i.e. 163,800.

**Q1.174b – e: 28.5%**
Because we are dealing with relative numbers all calculated from the total population, we don't actually need to do the full calculation (if you do, you will lose a LOT of time). Instead, using the letter N to mean the total population of 3,276,000, we can calculate the following:

For region B:
The male/female ratio is 3:1 therefore men represent 3/4 of the population in region B, which itself represents 20% of the national population. Therefore the number of males is 3/4 x 20% x N = 15% of N.

For region D:
The male/female ratio is 3:5 therefore men represent 3/8 of the population in region D, which itself represents 12% of the national population. Therefore the number of males is 3/8 x 12% x N = 4.5% of N.

For region F:
The male/female ratio is 3:2 therefore men represent 3/5 of the population in region F, which itself represents 15% of the national population. Therefore the number of males is 3/5 x 15% x N = 9% of N.

Therefore the males from regions B, D and F represent 15 + 4.5 + 9 = 28.5% of the total population N.


**Q1.174c – a: 1:0**
Let's call X the population of region C. The number of men in region C is 2/5 X. We know that 1/6 of them are literate, and 5/6 of them are illiterate.

Therefore the number of literate men is: 1/6 (2/5 X) = 2/30 X = 1/15 X and the number of illiterate men is 5/6 (2/5 X) = 10/30 X = 1/3 X.

Looking at the total population for the region, we know that 2/3 X are literate and 1/3 X are illiterate. Therefore we can deduce that:

Number of literate women = 2/3 X - 1/15 X = 10/15 X - 1/15 X = 9/15 X = 3/5 X

Number of illiterate women = 1/3 X – 1/3 X = 0

Hence a ratio of 1:0: i.e. all women are literate.

**Q1.174d – e: 15:14**
If N is the total population:

- The number of females in region G is: 4/7 x 9% x N.
- The number of females in region C is 3/5 x 8% x N.

The ratio is therefore (4 x 9 / 7) / (3 x 8 / 5) = (36 x 5) / (24 x 7)
Dividing by 12 on both sides gives (3 x 5) / (2 x 7) = 15/14.


**Q1.174e – a: 42:55**
Let's call X the population of region B last year, and Y the population of region F last year. We are looking for Y/X.

This year, the population of region B is therefore 1.12 X (an increase of 12% from last year) and the population of region F is 1.10 Y (an increase of 10% from last year). Therefore the ratio of the populations of F over B is (1.10 Y) / (1.12 X). We know from the pie chart that this ratio should be 15/20 i.e. 3/4.

So, this means that: 1.10Y / 1.12 X = 3/4. We can remove the decimal points by multiplying by 100, which gives 110Y / 112X = 3/4.

We can reverse the fraction by multiplying by 112/110 on both sides, which gives: Y / X = (3 x 112) / (4 x 110)

Since 112 = 14 x 8 and 110 = 55 x 2, we can simplify this fraction as follows: Y/X = (3 x 14 x 8) / (4 x 2 x 55)
Dividing by 8 on both sides gives: Y/X = (3 x 14) / 55 i.e. = 42 / 55.


**Q1.175a – c: 2002, 2003 and 2005**
The combined exports were as follows:

2000: 30 + 80 + 60 = 170.
2001: 60 + 40 + 90 = 190.
2002: 40 + 60 + 120 = 220.
2003: 70 + 60 + 90 = 220.
2004: 60 + 80 + 100 = 240.
2005: 40 + 80 + 100 = 220.
2006: 100 + 120 + 140 = 360.

The more observant candidates may have found a quicker way of answering the question: the values for 2006 are far higher than for other years, and so one can eliminate all the answers which contain 2006. That will only leave Option C.

**Q1.175b – e: +50%**
In 2004, the average value was (60 + 80 + 100) / 3 = 80.
In 2006, the average value was (100 + 120 + 140) / 3 = 120.
Thus, it has increased by 50%.

**Q1.175c – Graph B**
For this we can reuse the calculations made in 1.175a. The averages are:

| Year | Average | Increase from previous year |
|------|---------|------------------------------|
| 2000 | 170 / 3 = 57 | |
| 2001 | 190 / 3 = 63 | 6 |
| 2002 | 220 / 3 = 73 | 10 |
| 2003 | 220 / 3 = 73 | 0 |
| 2004 | 240 / 3 = 80 | 7 |
| 2005 | 220 / 3 = 73 | -7 |

We expect 2003 to show no increase (which eliminates Graphs C and D) and 2005 to show a negative increase (which also eliminates Graph C). Graph A has two negative increases so it can be eliminated. This now leaves us with only Graphs B and E. The only perceptible difference is the size of the bar for 2002. The bar for 2002 should be much taller than the bar for 2001, which points to Graph B.

**Q1.175d – c: 2002**
The bars show Redford in black, Blackbell in light grey and Blueridge in dark grey. Having identified that, you simply need to look at the relative sizes of each portion within each bar. So, for example, the values for 2000 are 30, 60 and 80. So you would expect the middle portion to be twice the size of the bottom portion (which it is). You would also expect the top portion to be 50% bigger than the middle portion, which it is.

The figures for 2002 are 40, 60 and 120. Therefore you would expect the top portion to be twice the size of the middle portion. However, they are of equal size. Hence 2002 is the year for which the graph was incorrectly drawn.


**Q1.176a – d: 200 g**
A Day 1 sourdough starter will contain 2/3 of wheat flour and 1/3 of water. Therefore, to make 300 g we require 200 g of wheat flour.


**Q1.176b – b: 25 g**
At the start of Day 3, we will need to throw away 3/4 of the current sour-dough starter and so we will be left with just 25 g. At that stage we are still in the "maintain-weight" feeding period and so we will need to feed it so that it, once again, weighs 100 g, i.e. we need to add a total of 75 g. We need to do that by adding 2/3 of flour and 1/3 of water. So the amount of water we need to add is 1/3 x 75 = 25 g.


**Q1.176c – c: 1.6 kg**
We know that the sourdough starter weighs 600 g. It would have weighed the same every day since Day 1 (with 75% of it being thrown away and replaced every day).

On Day 1, it contains 400 g flour + 200 g water (600 g with a 2/3 – 1/3 split).

On Day 2, we throw away 3/4 of the mix and thus need to replace 450 g of it. That would be done by adding 300 g of flour and 150 g of water.

On Day 3, we throw away 3/4 of the Day 2 mixture (which still weighs 600 g) and therefore also have to replace 450 g of it using a 300 g flour /150 g water mix.

In fact, every day after Day 1 we need to add 300 g of flour. By Day 5, we will therefore have used 400 g (Day 1) + 4 x 300 g = 1,600 g, i.e. 1.6 kg.


**Q1.176d – b: 25 g**
We are told that to make the bread, all we need to do is quadruple the weight of the starter the day before making the bread. So the amount of starter needed on Day 1 is 1/4 of the final desired amount, i.e. 100/4=25 g.

## Q1.176e – Column C

On Day 1, we have 2/3 flour and 1/3 water. We throw 3/4 of that away and replace it by fresh flour and water so that it makes up the same weight again. It means that the remainder of the sour starter will account for 1/4 of the new mix. That is only the case in Column C.


## Q1.177a – e: 532 Scott Road

From the Location column, Jane would have selected those with the three highest ratings, i.e. Headway Park, Elwater Road and Scott Road. Out of those, she will exclude the property with the lowest Interior rating, i.e. Elwater Road. And, out of the other two (Headway Park and Scott Road), she will choose the cheapest: Scott Road (£350,000 v. £485,000).


## Q1.177b – b: Exterior

If Jane has just bought a house in Pontefract Lane for £390,000 and her system is such that the final hurdle is to choose the cheaper of the two properties shortlisted, then there is only one option available for the property she discarded since there is only one property which is more expensive than 390,000: Headway Park with a price of £485,000.

Headway Park and Pontefract Lane happen to be the properties with the highest Space ranking of all properties. So that means that the third property she shortlisted could be any of the other three available. To find out which criteria she used for her first shortlisting, we must therefore find the columns where Headway Park and Pontefract Lane rank in the top three (excluding Space since this has already been used).

Interior – Not possible since Headway Park ranks fourth with a rating of 3.
Exterior – They rank in the top 3 (together with Scott Road).
Location: Not possible since Pontefract Lane has the lowest rating of all.

Hence her most important criterion was Exterior.


## Q1.177c – a: 0%

Since, at the end of her selection process, Jane always chooses the cheaper of two houses, she will never be able to buy the most expensive house. The only way it might have possibly happened is if, out of the three houses she originally shortlisted, she had to discard two of them because they both had the same lower rating. However, the ratings within any column are all different and therefore it cannot happen.

**Q1.178a – d: Week 1: 32 over target; Week 2: 2 over target**
In week 1 the total actual sales were 32 + 30 + 25 + 15 + 5 + 15 = 122 against a target of 15 + 25 + 20 + 10 + 10 + 10 = 90. Hence the company was over target by 32.

In week 2, the total actual sales were 35 + 40 + 24 + 12 + 9 + 24 = 144 against a target of 35 + 35 + 30 + 15 + 15 + 12 = 142. Hence the company was over target by 2.

**Q1.178b – c: South**
Sales are based on actual numbers.  Average per staff for the two weeks:
North: (32 + 35) / 8 = 67 / 8 = 8.4
East: (30 + 40) / 9 = 70 / 9 = 7.8
South: (25 + 24) / 5 = 49 / 5 = 9.8 – this is the highest.
West: (15 + 12) / 8 = 27 / 8 = 3.4
London: (5 + 9) / 6 = 14 / 6 = 2.3
Ireland: (15 + 24) / 4 = 39 / 4 = 9.75

At the exam, you will not have the luxury of a calculator and so you need to exclude some of the obviously wrong answers simply by looking at the ratios in order to minimise the number of calculations you need to do. Scanning down the list we can see two that clearly stand out: South has 49 sales with 5 staff, and Ireland has 39 sales with 4 staff members. Both have over 9 sales. All you then need to calculate by hand are the figures for South and for Ireland.

**Q1.178c – d: West**
The table shows (see calculation made for 1.178a) that the company was 2 over target in week 2. Once we remove one of the teams, it becomes 5 over target, an improvement of 3. Therefore the team that was removed was 3 under target in week 2, which matches the profile for the West team.

**Q1.179a – c: 310**
The answer is: 30 + 40 + 35 + 50 + 75 + 80 = 310.

**Q1.179b – b: Prof 2**
The prof with the average closest to 30 across the six years will be the prof with the total number of publications closest to 6 x 30 = 180.

Note: You can calculate the totals for all the professors; however, if you look carefully at the graph, you can see that Prof 4's average will be below 30 since his numbers are well below 30 each year, apart from one year where he peaks at 45 (but that is not enough to compensate for the lower numbers). You can see also that Prof 1 and Prof 6 have numbers that are far too high to qualify. Therefore you could limit yourself to calculating the totals for Profs 2, 3 and 5. For those who don't want to chance it, here are the totals for all professors:

Prof 1: 310; Prof 2: 235; Prof 3: 170; Prof 4: 115; Prof 5: 170; Prof 6: 295. Bearing in mind that the average needs to be over 30 (as stated in the question), the two profs with total publications of 170 will not qualify as their average will be below 30. Hence the next closest is Prof 2.

**Q1.179c – Graph D**
From the graph we can see that Prof 1 and Prof 6 have written a similar number of publications. Therefore we expect their portion of the graph to be roughly of the same size, but with Prof 6's section being slightly bigger.

This excludes:
- Graph A (since Prof 6's section is smaller than Prof 1's section)
- Graph B (since the two sections are of very different sizes)
- Graph E (since the two sections are of very different sizes).

(Note: You can also exclude Graphs A, B and E by looking at Prof 4 and noticing that he represents the lowest proportion of publications.)

We are now left with Graph C and Graph D. We can see that Prof 2 and Prof 5 should have sections of a similar size to each other, with Prof 5's section being slightly bigger. This excludes Graph C, where Prof 5's section is smaller than Prof 2's section.

(Note: You can also select Graph D over Graph C using the fact that Prof 3 has 2.5 more publications than Prof 4. In Graph C the section for Prof 3 is far too big compared to the section for Prof 4.)

**Q1.180a – c: 15%**
The journey from Paris to London is 2:15, i.e.135 minutes long.
The journey from Paris to Luxembourg is 2:39, i.e. 159 minutes long.
The difference is (159 – 135) / 159 = 24 / 159, i.e. 0.15, i.e. 15%.


**Q1.180b – b: 7:39**
The man made two London → Brussels trips (2:22 each) and one Brussels → London trip (1:56). In addition, he had 35 + 24 = 59 minutes of waiting time. Therefore in total his trip was 2 x (2 hr + 22 min) + (1 hr + 56 min) + 59 min = 4 hr 44 min + 1 hr 56 min + 59 min = 5 hr 159 minutes = 7 hr 39 min.


**Q1.180c – c: Charles**
Max: Paris to London (2:15) + 4-hour wait + London to Luxembourg (5:45) = 12 hours.

David: London to Paris (2:25) + 4-hour wait + Paris to Luxembourg (2:39) = 9 hours 4 minutes.

Charles: London to Luxembourg (5:45) + 4-hour wait + Luxembourg to Paris (2:16) = 12 hours 1 minute.

Tom: London to Paris (2:25) + 35-minute wait + Paris to London (2:15) = 5 hours 15 minutes.

So Charles's journey is the longest by 1 minute.


**Q1.180d – d: Max**
All trips are made in this triangular pattern using the same trains with the same journey times. The only difference between them is the waiting time.

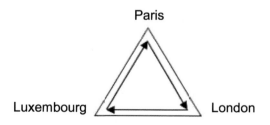

Paris

Luxembourg          London

304

Therefore all of them will have travelled the same distance overall; and the traveller with the fastest average speed will be the one who waited the least i.e. Max, who waited only 3 hours in total. All the other travellers waited 4 hours.

**Q1.181a – d: Those exercising strenuously once a week might as well exercise normally twice a week.**
Looking at the various statements:

*a: They are likely to lose weight through exercise.*
That may be true but it is not something that can be deduced from the chart as it does not deal with weight loss.

*b: They should avoid exercising more than 3 times a week.*
That is true only for strenuous exercise, but not for "any physical activity", therefore it cannot be generalised.

*c: They should increase their level of exercise gradually.*
It is probably true but not something we can deduce from the graph. The study does not deal with changes in the exercise regime.

*d: Those exercising strenuously once a week might as well exercise normally twice a week.*
The markers for both are roughly in the same place, halfway between 0.85 and 0.9, so this is correct.

*e: The risk of heart disease for inactive obese women is the same as the risk for inactive lean people.*
The inactive group is used as a reference. In other words, what we see on the graphs is the relative change in risk of heart disease for each group and how that change varies from weight group to weight group. It does not actually compare absolute values. Therefore this statement cannot be proven with the graphs (and it is probably false anyway).

**Q1.181b – e: 1, 2 and 3**
*1: The more they exercise, the lower their risk of heart disease, regardless of the intensity of the exercising.* This is true because on both graphs the line is going down.

*2: They can reduce their risk of heart disease by nearly 25% through exercising.* This is correct as the point for strenuous activity is at 0.76, i.e. a 24% reduction.

*3: The reduction in the risk of heart disease between 2-3/week and 4-6/week for lean women undertaking normal physical activity is lower than for obese women.* We can see that the line for lean women is less steep than the line for obese women. Hence lean women indeed experience a lower reduction in risk between those two frequencies of exercise.

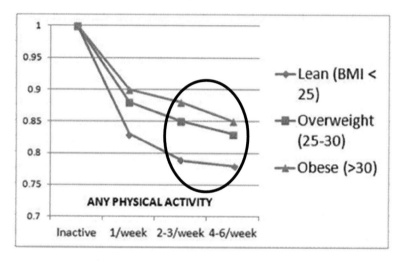

So, all three statements are correct.

**Q1.181c – d: 1 and 3 only**
For the graph and the study to have any meaning, it is important that people declare their true level of exercise; otherwise the data will be flawed. Also, if they change their exercise routine through the observation period (e.g. they increase it) then the results will be meaningless as we would not be able to measure the impact of individual exercise regimes on health.

As far as we are told, the level of exercise the women are doing is recorded once at the start of the study and that's it. So it must be assumed that they will stick to whatever they have declared. Hence Statements 1 and 3 are both correct.

Statement 2 is irrelevant because the study is not so much comparing the three categories of women. It is instead looking at the impact of different levels of exercise on each category separately. As such, if obese people find it hard to exercise, they will all have the same problem and so it will cancel out.


**Q1.182a – c: 50%**
Males represent 2 / (2+3) = 40% of all patients aged over 85.
The percentage of the total age group advised to do more exercise was 36%. For males it was 15%.

Therefore we have 0.40 x 0.15 + 0.60 x N = 0.36, where N is the percentage of female patients advised to do more exercise. This gives:

0.06 + 0.60N = 0.36
i.e. N = (0.36 – 0.06) / 0.60 = 0.5 or 50%.


**Q1.182b – a: 2 only**
*Statement 1: In 2005, 4% were advised to do more exercise.*
We know that 10% of the whole population was advised to do more exercise, and 16% of the male population was. In order to calculate the percentage of the female population that was advised, we would need to know the male: female ratio. In this case, the female percentage would be 4% if the male: female ratio was 50%. But since that ratio is not provided, we cannot conclude that this statement is correct.

*Statement 2: In 2005, fewer than 10% were advised to do more exercise.*
If the figure is 10% for the whole population and the figure is 16% (i.e. >10%) for males only, then the figure for females has to be lower than 10% to balance it out in the weighted average calculation, regardless of the male: female ratio. So this statement is true.

*Statement 3: The proportion advised to do more exercise was higher in 2015 than in 2010, and higher in 2010 than in 2005.*
We can see that the overall proportion increases and that the proportion for males decreases. However, without knowing the male:female ratio in each year we cannot conclude either way. For example, if the ratio was 1:1 (i.e. 50% of each) every year, then the female proportion would be 4, 2 and 8 for 2005, 2010 and 2015 respectively, which contradicts the statement.

**Q1.182c – c: 47%**
In 2015, in the age range 65–74, the percentage of all patients who were advised to exercise more was 60%. For males only, it was 15%.

If we call M the percentage of the population that is male and N the percentage of females in that age range who were advised to do more exercise, then we can write the equation:

M x 15 + (1–M) x N = 60
i.e. 15M + N – MN = 60
i.e. M(15–N) = 60 – N
i.e. M = (60–N) / (15–N).

Since the overall proportion of people in that age range who were advised to exercise is 60% and the percentage for males only is 15% then the percentage for females must be greater than 60% otherwise we would never get an average of 60% across both genders. Therefore 60%<N<100%.

If N = 60 then M = 0.
If N = 100 then M = 40 / 85 = 47%.
So the maximum value for M is 47%.

**Q1.183a – c: 5**
There were 25 graduates at the start and only 18 + 2 = 20 taking exams in Year 8, therefore 25 – 20 = 5 were dismissed.

**Q1.183b – c: 2**
We know that 3 graduates sat Exam 3 in Year 3. Anyone who was successful would have sat Exam 4 in Year 4. Only 1 person sat Exam 4 in Year 4, and since this was the first year it could have been taken then that number cannot include resits. Therefore 2 graduates failed Exam 3 in Year 3.

**Q1.183c – c: 12**
We know that 12 people had to resit Exam 1 in Year 2. The 2 who had to retake the exam in Year 3 are already included in those 12, so they should not be added otherwise we would be double-counting.

**Q1.183d – c: 23%**
Since this is the first year Exam 2 can be taken, those who passed Exam 2 in Year 2 will be the same ones who took Exam 3 in Year 3, i.e. 3. Therefore the pass rate is 3/13 = 23%.

**Q1.183e – e: 83.3%**
In Year 2, 12 people took Exam 1, but 2 had to resit it in Year 3. Therefore the pass rate is (12–2)/12 = 10/12 = 83.3%.

**Q1.183f – d: 100%**
Year 4 is the last year in which graduates can take Exam 2. Therefore those who failed it would have been dismissed. And since no one else could have been dismissed (since the others would be on either their first or their second attempt), the number of people dismissed at the end of the Year 4 exams is calculated as follows:

Total number of students who took an exam in Year 5 = 8 + 15 + 1 = 24
MINUS
Total number of students who took an exam in Year 4 = 3 + 20 + 1 = 24

Therefore no one was dismissed and so the pass rate was 100%.

**Q1.183g – e: 90%**
The pass rate is calculated as the number of people who passed Exam 2 in Year 3 divided by the number of people who took Exam 2 in Year 3 (which we know to be 20, from the table).

The number of people who passed Exam 2 in Year 3 is equal to the number of people who took Exam 3 in Year 4 for the first time. We know that the total number of people who took Exam 3 in Year 4 is 20, but that number will include those who are resitting Exam 3, having failed the previous year. The number of resits is 3 (Exam 3 in Year 3) – 1 (Exam 4 in Year 4) = 2.

Hence, 20 – 2 = 18 people were successful and the success rate is 18/20 = 90%

**Q1.184a – b: 29**
This is calculated as the number of diners who ate more than one dish (i.e. all except those in the four corners: 8, 7, 8, 1). The total is therefore: 4+3+3+2+4+4+2+2+5 = 29.

### Q1.184b – c: 14

Those who ate at least three dishes will be located in the central part of the diagram, as shown:

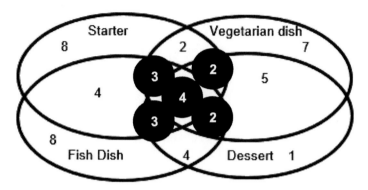

There are 14 people in total.

### Q1.184c – a: 0

The Starter area and the Dessert area do not intersect outside of other areas. So those who ate both a starter and a dessert all ate at least one main course and would have benefited from the better offers E or F.

### Q1.184d – a: £82.80

There are only 2 people who ate two main courses and a dessert only. These diners would have spent a total of 2 x (23 + 15 + 8) x 0.9 = £82.80.

### Q1.184e – c: £18.00

There are 8 diners who ate only a starter, and 9 diners who chose a main course + a dessert (4 chose fish + dessert, and 5 chose vegetarian + desert). Therefore only 8 people will be able to save money and 1 person who had main course + dessert will not be able to save anything.

Since the fish dish is more expensive than the vegetarian dish, the maximum saving will be achieved by using all 4 fish dishes and 4 out of the 5 vegetarian dishes.

The costs are calculated as follows:

Cost before pairing:
Starters = £9 x 8 diners x 1 (no discount) = £72
+ Veg & Dessert = £23 x 5 diners x 0.95 = £109.25
+ Fish & Dessert = £31 x 4 diners x 0.95 = £117.80

TOTAL= £299.05

Cost after pairing
Starter & Veg & Dessert = £32 x 4 diners x 0.90 = £115.20
+ Starter & Fish & Dessert = £40 x 4 diners x 0.90 = £144
+ Veg & Dessert = £23 x 1 diner x 0.95 = £21.85

TOTAL= £281.05

Saving: 299.05 – 281.05 = £18

**Q1.184f – e: 21 Type F + 4 Type B + 1 Type A**
In total the following number of dishes were ordered:

**26 starters + 28 fish dishes + 25 vegetarian dishes + 21 desserts.**

Therefore there is scope for 21 Type F discounts (i.e. the maximum possible discount which covers 1 starter + 2 mains + 1 dessert).

Once those discounts have been accounted for, we still need to allocate:
26–21=**5 starters** + 28–21=**7 fish dishes** + 25–21=**4 vegetarian dishes**. There is scope for 4 Type B discounts (i.e. starter + 2 main courses at 10% discount).

We are then left with 5–4=**1 starter** + 7–4=**3 fish dishes**. Putting the starter and one fish dish together will give a Type A discount, leaving two main dishes which need to be paid for in full.

Therefore the answer is: 21 Type F + 4 Type B + 1 Type A.

**Q1.185a – b: 67 litres**
This is calculated as: (1,000 million / 2) / 7,500,000 = 500 / 7.5 = 67.

**Q1.185b – b: 65%**
The production of German beer represents:
93,500 / (17,200 + 93,500 + 30,200 + 3,600) = 93,500 / 144,500 = 65%.

**Q1.185c – c: 79,900 million litres**
If Germans consume 200 litres per person per year, then they consume a total of 85,000,000 x 200 = 17,000 million litres.

80% of that consumption, i.e. 0.8 x 17000 = 13,600 million litres is local beer. Since they produce 93,500 million litres of beer locally, it means they export 93,500 – 13,600 = 79,900 million litres.

**Q1.186a – d: Structural**
The total profit made by the company (calculated by adding up all the numbers on the graph) is £80 million. 25% of that profit is £20 million, which is what the Structural division has made (7 + 8 + 5 = 20).

**Q1.186b – b: £11.25 million**
The Geotechnical division made a profit of £4.5 million in Europe. Therefore the turnover was 4.5 / 2 x 5 = £11.25 million.

**Q1.187a – c: Chiara plc**
Looking at the table, one can easily see that the largest difference is for Chiara plc: 1965 – 1250 = 715.

**Q1.187b – a: £155,000**
Yesterday, the share price for Eliad plc was 2525 / 1.01 = 2500. For Chiara plc, it was 1710 / 0.9 = 1900.

So 100 shares in Eliad would have cost 2500 x 100 = 250,000.
And 50 shares in Chiara would have cost 1900 x 50 = 95,000.
Hence a difference of 155,000.

**Q1.187c – d: £2,400**
Bravo plc paid a total annual dividend of 0.4 + 1.2 = £1.6 per share.
An investor with 1500 shares would therefore have been paid 1500 x 1.6 = £2,400.

**Q1.187d – b: £1 = 1.20 Euros**
The investor received 74,400 / 10 = 7,440 euros for 1 share in each company.

The cost of one share in each company yesterday (in £) was:
Amos: 1111/1.01 = 1100
Bravo: 201/1.005 = 200
Chiara: 1710 / 0.9 = 1900
Dross: 495 / 0.99 = 500
Eliad: 2525 / 1.01 = 2500

So a total of £6,200.

7440/6200 = 1.2. Therefore the exchange rate was £1 = 1.20 euros.


**Q1.187e – f: None. He is lying.**
Looking at the minimum and maximum prices, the only way the investor can get close to doubling his money by buying and selling his shares in the past 12 months would have been by buying Bravo plc shares at their minimum price and selling them at their maximum price. However, even if we include the value of the full dividends (0.4 + 1.2 = £1.6 per share), then the maximum he could have received per share would have been £220 + the dividend paid during the year = £221.6. If the investor had bought the shares at the minimum price of £111 then he would have been just short of doubling his money. Therefore he could not have "more than doubled" his money.


**Q1.188a – c: £12**
2.1 million vinyls generated £25.1m income. Hence the average per vinyl is 25.1 / 2.1 = £12.


**Q1.188b – e: Cannot be determined**
We know that the UK represents 17.1% of the worldwide market. But since we don't know how many albums were sold in the UK altogether we cannot calculate the size of the worldwide market.

### Q1.188c – a: 17.4 million
We know that Adele sold 17.4 million copies of her album in just six weeks. We are also told that her album was released on 19 November, which so happens to be six weeks exactly before the end of 2015. So that means that Adele's album sales for 2015 were 17.4 million.

### Q1.188d – c: 6
Revenue from streaming a video is 24.4 million / 27 billion.
Revenue from streaming an audio file is 146.1 million / 27 billion.
So the answer is 146.1 / 24.4 = 6.

### Q1.188e – a: Loss of £11
The revenue from 20 x 10 = 200 audio streams in 2015 was:
200 x 146.1 million / 27 billion = 29.22 / 27 = £1 approximately.
This compares to the revenue from a vinyl of 25.1 million / 2.1 = £12 approx.
Hence streaming the album instead of buying it led to a loss of £11.

### Q1.188f – b: 0.6 pence
The number of audio streams in 2014 was 27 / 1.82 = 14.8 billion.
Revenues from audio streams in 2014 were 146.1 / 1.69 = £86.4 million.
Hence the revenue per song was 86.4 / 14.8 / 1000 = 0.6 pence.

### Q1.189a – b: 10 km/h
Regardless of how he travels to work, he covers 20 km in 2 hours and therefore his average speed is 10 km/h.

### Q1.189b – d: 4 km
We know that his walking speed cannot be more than 6 km/h, which is 1 km every 10 minutes or 2 km every 20 minutes. This means that his walking portions of the route cannot have an angle steeper than this:

There are only two areas of the graph where this is the case: the first and the penultimate portions. In all other portions, he is either moving faster or he is stationary (flat line). Hence the maximum he can have walked is 2 x 2 km = 4 km.

**Q1.189c – d: 15 km/h**
The new bus would follow the new line below:

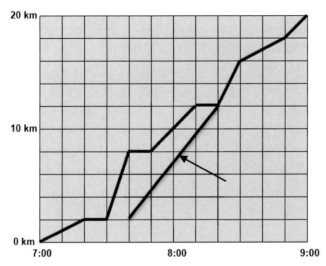

It would therefore drive 10 km in 40 minutes, hence an average speed of
10 x 60 / 40 = 15 km/h.

**Q1.189d – a: 8:50**
That bus covers 8 km between 8:20 and 9:00, i.e. in 40 minutes. If it drove
twice as fast, it would cover that distance in 20 minutes instead. We are told
that the bus is 10 minutes late picking up passengers, hence it would pick
up at 8:20 + 10 minutes = 8:30. Adding the 20-minute journey to that time
gives an arrival time of 8:50.

**Q1.190a – c: 40p**
The brother drives 90 miles in 90 minutes. He therefore drives at the speed
of 1 mile per minute, and the cost is 40p.

**Q1.190b – c: £677**
Travelling through Birmingham with the train on the Swiss side will cost:
2 x (40 x 0.4 + 155 + 120) = 2 x 291 = £582. Parking will cost £95.
Hence the total is 582 + 95 = £677.

**Q1.190c – a: Through Birmingham airport with taxi in Switzerland**
His actual travelling time was 7:15 – 2:20 = 4:55. If he travelled through Manchester, it would take 1:30 for the journey to the airport and 1:25 for the flight. This would add up to 2:55, leaving 2 hours for the transfer in Switzerland, which corresponds to neither of the possible options. Therefore he must have travelled through Birmingham.

The car and flight journey through Birmingham adds up to 0:50 + 1:15 = 2:05. This leaves 4:55 – 2:05 = 2:50 for the transfer at the end. Hence he took the taxi.


**Q1.190d – d: £115**
The maximum price he can pay is £30 x 9 = £270. The minimum price he can pay is £95 (for 7 days) + 2 x £30 = £155, which is cheaper than the £160 payable for 8–14 days. Hence the maximum saving is 270 – 155 = £115.


**Q1.190e – b: 65 miles**
It is £10 cheaper to fly from Manchester than from Birmingham. Therefore he would need to live further away from Birmingham by 10 / 0.4 = 25 miles. Hence a total distance of 40 + 25 = 65 miles.

You can also get this result by writing the equation: £36 + £145 = £155 + X (where X = cost of car trip to Birmingham).

This gives X = £26. So the total distance between his new home and Birmingham airport is 26 / 0.4 = 65 miles.


**Q1.191a – d: 99**
The total number of claims in 2009 was 915 x 1.2 = 1098.
Therefore the number of claims for theft was 9% x 1098 = 99.


**Q1.191b – a: A decrease of 4%**
The number of claims for leaking roofs in 2005 was 0.15 x 915.
For 2009, the number was 0.12 x 915 x 1.2. The ratio of 2009 claims over 2005 claims is therefore 0.12 x 1.2 / 0.15 = 0.144 / 0.15 = 0.96, i.e. a decrease of 4%.

**Q1.191c – c: 18.5%**
We are looking for N so that:
915 x 0.32 = 915(1+N) x 0.27.
Hence N = 0.32 / 0.27 – 1 = 0.185, i.e. 18.5%


**Q1.191d – d: 22%**
The total number of claims in 2009 was 915 x 1.2 = 1098. The additional percentage of gas leaks is 220 / 1098 = 20%. Hence after correction, gas leaks represent 20 + 2 = 22% of all claims in 2009.


**Q1.191e – c: 13%**
The total number of claims in 2005 should be 915 + 135 = 1050. Leaking roofs accounted for 0.15 x 915 = 137 claims. This represents 137 / 1050 = 13% of all claims.


**Q1.192a – b: Denmark**
The figure for survival rate at one week should be higher than the figure for one year. This is the case for all countries except Denmark.


**Q1.192b – a: 1 per thousand.**
The rate of stroke across all countries is:
(4+4+7+5+11) / (2.8+5.6+10.8+4.6+7.2) = 31 / 31 = 1 per thousand (we are dividing thousands by millions).


**Q1.192c – a: 1,500**
The number of people expected to die between one week and five years is found by taking away from the five-year figure those who died within one week. This gives: (0.92 – 0.62) x 5000 = 0.3 x 5000 = 1500.

**Q1.192d – c: Greece**
Taking Albania as an example: if 100 people have a stroke, 78 will survive one year, and 54 of those will survive until the five-year mark. Therefore the survival rate is 54 / 78 = 69%. Looking at all countries:

|         | 5 years | 1 year | Ratio         |
|---------|---------|--------|---------------|
| Albania | 54      | 78     | 54/78 = 69%   |
| Denmark | 72      | 91     | 72/91 = 79%   |
| Greece  | 74      | 84     | 74/84 = 88%   |
| Ireland | 62      | 87     | 62/87 = 71%   |
| Serbia  | 62      | 81     | 62/81 = 77%   |

Hence Greece has the best four-year survival rate for those who survived one year. Note that you can actually work out that the answer is Greece simply by looking at the numbers. All countries have high denominators of a similar order so the highest ratio will be achieved when the difference between the two numbers is at its smallest. When most countries have a difference of around 20 or more, Greece only has a difference of 10.

**Q1.192e – b: Denmark**
For this question we can interpolate the 4-year rate as being the 5-year rate + 25% of the difference between the 1-year and the 5-year rate, e.g. for Albania: 54 + (78–54)/4 = 60. So we get the following result for all countries:

|         | 5 years | 1 year | 4-year rate |
|---------|---------|--------|-------------|
| Albania | 54      | 78     | 60          |
| Denmark | 72      | 91     | 76.75       |
| Greece  | 74      | 84     | 76.5        |
| Ireland | 62      | 87     | 68.25       |
| Serbia  | 62      | 81     | 66.75       |

**Q1.193a – c: Grade 3**
This is stated in the last bullet point of the "Promotion from Grade 2 to Grade 3" paragraph.

Entrance at Grade 1 is possible for anyone who is suitable.
Entrance at Grade 2 is possible if there is no internal candidate.
Entrance at Grade 4 is possible if there is a requirement for it.

**Q1.193b – e: 14 years**
Regardless of the grade at which he joins, the employee will not be able to gain promotion to Grade 4 until he is 38 years old. So he will need to wait at least 14 years.

We also need to check that this is not slowed down by other requirements. The employee can't have joined at Grade 3, so he must have joined at Grade 1 or Grade 2. If he joined at Grade 1 then he could have been promoted to Grade 2 at the age of 26 (assuming he is promoted at the company's discretion and not automatically); and then promoted to Grade 3 at the age of 29 (three years of service required). So he would need to wait another 9 years to be promoted to Grade 4.

**Q1.193c – c: 31**
No one can be promoted to Grade 4 under the age of 38 and they must also have worked at Grade 3 for two years.

No one can be promoted to Grade 3 under the age of 35.

From those two statements we can see that if someone entered Grade 3 at the age of 35 then they would need to wait three years until they are 38 to be promoted to Grade 4. However, they would get a faster promotion if they entered Grade 3 at age 36 since they could reach Grade 4 in just two years.

Since the cap on the age requirement can be lifted, we can see that it is possible for someone to have the shortest possible career progression as follows:

Entry at Grade 1: 31
Promotion to Grade 2: 33 (Two years at Grade 1, with age exemption)
Promotion to Grade 3: 36 (Three years at Grade 2 + at least 35 years old)
Promotion to Grade 4: 38 (Two years at Grade 3 + at least 38 years old)

**Q1.193d – h: All of them**
*Statement 1: An employee with no or bad recommendations can never be promoted to a higher grade.* The paragraph explaining the criteria for promotion from Grade 1 to Grade 2 states that "An employee is automatically promoted if he/she has spent five years at Grade 1 AND there are no adverse reports about him/her AND the employee is at least 35 years old. So

it is possible for an employee with no recommendation to be promoted. As such, this statement is incorrect.

*Statement 2: No one below the age of 35 can be promoted.* This is incorrect because we know that the age limit can be lifted for promotion to Grade 2 in at least two ways: either at the discretion of the company with more than two years of service or if the employee has good references.

*Statement 3: If an employee is Grade 3 then he must have at least five years of service with the company.* This is incorrect. That statement would be true if the employee joined at Grade 1 (since they could have become promoted to Grade 2 within two years and then to Grade 3 three years thereafter – hence a total of five years). However, it is possible for employees to join the company at Grade 2, in which case they would only have a minimum of three years of service when they start their Grade 3 post.

### Q1.194a – c: 30 million
There are 1 million unemployed men (representing 5% of the male work-force) and 1 million unemployed women (representing 10% of the female workforce). Therefore the total workforce is 1/0.05 + 1/0.10 = 20+10 = 30 million.

### Q1.194b – d: 200,000
The number is calculated as (all numbers in thousands):
(1300 + 1000 + 1100 + 600) – (1100 + 1000 + 900 + 800)
= 4000 – 3800 = 200. So there were 200,000 more unemployed women than men.

### Q1.194c – f: 2 and 3 only
*Statement 1: In France, women are 2% more likely to be unemployed than men.* We know that 8% of men are unemployed and 10% of women are unemployed. Therefore women are 25% more likely to be unemployed than men, and not 2% (which is the absolute and not the relative difference).

*Statement 2: In Italy, women are twice as likely to be unemployed as men.* This time the comparison is 5% versus 10%, hence women are twice as likely to be unemployed as men.

*Statement 3: The figures shown for the UK unemployed population are not correct.* If we calculate the size of the workforce we get: 800/0.03 + 600/0.01 = 27 million + 60 million = 87 million, which is more than the entire population. So these figures are incorrect.

### Q1.195a – e: 75%

The recruitment firm wants to recruit people who fulfil both the degree and the work experience criteria. Therefore it will recruit from the pool of people that features in the intersection of the two circles. Anyone outside of that area will not be recruited. There are 40 circles, 10 of which are in the intersection of the two circles; therefore the probability of not being recruited is (40 – 10) / 40 = 30 / 40 = 75%.

### Q1.195b – b: 20%

The population with under three years' work experience will be represented outside of the work experience circle. The population with no university degree will be represented outside the university degree circle. Therefore the population that fulfils both criteria will be represented by the dots sitting outside of both circles, i.e. the eight circles on the right-hand side. The probability is therefore 8/40 = 20%.

### Q1.196a – e: 800

The graph shows that 60 + 20 = 80% of people did not purchase anything on Monday, i.e. 800 people.

### Q1.196b – b: 6%

The only population the graph represents are those who first went to the site. You can see from the legend of the graph that two of the three categories of shoppers do not revisit the site the next day. Only those in the black section actually come back the next day. Therefore the shoppers shown on Tuesday are those who were in the black section on Monday. Similarly, the shoppers represented on Wednesday are those who were in the black section on Tuesday. The important thing to remember is that there are no new shoppers on Tuesday or Wednesday.

The first bar shows that, on Monday, only 20% of shoppers revisited the site the next day.

The second bar shows that, out of those who revisited on Tuesday, 30% purchased an item. Hence the percentage of people who bought an item on Tuesday is 20% x 30% = 6%.

**Q1.196c – b: 1.2%**
The first bar shows that, on Monday, only 20% of shoppers revisited the site the next day.

The second bar shows that out of those who visited the site on Tuesday, 30% revisited on Wednesday.

The third bar shows that out of those who visited the site on Wednesday, 20% revisited on Thursday.

Therefore the proportion of shoppers who visited the site on Thursday was 20% x 30% x 20% = 1.2%.

**Q1.196d – e: It is not possible as it would need to be over 100%**
The percentage of people who purchased a substitute item on each day is as follows:

Monday: 20%
Tuesday: 20% x 30% = 6%
Wednesday: 20% x 30% x 60% = 3.6%
Thursday: N (this is the number we are looking for).

Hence a total of 29.6% + N purchased a replacement item.

We also know that the percentage of Monday shoppers who visited the site on Thursday is 20 x 30 x 20 = 1.2%. So the total percentage of people who purchased a replacement item can only be as high as 29.6 + 1.2 = 30.8%.

If the recommended utensil cost £10 and, say, 100 people visited the site on Monday, then if everyone had bought it the online website would have taken £1,000.

Instead if 30.8% purchased the substitute item at a cost that is 25% higher, then the online shop can only hope to make 100 x 0.308 x 10 x 1.25 = £385. The shop would have to sell the substitute item at more than three times the price of the original recommended item in order to take the same amount of money.

**Q1.197a – a: 13%**
The minimum percentage of Maltese people who visited both a library and a zoo is calculated as 65 – (100–48) = 65 – 52 = 13%.

**Q1.197b – d: 1 and 2 only**
*Statement 1: The proportion of the Italian population that lives close to either a museum or a theatre is greater than in the UK.* A higher percentage of the population goes to museums and theatres in Italy than in the UK. The fact that these places are closer to the population could help explain this fact.

*Statement 2: Out of all the countries listed, Spain has the fewest zoos per capita.* The table shows that Spain is the country where the smallest percentage of the population goes to zoos. This could be explained by the fact that there are relatively fewer zoos per capita (e.g. if there are not many zoos, people may be living too far away to visit them).

*Statement 3: Entry to museums is free in the UK.* If anything, this should ensure that a large proportion of the population visits museums. But that is not the case as the table shows that the UK in fact has the lowest proportion of all countries.

**Q1.198 – e: 1 and 2 together are not sufficient. More data is needed**
To solve the problem, we will need to know the actual price of the book at some stage in its shelf life. So Statement 1 would be useful for that; but it would not be sufficient. Indeed, once we know P, to calculate the saving we need to calculate the price at which Josie has bought the book. This is calculated as:
P x (1+A/100) x (1-B/100).

Knowing the value of B – A will only help us substitute one for the other in the equation but without one or the other's absolute value we will not be able to estimate the price and the savings. Hence we need additional data.

324 BMAT Practice Questions

**Q1.199 – b: 2 only**
*Statement 1: If 3 cats were added, there would be more cats than dogs.*
If we list the possible answers to the problem posed giving a 3:2 ratio, we get:

    i.    3 dogs + 2 cats
    ii.   6 dogs + 4 cats
    iii.  9 dogs + 6 cats
    iv.  12 dogs + 8 cats, etc.

If we add 3 cats to (i), we obtain 3 dogs and 5 cats and therefore there are indeed more cats than dogs.

If we add 3 cats to (ii), we obtain 6 dogs and 7 cats and therefore there are also more cats than dogs.

Given that we have identified two possible answers, we can conclude that Statement 1 is helpful but not sufficient.

*Statement 2: If 5 cats and 3 dogs were added, there would be more cats than dogs.* Again if we look at the possible options using a 3:2 ratio:

    i.    3 dogs + 2 cats
    ii.   6 dogs + 4 cats
    iii.  9 dogs + 6 cats
    iv.  12 dogs + 8 cats, etc.

For (i), adding 5 cats and 3 dogs gives a total of 7 cats and 6 dogs, which satisfies Statement 2 as we then have more cats than dogs.

For (ii), adding 5 cats and 3 dogs gives a total of 9 cats and 9 dogs and Statement 2 is no longer valid.
So, if Statement 2 is true then it is sufficient to solve the problem as it gives a unique solution.

**Q1.200a – b: 187,500**
The number of total page views in the last two weeks of February was 350,000 + 400,000, i.e. 750,000. We know from the first table that the front page represented 25% of total page views, i.e. 750,000 x 0.25 = 187,500.

## Q1.200b – b: 2 only

*Statement 1: Ahmed was the most popular blogger in February when looking at the total monthly page views.* The percentage of the website's total page views attributed to Ahmed is 10 + 9 + 7 = 26% and it is true that it is higher than for the other three bloggers (Paul = 14, John = 6, Nazia = 7). However we have no information about the other three bloggers' performance in the first two weeks of February and so we are unable to conclude whether the statement is correct.

*Statement 2: At least five of the nine blog articles viewed most often during the second half of the month were posted during those two weeks.*
- Ahmed has three blog articles that appear in the top 10 and all three were posted in the last two weeks of February since he wasn't there before.
- Nazia has two blog articles in the top 10, and we know that she only wrote one blog article in the first two weeks of February. Therefore at least one of her blogs was written in the second half.
- John has two blog articles in the top 10 and we know that he only wrote one blog article in the first two weeks of February. Therefore at least one of his blog articles was written in the second half.
- Paul has two blog articles in the top 10 but we know that he wrote six blog articles in the first half of the month and one in the second half. Therefore we have no way of finding out if he wrote either of his two top 10 blogs in the second half of February or not. It is indeed possible that both were written in the first half of the month.

In total, we know that at least 3 + 1 + 1 = 5 blogs were written in the second half of February. So Statement 2 is correct.

*Statement 3: The site was stickier during the second half of the month than during the first half.*
The text defines 'stickiness' as ensuring that people view more pages once they are on the site. As such, a measure of it would be the ratio of the number of page views over the number of site visits. We can see, however, that this ratio was at or over 2:1 (300,000:150,0000 and 340,000:160,000) for the first two weeks of February, and that it was slightly below 2:1 for the second half (350,000:180,000 and 400,000:220,000). Therefore the site was stickier in the first half of February and not the second half.

# 1G Aptitude and Skills
## Understanding Arguments - Answers

**Q1.201 – c: The tariff charge imposed on a vacuum cleaner imported from China into India is at most 10% of the manufacturing cost in India.**
If we take the Indian manufacturing cost to be 100, then the Chinese cost will be 90. Therefore to make it worthwhile importing the goods from China to India, the combined cost of transport and tariff charge cannot be more than 10, i.e. 10% of the Indian manufacturing cost. Since the 10% covers both the tariff charge and the transport charge then it is correct to say that the tariff charge is at most 10% of the manufacturing cost in India. The tariff charge could be as high as 10% if there is no transport cost.

Note that, expressed as a percentage of the Chinese cost, this represents 10 / 90 = 11%, hence Option d will only be correct if the transport charge accounts for at least 1%, but nothing in the text suggests this is the case. Hence Option d is not valid.

Option e is incorrect because, although the transport cost could be as high as 11% (see above reasoning using transport cost instead of tariff charge), it could also be well below, and in fact as little as 0.

Option a cannot be deduced from the text as the lower cost could also be linked to cheaper components.

Option b cannot be deduced since the 10% is the difference in manufacturing cost and has nothing to do with employment levels.

**Q1.202 – d: It presupposes the number of pregnant women in the random sample.**
We will only get a vast majority of women who test positive to be pregnant if there are enough pregnant women in the sample in the first place.

Let's assume that the sample of 200 women contains 100 pregnant women and 100 non-pregnant women.

Out of the 100 pregnant women, 99 will test positive.

Out of the 100 non-pregnant women, 10 will test positive.

So in total we will have 109 women testing positive with the vast majority being pregnant.

But let's assume instead that we have 10 pregnant women and 190 non-pregnant women in the group.

Out of 10 pregnant women, 9.9 will test positive (so say 10).
Out of 190 non-pregnant women, 19 will test positive.

So a total of 29 women will test positive, only 10 of which (so just about a third) will actually be pregnant.

Option a: This is incorrect because, in fact, the entire issue in this situation is the margin of error.

Option b: Whether there is interference from other factors or not is irrelevant since the statistics are whatever they are, regardless of the reason for being as such. It is very possible that other factors may come into play (in fact those factors may well be what is causing the margin of error). So this is not a flaw.

Option c: The conclusion of the argument is about women who test positive and their chances of being actually pregnant. It is not about women who do not test positive. As such this objection is not relevant.

Option e: In fact, the text suggests the total opposite.


**Q1.203 – c: The charge will not push residents to dump their rubbish in surrounding forests.**
The conclusion reached by the council only makes sense if the charge actually has the intended effect. So it assumed that people will actually pay it rather than find ways to get around it. Hence Option c is the correct answer.

Option a: In fact, the council will almost be hoping that the charge does have some kind of financial impact on households so that residents are forced to take action to reduce the rubbish they throw away. So this cannot be an assumption made to reach the conclusion.

Option b: This may be what some people do but this is not an assumption that is needed for the conclusion to hold. There are other ways in which people may be able to throw away less rubbish, e.g. by recycling more or purchasing products with less packaging.

Option d: This does not need to be true for the new policy to work. The threat of a high charge may be sufficient to reach the desired effect whether or not people care about the environment.

Option e: If it were assumed that people could use landfill sites in other countries then it would make the policy ineffective.

**Q1.204 – d: The quality of the service rendered can be ignored when measuring productivity.**
The wording of the question is slightly complex as it is asking what the author is doubting the most. Therefore we are looking for the statement that is most likely to be incorrect. The author is essentially saying that it is all very well measuring numbers of patients, but is asking what the point of using such measures is if it means that whatever service is provided is of poor quality. As such he is objecting to the quality of the service being ignored and therefore Option d is correct.

Option a: The author is never questioning or implying that doctors are not representative of service workers in general. In reality, the fact that he is using them as an example suggests he may feel they are representative.

Option b: The various activities are only used as illustrations of a point. Whether they are the primary activities of a hospital is actually irrelevant to the argument.

Option c: Any argument opposing groups and single individuals would only be relevant if we were discussing a lack of representativity of the sample. But there is no issue with it here. In any case, this statement is the wrong way round because it is likely something the author would agree with rather than doubt.

Option e: The author is quoting the four-hour target as an example of what is being done. He gives no indication that he disagrees with that target in particular as being relevant. His only gripe is with the fact that other factors should also be taken into account.

**Q1.205 – d: For the past 5 years, a survey of language students has shown that most are put off applying to lecturer posts because, in the private sector, they can earn as much as a maths lecturer.**
The text seeks to demonstrate that the cuts are responsible for a shortage in the number of language lecturers. It explains this statement through two arguments:

1) The salaries of language lecturers have become lower than the salaries paid to lecturers in other disciplines.
2) Their working conditions have not improved, whereas their colleagues' have.

The question asks you to determine which of the options given would best support the claims made. This means that you must find which of the statements, if assumed to be true, would help you validate some or all of the claims made in the text.

Option a: The fact that students are put off applying for language courses because of a worsening of the lecturer-to-student ratio may well be a consequence of the shortage of lecturers. It does not, however, validate any of the arguments found in the text. It is an effect rather than a cause.

Option b: The fact that all current lecturers are happy with their working conditions and salary does not say anything about the reasons that caused the others to resign. For a start, those who decided to remain in their job are more likely to be happy about their pay and conditions than those who left; so they are a self-selected group and the survey is biased. In addition, it is perfectly possible that those who resigned might have been happy with their pay and working conditions, too, but resigned for other reasons, e.g. work-life balance.

Option c: The fact that all lecturers take up posts which are better paid is no indication of their reason for leaving their lecturer post (in fact, most people who leave any job would be moving into a better paid job). As well as disillusion, reasons for leaving could be geographical or wanting more responsibility. It may be that money is a driving factor, but it is not supported by that statement. The problem that language lecturers face is that their salary is lower than their colleagues', but not that it is lower than in the private sector. Indeed it is possible that, even with a 30% increase, their private sector salary is lower than the salary earned by a lecturer from a different field.

Option e makes it hard to draw any conclusions since the two reasons for leaving might not be mutually exclusive. It could be, for example, that the 20% who complained about a worsening of the working conditions were part of the 30% complaining about pay conditions, in which case we would only have a total of 30% of leavers falling into the category described in the text. The worst-case scenario would be 50% of disgruntled language lecturers for pay or working conditions reasons. This may not be the main cause of the shortage. We would need to know the reasons for leaving that the others invoked. Finally, note that the fact that people are leaving the profession does not mean that there is a shortage. If lecturers are replaced through a constant recruitment stream then, though maybe conditions are poor and pay is lower, this would not result in a shortage.

Option d approaches the problem from a different angle. It explains that there is a recruitment shortage due to the fact that those who study languages do not subsequently take up lecturer posts because, in the private sector, they can earn as much as lecturers from other fields. This would explain the shortage and validate the claims made about poorer pay because it offers a direct contrast between the pay of language lecturers and that of other teachers. Note that this option does not provide any support for the claim made about working conditions but, since it is the only option that actually strengthens any argument, it has to be the best option.

**Q1.206 – c: The distortion of reality present in medical dramas can exacerbate the anxiety experienced by hypochondriacs.**
In this question you are asked what can be safely inferred from the text. This means that you must gauge the validity of each statement solely in relation to the information contained within the text and nothing else.

Option a: Although it is clear that hypochondriacs would present with concerns that may be unjustified and that they, therefore, would be taking time that may be better spent dealing with patients with "real" problems, nothing in the text deals with the idea of "waste" of time. It is indeed a subjective judgement. In fact, one could argue that, since they have an abnormal anxiety, they do have a real problem to deal with.

Option b: The text only talks about the impact that medical dramas have on hypochondriacs who watch them, not about the proportion of viewers within the hypochondriac population and the rest of the population.

Option d is a bit trickier. The text suggests that the inaccuracies may make the problem worse, which may then imply that removing such inaccuracies could soften the impact of TV dramas on hypochondriacs. However, the use of the word "substantial" makes the option unsuitable since the text only mentions that the problem "is not helped" by the inaccuracies. That suggests that the bulk of the anxiety does not come from watching dramas. It is simply accentuated by them.

Option e cannot be concluded from the text since it does not mention anything about the origins of the condition. Indeed, there may be a combination of genetic and experiential factors.

Option c is the only one that is directly implied by the text.


**Q1.207 – c: Heart disease may affect employees in any business.**
The text states that "all employers can expect to have amongst their employees a non-negligible number of employees who suffer from one form or another of it".

Option a: All we know from the text is that those who have had a heart attack should avoid heavy and/or stressful work, but that does not mean that these are possible causes of a heart attack. It could be, for example, that those involved in stressful work tend to have bad dietary habits as a result of which they develop heart disease. The reason why stressful work should be avoided could be that those who have had a heart attack tend to tire more easily and suffer headaches when put under pressure. In essence, the fact that there is a link between the two does not necessarily mean that there is a cause and effect relationship.

Option b: We know that the majority of people (70%) are allowed to return to work, but we also know that there are conditions imposed with regard to the type of work they can and can't do. So we don't know if they actually do.

Option d: Nothing in the text suggests any link between heavy physical work and stress. They are presented as two separate issues.

Option e: Nothing in the text addresses the issue of age.

**Q1.208 – e: Using the foil-lined vest correctly reduces the level of radiation reaching the organs of a user in the body scanner.**
The main argument is that there are unknown health risks of the radiation given out by airport body scanners. However, the correct positioning of the special vest allows a potential reduction in the dose of radiation reaching the internal organs. Thus option e is correct.

Option a: All we know from the text is that there is no conclusive evidence that scanners have adverse effects in the short term. We know nothing about long-term health risks due to the radiation.

Option b: This statement is incorrect for two reasons. First it is unclear as to what "protected" actually means. Most people would infer that this means that it leads to a substantial if not total reduction in radiation reaching the body; however, the text only mentions a negligible to small reduction. Second, the statement does not differentiate between vests worn correctly and those worn incorrectly. The text implies that those who wear the vest incorrectly will only see a negligible reduction in radiation; as such it cannot be argued that those who wear the vest are protected.

Option c: The text says nothing about the way in which the vest works. It could equally work by absorbing the radiation.

Option d: The text says that the level of radiation reaching the organs varies depending on whether the vest is being worn correctly. What the author attempts to say here is that it is the manner in which the vest is worn which determines whether there is a reduction or not (in the text, the organs are considered collectively). The text does not imply that different organs may be affected in different ways.

**Q1.209 – c: Breakfasts eaten at home are usually unhealthy.**
The text implies that breakfast clubs are linked to a healthy breakfast, which in turn improves attendance and behaviour. This implies that breakfast clubs are able to provide something parents don't tend to provide: a healthy breakfast. Option c reflects that.

Option a might have been a possibility but the text makes a clear link with the healthiness of the breakfast rather than whether it is provided at all. It would be logical to assume that some children go to school without having eaten breakfast, but the text does not support this. Option c has a broader spectrum and therefore is more appropriate (in fact, if we consider that having no breakfast is similar to having an unhealthy breakfast, Option c encompasses Option a).

Option b might also be true but it highlights a flaw in the argument and is therefore not something that can be deduced from the text. The text does not raise any doubts about the healthiness of school breakfasts. This option might have been a possibility if the text had talked about the fact that some parents had objected to the purpose of breakfast clubs on the basis of quality. The only objection raised in the text is about who should take responsibility and not about the quality of the breakfast.

Option d is not supported by the text. All we know is that the creation of breakfast clubs is taking money away from educational resources, implying that fewer textbooks, for example, may be purchased as a result. We know nothing about the actual cost of textbooks.

Option e: The cost of breakfast to the school in relation to the cost to parents has no bearing on the argument. The argument relates solely to the fact that the breakfast money could be better used towards educational resources instead. The matter of parent responsibility refers to a moral responsibility rather than financial. The text does not deal directly or indirectly with the relative cost to both parties.

### Q1.210a – d: To make flag burning illegal is to criminalise what the flag represents.
The speaker maintains that to burn a flag is an act of freedom of speech and not an act of disrespect against the values of society. This, therefore, implies that it is not right to criminalise the act as this would infringe on freedom of expression. As such, Option d is the closest conclusion to the argument.

Option a states that those who served in the army care about flag burning. First, although the text mentions the fact that people have fought and died for the flag, this is not the main conclusion of the argument but an argument towards it (the conclusion of the argument being that burning the flag seems contradictory). Second, although we are told that some fought and died for the flag, this is not the same as saying that those who served in the army actually care about flag burning.

Option b: This option essentially states that flag burning is such a rare event that it isn't worth bothering about criminalising it. However, the argument in the text is based on the emotions of the people involved and the right to freedom of speech. It is not linked to the rarity of the event.

Option c: There is no mention of an election or of major disagreements with other political parties.

Option e: The text argues implicitly for decriminalisation, not criminalisation, in the UK.


**Q1.210b – a: The world's relevant authorities do not consider a physical action as being freedom of expression.**
If a physical action (such as flag burning) is not considered freedom of expression, then it weakens the argument that flag burning should be decriminalised on that account.

Option b: This argument is irrelevant since the discussion is on whether flag burning should be criminalised because of what it represents rather than as a preventive measure against other possible crimes.

Option c: In the context of the option, draping the flag in mud is done as part of a ceremony designed to mark respect. This does not justify doing it out of disrespect or hatred.

Option d: The author is in favour of flag burning because it represents freedom of expression. This statement does not weaken the conclusion because it does not address that issue in particular.


**Q1.211 – g: None of the above.**
Option a: This would only be true if the number of low-income earners was equal to the number of high-income earners, but it would not be true for any other split. For example, if there were:

- 100 low earners, 40% of whom smoked 40 cigarettes per day
- 10 high earners, 20% of whom smoked 20 cigarettes per day

the total number of cigarettes smoked by low earners would be 40% x 100 x 40 = 1600, whereas for high earners it would be 20% x 10 x 20 = 40 cigarettes, giving a ratio of 40.

Option b: All we know is that there are a greater proportion of smokers amongst low earners than amongst high earners. We cannot conclude anything without knowing absolute numbers.

Option c: The fact that people who earn less tend to smoke more cannot lead to conclude that those who smoke earn on average less. It would very much depend on the numbers included within each group. For example, consider the following data (low earners in grey):

| Salary (£ '000) | 10 | 14 | 50 | 60 | 70 | 80 | 90 | 100 | 100 | 200 |
|---|---|---|---|---|---|---|---|---|---|---|
| Smoke? | No | Yes | No | No | No | No | No | No | Yes | Yes |

The table has a 50% proportion of smokers in low incomes and 25% of smokers in high incomes. Average salary of smokers = £105. Average salary of non-smokers = £66. Much will, in fact, depend on the salaries and proportion of smokers at the high end of the high-earners group.

Option d: This is just speculation, which cannot be confirmed by the text. It may be that they are very aware but choose to ignore the knowledge they have, with the attitude that: "You might die by getting run over by a bus tomorrow, so you might as well enjoy your life."

Option e: Whether this is true or not, it cannot be drawn from the text.

Option f: This cannot be concluded from the text for two reasons: (i) we do not have absolute numbers, only proportions within each group and (ii) it is perfectly possible to consider that low earners may die of something else (e.g. heart disease) before they even get lung cancer.

**Q1.212 – c: The low fees charged by the audiology schools at Helina city are the primary reason why students from Bailey city move to these colleges.**
The author's argument is that an equalisation of fees will lead to Bailey city students preferring to study in Bailey city rather than moving to Helina city. The underlying assumption is that students in Bailey city currently go to Helina city to pursue their studies because school fees are cheaper there.

If the fees are equal, then the fee level will no longer be an incentive to travel to Helina unless Helina's colleges offered a superior level of education or there was a shortage of places in Bailey. If Helina offered superior education (Options a, b and d) then, with the fee level being equal, there is no reason to think that people would move back to Bailey; indeed they would remain in Helina to enjoy the education received there for the same price. The number of colleges on either side (Option e) is irrelevant; it would only matter if the number of places in Helina were to be cut.

**Q1.213 – d: Many people who are regarded as wise care more about their principles than about their economic status.**
The reviewer feels that wisdom and poverty are incompatible. He would therefore deduce that the book is wrong in one of two ways: either Lenin was richer than thought, or he was not wise. Option d is a good counterargument.

Option a is looking at the argument the wrong way round. The fact that rich people are usually wise does not imply that everyone who is wise has to become rich. It would merely imply that those who are not wise have a lesser chance of becoming rich. Option b is irrelevant as it confuses the concepts of influence and wealth. Option c is flawed because the notion of poverty would have been looked at in the context of the time when it happened and not the current context. Option e is also wrong because the fact that Lenin had wealthy friends on whom he depended does not mean he wasn't poor.

**Q1.214 – e: All of them**
The author says that since one of the buildings was not built until 1503 then Leonardo can't have started his painting before 1503. However, all we can deduce from that is that he did not finish it until after 1503. He could well have started painting it before and then added the building after 1503, once it had been built. Therefore the only way the author could draw that conclusion using the building is if the building was one of the first things he had painted; i.e. Statement 3.

The author also says that since Leonardo used a pigment which ceased to be produced after 1506 then he can't have finished the painting after 1506. However, there are two problems with that:

i.   It is perfectly possible that Leonardo bought a stock of that pigment, which then allowed him to continue using it well after it had ceased to be produced. Therefore the argument only holds if Leonardo had no stock left. Hence Statement 2 would strengthen the author's point.

ii.  It is possible that he did only use that pigment before 1506 but then did the rest of the painting using other, newer pigments, or using only some of the other pigments he already had that had not ceased to be produced. Therefore if we knew that most of the painting required the abandoned pigment, this would strengthen the author's case (Statement 1).

**Q1.215 – a: The fact that cows are mammals does not mean that cats are not mammals too.**
The author is saying that since hot winters can be followed by hot summers, then it is not true that cold winters are always followed by hot summers. All the author has found evidence for is that a hot summer can be preceded by either a cold or a hot winter. But it does not prove that a cold winter is not always followed by a hot summer.

That is equivalent to saying that if a cow is a mammal (if a hot winter is followed by a hot summer) then it doesn't mean that a cat cannot be a mammal too (a cold winter can't be followed by a hot summer too), which is Statement a.

All the author would need to do is find one single example where a cold winter was followed by a cold summer to disprove the claim. As such Statement d is incorrect on two counts: first, because a single example *would* be sufficient to disprove the claim and, second, because the author is choosing the wrong example anyway.

Statement e is also incorrect because the following winter is irrelevant. This statement deals with the sequence summer–winter, whereas we are interested in the winter–summer sequence.

Statement b would be equivalent to saying that if both a hot and a cold winter can lead to a hot summer then we cannot conclude that a hot winter is a cold winter. That is not what the author is saying.

Statement c is equivalent to saying that if we know that all hot winters lead to hot summers then we cannot conclude that a cold winter leads to a cold summer. This statement is incorrect on two counts. First, the author is not arguing that all hot winters lead to hot summers, but only that he has found some examples of it. Second, the author is not trying to prove that cold winters lead to cold summers anyway.

**Q1.216 – a: Make a subsidiary located in a high-tax rate country buy services from a subsidiary located in a low-tax country at a high price.** To be most effective, as much profit as possible needs to be taken out of high-tax countries and placed in low-tax countries. In effect this will mean that a subsidiary located in a high-tax country will need to be charged as much as possible by a subsidiary located in a low-tax country (Option a).

Note that Option e is also a possible candidate as it charges inflated fees to a subsidiary in a high-tax country. However, we are not told where the money is going. If it goes to another high-tax country, then it is pointless.

**Q1.217 – b: It has been many years since the hunting cap on snow rabbits has led to the hunting season for snow rabbits being closed earlier than the scheduled date.**
The author assumes that by dropping hunting restrictions for the snow rabbit, many more of them would be killed and they would pose less of a threat to Arctic birds. However, if the cap has not actually been reached for many years then it is effectively pointless; therefore removing it will have no effect at all.

All Option a does is explain that the restrictions were imposed to protect the rabbits and so we can conclude that those restrictions were successful in achieving their aim. From that, we might also infer that dropping the restriction would help cull more rabbits, but that supports the argument made by the author; it does not undermine it.

Option c could mean that the number of hunters has increased or that the overall number of rabbits has increased (hence the 5% quota has also increased with it). Either way, it doesn't undermine the fact that the removal of the 5% quota would allow the bird population to recover.

Option d just means that the rabbits have settled more substantially and so would argue in favour of a larger cull; hence it doesn't undermine the argument for the removal of the 5% quota.

Option e again points to the risk of an ever-expanding rabbit population and so it actually justifies the need for a larger cull if the birds are to be protected.

**Q1.218 – b: Major accidents on high-speed racetracks occurred at about the same rate between 1965 and 1980 as they did before 1965.**
If the rate of major accidents remained stable, then it would make it easier to measure the impact of the new safety features introduced on cars through the reduction in fatalities. This, in turn, would show an increase in longevity and therefore a gradual increase in the average age of drivers.

Important note: By itself a stable rate of major accidents would not be sufficient to help reach a conclusive answer as to whether the safety measures introduced helped reduce fatalities; it would merely be a helpful point. A decrease in fatalities could happen as a result of drivers simply becoming more cautious or if the track itself had been modified. However, the question is not asking for a conclusive statement; it is only asking for evidence that would be useful.

Option a would help explain an increase in the average age (most likely through high-risk-taking behaviour exhibited by the younger drivers) but would in no way be useful to support the fact that the safety measures had an impact.

Option c supports a lowering of the average age.

Option d is irrelevant to the debate.

Option e would explain a decrease in fatalities and therefore an increase in the average age but not the usefulness of the new in-car safety measures; in fact, if other safety measures were introduced to the track and the uniforms, it would make it harder to determine how much of an impact the in-car safety measures had.

**Q1.219 – c: Intestinal polyps cause a change in body chemistry that results in greater secretion of potassium.**
The researchers' recommendation is based on the assumption that low-potassium leads to the development of polyps and that, therefore, increasing the level of potassium should reduce the risk of polyps developing. However, if the polyps themselves actually increase the secretion of potassium by the body, then someone with polyps would not be expected to have a low level of potassium; increasing the level of potassium in the diet would not change much. The indication here is that the low level of potassium could be caused by something else altogether.

Option a has a degree of validity; however, it is not clear which compounds are difficult to digest.

Option b: The fact that polyps may disappear by themselves is irrelevant. First, it is not a guarantee; second, it does not mean that other means of action are not effective. But, most importantly, the researchers are trying to find ways to reduce the risk of polyps; letting them disappear may be a way of dealing with them once they are present, but not a way of preventing them.

Option d is incorrect because it refers to fresh vegetables not being available in all seasons whereas the text refers to green, leafy vegetables. Those may be available in frozen form. But even if they were not, it would still be possible to use dairy products whenever vegetables are not available.

Option e is irrelevant. The fact that the problem can be remedied by vitamin pills does not mean that the suggested approach is ineffective.

**Q1.220 – d: Drinking unhygienic tap water is the only way to get food poisoning.**
The text states that drinking unhygienic tap water always causes stomach infection or food poisoning. That does not mean that food poisoning cannot be caused by other things. Therefore, in order to conclude that Richard's food poisoning is caused by the water, one has to assume that unhygienic water is the only possible cause.

Option a serves to reinforce the possibility that the water may be the culprit; but it does not lead to the definite conclusion that the author draws. Option b might help link Richard's food poisoning to the water he recently drank but does not help reach a definite conclusion. Option c is irrelevant. Option e merely explains the reason why unhygienic water can cause food poisoning or stomach infection; it doesn't in any way exclude the fact that those can be caused by other things.

**Q1.221 – c: Most UK citizens who are not members of a company's pension scheme are discouraged to save for their retirement because the high-street banks' savings accounts offer poor interest rates.**
If the reason people do not invest in the long term is that high-street banks offer low rates on normal savings accounts, then the government's offer to pay a similar interest rate and make it non-taxable will be attractive and is likely to increase the amount people want to save.

Option a actually implies that people haven't got the means to save in the first place; so the new type of account will not encourage them to save.

Option b implies that many people are likely to withdraw the money before they reach the age of 60. It could be argued that if people have children late then they may be able to hold on to the money until they are over the age of 60. However, it is another assumption we need to make; and, in any case, the money would not be for the needs of the parents themselves, but for the children. So that would not really address the core issue of people saving for their long-term needs. At best this option is ambiguous and therefore not necessarily the strongest.

Option d indicates there may be a need for the new account or, on the contrary, that people simply have no money to invest.

Option e means that people are already saving their money. Creating a new tax-free account would mean they might transfer some of that money into it but it doesn't imply that it will increase the amount they save in the first place, which is what the Chancellor of the Exchequer is hoping to achieve (see first sentence).

**Q1.222 – c. Fresh grass clippings mixed into soil decompose rapidly, generating high levels of heat that kill beneficial soil bacteria.**
Option a: That would imply that wet grass may be better than dry grass, unless the wetness promotes toxic bacteria too and it cancels out. Either way, without further detail, it does not really help explain the difference.

Option b: If lawn fertilizer is present in dry grass then it will also inevitably be present in wet grass. So this does not help.

Option d is an observation but does not explain the difference in plant growth.

Option e would not explain why wet grass is harmful for growth and dry grass isn't.

**Q1.223 – c: The majority of professionals who eat lunch at their desk whilst working are overweight.**
Consider the following logic:

- Statement: "Most red shoes are Russian." If we looked at a large batch of red shoes and found that most of them were Russian then this would support the statement.
- However, if we looked at a batch of Russian shoes and found that most of them were red, all we could conclude is that most Russian shoes are red. That would not mean red shoes could not come from other countries as well.

Similarly here, the statement "Most people who eat at their desk become overweight" can be supported by taking a group of people who eat at their desk and seeing that a majority of them are overweight (Option c). However, if we take a group of overweight people and notice that they all eat at their desk, then all we can conclude is that most overweight people eat at their desk; there could equally be many thin people eating at their desk. Hence options a and e are incorrect.

Note, however, that Option c, though correct, is not sufficient to prove the point. Indeed we would also need to prove that people who eat properly do not get overweight. But it is something that can be used to support the point; whereas Options a and e contribute to a different point altogether.

Option b is irrelevant and Option d actually contradicts the point.


**Q1.224 – a: He contradicts himself.**
The author says that the fuel duty would raise £59 billion based on current consumption, which would just cover the deficit. However, in the next sentence he talks about the fact that the higher tax would reduce consumption, with environmental benefits. This therefore suggests the 1p increase will not be sufficient to cover the deficit, contradicting his first point.

Option b is incorrect because the text says clearly that the reduction in demand will be due to the higher tax (i.e. a financial consideration rather than an ethical one). So he is not assuming anything about people's feeling for the environment.

Option c is incorrect because nothing suggests that the data is incorrect. It is the application of that data which is incorrect.

Option d is incorrect because he is drawing the wrong conclusion about the effect but he is not mistaking it for a cause.

Option e is incorrect because, since the increase is the same for both types of fuels, we don't need to know the split in consumption to work out the total tax raised.


**Q1.225 – a: The Perez Hotel has five different entrances, which are used equally by all customers, whereas the other hotel has only two.**
For Durasin to argue that their carpets are more resistant, the comparison needs to be fair. If the Perez Hotel has five entrances that are used equally then each entrance's carpet will wear out more slowly than if the same number of people use only two entrances at the Oaxaca Hotel.

Option b is not relevant as the question is solely about the comparison between the current carpets in both hotels. The fact that the Durasin carpet currently in place is not the most durable in the range is not relevant.

Option c either makes no difference to the argument or actually strengthens the case. If the people going directly to the restaurant are in addition to the footfall that the passage mentions, then it makes no difference to the lifespan of the actual hotel's carpets mentioned in the text since we will still have the same footfall on both sides, allowing a direct comparison. However, if the people going directly to the restaurant at the Oaxaca Hotel are included in the footfall mentioned, then it means that the footfall in the Oaxaca Hotel itself is lower than at the Perez and therefore it reinforces the case that the carpet installed at the Oaxaca Hotel is weak (since it needs to be replaced earlier despite a lower footfall).

Option d is irrelevant as it does not deal with the two carpets that are being compared.

Option e, at worst, strengthens the message as it shows that Durasin carpet is hard-wearing.

**Q1.226 – c: The advantages afforded by integrated hands-free sets do not outweigh the risks of hazardous driving created by them.**
The author balances practicality and danger, and opts to ban hands-free sets because of the danger they pose. Therefore it is clear that, in his opinion, the benefits do not outweigh the risks.

Option a: The text does indeed talk about phones being popular because people can have easy access to them if they have had an accident. However, this is presented as an aside as opposed to a main benefit. And in any case, this is merely outlining a benefit of phones as opposed to backing up his opinion.

Option b and Option d may be correct but they are merely illustrations of what could make the driving hazardous and are pure speculation as to what the author might be thinking.

Option e merely ranks two benefits of hands-free phones. Not only can it not be deduced from the text but it also does not provide any clarification for the reasons behind his opinion.


**Q1.227 – b: A survey of readers shows that 95% of them regularly access online resources which deal with rare wild flowers.**
The argument is that mentioning rare wild flowers in the magazine leads to people collecting them from the wild and that avoiding that topic would help preserve rare wild flowers. However, since the vast majority of readers also regularly access other resources on the same topic, that policy is unlikely to yield much success unless those resources followed a similar policy too.

Option a only deals with new gardeners and points to the fact they get discouraged because of their lack of skills. That has nothing to do with the preservation of rare wild flowers.

Option c implies that, even when the demand for rare wild flowers is satisfied, there are still some left. All it really means is that the flowers are not so endangered that they will disappear altogether, but it does not mean that the policy will have a limited effect.

Option d is irrelevant.

Option e hints at the fact that there may be a way to make rare flowers less rare and it may be a good preservation tool. But it does not mean that the magazine's policy cannot have an impact on the demand for those flowers in the first place.


**Q1.228 – a: The hospitals reviewed by the book are likely to have been carefully selected to suit the argument.**
This criticism is the most likely because it is the only one that is actually relevant to the argument and is plausible. The author is trying to prove that the design of European hospitals is more complex than the design of American hospitals by using a sample of 25 hospitals on each side. Given that this is a small sample, it would be legitimate to suspect that those hospitals were picked to suit his purpose. Note that it may not be true but it is a legitimate concern.

Option b: This assertion is entirely correct, e.g. most people would probably rank quality of care above hospital design, but it does not directly criticise the argument the author makes. It simply introduces a different dimension.

Option c: This is a statement which implies that a bias against European healthcare would be more likely to make the author criticise the design of European hospitals. However, we can't actually work out from the text whether a simple design is a good thing or a bad thing. It could be a bad thing if it meant that many facilities were missing. Or it could be a good thing if it meant that it was easier to navigate. As such, Option c is a possible criticism but it doesn't directly address the logic of the argument and it could also be interpreted in several ways.

Option d: This statement may be true, but just like Option b it adds a different dimension to the debate (i.e. querying whether looking at design is the right thing to do in the first place) but does not actually criticise the arguments made by the author.

Option e: There are several problems with this option: (i) it narrows design down to aesthetics and so does not quite deal with the statement as a whole; (ii) it deals with the claim made but not with the way the author tries to prove his claim; and (iii) rather than a criticism it is merely explaining why the author may be thinking that way, which weakens it.

**Q1.229 – d: Burglar alarms tend to be installed in burglary-prone areas.**

The question invites us to find an explanation for the fact that, although burglar alarms are supposed to protect homeowners against burglaries, houses with an alarm tend to be burgled more than those without. Option d is a good explanation. In effect, what it helps conclude is that the rate of burglaries for houses with an alarm is lower than what it would be without an alarm, but not as low as it would be in an area that was less vulnerable and where an alarm therefore might not be needed.

A possible way of illustrating this point is as follows: imagine an area where people all have very expensive possessions (let's call it the "rich area") and another area where people have very few possessions (let's call it the "poor area"). In the rich area people would be burgled often and so would aim to install burglar alarms. In the poor area, people would not be burgled often and so would not bother with an alarm. Someone who lived in the rich area would aim to install an alarm to reduce the risk of burglary and therefore the insurance premium. But those living in the rich area still have a higher chance of being burgled than someone living in the poor area, who has nothing worth stealing.

Options a, b and c explain why burglar alarms may be ineffective but do not explain the higher burglary rate in houses with alarms.

Option e deals with the feelings of home owners, which are irrelevant in the context of the argument we are discussing.

**Q1.230 – d: Effectiveness is not the only criterion that should be considered when deciding whether to use Proxyform.**

The physician's argument is that Proxyform cannot be used simply because it may be effective but that cost and side effects should also be considered. Hence Option d is the best fit.

Option a: Although it would be true to say that the dilemma in question would mostly arise when the most effective drugs are also the most expensive (and therefore one might need to settle for a less effective but more affordable alternative), it is an assumption required to justify the fact that there is an issue in the first place, but it does not summarise the physician's point of view. In any case, it does not address the issue of side effects.

Option b is not actually demonstrated by the text since all we are told is that the drug has a degree of effectiveness but we don't know about the effectiveness of other drugs. In any case, it does not describe the issue fully since it ignores the dilemma of integrating costs and side effects into the equation. Option c also points to the effectiveness of the drug but not the dilemma that ensues.

Option e is not actually part of the argument, but it may be what is causing it. It is not, however, paraphrasing the issue as it is merely an assumption.

**Q1.231 – e: A different study shows that adults who watch no TV and behave aggressively towards others tend to choose programmes that contain a high level of violence when they are given the chance to watch TV.**
Option e says that those who are naturally violent tend to be attracted to violent programmes. Therefore if we take a group of people who watch violent programmes, there will be a sizeable number of people in that group who are violent, whereas in a group of people who watch non-violent programmes there may be comparatively fewer. Without proving anything categorically, Option e opens up the possibility that TV may not be causing the violence but that the group of people who opt for violent programmes is self-selecting. As such it undermines the author's conclusion.

Option a simply says that the level of violence varies between programmes and does not undermine or back up the author's conclusion.

Option b says that some people in the LVC group were exposed to no violence at all, which does not add anything to the debate.

Options c and d might be of social interest but are irrelevant to determine whether it is the TV that causes violence.

**Q1.232 – f: 2 and 3 only.**
Statement 1 can be excluded straight away because there is no indication in the text as to why the score was as low as it was when the Devils formation was used.

Statement 2: The ratio of points scored per minute played is:
60/54 for the Angels formation (which is >1) and 40/46 for the Devils formation (which is <1). Therefore Statement 2 is true.

Statement 3: Looking only at the period from the moment the first point was scored, the ratio for the Angels formation was 60/54 = 1.1 (no change since they scored from the beginning). We don't know exactly when the Devils formation's first point was scored in each match, but we know it was always in the second half. So the minimum ratio they can achieve is 40 / (46 x 0.5) = 1.7. That ratio is even higher if the first point in each match was later than half-time.

**Q1.233a – d: The agencies' ways of working were not flexible enough.**
One of the aims of the new recruitment programme is to promote a "flexible working culture" taking better account of childcare issues. This, therefore, suggests this was an issue before.

Option a is not correct. The lowering of the grade requirement is designed to cast the net wider so as to increase the number of women applicants and therefore women recruits. It is, in fact, very possible that most women had grades above 2:1 but that those women were put off applying because of childcare issues.

Option b is also incorrect. First of all, it is hard to define what is meant by 'male' skills without sounding remotely sexist. The only phrase in the text that may relate to male and female skills is the fact that the recruitment is meant to be emphasising more the "high emotional intelligence" issue. However, that does not mean it was not present before; it simply implies it should be highlighted more prominently, which is why Option e is also incorrect.

Option c is incorrect because nothing suggests that promotion was limited. The low percentage of women at senior level may be due to a low number of applicants (a fact supported, in part, by the fact that the recruitment process is not trying to select more women out of the normal bunch of applicants, but is trying to encourage more women to apply).

**Q1.233b – a: None of them.**
Statement 1: We are told that the target increased to 41% so it was lower before. The 4% drop refers to a drop in women recruits and has nothing to do with the target.

Statement 2: Before 2016, the target for MI5 was 46 – 5 = 41%. We know that the target for MI6 increased to 41% and so it was below that level before. Hence the target for MI5 was actually higher than for MI6.

Statement 3: The only figure we are given for GCHQ refers to the number of applications (40% of applications were from women) and not the actual recruitment target. Therefore we cannot conclude whether this statement is true or not.

**Q1.234 – d: A report commissioned by the local council observed that swerving could be avoided by reducing traffic on the bridge to one lane instead of the two lanes that are currently being used. This could safely be done as an interim measure for a few months.**
The main argument we are discussing is whether there is enough justification to close the bridge. Option d provides an indirect clue that it is possible to repair the bridge by reducing traffic to one of the two lanes on the bridge, allowing one lane to be repaired whilst the other one is being used for traffic.

Options a and b are both inconveniences that would result from the closure of the bridge. However, they are not reasons not to close the bridge. Indeed, if the bridge could not be closed for repair, it would become permanently unusable and the issue of congestion in the town centre and increased journey times would then become a lot worse.

Option c is irrelevant. If it is true then it simply means there will be less scope for repairs but the issue here is not whether or not the repairs are affordable (and for all we know they could be funded out of what is left of the budget anyway) but whether the bridge should be closed. The same logic applies to Option e.

**Q1.235 – e: Bronchodilators are the single most prescribed treatment for asthma.**
We know that bronchodilators account for roughly 50% of the prescriptions. We also know that inhaled steroids account for roughly 10% of prescriptions. Therefore, any other treatment could only account for a maximum of 100 – 50 – 10 = 40% of asthma-related prescriptions. Hence bronchodilators are the single most prescribed treatment for asthma.

Option a is not true because the text says that the move away from bronchodilators to inhalers is occurring for all but the mildest asthmatics. That indicates that inhalers are most effective for those who are not mild asthmatics.

Option b is incorrect because it peaked in 1995.

Option c: There are 10 million prescriptions, not asthma sufferers. There could be fewer than 10 million asthmatics if they each receive more than one prescription. Or there could be more if we consider that only those who are diagnosed are recorded in the statistics.

Option d: Nothing in the text provides any indication of the form in which bronchodilators are provided.

**Q1.236 – e: *Abacus* has lost 50% of its readers spread equally across all ages to a rival magazine written in a more fun fashion.**
There are two things that *Abacus* is trying to achieve: (i) increase its popularity with young readers and (ii) increase its number of subscribers. By switching to a new style of writing, *Abacus* may well gain more young readers but is at risk of losing the older ones. Option e indicates that the majority of the losses were likely due to using the wrong style of writing, and that this affects all ages equally, meaning in effect that the result of the young adult survey could equally apply to other readers. Hence Option e would reinforce the need for *Abacus*'s policy to switch to a new style.

Option a: That is probably true but there is no indication that *Abacus* is looking for an instant increase in readership.

Options b, c and d: There will always be exceptions to the rule. But the fact that *Abacus* may lose a handful of current readers by switching to a new style should not be a deterrent to introducing the change if they end up gaining more readers than they lost. In any case, these statements would weaken the case, not reinforce it.

Option f: If the majority of readers are young adults, any change of policy will have a big impact on the readership but we cannot predict what that impact is. All we know from the text is that some young adults find the old style uninteresting, but we are not told in what proportion. If, for example, *Abacus* had lost 10% of those readers because they preferred a more fun style of writing, they may well get those 10% back but lose the other 90% who preferred the more journalistic style.

**Q1.237 – c: Studies of Uttarakhand lake sediment cores provide conclusive evidence that there are only four factors that might cause Indian cities to be abandoned between 800 and 1000 AD: invading forces, internal revolts, disease and weather.**
Option c says there are only four ways for a city in that time period to be abandoned, but further evidence from the archaeologists in the paragraph itself show no reason to support abandonment due to invasion, revolt or disease. Thus, weather changes are the only possible cause. This most strongly supports the archaeologists' theory.

Option a states that neither warfare nor revolt result in abandonment of the cities, thus leaving disease and drought as possible causes of depopulation. This strengthens the argument somewhat, but not as much as Option c.

Option b only proves that the cities were abandoned (assuming that, as cities are abandoned, no inscription can subsequently be made), but does not help define the reasons behind it.

Option d says that there is drought happening but we cannot directly link it to the abandonment of the city.

Option e only deals with one city and does not provide information about the causes of the abandonment.

**Q1.238 – d: The author makes no distinction between coincidence and causality.**
The author links the violence to freakish weather conditions by noting the timeline of violent behaviour, then noting the weather conditions at the time, and then trying to link the two. But the initial link between the violent behaviours and the weather itself may be due to coincidence; hence Option d is the best description of the flaw.

Option a: A degree of evidence is presented. The text quotes several studies with regard to weather pattern, for example, and states conclusively that grain can cause ergotism – a fact that seems to come from a reliable source since the author is normally open about areas where he speculates (e.g. use of "most likely" in the conclusion) but is quite categorical here. So Option a is, at best, ambiguous and not as clear-cut as Option d.

Option b: There are clear links drawn between cause and effect in the plausible theories, but it is association of weather patterns with violence that is incorrect. The author is jumping to conclusions.

Option c is just a judgement on historical speculation but does not highlight a particular flaw in the rationale proposed by the author.

Option e does not actually matter.

**Q1.239 – b: Add more weight to Arnie's argument that the number of flights should be reduced.**
Clara's statement offers another argument to reduce the number of commercial flights: this time on the basis that they are heavy polluters. Note that Arnie and Clara seem to hint at the same solution but using slightly different points of focus since Arnie focuses on carbon dioxide emissions specifically whilst Clara focuses more broadly on the issue of pollution, which could be caused by carbon dioxide, though not exclusively (which is why Option d is not correct).

Option a is incorrect because Clara does not offer an alternative solution. Both point towards the need to reduce the number of commercial flights.

Options c and e are incorrect since Clara does not question anything but merely adds an example to the debate, pointing in the same direction as Arnie.

**Q1.240 – e: That all job applicants who were rejected had fewer qualifications than those who were given a job.**
As explained by the trade union representative, sexual discrimination is the fact that women (or men) are denied a job because of their gender. The fact that most employees are men does not necessarily mean that discrimination has taken place; it is very possible some sectors only attract men or women (e.g. most builders are men but most journalists are women). So, in order to demonstrate or refute discrimination on the basis of gender, one would need to look at whether applicants have been considered fairly during the recruitment process. Option e would show that all those who were rejected were less qualified, which would be a non-gender discriminatory process.

Option a does not exclude the fact that some women with the same or higher level of qualification might have been excluded during the recruitment process.

Option b focuses on pay equality, which is a different issue to the one raised in the text (which is about recruitment).

Option c might be a reasonable explanation as to why there are only 7 women out of 70 managers, i.e. the ratio of men to women within the company reflects the ratio of men to women amongst applicants. This would be valid if one could prove that all applicants had a similar profile; however, that does not prove that women were not discriminated against. Indeed, one could envisage a situation where all women who applied were better qualified than men and where, therefore, they would secure all the jobs within the company.

Option d explains why some women may be more reluctant to apply for the job, but that does not deal with single women who have no children, or women in general who are better qualified than men and have still been discriminated against.

### Q1.241 – b: That they only aim to punish and not prevent.
That section of the public is quite happy for people to go to jail but does not really want to deal with the aftermath in any way that could see a lower reoffending rate. Therefore Option b is a good fit.

Option a would also be a good candidate but it is a lot broader. The fact that people are rejecting the proposed idea does not mean that they are not interested in prevention through other means.

The other options are not supported by the text as they deal either with emotions, which do not appear to be a driver for the public reaction, or with money, which is also not an argument involved in their decision to oppose the plan.

### Q1.242 – b: Migraines start well before the person can feel it. Those who develop a migraine tend to crave sweet foods before they can feel the migraine.
If migraines give people a craving for sweet food, then that would explain why they eat chocolate before the migraine kicks in properly. In effect, the

chocolate craving is a sign that a migraine is coming rather than its cause. Therefore it weakens the argument that people should stop eating chocolate.

Option a: If chocolate contains caffeine, then all we know is that this may be a possible explanation for the fact that chocolate causes migraines. It does not weaken the argument.

Options c and e: The fact people develop migraines without ever eating chocolate does not mean that chocolate cannot cause migraines.

Option d points to the fact that it may be the coffee rather than the chocolate which could cause the issue. Therefore it raises the prospect that the chocolate may not always be the culprit. However, this is far more speculative than Option b, and it also does not explain how this relates specifically to people who get migraines. Therefore it would not be the option that weakens the argument the most.

**Q1.243 – d: Some natural substances used in food can be harmful.**
The company claims that the fact they only use natural ingredients implies their food is safe. That claim would be compromised if it were true that some natural ingredients can also be harmful. The fact that artificial ingredients can be harmful does not in any way imply that anything that is not artificial is safe.

Option a: This backs the company's position that natural foods are safe.

Option b: This is irrelevant here since we are trying to assess whether natural foods are safe or not.

Option c: This is irrelevant as it deals with flavour and not health.

Option e: This is exactly the reason why the company is trying to convince people that their food is safe.

**Q1.244 – c: The fruit can only be used in salads.**
The passage mentions salads as a possible way of eating the new fruit. There is no assumption that this is the only way. The focus is on the sourness of the fruit rather than its use.

Option a: The text says that removing the sour taste will make it acceptable to American tastes, hence why, since the introduction of the new sour taste removal technique, they have started to grow it. That assumes there is nothing else which may prevent its acceptability.

Option b: If the fruit is intended to be marketed as a source of vitamin C, if a method has been found to make it less sour and production has started, one can only assume that there is a market for it.

Option d: If the new process removed a significant part of the vitamin C content then the fruit would lose its marketability factor. So it can be safely assumed that is not the case.

Option e: No one would go to such trouble if Americans ate sour foods readily.

**Q1.245 – a: The flute seems to be made from a bear's femur bone which would have been long enough to make the flute capable of playing a complete diatonic scale of seven notes.**
If this is true then it means Homo sapiens could well have been in possession of a flute that could play the diatonic scale. There is no certainty about it, but it is the statement which most supports that fact.

Options b and e: This basically tells us that there is no other evidence available, so it cannot support the belief that Homo sapiens discovered the diatonic scale or even played music. So those statements may, in fact, weaken the case.

Options c and d are not relevant to determine whether Homo sapiens discovered the diatonic scale. They add nothing in terms of proof.

**Q1.246 – b: The higher the quality of the wooden frames, the less likely they are to fall into disrepair and the less likely the building is to be demolished or abandoned.**
The author says that his observations are based on his travels this year. Therefore he will only have had a chance to test the hotels that are still standing. If the above sentence is true, then he will have seen the best of the pre-1940 buildings (i.e. those that have not collapsed yet) but a mix of

good and bad from the post-1940 era). Therefore this introduces a bias in his observations and weakens his conclusion.

Option a: The fact that, post 1940, carpenters had to work faster (and therefore possibly cut corners as is implied here) would back the author's opinion that post-1940 buildings were not as well built.

Option c: The newer hotels being bigger does not necessarily imply anything either way with regard to the quality of the work.

Option d: The duration of apprenticeships does not reflect the quality of the learning during that time.

Option e: If the quality of the materials was the same pre-and post-1940 then the author is right. The difference could be due to poorer craftsmanship. So this does not weaken the argument.


**Q1.247 – b: Planes use air corridors, which are similar to train tracks and can only link one airport to another, with airports not being as conveniently located as train stations.**
The author argues that planes are more convenient because they can go anywhere and are just as fast as HS2 trains. If, however, they can be compared to trains because they can actually only go where there is an airport (station), they have to stick to air corridors (train tracks) and they travel just as fast but the airports are not as conveniently located as train stations, then it takes away their appeal. Hence Option b weakens the argument.

Option a: The argument is about whether the government should have developed air travel instead of trains. It has nothing to do with cars or buses.

Option c: The method of driving is irrelevant as the argument we are trying to weaken is that cars, buses and planes can take you anywhere whereas trains can't.

Options d and e would back the author's argument rather than weaken it.

**Q1.248 – d: The local police station has been closed and people who wish to report a non-serious crime need to travel 5 miles along a busy road to reach the next available police station.**
The councillor's argument is that burglaries have reduced as a percentage of the population but have gone up in absolute numbers because the population has increased. If the police station where it's necessary to report non-serious crimes has moved to a place it is harder for the population to travel to then the number of burglaries is underreported. So it means that the number of burglaries is even higher than it appears.

Option a: The fact that the rate of burglaries is higher amongst the elderly and lower amongst younger people does not help us conclude anything about the trend over the whole population and does not weaken the councillor's argument.

Option b: If people are now more likely to report burglaries, that would explain why the number of burglaries appears to have increased and it would, in fact, weaken Mrs Khan's argument that the increase is due to poor policing. However, it strengthens the councillor's argument because if part of the increase in the number of burglaries is due to better reporting, but the burglary rate has gone down, then it means the police are doing an even better job than it looks because they have managed to lower the rate of burglaries despite being swamped by more reports.

Option c is pointless because it does not address the impact the recruits may have on burglaries.

Option e does not help us draw any conclusions about decreasing non-serious crime rates.

**Q1.249 – b: For the past 5 years, commercial fishermen have been using sonar equipment enabling them to locate lobsters with great accuracy.**
If commercial fishermen use sonar equipment to locate lobsters then they will be placing their traps in locations where they are likely to catch a large number of lobsters; whereas, in the past, they might have placed traps in locations where there were no lobsters at all. If, despite the increased probability of catching lobsters, the LPT remains the same, then it actually suggests that the lobster population has decreased and so it weakens the argument.

Option a: The text compares the LPT today with the LPT 15 years ago. Intermediate values of the LPT have no effect whatsoever on the conclusion that the lobster population has remained the same.

Option c: If this is true, it tells us nothing about the current lobster population, which could have replenished itself (or not) to the same level as 15 years ago.

Option d: If the number of traps has remained constant then it might actually strengthen the conclusion that the population of lobsters is the same now as it was 15 years ago as it means the sampling methods are similar.

Option e: If demand has dropped this may imply that fewer traps are laid to catch lobsters. However, that would not affect the LPT, which is calculated as an average caught per trap. Fewer traps and fewer lobsters caught would result in a similar LPT but would give no indication about the number of lobsters available.

### Q1.250 – d: 1 or 3.
The aim of the marketing campaign was to entice people away from competing fitness centres, and not simply to increase membership. So the marketing campaign will only be a success if we can find out how many of those who joined have come from competing fitness centres. All we have been given in the text is the number of new members and the fact they represent an increase of 20% on the membership before the marketing campaign was implemented.

Statement 1: If we know the number of people who have just joined Moving It and have never visited another local fitness club before then we know that the difference between that number and the 100 new joiners have visited a local fitness club before. Therefore that will give us the indication we need to determine how many people were enticed to join from competing fitness centres.

Statement 2: This will only give an idea of the percentage of people who have left rival clubs but without the possibility of ascertaining how many then joined Moving It. Besides, knowing the percentage without knowing the total membership of rival clubs is a pointless figure.

Statement 3: That would be the most direct measure.

Therefore we only need 1 or 3.

**Q1.251 – b: It fails to consider that atorvastatin may reduce the risk of heart disease but not as a consequence of its lowering cholesterol levels.**
The author implies that high cholesterol is a cause of heart disease, hence lowering its level would also lower the risk of heart disease. However, the text only states that it is the atorvastatin which reduces the risk of heart disease, and not the lowering of the level of cholesterol. The two could be happening separately. Hence Option b is highlighting the flaw of the argument.

Option a: The argument does not revolve around side effects. The only side effect that would be of interest would be the fact that it lowers the risk of heart disease, but that is not something one would call "severe".

Option c: The author does use data from a recent study.

Option d: In actual fact the author does state that atorvastatin does decrease cholesterol levels and then extrapolates that by saying that lowered cholesterol reduces heart disease.

Option e is irrelevant.


**Q1.252 – d: Most of the projected increase in the number of passengers is expected to occur at off-peak times when hardly anyone uses the Tube.**
In this question what we are asked to find is the argument that would allow us to make sense of what seems to be a paradox, i.e. what would enable the Tube to cope with a 25% increase in passengers with only an 8% increase in capacity. One possible answer is that some of the additional journeys will be absorbed by spare capacity in the system and Option d provides an opportunity for that to happen. If most of the projected increase in passengers is at off-peak times when there is spare capacity, then the Tube may only need to create a smaller percentage of additional capacity to be able to cope.

Option a: The issue is not cost. It is whether the additional planned capacity is sufficient. This option does not provide a reason for believing that the system could cope with the additional capacity if it was increased by 8%.

Option b: Similarly to Option a, this deals with costs and not the difference between the planned increase in capacity of 8% and the planned increase in passengers of 25%.

Option c: This actually suggests that those who are using the Tube and contribute to the overcrowding will have no choice but to continue to use the Tube. If alternative modes of transport were available, then some passengers may have stopped using the Tube altogether and this could have helped bring down the 25% predicted increase.

Option e: Increasing the number of bus routes that link to Tube stations could either encourage passengers to use the bus for part of their journey, or could bring more passengers into the Tube. So this cannot be a justification.

**Q1.253 – b: There are more calories in one pear than in one apple.**
If we call each fruit by its initial, the text gives us: A>O and P>M.
We want to find the options that enable us to conclude that A>M.

Option a: If A = P: since P>M, then (P=A)>M.
Option c: If O=P: since A>O and P>M then we can write A>(O=P)>M.
Option d: If O>M: since A>O then A>O>M.
Option e: If O>P: since A>O and P>M then A>O>P>M.

**Q1.254 – c: Relative brain size is a better indicator of intelligence than absolute brain size.**
The text talks about the fact that the level of intelligence is linked to how the size of the brain compares to the size of the body.

Option a cannot be deduced because corvids are only given as an example of intelligent birds. The text does not deal with other types and nor does it compare corvids to other birds.

Option b: Creating tools is certainly given as an indication that an animal may be intelligent but there is no hint that there is a scale on which this can be measured to define intelligence.

Options d and e are incorrect as they both deal with absolute sizes.

**Q1.255 – e: The percentage of high achievers in science, sport, theatre and music who are left-handed is well over 10%.**
The fact that amongst high achievers there is a higher proportion than expected of left-handed people weakens the fact that they should be considered as having a disability.

Options a and b do not reinforce or weaken the argument. They are simply facts that would represent a burden to left-handed people.

Options c and d tend to strengthen the conclusion that left-handed people suffer from a disability.

**Q1.256 – e: None of the above.**
Option a: All we know is that people who work in those places are underpaid and work in boring jobs. But that does not mean that a boring job is always underpaid. One does not have to cause the other.

Option b: This is incorrect for the same reason as Option a.

Option c may well be true but it is not something we can conclude from the text. The link between levels of pay and social class is not necessarily automatic (e.g. it is possible that fast food outlets employ mainly students from all social classes on short-term contracts whereas factories may employ people from a particular social class on longer contracts).

Option d is incorrect because the text talks about the type of work and about remuneration without actually comparing physical working conditions. The only mention of working conditions is in the fact that workers cannot complain about them, but it does not mean they are the same.

**Q1.257 – d: The health improvements noted by surveys are in medical fields where online sources match medical advice.**
The text argues that, since people tend to take information from online sources and their health has improved, there must be a cause and effect relationship between the two and therefore formal medical advice is pretty much pointless. However, if it were true that health improvements were noted in the fields where the online advice and the medical advice matched then it would indicate that, in those fields, people can be safe listening to either source of advice, but that, in the other fields, people's health has not

improved when people switched to online rather than formal medical advice. Hence this weakens the argument.

Options a, b and e explain why people might switch off from medical advice but it does not help with the conclusion of the text that people are better off switching to online resources if they want better health.

Option c also explains why people may want to gain more control over their health but does not address the issue of actual improvement in health and well-being.


**Q1.258 – b: 1 and 4.**
Each statement can be worded as follows:
Statement 1: Number of taxis is greater than or equal to number of buses.
Statement 2: Number of taxis is lower than or equal to number of buses.
Statement 3: Number of taxis is strictly lower than number of buses.
Statement 4: Number of taxis is greater than or equal to number of buses.


**Q1.259 – c: Speaking another language to improve one's chances in life is not a new consideration.**
We are told that, for hundreds of years, people have needed to know at least one extra language to be able to trade so the concept of multilingualism is not new if one wants to improve one's chances in life.

Option a: All we know is that English is the most commonly spoken language but that will include people who only speak English and may not be multilingual. So we cannot conclude from such a statement that most multilingual people speak English.

Option b: There is no indication this may happen.

Option d: There is no mention in the text of travellers.

Option e: Social media is not hinted at or mentioned, so this is pure speculation.

**Q1.260 – c: It attacks the owner's motives rather than the reasons.**
The author does not actually seek to examine whether the owner may have a point. He simply criticises her motives, which is an entirely different point. In other words, it may be a publicity stunt but it does not mean that the owner does not have a valid point. The author's argument would only make sense if he sought to counter the owner's arguments directly; for example by demonstrating the meat may be lean but actually high in cholesterol

Option a is actually incorrect since the author says he does not know whether the species is protected.

Option b is incorrect because neither the owner nor the author actually raises the issue of sustainability. That would be a relevant issue if we were told that the dish was very popular but all we know is that it is on the menu.

Option d is incorrect because if puffins don't have natural predators then that might make it more acceptable to eat them since the population would grow in size in a possibly uncontrollable manner. As such, it may justify the owner's stance but it does not contradict the argument that this is all a publicity stunt.

Option e: Whether animals are worth eating is not a debate that depends on how damaging they might be. And, in any case, it does not address the discrepancy between the two opinions.

**Q1.261 – b: The statistic quoted is not representative of the whole population.**
The statistic is only for Londoners whereas the conclusion is to invest nationwide.

Option a: Since the conclusion does not specify whether the investment should be in buses or trains, then the fact the survey does not do so is not a major flaw. For a similar reason, Option d is also incorrect.

Option c: The reason for the remaining 25% to continue using the car is irrelevant. It does not take away the impact the investment will have on the remaining 75%. For a similar reason Option e is irrelevant.

**Q1.262 – b: It confuses a correlation with a cause.**
A correlation is when there may be an external factor that links everything up. For example, it is possible that most FTSE 100 chief executives are people who are in their 50s and that, at the time they were born, many boys were called David, Paul or Kevin because it was the fashion at the time.

Note that it might have been tempting to answer Option e: It generalises from anecdotal evidence. However, there is a difference between generalisation and confusing a correlation with a cause.

Generalisation is simply transferring a concept to a larger group of people. So, for example, a generalisation would be that 25% of CEOs of all companies are called David.

Here the situation is slightly different because the argument is actually that it is the name which leads to success. So there is an additional element of flawed logic, which lies in the way the different items of data are connected.

**Q1.263 – b: 4-year degrees will be a condensed version of the same content as 5-year degrees.**
The author is basically arguing that it is already a struggle to make the 5-year degree work and so a 4-year degree will be even more problematic. For the argument to work, we need to assume that the content of the two degrees is the same. If it isn't (e.g. if it is easier or it teaches a reduced but carefully selected syllabus) then this may not be such a problem.

Option a is not actually a necessary assumption since all we need to know is that students are lacking the relevant knowledge. Why they are lacking it is irrelevant to the argument.

Option c is irrelevant to the argument since it is not about application ratios or the difficulties of getting into medicine.

Option d is irrelevant since student preferences do not impact in any way on making a 4-year degree work.

Option e simply reinforces the argument but it is not a necessary assumption. What it tells us is that students are not as educated now as they were 30 years ago at the same stage. Even if biology was simply just as important as before (instead of more important), that would still be a problem.

**Q1.264 – c: In countries where such images are displayed, tobacco is highly taxed and there is a ban on tobacco advertising.**
The argument is that bad pictures put people off in some countries and therefore the idea should be extended to other countries. But if those countries have high tobacco taxes and ban advertising then it is possible that the reduction in smoking is due to those factors rather than the bad pictures. Or at least it could be argued that the effect of bad pictures may only be minor and therefore adopting such policy in countries where taxes are low and advertising is permitted may not have the same impact.

Option a is irrelevant to the argument.

Option b may mean that governments may be reluctant to introduce such policy but it does not mean that the policy does not make sense.

Option d reinforces the point.

Option e shows that people are quitting "proper" smoking in favour of e-smoking but that does not weaken the fact that pictures would help.


**Q1.265 – e: The increase in the number of apartments available would exceed the number of new potential tenants.**
The argument relies on the fact that "potential tenants will have a greater selection". So, that assumes that the number of apartments available for each potential tenant will increase and therefore that the number of apartments available will increase at a higher rate than the number of potential tenants.

Option a: The argument is about supply and demand for apartments in the long term and has nothing to do with the immediate needs of current residents.

Option b is merely philosophical and does not impact on the argument.

Option c: This is not an assumption since the whole point is that, in the long term, this should lead to increased availability and therefore lower prices and so may benefit everyone. It is possible that things will pan out in such a way that only current owners may benefit but (i) it is a "may" and not an "only" and (ii) this would be a consequence rather than an assumption.

Option d is irrelevant to the supply and demand argument.

**Q1.266 – d: There are many strains of the cold virus (new ones are, in fact, found every year), and children develop resistance to individual strains.**
The theory is that, through repeated exposure, children become resistant to colds. However, if there are several strains and new ones keep appearing they are unlikely to get much repeated exposure to the same strain and so this weakens the theory.

Options a and b are irrelevant.

Option c: This deals with the alleviation of a symptom but not the fact that they catch a cold in the first place.

Option e: This supports the theory instead of weakening it.

**Q1.267 – c: Locke's contributions to the development of European thought have been greatly exaggerated.**
The author argues that much of Locke's work was copied from others and that the others are not being recognised. As such he is arguing that Locke's contribution has been exaggerated. Option d would be a suitable option too but it goes one step further in the judgement we can bear on the text and cannot be argued to be a direct conclusion we can draw from the text. It may end up being a consequence at some stage.

Option a is restating a fact and, as such, is not really a conclusion. In any case, it is unclear from the text as to whether Locke had acknowledged his sources or not.

Option b is incorrect because all we can deduce is that the author is re-evaluating Locke's work. The only mention of current historians is in relation to the fact they are neglecting Locke's predecessors.

Option e is not addressed in the passage.

**Q1.268 – b: 1 only**
*Statement 1: If a house does not have a large bay window then it does not have a view onto the park.*

This is true since we know that all houses with a view on the park have large bay windows. This illustrates the most fundamental rule of logic you need to know for the BMAT, which is that:

> If A implies B then (not A) implies (not B)

And so in this case:

> (House with a view) implies (large bay window)
> therefore
> (No large bay window) implies (house with no view)

*Statement 2: If a house has a white bay window then it has a view onto the park.*
The fact that all houses with a view onto the park have white or brown windows does not mean that there can't be houses elsewhere which use the same colours. So this is false.

*Statement 3: If a house does not have a view onto the park, then it does not have a large bay window.*
The fact that all houses on the park have a large bay window does not mean there can't be houses elsewhere with large bay windows too. So this statement is false.

*Statement 4: If a house does not have a view onto the park, then it has a large bay window but that bay window can be of a different colour than white or brown.*
Similarly to Statement 3, we cannot reach any conclusion with regard to houses with no view on the park. They may or may not have large bay windows.

**Q1.269 – c: Set up a programme of preventive maintenance for major pieces of machinery recently ordered and delivered.**
The motto essentially means that there is no point dealing with a problem unless it has come to light. All of the options entail dealing with a current problem, except Option c, which is "preventive".

**Q1.270 – b: The expansion of health insurance services to those below the poverty line will not address health problems caused by substandard housing.**
The issue is caused both by lack of preventative care (due to lack of insurance) and by substandard housing. The author argues that expanding health insurance will increase life expectancy, but without addressing the issue of substandard housing this may prove pointless if they are still exposed to harmful substances. For example, there is no point in encouraging people to take statins to reduce the risk of heart disease if they are going to die of respiratory problems linked to asbestos at the age of 50 anyway.

Option a is not that much of a flaw with regard to the argument that health insurance should be expanded. It merely raises a question as to how cost-effective this will be. It would be a flaw if it hinted that it may not be cost-effective, but that is not the case.

Option c does not actually address the argument, which is about preventative medicine rather than treatment. If anything, it strengthens the case for preventative medicine.

Option d focuses on the wrong point. It does not actually matter what the exact number of people below the poverty line is as long as the investment made to deal with their issues is cost-effective.

Option e is irrelevant because the author deals with the expansion of health insurance rather than the housing issue.

# Section 2

# Scientific
# Knowledge
# & Applications

# 302
## Practice Questions
## & Answers

# 2A Scientific Knowledge and Applications Introduction & Advice

## Format of Section 2 of the BMAT

Section 2 of the BMAT, "Scientific Knowledge and Applications", consists of 27 questions, which you must answer within 30 minutes. This gives you just over one minute per question.

The questions can be in a multiple-choice format – you are typically given four to six options to choose from – but some questions can be in a short answer format, meaning that you must write down the answer in the box provided, without being able to choose from a given list of options.

This section draws upon your knowledge of Biology, Physics, Chemistry and Mathematics and tests your ability to apply scientific knowledge up to and including National Curriculum Key Stage 4. You will find, however, that, in order to differentiate between candidates, some questions may appear to be more stretching as they require candidates to demonstrate an ability to apply their knowledge rather than simply demonstrate that they have assimilated the GCSE syllabus.

The allocation of questions between topics is typically as follows:

- Biology: 7 questions
- Physics: 7 questions
- Chemistry: 7 questions
- Mathematics: 6 questions

The allocation varies from year to year (+/- 1).

## Revision and practice

Section 2 of the BMAT requires a good knowledge and understanding of a wide range of topics. The first step in your preparation is therefore to ensure that you are totally secure in your knowledge of science and mathematics at GCSE level; as such, revising from your textbooks will prove invaluable.

More importantly, many of the exercises test your understanding of that knowledge and how it can be applied to concrete situations. Practising answering hundreds of questions will help you achieve that.

In this section of the book we have set out 302 questions. This is equivalent to 10 exams and will give you all the practice you need.

| Section | No of exercises* | No of questions | Questions Page | Answers Page |
|---|---|---|---|---|
| Biology | 60 | 68 | 372 | 479 |
| Physics | 80 | 82 | 398 | 499 |
| Chemistry | 61 | 66 | 429 | 522 |
| Mathematics | 86 | 86 | 451 | 541 |

(*) Some exercises contain several questions

# Important tips

- Although you are allowed 1 minute per question, aim for a shorter time so that you have time to review your answers. If you feel that a question may take you a long time, skip it and go back to it. The test is paper-based so that is easily done.

- Every question carries the same weight and you can answer them in any order. Start with your strong topics and leave the difficult ones until the end.

- On the day of the exam, you will not be allowed to use a calculator. If a question looks as if it may require a lot of calculations, look for a more "clever" alternative; see if you can simplify the problem.

- If you are stuck, try to eliminate some obvious wrong answers and guess amongst the remaining options. This is easier if the options given are far apart and you have some idea of the order of magnitude.

## 2B Scientific Knowledge and Applications
## Biology – 68 Questions

### Answers from page 479

**Q2.1** The diagram below applies to questions Q2.1a and Q2.1b. It shows the genetic inheritance of Achondroplasia in a family pedigree. Achondroplasia results in dwarfism.

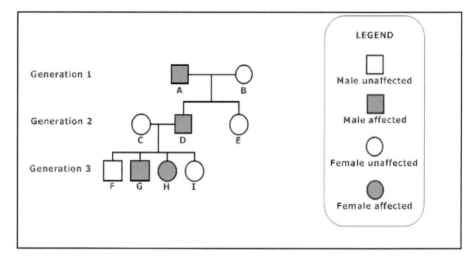

**Q2.1a** What is the pattern of inheritance for Achondroplasia?

    **a.** Autosomal dominant
    **b.** Autosomal recessive
    **c.** X-linked dominant
    **d.** X-linked recessive

**Q2.1b** Which individuals must be heterozygous for Achondroplasia?

    **a.** A and D
    **b.** A and B
    **c.** D and E
    **d.** C and H
    **e.** B and C

**Q2.2** Colour blindness is an X-linked recessive trait. A woman who is a carrier for the trait has two boys with a colour-blind man.

**Q2.2a** Assuming the boys' births are independent, what is the probability that both boys are colour-blind?

    a.  0%
    b.  25%
    c.  50%
    d.  75%
    e.  100%

**Q2.2b** If they have two further daughters born to the family, who are now 3 and 5 years old respectively, what is the probability that both girls are carriers?

    a.  0%
    b.  25%
    c.  50%
    d.  75%
    e.  100%

**Q2.3** Sickle cell anaemia is an autosomal recessive disorder. A male with the disease, and a female who is not diseased but carries the trait, produce two girls.

What is the probability that neither girl's genotype contains the sickle cell allele?

    **a.**  0%
    **b.**  12.5%
    **c.**  25%
    **d.**  66%
    **e.**  100%

**Q2.4** The diagram below shows the genetic inheritance of haemophilia in a family pedigree. Haemophilia is a sex-linked recessive disease. $X^H$ is the normal allele and $X^h$ is the haemophilia allele.

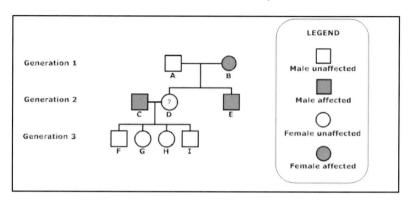

What is the genotype of the female marked D?

a. $X^HX^h$
b. $X^HX^H$
c. $X^hX^h$
d. $X^HY$
e. $X^hY$

**Q2.5** The human genome is formed of DNA comprising four different nucleotides (adenine, guanine, cytosine and thymine). A codon, or triplet repeat, is a string of three nucleotides, which are read together to encode an amino acid. Up to 64 different permutations of codon can exist; however, only 20 different amino acids are encoded. This is because an amino acid can be encoded by more than one codon, e.g. valine is coded by both 'GTG' and 'GTT'.

What property of the genetic coding does this represent?

a. The genetic code is degenerate
b. The genetic code is unambiguous
c. The genetic code is non-overlapping
d. The genetic code is universal
e. None of the above

**Q2.6** In English roses, the allele for red petals (R) is dominant to the allele for white petals (r), and the allele for large thorns (T) is dominant to the allele for small thorns (t). When a rose of unknown genotype is crossed against a white rose that has small thorns, the phenotypic ratio is as follows:

- 25% Red petals, Large thorns
- 25% Red petals, Small thorns
- 25% White petals, Large thorns
- 25% White petals, Small thorns

What is the genotype of the unknown parent?

a. RrTT
b. rrTt
c. Rrtt
d. RrTt
e. Cannot be determined from the information given

**Q2.7** An experiment is performed on a field pea plant. There are 2 alleles that determine the size of the pea: P (large pea size trait) and p (small pea size trait). The P allele is autosomal dominant. How many genotypes and phenotypes are possible?

a. 3 genotypes and 3 phenotypes
b. 3 genotypes and 2 phenotypes
c. 2 genotypes and 3 phenotypes
d. 2 genotypes and 2 phenotypes
e. None of the above

**Q2.8** Ignoring the possibility of mutations that arise spontaneously, which of the following statements applies to a sex-linked recessive disorder that is lethal in infancy?

a. Only male infants will die from the disorder
b. Both male and female infants can die from the disorder
c. Only female infants can die from the disorder
d. Male children of male carriers are always carriers
e. 100% of all male infants born from carriers will die

**Q2.9** A new genetic disease is discovered. The associated family tree is shown, with disease phenotype in black and normal genotype in white.

What is the mode of inheritance of this disease?

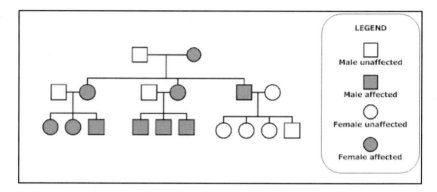

LEGEND

Male unaffected

Male affected

Female unaffected

Female affected

    **a.** X-linked recessive
    **b.** Co-dominant
    **c.** Autosomal dominant
    **d.** X-linked dominant
    **e.** Mitochondrial

**Q2.10** As the world's population growth is exponential, some people believe that, once a critical population density level has been reached, everyone should become a vegetarian. Using your knowledge of food chains, which of the following arguments backing this claim up is most likely to be true?

    **a.** Switching to vegetarianism would help support a greater number of people.

    **b.** Eating too much meat is not healthy.

    **c.** Plant foods contain all the nutrients needed for human survival.

    **d.** Biodiversity in the ecosystem would be increased.

**Q2.11** DNA is a nucleic acid and can be double stranded (ds) or single stranded (ss). Each DNA is composed of four bases of either guanine (G), adenine (A), thymine (T) or cytosine (C). According to DNA base pairing rules, A binds with T and C binds with G via hydrogen bonds if it is double stranded. RNA is also a nucleic acid, which can be single or double stranded, and contains the bases G, A, C and U (uracil) only. According to RNA pairing rules, A binds with U and C binds with G if it is double stranded.

The following table provides the composition of bases in four different nucleic acid specimens. Of what type is each of the four specimens shown in the table?

| | Base (%) | | | | |
|---|---|---|---|---|---|
| | A | T | G | C | U |
| Specimen 1 | 37 | 37 | 13 | 13 | 0 |
| Specimen 2 | 16 | 34 | 34 | 16 | 0 |
| Specimen 3 | 43 | 0 | 7 | 7 | 43 |
| Specimen 4 | 33 | 0 | 22 | 5 | 40 |

a.  (1) dsDNA  (2) ssDNA  (3) dsRNA  (4) ssRNA
b.  (1) dsDNA  (2) ssRNA  (3) dsDNA  (4) ssDNA
c.  (1) ssDNA  (2) dsDNA  (3) ssRNA  (4) dsRNA
d.  (1) dsDNA  (2) ssRNA  (3) ssDNA  (4) ssDNA
e.  (1) dsRNA  (2) dsRNA  (3) ssRNA  (4) ssRNA

**Q2.12** Sherpas are a people living in the Himalayas at an altitude significantly above sea level. Which of the following statements regarding their respiratory system is likely to be true?

a.  Sherpas have greater vital capacity and enlarged thoracic cavity.

b.  Sherpas have reduced vital capacity and decreased thoracic cavity.

c.  Sherpas inhale a smaller amount of air than people living at sea level.

d.  Sherpas have a reduced concentration of red blood cells than people living at sea level.

**Q2.13** Crossover values (COVs) are the percentages of offspring showing recombination among the total offspring of a given cross. They indicate the amount of crossing over that has occurred and therefore, in effect, indicate the relative distance between genes. COVs are used to help construct chromosome maps.

Four genes, called S, T, U and V, are found on the same chromosome. Use the following COVs to work out the sequence of the four genes.

S to T = 25; T to U = 8; U to V = 7; S to V = 10; S to U = 17

    **a.** U V S T
    **b.** U S T V
    **c.** S T V U
    **d.** T U V S
    **e.** T V U S

**Q2.14** Plant cells comprise cytoplasm: a cell membrane encompassed by a cell wall made of cellulose. A stick of celery stalk is placed in water. Cellulase is added to the water, to fully dissolve the cell walls. Assuming that cellulase has no effect on solute concentration in water, what would happen to the cells of the part of the stalk placed in the water?

1. The cells would separate.
2. The cells would undergo lysis.
3. The cells would shrink.
4. The cells would lose their structure.
5. The cells would become turgid.

    **a.** 1, 3 and 5 only
    **b.** 1, 4 and 5 only
    **c.** 2, 4 and 5 only
    **d.** 1, 3 and 4 only
    **e.** 1, 2 and 4 only

**Q2.15** Listed are some features of plant, bacterial and animal cells:

1. Cell membrane.
2. Cellulose cell wall.
3. Chloroplast.
4. Chromosomal DNA.
5. Flagella.
6. Vacuole.
7. Mitochondrion.

Which of the above are exclusive to plant cells?

   **a.** 2, 3 and 4 only
   **b.** 1, 6 and 7 only
   **c.** 2, 3 and 6 only
   **d.** 1, 2 and 6 only
   **e.** All options

**Q2.16** A newly discovered retrovirus can divide every hour. Assuming that this retrovirus has 3 million nucleotide base pairs in its genome and that the mutation rate is at $1\times10^{-6}$ per base pair, how many mutations will occur in 3 hours?

   **a.** 3
   **b.** 6
   **c.** 9
   **d.** 12
   **e.** 15

**Q2.17** Human chorionic gonadotropin hormone (hCG) is produced by women when they are pregnant. A quantity of hCG hormone is injected into the blood of a mouse. Antibodies from white blood cells are produced in the mouse's blood in response to the injected substance. What could the serum from this mouse's blood be most useful for?

   **a.** Treatment of infertility
   **b.** Pregnancy test
   **c.** Prevention of fertilisation
   **d.** Paternity test
   **e.** None of the above

**Q2.18** Stem cells are undifferentiated cells that have the remarkable potential to be self-renewing, dividing by mitosis to produce specific body cell types. Which of the following statements regarding the two types of stem cells (adult and embryonic) is correct?

   a. An injury to the nerves of the spinal cord can always be corrected by using adult stem cells

   b. Embryonic stem cells cannot differentiate into adult nerve cells

   c. Embryonic stem cells can potentially replace damaged nerve cells in the spinal cord

   d. All of the above statements

   e. None of the above statements

**Q2.19** Huntington's disease is a rare inherited neurodegenerative disorder caused by an autosomal dominant allele on chromosome 4. The disorder causes part of the DNA called a CAG base sequence to repeat many more times than it is supposed to (so-called "tri-nucleotide repeat"). Normally, this section of DNA is repeated fewer than 26 times. But, in people with Huntington's disease, it is repeated 40 times or more. As the gene is passed down through families, the number of times that the CAG tri-nucleotide repeats tends to increase. If a married couple has four children, and two of the children have the disorder, which of the following statements about the genotypes of the parents is correct?

   a. Both parents are heterozygous for the disorder

   b. One parent is homozygous for the disorder and the other parent does not have the disorder

   c. One parent is heterozygous for the disorder and the other parent does not have the disorder

   d. Both a and c could be correct

   e. None of the above

**Q2.20** The enzyme trypsin is released by the pancreas and catalyses the hydrolysis of peptide bonds formed by the carboxyl groups between the amino acid lysine (Lys) and arginine (Arg). Pepsin is a stomach enzyme, which catalyses the hydrolysis of peptide bonds formed by amine groups of aromatic amino acids phenylalanine (Phe) and tyrosine (Tyr). The carboxyl group is denoted by the COOH side chain in the amino acid and the amine group is reflected by an $NH_2$ side chain.

Taking this into account, find out what will be formed from the following polypeptide in the stomach and subsequently in the small intestine?

$NH_2$ – Gly – Lys – Met – Thr – Phe – Tyr – Arg – Pro – COOH

|  | **Stomach** | **Small intestine** |
|---|---|---|
| **a.** | Gly – Lys – Met – Thr – Phe<br>Tyr – Arg – Pro | Gly<br>Lys – Met<br>Thr – Phe<br>Tyr – Arg – Pro |
| **b.** | Gly – Lys – Met<br>Thr – Phe – Tyr – Arg – Pro | Gly – Lys – Met<br>Thr<br>Phe<br>Tyr – Arg<br>Pro |
| **c.** | Gly – Lys – Met – Thr<br>Phe<br>Tyr – Arg – Pro | Gly – Lys<br>Met – Thr<br>Phe<br>Tyr – Arg<br>Pro |
| **d.** | Gly – Lys<br>Met – Thr – Phe – Tyr – Arg<br>Pro | Gly – Lys<br>Met – Thr – Phe<br>Tyr – Arg<br>Pro |

**Q2.21** A woman is started on a new contraceptive device: subcutaneous oestrogen therapy (injections of oestrogen into the skin of her left thigh). Which of the following choices represents a possible sequence for a direct route from the site of absorption to its site of action?

    **a.** Skin capillaries > superior vena cava > left atrium > left ventricle > aorta > ovaries

    **b.** Leg veins > inferior vena cava > right atrium > right ventricle > left ventricle > carotid artery > pituitary

    **c.** Skin capillaries > hepatic portal vein > inferior vena cava > right atrium > pulmonary artery > left ventricle > aorta > pituitary

    **d.** Leg veins > inferior vena cava > pulmonary artery > left atrium > left ventricle > pulmonary vein > carotid artery > pituitary

    **e.** Skin capillaries > inferior vena cava > right atrium > right ventricle > left ventricle > carotid artery > ovaries

**Q2.22** Enzymes act as biological catalysts and aid in the breakdown of food during digestion. Which of the following is not an enzyme?

    **a.** Amylase
    **b.** Hydrochloric acid
    **c.** Protease
    **d.** Lipase
    **e.** None of the above

**Q2.23** The DNA of an organism was found to contain 30% adenine. What is the difference between the percentage of base pairs of adenine and guanine present in the DNA of that organism?

    **a.** 0%
    **b.** 5%
    **c.** 10%
    **d.** 20%
    **e.** 30%

**Q2.24** The diagram below applies to questions Q2.24a to Q2.24c. It shows a simplified kidney tubule and associated blood vessels. Use the letters A to H from the diagram to answer the following questions. Some letters may be used more than once.

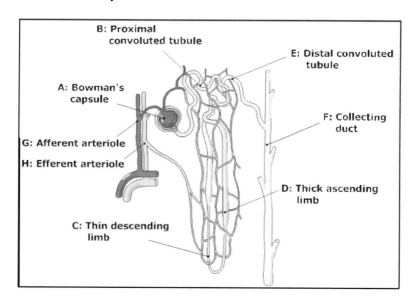

**Q2.24a** What part of the tubules contains the highest concentration of urea?

**a.** A    **b.** B    **c.** C    **d.** D    **e.** E    **f.** F    **g.** G    **h.** H

**Q2.24b** What part of the tubules absorbs the largest amount of sodium?

**a.** A    **b.** B    **c.** C    **d.** D    **e.** E    **f.** F    **g.** G    **h.** H

**Q2.24c** What part of the tubules absorbs the largest amount of glucose?

**a.** A    **b.** B    **c.** C    **d.** D    **e.** E    **f.** F    **g.** G    **h.** H

**Q2.25** A patient comes to the local GP. A urine dipstick test shows that there is glucose in the patient's urine sample. This means that:

    **a.** Glucose transporters in the loop of Henle are not functioning properly

    **b.** The patient is healthy, since glucose normally appears in the urine

    **c.** The proximal tubule is over-secreting glucose

    **d.** Glucose influx into the filtrate is occurring faster than it can be reabsorbed

    **e.** None of the above

**Q2.26** Which of the following is a function of the liver?

    **1.** Removal of glucose from the blood
    **2.** Removal of urea from the blood
    **3.** Breakdown of hormones
    **4.** Synthesis of cholesterol

    **a.** 4 only
    **b.** 1, 3 and 4 only
    **c.** 1, 2 and 3 only
    **d.** 2 and 3 only
    **e.** All of the above

**Q2.27** Normal working kidneys produce the hormone erythropoietin, which drives haematopoiesis (red blood cell production) in the bone marrow. When kidneys fail, they stop producing erythropoietin. In addition to profound effects on electrolyte management and the disposal of metabolic waste products, which process does renal failure compromise?

    **a.** Oxygen carriage in the bloodstream
    **b.** Myocardial contractility
    **c.** Cognition
    **d.** Pulmonary gas exchange
    **e.** All of the above

**Q2.28** An 18-year-old student becomes stranded in the desert when he gets lost during his Duke of Edinburgh hike. After 4 hours of walking in temperatures of 29 degrees Celsius, he comes across a petrol station and finds help.

During his hike, which of the following played a role in an endocrine mechanism to lower his plasma osmolarity?

    **a.** Pituitary
    **b.** Collecting duct
    **c.** Hypothalamus
    **d.** Kidneys
    **e.** All of the above

**Q2.29** The Bowman's capsule assists in clearing urea from the blood by:

    **a.** Actively transporting urea into the filtrate using ATP-driven pumps
    **b.** Exchanging urea for glucose in anti-port mechanism
    **c.** Allowing urea to diffuse into the filtrate under filtration pressure
    **d.** Converting urea to amino acids
    **e.** None of the above

**Q2.30** The epithelial cells of the proximal convoluted tubule contain a brush border similar to the brush borders of the small intestine.

What is the function of the brush border?

    **a.** Increase the amount of filtrate that reaches the loop of Henle
    **b.** Increase the surface area available for absorption
    **c.** Slow the rate at which the filtrate moves through the nephron
    **d.** Move the filtrate through the nephron with cilia-like action
    **e.** Slow the rate at which substances can be absorbed

**Q2.31** Which of the following is the correct sequence of structures through which urine flows?

    **a.** Urethra → Urinary bladder → Ureter → Collecting duct
    **b.** Collecting duct → Urinary bladder → Urethra → Ureter
    **c.** Collecting duct → Ureter → Urinary bladder → Urethra
    **d.** Ureter → Collecting duct → Urethra → Urinary bladder
    **e.** Collecting duct→ Urethra → Urinary bladder → Ureter

**Q2.32** The diagram represents the view from the front side of a section through the heart, and associated blood vessels.

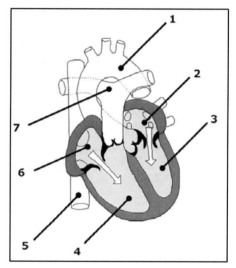

Which sequence of numbers shows the course of blood flow from the point of entry to the heart from the rest of the body to the blood being pumped out of the heart to the rest of the body?

    **a.** 2 → 3 → 1 → 6 → 5 → 4 → 7
    **b.** 6 → 4 → 7 → 5 → 2 → 3 → 1
    **c.** 2 → 3 → 7 → 1 → 5 → 4 → 6
    **d.** 5 → 6 → 4 → 7 → 2 → 3 → 1
    **e.** 5 → 6 → 4 → 7 → 1 → 2 → 3

**Q2.33** Which chambers of the heart pump oxygenated blood?

    **a.** The right and left atria
    **b.** The right and left ventricles
    **c.** The right atrium and the left ventricle
    **d.** The left atrium and the left ventricle
    **e.** The left atrium and right ventricle

**Q2.34** The diagram below shows a simplification of the human circulatory system.

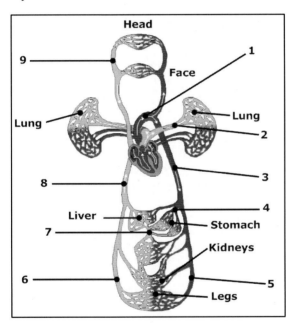

Which one of the following represents a path that might be taken by blood passing from the stomach to the head?

    **a.** $6 \rightarrow 8 \rightarrow 9 \rightarrow 1$
    **b.** $4 \rightarrow 3 \rightarrow 2 \rightarrow 1$
    **c.** $4 \rightarrow 3 \rightarrow 1 \rightarrow 2 \rightarrow 9$
    **d.** $7 \rightarrow 8 \rightarrow 2 \rightarrow 9$
    **e.** $7 \rightarrow 8 \rightarrow 2 \rightarrow 1$

**Q2.35** The capillary network comprises the greatest cross-sectional area of blood vessels in the body with the highest resistance to blood flow. In a healthy individual, the highest blood pressure would most likely be found in:

    **a.**   The aorta
    **b.**   The vena cava
    **c.**   The systemic capillaries
    **d.**   The pulmonary artery
    **e.**   The pulmonary vein

**Q2.36** Gas exchange between the blood and tissues occurs:

    **a.**   Throughout the circulatory system
    **b.**   In the arteries, arterioles and capillaries
    **c.**   In the systemic arteries only
    **d.**   In the capillaries only

**Q2.37** In the congenital heart defect known as patent ductus arteriosus, the ductus arteriosus (a blood vessel that connects the aorta and the pulmonary arteries during foetal development) fails to close at birth. This will likely lead to all of the following EXCEPT:

    **a.**   Equal, or increased, oxygen concentration in the blood that reaches the systemic tissues
    **b.**   Increased oxygen concentration in the blood that reaches the lungs
    **c.**   Increased workload imposed on the left ventricle
    **d.**   Increased workload imposed on the right ventricle

**Q2.38** Which of the following options describes the physiological order of blood flow through the heart?

    **a.**   Right ventricle > left ventricle > right atrium > left atrium
    **b.**   Vena cava > left atrium > right atrium > aorta
    **c.**   Right atrium > left atrium > right ventricle > left ventricle
    **d.**   Right ventricle > right atrium > left ventricle > left atrium
    **e.**   Right atrium > right ventricle > left atrium > left ventricle

**Q2.39** Which of the following is not related to the low speed of blood flow across the capillary beds?

    **a.** Efficient metabolic substrate diffusion
    **b.** Systolic blood pressure
    **c.** Precipitous drop of blood pressure
    **d.** Efficient gas diffusion
    **e.** None of the above

**Q2.40** Haemoglobin in red blood cells is responsible for carrying oxygen around the body. At which location does this molecule bind most strongly to oxygen?

    **a.** Aorta
    **b.** Venules in the arm
    **c.** Capillaries in the legs
    **d.** Pulmonary artery
    **e.** Pulmonary veins

**Q2.41** Atherosclerosis is a major cause of disease in modern "western-ised" countries. Atherogenesis, which is the process of developing atherosclerotic plaques, takes place in the wall of the blood vessels.

The endothelium, which is the innermost layer of the vessel artery, overlies the atherosclerotic plaque. When this cell layer ruptures, plaque contents rush into the bloodstream and cause rapid clot formation. This can cause sudden heart attacks.

Which vessel type is least likely to develop atherosclerotic plaques?

    **a.** Aorta
    **b.** Common carotid artery
    **c.** Femoral artery
    **d.** Common iliac artery
    **e.** Saphenous vein

**Q2.42** Patients who undergo liver resections for liver cancer often have diminished bile production. Over time, the remaining liver up-regulates bile production and makes up for the shortage. However, during the first few weeks, these patients' faecal material is typically pale, foul-smelling and difficult to flush away.

What accounts for this change?

    a.    Lack of lipid emulsification
    b.    Lack of lipase secretion
    c.    Poor intestinal lipid absorption
    d.    Post-operative bleeding
    e.    All of the above

**Q2.43** Which of the following are correct examples of negative feedback?

    1.    Secretion of glucagon by pancreas when glucose levels are high
    2.    ADH secretion when water concentration in the blood is low.
    3.    Dilation of blood vessels near your skin when your body temperature is low.

    a.    2 only
    b.    1 and 2 only
    c.    2 and 3 only
    d.    1, 2 and 3
    e.    None of the above

**Q2.44** A patient's tidal volume (i.e. the amount of gas a person can inhale/exhale in one breath at rest) is 600 $cm^3$. He takes 15 breaths per minute. Assuming the air he inhales contains 20% oxygen. Approximately how much oxygen would he inhale in 2 minutes if his breathing rate remained constant?

    a.    1.8 $dm^3$
    b.    3.6 $dm^3$
    c.    7.2 $dm^3$
    d.    18 $dm^3$
    e.    36 $dm^3$

**Q2.45** The image below shows components of the digestive system. It applies to questions 2.45a and 2.45b.

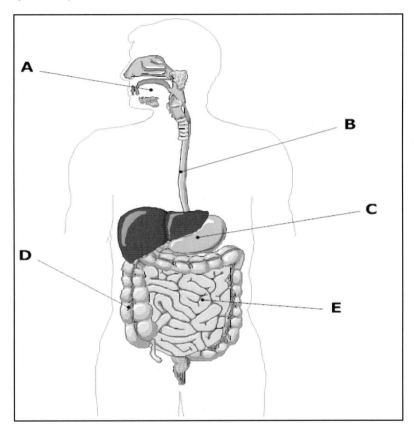

**2.45a** In humans, in which of the indicated areas does most chemical digestion of food occur?

a. A      b. B      c. C      d. D      e. E

**2.45b** In humans, in which of the indicated areas does most digestion of proteins occur?

a. A & C      b. C & D      c. C & E      d. D & E

**Q2.46** A 68-year-old man is diagnosed with "cancer of the large intestine". In which structure could this not be located?

    **a.** Sigmoid colon
    **b.** Transverse colon
    **c.** Appendix
    **d.** Caecum
    **e.** Ileum

**Q2.47** Which of the following sections of the gut is not primarily involved with water and salt absorption?

    **a.** Caecum
    **b.** Rectum
    **c.** Sigmoid colon
    **d.** Ascending colon
    **e.** None of the above

**Q2.48** Which of the following is not a process that adds carbon dioxide to the atmosphere?

    **a.** Respiration in plants
    **b.** Respiration in animals
    **c.** Decomposition
    **d.** Combustion
    **e.** Kidney excretion

**Q2.49** Which of the following statement about the liver is correct?

    1. It stores bile in the gallbladder
    2. It contains sinusoids
    3. It receives blood from the intestine and heart.

    **a.** 1 only    **b.** 2 only    **c.** 3 only    **d.** 1, 2 and 3    **e.** None

**Q2.50** A dominant gene which controls flower colour in the plant, S, gives flowers a violet colour. The recessive gene s gives a yellow colour. Two heterozygous plants were crossed to give 2000 offsprings. How many more purple-flowered than white-flowered offsprings would you expect?

    **a.** 250    **b.** 500    **c.** 1,000    **d.** 1,500    **e.** 17,500

**Q2.51** A person accidentally pricks his finger on a sharp pin. The hand automatically moves away from the pin. This diagram shows the parts involved in the reflex action and applies to Q2.51a and Q2.51b.

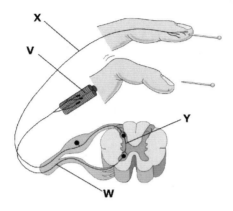

**Q2.51a** Which of the following below correctly identifies the neurones in the reflex pathway?

|    | Sensory neurone | Relay neurone | Motor neurone | Effector |
|----|-----------------|---------------|---------------|----------|
| a. | Y | X | W | V |
| b. | W | Y | V | X |
| c. | X | Y | V | W |
| d. | V | W | X | Y |
| e. | X | Y | W | V |

**Q2.51b** Which row in the table shows how information passes from X to Y, Y to W and W to V?

|    | From X to Y | From Y to W | W to V |
|----|-------------|-------------|--------|
| a. | Chemical | Impulse | Impulse |
| b. | Chemical | Chemical | Impulse |
| c. | Chemical | Chemical | Chemical |
| d. | Impulse | Impulse | Impulse |
| e. | Impulse | Chemical | Impulse |
| f. | Impulse | Chemical | Chemical |

393

**Q2.52** A certain chemical in grapefruit and grapefruit juice can interact with medications by inhibiting the liver enzyme CYP3A4. Warfarin is a drug that prevents blood from clotting, and is broken down by the liver enzyme CYP3A4. The effect of warfarin is measured by the blood's INR (International Normalized Ratio), with a higher value meaning that the blood takes longer to clot.

What does the following information suggest might happen to people who take warfarin with grapefruit juice?

|  | Concentration of CYP3A4 | Concentration of warfarin in blood | INR |
|---|---|---|---|
| a. | Same | Same | Same |
| b. | Same | Increase | Decrease |
| c. | Same | Increase | Increase |
| d. | Decrease | Increase | Increase |
| e. | Decrease | Increase | Decrease |
| f. | Decrease | Decrease | Decrease |
| g. | Increase | Increase | Same |

**Q2.53** A volunteer was plunged into an ice bath at time X, and was retrieved at time Y. Their body temperature was measured throughout and plotted in the diagram below. If someone had impaired temperature response, how would the diagram differ?

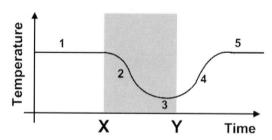

| a. | 1 would be at a higher set point |
|---|---|
| b. | 2 would be less steep |
| c. | 3 would be later |
| d. | 4 would be steeper |
| e. | 3 would be lower |

**Q2.54** The following diagram applies to questions 2.54a and 2.54b. It shows a section through the thorax.

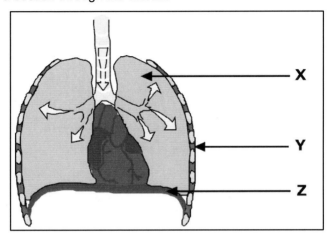

**Q2.54a** When breathing in (inspiration), what happens to the muscles at Y and Z and the pressure at X?

| Answer | Pressure X | Muscle Y | Muscle Z |
|--------|-----------|----------|----------|
| a. | Increases | Relaxes | Contracts |
| b. | Increases | Relaxes | Relaxes |
| c. | Increases | Contracts | Relaxes |
| d. | Decreases | Relaxes | Relaxes |
| e. | Decreases | Contracts | Contracts |

**Q2.54b** When breathing out (expiration), what happens to the muscles at Y and Z and the pressure at X?

| Answer | Pressure X | Muscle Y | Muscle Z |
|--------|-----------|----------|----------|
| a. | Increases | Relaxes | Contracts |
| b. | Increases | Relaxes | Relaxes |
| c. | Increases | Contracts | Relaxes |
| d. | Decreases | Relaxes | Relaxes |
| e. | Decreases | Contracts | Contracts |

**Q2.55** The spinal cord and spinal nerves are portions of which division of the nervous system?

    **a.** Peripheral nervous system
    **b.** Central nervous system
    **c.** Peripheral nervous system and central nervous system
    **d.** Basal ganglia
    **e.** Cortical

**Q2.56** Sustained heavy exercise results in all of the following changes to blood chemistry EXCEPT:

    **a.** Lowered pH
    **b.** Raised $CO_2$ levels
    **c.** Increased temperature
    **d.** Decreased carboxyhaemoglobin
    **e.** Increased lactate levels

**Q2.57** A cube of meat is placed in test tubes containing a set volume of water. Other substances are added to it (see table below), including solution X, which may or may not be an enzyme. The tubes are left for 12 hours and then tested for the presence of amino acids.

| Tube | Solution(s) added | Result of test for amino acids |
|------|-------------------|-------------------------------|
| 1 | Acid | Traces |
| 2 | Alkali | Traces |
| 3 | None | Absent |
| 4 | Solution X | Absent |
| 5 | Solution X + acid | Large amounts |
| 6 | Solution X + alkali | Absent |
| 7 | Boiled solution X + acid | Traces |

Which two test tubes would best point to the fact that solution X is likely to be an enzyme?

    **a.** 1 and 4
    **b.** 1 and 7
    **c.** 2 and 6
    **d.** 5 and 7

**Q2.58** Which of the following associations between the steps of respiration and the contraction of muscles is correct?

    **a.** Exhalation – diaphragm contracts
    **b.** Exhalation – intercostal muscles relax
    **c.** Inhalation – diaphragm relaxes
    **d.** Inhalation – intercostal muscles relax

**Q2.59** Which one of the following represents the likely sequence of structures followed by air molecules during inhalation?

    **a.** Larynx → Pharynx → Trachea → Bronchi → Alveoli
    **b.** Pharynx → Larynx → Trachea → Bronchi → Alveoli
    **c.** Pharynx → Trachea → Bronchioles → Bronchi → Alveoli
    **d.** Pharynx → Trachea → Larynx → Bronchi → Alveoli
    **e.** Larynx → Pharynx → Bronchioles → Bronchi → Alveoli

**Q2.60** The table shows the breathing rate, heart rate and body temperatures of four different mammals.

| Mammal | Breathing rate (inhalations/min) | Heart rate (beats/min) | Body temperature (degrees centigrade) |
|--------|----------------------------------|------------------------|----------------------------------------|
| A | 10 | 30 | 35.9 |
| B | 30 | 200 | 38.3 |
| C | 15 | 45 | 37.2 |
| D | 200 | 550 | 36.5 |

Rank the animals A to D in descending order of surface area per unit volume of the body.

    **a.** A<B<C<D         **f.** D<A<B<C
    **b.** A<C<B<D         **g.** C<D<B<A
    **c.** A<D<B<C         **h.** C<B<A<D
    **d.** D<C<B<A         **i.** B<A<C<D
    **e.** D<B<C<A         **j.** B<D<C<A

## 2C Scientific Knowledge and Applications
## Physics – 82 Questions

### Answers from page 499

**Q2.61** A runner is running on the road when the alarm system of a stationary car he has just passed goes off. How fast is he running if he hears the sound at 97.5% of the frequency heard by someone standing still? (Take the speed of sound in air as 340m/s)

    a.  He is not running
    b.  2.5 m/s
    c.  8.5 m/s
    d.  15 m/s
    e.  None of the above

**Q2.62** A computer speaker is used to play two notes. The second note has half the wavelength of the first note. Which of the following correctly describes the property of the second note produced in comparison to the same property of the first note?

    a.  The amplitude of the second note is half
    b.  The frequency of the second note is the same
    c.  The intensity of the second note is lower
    d.  The frequency of the second note is double
    e.  The amplitude of the second note is double

**Q2.63** A mini-submarine sends out a sonar signal in a direction directly below it. It takes 2.1 s for the sound wave to travel from the submarine to the ocean bottom and back to the submarine.

How high up from the ocean floor is the mini-submarine? (Take the speed of sound in water to be 1490 m/s)

    a.  1,565 m
    b.  3,129 m
    c.  4,066 m
    d.  6,258 m
    e.  9,517 m

**Q2.64** An ambulance van speeds towards you at 72 km/h. Its siren emits a sound at a constant 400 Hz frequency. You are standing still at the roadside. What is the frequency of the sound that you hear?

    **a.**   Less than 400 Hz
    **b.**   400 Hz
    **c.**   More than 400 Hz
    **d.**   Cannot be determined from the information given

**Q2.65** A scientist puts object X on a beam balance and, separately, on a spring balance. At the equator, the strength of the gravitational field strength is lower than at the South Pole; he performs the experiment in both places.

    **Beam balance**               **Spring balance**

How do the readings at the South Pole compare with those at the equator for both balances?

| | Beam balance | Spring balance |
|---|---|---|
| a. | Different | Same |
| b. | Same | Same |
| c. | Different | Increased at equator |
| d. | Same | Increased at equator |
| e. | Different | Decreased at equator |
| f. | Same | Decreased at equator |

**Q2.66** If a wave generator makes waves that hit the side of a swimming pool once every five seconds, and the wave peaks are 10 m apart, at what velocity are the waves moving?

    **a.**   2 m/s
    **b.**   4 m/s
    **c.**   12 m/s
    **d.**   20 m/s
    **e.**   48 m/s

**Q2.67** Sound waves are an example of:

    a.  Longitudinal waves because the medium moves perpendicularly to the propagation of the wave
    b.  Longitudinal waves because the medium moves parallel to the propagation of the wave
    c.  Transverse waves because the medium moves perpendicularly to the propagation of the wave
    d.  Transverse waves because the medium moves parallel to the propagation of the wave

**Q2.68** When the frequency of a sound wave is increased, which of the following options is correct?

|    | Wavelength | Period | Amplitude |
|----|------------|--------|-----------|
| a. | Increase | Increase | Increase |
| b. | Increase | Increase | No change |
| c. | Increase | Decrease | No change |
| d. | Decrease | Increase | No change |
| e. | Decrease | Decrease | No change |
| f. | Decrease | Decrease | Decrease |

**Q2.69** A wave is travelling through air before passing through water. Which of the following characteristics of the wave change when it enters the water?

    a.  Frequency only
    b.  Speed only
    c.  Frequency and speed
    d.  Frequency and wavelength
    e.  Speed and wavelength
    f.  Frequency, speed and wavelength

**Q2.70** An inclined ramp is a flat machine whose endpoints are at different heights. Using a ramp enables objects to be moved upwards by moving further along a horizontal distance, rather than totally vertically.

Ignoring friction, which of the following is true about moving an object with a given force (X) up a ramp versus without a ramp?

| | Work done | Final momentum |
|---|---|---|
| a. | Same | Same |
| b. | Same | Increased |
| c. | Less | Increased |
| d. | Less | Same |
| e. | More | Increased |
| f. | More | Same |
| g. | None of the above | |

**Q2.71** A force is applied to a block with mass (m). Which of the following changes will produce the greatest increase in the block's acceleration?

| | Force | Mass |
|---|---|---|
| a. | Triple | Halve |
| b. | Double | Triple |
| c. | Double | Double |
| d. | Halve | Double |
| e. | Double | Halve |

**Q2.72** A space shuttle weighing 5000kg is travelling at 100m/s upwards. A force of 10000N acting in the direction of its travel is then applied to it for 6 seconds. What is the resulting change in velocity?

    **a.**   3 m/s
    **b.**   6 m/s
    **c.**   12 m/s
    **d.**   112 m/s
    **e.**   120 m/s

**Q2.73** Balloons filled with helium float because helium is lighter than the air surrounding it. However, some balloons are filled with hot air and they also float. Which of the following best explains why a hot air balloon rises?

    **a.** The total mass of air in the balloon is greater than the mass of air outside the balloon
    **b.** The density of hot air is lower than that of the air surrounding the balloon
    **c.** The heat in the balloon pushes on the fabric of the balloon, which forces the balloon upwards
    **d.** The hot air balloon has a hole at the bottom
    **e.** None of the above

**Q2.74** An Olympic weightlifter lifts a 250 kg barbell from the ground to a height of 2 m. How much work has he done, and how much work is required to hold the weight at that height? (Take gravity to be 10 m/s$^2$)

| | Work done (J) | Work on holding (J) |
|---|---|---|
| **a.** | 5000 | 0 |
| **b.** | 5000 | 5000 |
| **c.** | 2500 | 0 |
| **d.** | 2500 | 2500 |
| **e.** | 500 | 500 |

**Q2.75** Which of the following statements regarding electricity is true?

   **a.**  As the electric potential difference between two points decreases, the electrical power decreases

   **b.**  As the current flowing between two points decreases, the electrical power increases

   **c.**  As the charge passing through two points increases per unit time, the electrical power decreases

   **d.**  None of the above

**Q2.76** Given the following formula for calculating resistance:

$$\text{resistance (R)} \ (\text{Ohm, } \Omega) = \frac{\rho \ (\text{resistivity, } \Omega m) \times l \ (\text{length, m})}{A \ (\text{cross sectional area, m}^2)}$$

which of the following would increase the total resistance of a cylindrical wire the most?

|     | Length of wire | Diameter of wire |
| --- | --- | --- |
| **a.** | Halving | Same |
| **b.** | Doubling | Same |
| **c.** | Same | Halving |
| **d.** | Same | Doubling |
| **e.** | None of the above | |

**Q2.77** A medical student drinks hot coffee from a thermos flask which is a doubled glass-walled vessel containing a hot liquid. There is a space in between the glass walls of the flask.

What action would reduce the heat loss caused by radiation?

   **a.**  Painting surface A silver

   **b.**  Painting surface A black

   **c.**  Painting surface B black

   **d.**  Painting surface C black

   **e.**  Create a vacuum between the glass walls.

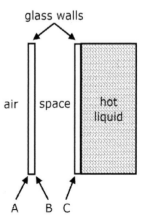

403

**Q2.78** A student arranges four 6Ω resistors. How many functionally different resistors can be made if all resistors are used in each circuit configuration?

    **a.**  3      **b.** 4      **c. 5**      **d.** 6      **e.** 7

**Q2.79** The circuits below show identical filament bulbs designed to work at 12 V.

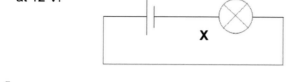

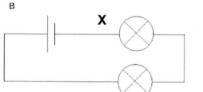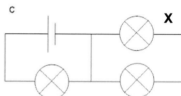

If all three circuits use the same 12V battery, which of the bulbs marked X will produce the most light?

    **a.**   A
    **b.**   B
    **c.**   C
    **d.**   A, B and C produce the same amount of light

**Q2.80** The total resistance of a circuit is related both to the resistance of individual resistors and to the composition of the circuit. A circuit currently consists of two 6Ω resistors in parallel. If the resistors were rearranged so that they are placed in series instead, how would the total resistance of the circuit change?

    **a.**   Decrease twofold
    **b.**   Decrease fourfold
    **c.**   Increase twofold
    **d.**   Increase fourfold
    **e.**   Increase eightfold

**Q2.81** A battery has a measured voltage of 6 volts if no circuit is connected to it. When it is connected to a 10Ω resistor, the current is 0.5 amps. What is the internal resistance of the battery?

    **a.**   0.005Ω
    **b.**   0.05Ω
    **c.**   0.5Ω
    **d.**   2Ω
    **e.**   5Ω

**Q2.82** The circuit below has 3 resistors connected in series to a 12V battery, and a further resistor connected in parallel to those, but on a branch of the circuit which has not yet been switched on

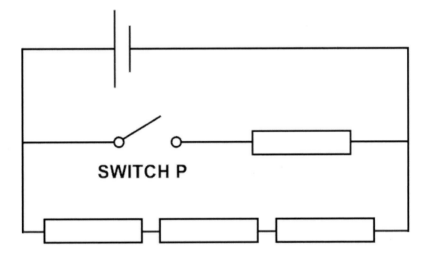

SWITCH P

When switch P is closed, which of the following statements is true?

    **a.**   The voltage produced by the battery will be increased
    **b.**   The voltage produced by the battery will be decreased
    **c.**   The current produced by the battery will be decreased
    **d.**   The power produced by the battery will be increased
    **e.**   None of the above

**Q2.83** A charged particle is sitting still in a magnetic field. What is the orientation of the magnetic force acting on the charged particle?

    **a.** In a direction perpendicular to the right of the magnetic field
    **b.** In the direction of the magnetic field
    **c.** In a direction perpendicular to the left of the magnetic field
    **d.** There is no magnetic force acting on the particle
    **e.** In the direction opposite to the magnetic field

**Q2.84** A magnetic field is directed perpendicular to a wire loop. If the magnetic field is increased steadily, which of the following is true?

    **a.** An electromotive force will be created
    **b.** A second magnetic field will be produced in a direction opposite to the increasing magnetic field
    **c.** The current through the wire will be constant
    **d.** All of the above
    **e.** None of the above

**Q2.85** Which of the following statements regarding a magnetic rod is true?
    I.      The rod must have a north and a south pole
    II.     There is no current within the rod
    III.    Magnetic rods are monopolar

    **a.** I only
    **b.** I and II only
    **c.** II and III only
    **d.** III only
    **e.** None of the above

**Q2.86** Bees can see a higher frequency of electromagnetic waves than humans. Consequently, which of the following colours are bees more likely to be attracted to?

    **a.** Red
    **b.** Yellow
    **c.** Green
    **d.** Blue
    **e.** Violet

**Q2.87** A copper soup ladle is heated at one end in a pot of boiling water. After a while, the other end become hot.

Which statement describes how heat transfer occurs in the soup ladle?

    **a.** Energetic copper molecules move from the cooler end to the hotter end

    **b.** Energetic copper molecules move from the hotter end to the cooler end

    **c.** Energetic free electrons move from the cooler end to the hotter end

    **d.** Energetic free electrons move from the hotter end to the cooler end

    **e.** None of the above

**Q2.88** Which of the following is not a possible light ray through a glass lens?

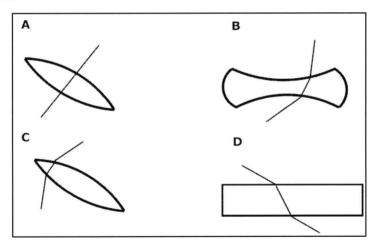

    **a.** A
    **b.** B
    **c.** C
    **d.** D
    **e.** B and C
    **f.** None. All are possible

**Q2.89** Rank the following by their wavelengths, from lowest wavelength to highest wavelength:

I  -  Indigo
II  -  Infrared
III -  Orange
IV -  Ultraviolet
V  -  X-rays

    **a.**   V, IV, III, I, II
    **b.**   IV, II, I, III, V
    **c.**   V, I, II, IV, III
    **d.**   II, IV, III, I, V
    **e.**   V, IV, I, III, II
    **f.**   II, I, III, IV, V

**Q2.90** Milk is poured into four separate dishes, two of which have a small surface area and the other two have a large surface area. Some of the milk is hot, some is cold. From which dish does the milk evaporate the quickest if the volume poured is exactly the same?

| | Surface area | Temperature |
|---|---|---|
| **a.** | small | cool |
| **b.** | small | warm |
| **c.** | large | cool |
| **d.** | large | warm |

**Q2.91** If an object is released from rest 19.6 m above the ground, how long does it take the object to reach the ground?

    **a.**   1 second
    **b.**   2 seconds
    **c.**   3 seconds
    **d.**   4 seconds
    **e.**   20 seconds

**Q2.92** Which of the following will substantially alter the density of a solid?

    **a.** Move the solid to the Moon where the gravity is different
    **b.** Submerge the solid at the bottom of a swimming pool
    **c.** Double the volume and mass of the solid
    **d.** All of the above
    **e.** None of the above

**Q2.93** An astronaut in space squeezes water out of a tube and allows it to settle. Given that water's cohesive forces are stronger than adhesive forces in space as there is no gravity, what shape will the water take?

    **a.** A perfect sphere
    **b.** A flat thin sheet that expands in all directions
    **c.** A tubular shape
    **d.** A tear shape
    **e.** None of the above

**Q2.94** Consider 3 liquid substances, A, B and C, with different densities.
- A solid block is able to float in a bucket of substance A.
- When the same block is placed in a bucket of substance B, it quickly sinks to the bottom.
- Substance A is less dense than substance C.

If a cylinder is filled with substances A, B and C, which of the following describes the order of the materials from bottom to top?

    **a.** A, B, C
    **b.** A, C, B
    **c.** B, A, C
    **d.** B, C, A
    **e.** C, A, B
    **f.** C, B, A

**Q2.95** An object is thrown vertically upwards with a speed of 10 m/s while an identical object is thrown vertically downwards with a speed of 20 m/s. Ignoring friction, which object undergoes a greater change in speed in 2 seconds?

    **a.** The object being thrown upwards
    **b.** The object being thrown downwards
    **c.** Both are the same
    **d.** Cannot be determined

**Q2.96** A cannonball is shot straight up in the air (the cannon is 1 m off the ground level). If the velocity as it leaves the cannon is 5 m/s, how high does the cannonball get, as measured from the ground? (Take gravity to be 10 m/s$^2$)

    **a.**   1.00 m
    **b.**   1.25 m
    **c.**   2.00 m
    **d.**   2.25 m
    **e.**   2.50 m

**Q2.97** A cannonball (mass = 1 kg) is shot up vertically at the same time as a bullet (mass = 0.01 kg) is shot horizontally.

If they both start from the same height, which of the following statements is true?

(Ignore friction and take gravity to be 10 m/s$^2$)

    **a.**   The cannonball will reach the ground first
    **b.**   The bullet will reach the ground first
    **c.**   Both will reach the ground at the same time
    **d.**   More information is needed to answer this question

**Q2.98** If the initial height of a tennis ball in free fall is increased by a factor of 4, by what factor will the final velocity increase at the point that it hits the ground?

(Ignore air resistance)

    **a.**   2
    **b.**   4
    **c.**   8
    **d.**   1 (i.e. the velocity will be the same)
    **e.**   The increase depends on the value of the initial height

**Q2.99** A Canadian woodcutter is using an axe to split tree trunks into fire-wood. That work involves the following energy forms:

1. Chemical (muscle) energy.
2. Chemical (binding) energy of wood, heat energy, sound energy and kinetic energy.
3. Mechanical kinetic energy of the axe.
4. Mechanical potential energy of the axe.

Which is the most likely chronological sequence in which these energy exchanges take place?

    **a.** $1 \rightarrow 2 \rightarrow 4 \rightarrow 3$
    **b.** $1 \rightarrow 4 \rightarrow 3 \rightarrow 2$
    **c.** $4 \rightarrow 1 \rightarrow 3 \rightarrow 2$
    **d.** $1 \rightarrow 2 \rightarrow 3 \rightarrow 4$
    **e.** $3 \rightarrow 4 \rightarrow 1 \rightarrow 2$

**Q2.100** If the sun were to disappear suddenly at once, what would be the effect of its disappearance on the orbit of the Earth?

    **a.** The orbit would remain unchanged, due to the absence of an external force

    **b.** The orbit would slowly decay until the Earth was stationary

    **c.** The Earth would immediately become stationary

    **d.** The Earth would move in a straight line tangential to its previous orbit

    **e.** The Earth would fall toward the sun's former position

    **f.** The Earth would accelerate into space

**Q2.101** The graph below represents a car moving in a straight line. When t = 0, the displacement of the car is 0.

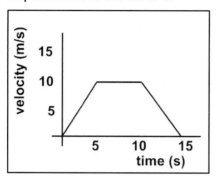

**Q2.101a** Which of the following statements about the car is not true?

a.   The car has moved 100 m
b.   The car moves with constant acceleration from t=0 to t=5s
c.   The car moves with constant velocity from t=5s and t=10s
d.   The car is reversing from t=10s and t=15s

**Q2.101b** Which of the following graphs best represents displacement versus time for the car above?

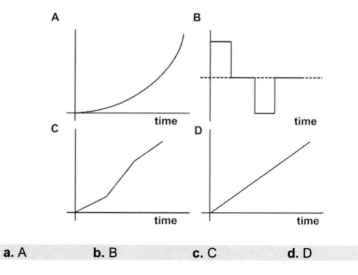

a. A          b. B          c. C          d. D

**Q2.101c** Which of the graphs below best represents the graph of acceleration versus time for the car above?

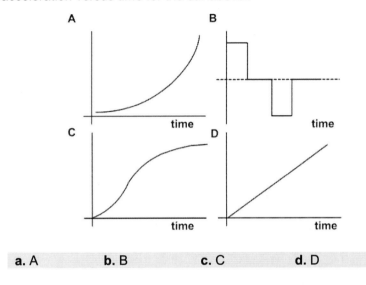

**a.** A　　　　　**b.** B　　　　　**c.** C　　　　　**d.** D

**Q2.102** Which of the following is the most probable situation to describe the motion of the object depicted in the graph below?

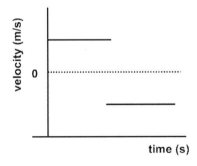

**a.**　A car accelerating then decelerating in a straight line
**b.**　The Earth in orbit
**c.**　A pendulum
**d.**　A rounders ball thrown by the pitcher and hit by a batter
**e.**　A golf ball being hit from stand still

413

**Q2.103** An individual person is riding an elevator, which is going up at a constant speed. Which of the following correctly describes the force acting on his feet?

    **a.** The force of the floor is lower than the force of gravity against his feet

    **b.** The force of the floor is the same as the force of gravity against his feet

    **c.** The force of the floor is greater than the force of gravity against his feet

    **d.** More information is needed to answer this question

**Q2.104** A car is travelling at 45 km/h. The driver brakes, bringing the car to rest in a time of 3.6 seconds. What's the magnitude of the average acceleration of the car in units of km/h$^2$?

    **a.**    450 km/h$^2$
    **b.**  12,000 km/h$^2$
    **c.**  24,000 km/h$^2$
    **d.**  45,000 km/h$^2$
    **e.**  60,000 km/h$^2$

**Q2.105** A car can drive one perimeter of a circular track of radius 1,000 m in 6 minutes. What is his average velocity?

    **a.** 2.8 m/s
    **b.** 7.0 m/s
    **c.** 7.5 m/s
    **d.** 17.5 m/s
    **e.** 20.5 m/s

**Q2.106** A driver sees an accident ahead on the motorway. He brakes from 20 m/s and decelerates at a constant rate of -5 m/s$^2$. How far does the car go before it comes to a complete halt?

    **a.** 4 m
    **b.** 8 m
    **c.** 15 m
    **d.** 30 m
    **e.** 40 m

**Q2.107** A car is pulling into a motorway petrol station and has slowed to a complete stop. Whilst the car was slowing down, which of the following options was true?

|     | Velocity | Acceleration |
| --- | --- | --- |
| a.  | Positive | Positive |
| b.  | Positive | Negative |
| c.  | Negative | Positive |
| d.  | Negative | Negative |

**Q2.108** Which of the following graphs best represents a car with a constant velocity?

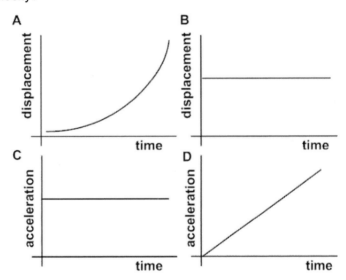

**Q2.109** A car travels at a speed of 10 km/h and, upon seeing a road sign, it brakes and comes to a stop after 10 metres. If the car had initially been travelling at 100 km/h and it had decelerated at the same rate, how long would it have taken to come to a stop?

    a.    10 m
    b.    40 m
    c.    50 m
    d.    100 m
    e.    1000 m

**Q2.110** The graph below represents the distance travelled in a straight line by a car. What is the total distance travelled by the car from t = 0 to t = 10 seconds?

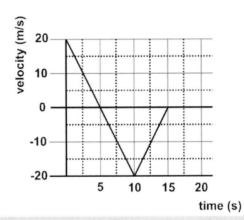

a.   15 m
b.   25 m
c.   50 m
d.   100 m
e.   150 m

**Q2.111** A truck is travelling at 40 m/s when it passes the 200 m marker. The truck accelerates at 0.02 m/s² for the following 400s. What metre marker will the truck pass at that time?

a.   8,000 m
b.   12,000 m
c.   17,400 m
d.   17,600 m
e.   17,800 m

**Q2.112** A car is driving at a speed of 10 m/s. If 2 people weighing 980N each jump out of the car, by how much does the kinetic energy of the car change?

a.   - 5,000 J
b.   - 10,000 J
c.   0 J
d.   5,000 J
e.   10,000 J

**Q2.113** Which of the following statements is true regarding the force of friction?

    **a.**  Friction is an example of a non-conservative force
    **b.**  The force of friction is always in the opposite direction of motion
    **c.**  Heat is the form of energy released by friction
    **d.**  Friction causes a loss of kinetic energy
    **e.**  All of the above

**Q2.114** A toy tyre rolls down a slope that is 10 m high. The speed of the toy tyre at the bottom of the ramp is 12 m/s. The radius of the toy tyre is 40 mm. What is the tyre's speed in revolutions/seconds at the bottom of the ramp?

    **a.**  6 revolutions/second
    **b.**  12 revolutions/second
    **c.**  24 revolutions/second
    **d.**  48 revolutions/second
    **e.**  96 revolutions/second

**Q2.115** Which one of the following objects is likely to be the best emitter of thermal radiation? Assume that all objects have the same mass and all objects are made and filled with one single type of metal.

    **a.**  A cylinder made of black metal
    **b.**  A cuboid made of white metal
    **c.**  A sphere of black metal
    **d.**  A sphere of white metal
    **e.**  A thin, flat disc of black metal
    **f.**  A thin, flat disc of white metal

**Q2.116** Which of the following serves as a concise definition for a generator?

    **a.**  Two parallel plates, separated by a magnetic field
    **b.**  A straight conductor surrounded by a magnetic field
    **c.**  A conducting plate, surrounded by an insulating coil
    **d.**  A conducting coil rotating in a magnetic field
    **e.**  A toroidal magnet with a potential difference applied
    **f.**  A magnetic field surrounding a capacitor

**Q2.117** A 2,000 kg car travelling at 30 m/s crashes into a 5,000 kg truck that is originally at rest. What is the speed of the truck after the collision, if the car comes to rest at the point of impact? (Ignore friction)

    **a.**   2 m/s
    **b.**   4 m/s
    **c.**   8 m/s
    **d.**   10 m/s
    **e.**   12 m/s

**Q2.118** A cannonball of mass 10kg is sitting on the floor of a lift. The lift accelerates downwards at 4 m/s$^2$. How much would the cannonball weigh (in N) if measured in the lift? (g=10 m/s$^2$).

    **a.**   2.5 N
    **b.**   5 N
    **c.**   20 N
    **d.**   40 N
    **e.**   60 N

**Q2.119** A ball is initially rolling up a ramp at 0.5 m/s. It decelerates constantly at a rate of 0.1 m/s$^2$. How long does the ball take to come to a complete stop?

    **a.**   0.25 s
    **b.**   1.5 s
    **c.**   2 s
    **d.**   2.5 s
    **e.**   5 s

**Q2.120** A lift with weight X moves upwards at a constant speed. The entire weight of the lift is supported by a single cable. The tension in the cable is:

    **a.**   Equal to X
    **b.**   Greater than X
    **c.**   Less than X
    **d.**   Cannot be found

**Q2.121** A hollow Styrofoam ball takes 3.7 seconds to reach the ground after having been dropped from the top of a building. A lead ball of the same size takes 3.05 seconds to reach the ground. Which one of the following statements best accounts for this discrepancy?

    **a.** There is gravitational force between the Styrofoam ball and the building as it falls, slowing the ball down

    **b.** Air resistance acting on the Styrofoam ball is greater than the air resistance on the lead ball and thus slows it down more

    **c.** The force of gravity on the hollow Styrofoam ball is greater than on the lead ball

    **d.** The lead ball does not reach terminal velocity

**Q2.122** A Formula 1 car is accelerating from the starting line after the lights have turned green. What is the force that causes the car to accelerate?

    **a.** The oblique force of the road on the wheels
    **b.** The horizontal force of the road on the wheels
    **c.** The perpendicular force of the road on the wheels
    **d.** The horizontal force of the wheels on the road
    **e.** The vertical force of the wheels on the road

**Q2.123** Due to a mechanical failure, the engine of a moving Formula 1 car has completely stopped and exerts no force on the car's axels. The car is slowing down as it coasts towards the exit. Which of the following is true about the forces acting on the car?

    **a.** There are no forces acting on the car
    **b.** The net force acting on the car is backwards
    **c.** The net force acting on the car is upwards
    **d.** The net force acting on the car is forwards
    **e.** None of the above

**Q2.124** This is a reading of a patient's left ventricular blood pressure.

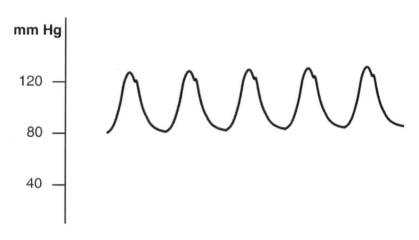

Which of the following statements is correct?

    **a.**   The reading has an amplitude of 50 mmHg
    **b.**   There are 6 complete wavelengths shown
    **c.**   The object is in simple harmonic motion
    **d.**   All are correct
    **e.**   None are correct

**Q2.125** A rugby player weighing 100kg accelerates uniformly from rest to a speed of 12m/s in 12 seconds. How much distance does he cover during those 12 seconds?

    **a.**   12 m
    **b.**   24 m
    **c.**   36 m
    **d.**   72 m
    **e.**   154 m

**Q2.126** A rugby player weighing 100 kg accelerates uniformly from rest to a speed of 12 m/s in 12 seconds. What is the magnitude of the net force on the player?

    **a.** 12 N
    **b.** 50 N
    **c.** 100 N
    **d.** 120 N
    **e.** 240 N

**Q2.127** Which of the following graphs shows the rate of heat transfer from the heating element in the kettle to the water (with respect to time) for a kettle that is boiling water from room temperature?

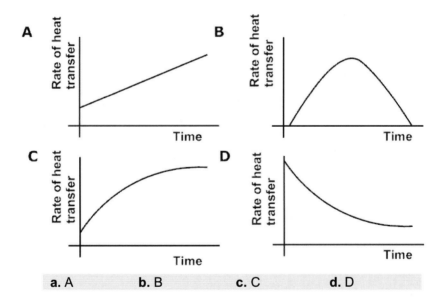

    **a.** A        **b.** B        **c.** C        **d.** D

**Q2.128** During a small earthquake, the people in the park did not notice it happening. However, during this minor earthquake, a single statue was completely demolished. What is the most likely explanation for this?

    **a.** The epicentre was focused at a point directly beneath the statue

    **b.** The amplitude of the earthquake was only large enough to transfer enough energy to collapse that one statue

    **c.** The frequency with which the earthquake was shaking was at the natural frequency of the statue

    **d.** All of the above

    **e.** None of the above

**Q2.129** Which of the following graphs best represents the radioactive decay of $^{201}$Hg?

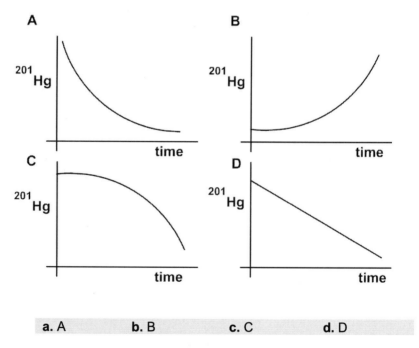

    **a.** A         **b.** B         **c.** C         **d.** D

**Q2.130** An analysis of a sample of Asteroid 9347 shows that it contains 6% of substance A and 44% of substance B by mass. Substance B is formed from the decay of substance A with no loss of mass and is not normally found on an asteroid.

The half-life of substance A is 400 years. What is the approximate age of the asteroid?

    **a.**    300 years
    **b.**    400 years
    **c.**    800 years
    **d.**    1000 years
    **e.**    1200 years
    **f.**    2400 years

**Q2.131** The graph below shows the volume and density of several different surgical instruments. Which of the following instruments have the same mass?

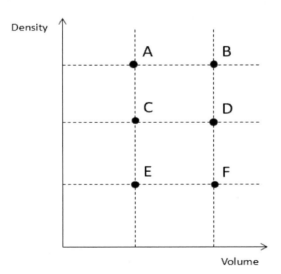

    **a.**    A & D
    **b.**    A & F
    **c.**    B & E
    **d.**    C & D
    **e.**    C & E
    **f.**    C & F

**Q2.132** The table shows the properties of certain radioactive isotypes. Which of the following would be the best isotype to use as a tracer in the human body?

| | Isotype | Type of radiation emitted | Half-life |
|---|---|---|---|
| a. | Americium 241 | Alpha | 141 years |
| b. | Polonium 210 | Alpha | 210 days |
| c. | Neptunium 231 | Alpha | 1 hour |
| d. | Thallium 204 | Beta | 4 years |
| e. | Tin 113 | Beta | 113 days |
| f. | Substantium 78 | Beta | 3 hours |
| g. | Sodium 22 | Gamma | 3 years |
| h. | Cubstantium 89 | Gamma | 78 days |
| i. | Technetium 99 | Gamma | 5 hours |

**Q2.133** A scientist investigates how the count rate of the nuclear radiation emitted by a particular radioactive source changes with time. He places a radiation detector 30 cm from the source, and records the count rate every 2 hours for 12 consecutive hours. This gives the following results:

| Time (hours) | 2 | 4 | 6 | 8 | 10 | 12 |
|---|---|---|---|---|---|---|
| Count (counts/minute) | 164 | 120 | 83 | 58 | 41 | 30 |

Which of the following below is true?

| | Count rate at 0 | Type of radiation emitted | Half-life |
|---|---|---|---|
| a. | 0 counts/second | Alpha | 120 minutes |
| b. | 240 counts/minute | Alpha | 240 minutes |
| c. | 4 counts/second | Beta | 120 minutes |
| d. | 120 counts/second | Beta | 160 minutes |
| e. | 240 counts/second | Beta | 240 minutes |
| f. | 4 counts/second | Gamma | 240 minutes |
| g. | 12 counts/second | Gamma | 120 minutes |
| h. | 240 counts/minute | Gamma | 160 minutes |

**Q2.134** Which three of the following effects can be attributed to thermal expansion?

1. A computer ceasing to function at high temperatures.
2. An object floating in cold water, but sinking in hot water.
3. Hot air rising above a radiator.
4. The burning of wood in a stove.
5. A ring of coffee mark on the inside of a cooling cup of coffee.
6. Melting of a plastic toy left in the sun.

    **a.** 1, 2 and 5
    **b.** 1, 3 and 5
    **c.** 1, 3 and 6
    **d.** 2, 3 and 4
    **e.** 2, 3 and 5
    **f.** 2, 4 and 5
    **g.** 3, 4 and 6
    **h.** 3, 5 and 6

**Q2.135** Figure X shows a uniform aluminium disc with a hole at the centre. Which one of the following diagrams shows how the disc will appear once it is put in an oven at 300 degrees Celsius?

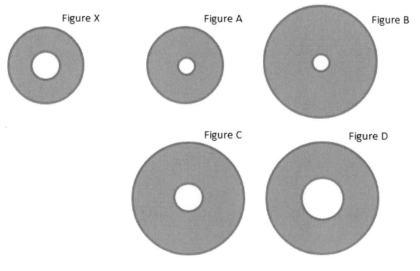

Figure X      Figure A      Figure B

Figure C      Figure D

**Q2.136** The nuclei of a radioactive element decay into the nuclei of another element at a rate proportional to the number of nuclei in the first element.

Consider that a radioactive element X decays into another radioactive element Y, which further decays into a non-radioactive element Z.

If you start with a pure sample of element X, and a plot of the number of the nuclei of Y as a function of time (t), which of the following graphs do you expect to obtain?

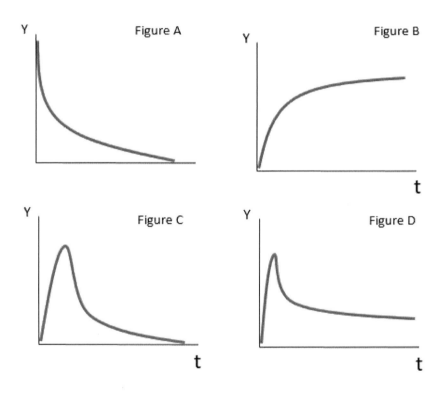

**Q2.137** An astronaut is sitting in a space shuttle on the ground. The shuttle takes off and accelerates to an altitude of 5,000m. During this time, what happens to the mass and to the weight of the astronaut?

|    | Weight    | Mass      |
|----|-----------|-----------|
| a. | decreases | decreases |
| b. | increases | Increases |
| c. | increases | decreases |
| d. | decreases | increases |
| e. | unchanged | increases |
| f. | unchanged | decreases |
| g. | decreases | unchanged |
| h. | increases | unchanged |

**Q2.138** Which of the following statements is false regarding liquids?

    **a.** Liquids are a condensed phase

    **b.** As miscibility of two fluids increases, emulsion formation increases

    **c.** Liquids result from molecular interactions

    **d.** Liquids are more disordered than solids

    **e.** They have little intermolecular space, which makes them relatively non-compressible

**Q2.139** A phase diagram is used to show the conditions under which a substance is in its solid, liquid or gaseous phase.

What are the axes of the phase diagram?

    **a.** X= pressure; Y = freezing point
    **b.** X= pressure; Y = temperature
    **c.** X= vapour pressure; Y = temperature
    **d.** X= pressure; Y = boiling point
    **e.** None of the above

**Q2.140** Two balls are dropped from a building. The balls are the same size, but ball A has greater mass than ball B.

When both balls reach terminal velocity, which of the following is true?

    **a.**   The force of air resistance on either ball is zero
    **b.**   Ball A has greater air resistance
    **c.**   Ball B has greater air resistance
    **d.**   The acceleration of both balls is 9.8 m/s$^2$
    **e.**   Ball B has greater velocity

# 2D Scientific Knowledge and Applications Chemistry – 66 Questions

## Answers from page 522

**Q2.141** Carbon-11 is an isotope of Carbon-12 and decays into Boron-11 by emitting a single proton. Which of the following is true?

    **a.** Carbon-11 has more protons than Carbon-12
    **b.** Boron-11 has a greater atomic number than Carbon-11
    **c.** Carbon-11 has the same atomic weight as Carbon-12
    **d.** Carbon-11 has the same atomic number as Carbon-12
    **e.** None of the above

**Q2.142** Which of the following correctly describes the molecules in an amino acid solution that is very dilute and mixed fully, at room temperature?

|  | amino acid molecules | water molecules |
|---|---|---|
| **a.** | widely separated not moving | widely separated randomly moving |
| **b.** | widely separated randomly moving | close together not moving |
| **c.** | widely separated randomly moving | close together randomly moving |
| **d.** | close together randomly moving | close together randomly moving |
| **e.** | close together not moving | widely separated not moving |

**Q2.143** In which of the following reactions is water a product?
    I.    Ethanol + Oxygen to give ethanoic acid
    II.   Combustion of ethanol
    III.  Fermentation of glucose

    **a.** I and II only
    **b.** I and III only
    **c.** II and III only
    **d.** All three reactions
    **e.** None of the above.

**Q2.144** A drop of liquid bromine is placed in the bottom of a gas jar. Brown fumes of bromine vapour slowly spread through the covered gas jar. Why does this happen?

    **a.** Bromine vapour is less dense than air.
    **b.** Bromine molecules and the molecules in the air are always moving around.
    **c.** Bromine molecules are smaller than the molecules in the air.
    **d.** Bromine molecules move faster than the molecules in the air.
    **e.** Bromine molecules is more dense than air molecules.

**Q2.145** A natural sample of Tanium contains 96% of $^{150}$Tanium. How many moles of $^{150}$Tanium are likely to be found in a 78g sample obtained from nature?

    **a.** 0.1   **b.** 0.25   **c.** 0.5   **d.** 2.5   **e. 5**

**Q2.146** The diagram shows elements of the Periodic table.

| | Neutrons | Protons | Electrons |
|---|---|---|---|
| A. | 6 | 6 | 6 |
| B. | 5 | 6 | 5 |
| C. | 5 | 6 | 6 |
| D. | 6 | 5 | 5 |
| E. | 6 | 5 | 6 |

**Q2.146a** Which of the above options correctly describes Carbon-12?

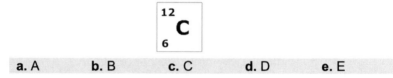

    **a.** A    **b.** B    **c.** C    **d.** D    **e.** E

**Q2.146b** Which of the above options correctly describes Boron-11?

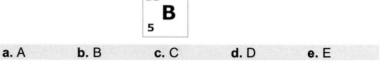

    **a.** A    **b.** B    **c.** C    **d.** D    **e.** E

**Q2.147** Which of the following statements is true when a solution is saturated?

    **a.**  The solvent changes to solute, and the solute changes to solvent at an equal rate
    **b.**  The concentration of the solvent is at a maximum
    **c.**  The concentration of the solvent is at a minimum
    **d.**  None of the above

**Q2.148** Solution A contains 1 mole of sodium chloride in 1 litre of water. Solution B contains 1 mole of potassium chloride in 1 litre of water. Both solutions are heated and the boiling point is measured. Which of the following statements is correct?

    **a.**  Solution A has a higher boiling point
    **b.**  Solution B has a higher boiling point
    **c.**  Both solutions will have the same boiling point
    **d.**  More information is required to determine the relative boiling points

**Q2.149** Which of the following compounds has the greatest heat of combustion?

    **a.**  Carbohydrates
    **b.**  Proteins
    **c.**  Unsaturated fats
    **d.**  Saturated fats

**Q2.150** Which molecule has the largest number of electrons involved in covalent bonds?

    **a.**  $C_2H_4$
    **b.**  $NH_3$
    **c.**  $CH_3OH$
    **d.**  $N_2$
    **e.**  $Cl_2$

**Q2.151** Compounds A and B are both alkanes. Compound A has a higher boiling point than compound B.

Which of the following could be the formulae of compounds A and B?

| | Compound A | Compound B |
|---|---|---|
| a. | $C_4H_{10}$ | $C_5H_{12}$ |
| b. | $C_3H_8$ | $C_4H_{10}$ |
| c. | $C_4H_{10}$ | $C_3H_8$ |
| d. | $C_5H_{12}$ | $C_4H_8$ |

**Q2.152** A reaction is carried out in a container. A pure compound X is shown at the start of the experiment. Compound X undergoes a first order reaction to form compound Y, with no reverse reaction.

Which of the following might represent the container at 20 minutes? The diagram shows the number of molecules of each sample X and Y.

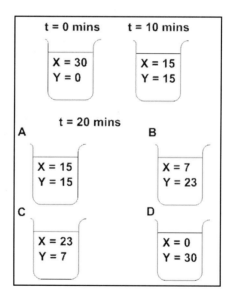

432

**Q2.153** A reaction begins with only its reactants and moves into eventual equilibrium. Which of the following options is happening during the reaction until equilibrium is reached?

|   | Rate of forward reaction | Rate of reverse reaction |
|---|---|---|
| a. | Decreases | Decreases |
| b. | Increases | Increases |
| c. | Decreases | Increases |
| d. | Increases | Decreases |

**Q2.154** Calcium carbonate decomposes into calcium oxide and carbon dioxide gas via the following reversible reaction:

$$CaCO_3 \text{ (s)} \leftrightarrow CaO \text{ (s)} + CO_2 \text{ (g)}$$

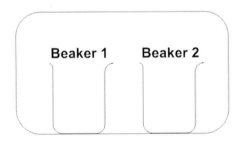

Beaker 1     Beaker 2

Beaker 1 contains pure $CaCO_3$ and Beaker 2 contains pure CaO. The container is sealed with room air.

Which of the following statements is true about the system upon achieving equilibrium?

    a.    Beaker 1 is empty
    b.    Beaker 2 is empty
    c.    The number of calcium atoms in Beaker 2 has increased
    d.    The number of calcium atoms in Beaker 2 has decreased
    e.    Beaker 2 contains a mixture of $CaCO_3$ and CaO

**Q2.155** Two gas containers, one containing butane and one containing propane, are placed at the same distance from a naked flame in a burning barbecue pit. Both gases are released at the same time and at the same rate. The propane gas reaches the flame and catches fire before the butane gas reaches the flame.

Which of the following statement explains this?

a. Each propane molecule has a higher proportion of hydrogen than each butane molecule.
b. Propane does not have isomers; butane does.
c. Propane has a higher boiling point than butane.
d. Propane molecules have a smaller mass than butane molecules.

**Q2.156** Which of the following is true of a catalysed reaction?

a. At equilibrium, a catalyst drives the forward reaction and so more product is produced
b. At equilibrium, a catalyst drives the back reaction and so more reactants are produced
c. The catalysed reaction pathway has a lower energy of activation than the uncatalysed reaction pathway
d. A catalyst may be the limiting reagent
e. None of the above

**Q2.157** Which of the options is the catalyst for the following two-step reaction?

Reaction 1: $Cl + O_3 \rightarrow ClO + O_2$
Reaction 2: $ClO + O \rightarrow Cl + O_2$

a. $Cl$
b. $O_2$
c. $O$
d. $O_3$
e. $ClO$

**Q2.158** Consider the following table:

|  | Rate of reaction | Activation energy | Time taken for reaction to complete |
|---|---|---|---|
| **a.** | Increases | Decreases | Decreases |
| **b.** | Increases | No change | Decreases |
| **c.** | Decreases | Decreases | Increases |
| **d.** | Decreases | No change | Increases |
| **e.** | No change | Increases | Decreases |
| **f.** | No change | Decreases | Decreases |

**Q2.158a** If the temperature of a chemical reaction is increased, which of the above normally occurs?

a. A    b. B    c. C    d. D    e. E    f. F

**Q2.158b** If a catalyst is added, which of the above always occurs?

a. A    b. B    c. C    d. D    e. E    f. F

**Q2.159** On which of the following does the rate of reaction depend?
I      Temperature.
II    Concentration of reactants.
III   Concentration of catalyst.
IV   Surface area of a catalyst.

a.   I
b.   I, II and III
c.   III and IV
d.   I and IV
e.   I, II, III and IV

**Q2.160** Which of the following atoms is most often found acting as a hydrogen bond acceptor?

a.   Hydrogen
b.   Carbon
c.   Calcium
d.   Oxygen
e.   All of the above

**Q2.161** What is the difference between a strong acid and a weak acid in an aqueous solution?

    **a.**   In a strong acid, the ions completely separate, while only a fraction of them separate in a weak acid

    **b.**   Strong acids always have a higher pH than weak acids

    **c.**   In a weak acid, the ions completely separate, while only a fraction of them separate in a strong acid

    **d.**   None of the above

**Q2.162** Two reactions involving water are shown below:

- Reaction 1: $NH_4^+ + H_2O \rightarrow NH_3 + H_3O^+$
- Reaction 2: $NaH + H_2O \rightarrow Na^+ + OH^- + H_2$

Which of the following is true regarding the role of the water in the two reactions?

|  | Reaction 1 | Reaction 2 |
|---|---|---|
| **a.** | Acts as a base | Acts as an acid |
| **b.** | Acts as an acid | Acts as a base |
| **c.** | Acts as an acid | Acts as an acid |
| **d.** | Acts as a base | Acts as a base |

**Q2.163** Ammonia is made from the Haber process between reacting nitrogen and hydrogen. The process is usually carried out at a temperature of 450°C:

$$N_2(g) + 3H_2(g) \leftrightarrow 2NH_3(g) \quad \Delta H = -92kJ/mol$$

Which row correctly shows the effect of increasing the temperature to over 450°C on the position of the equilibrium and on the rate of the reaction?

|  | Position of equilibrium | Rate of reaction |
|---|---|---|
| **a.** | Moves to right | Decreases |
| **b.** | Moves to right | Increases |
| **c.** | Moves to left | Decreases |
| **d.** | Moves to left | Increases |

**Q2.164** How many times bigger is the volume of 2 moles of Oxygen ($O_2$) compared to the volume of 1 mole of Argon gas (Ar)? Assume that temperature and pressure are equal.

    **a.** 4      **b.** 2      **c.** 0.25      **d.** 0.5      **e.** 1

**Q2.165** A scientist has made a tube containing various levels of filters, designed to treat impure water and transform it into drinkable water. The filters are arranged as follows:

| Impure water |
|:---:|
| **Filter 1 - Gravel (2-3mm)** |
| **Filter 2 - Gravel (0.5-1mm)** |
| **Filter 3 - Carbon** |
| **Filter 4 - Chlorine gas** |
| **Drinkable water** |

Which of the following will not be removed from the impure water by this filtering process?

    **a.**   Odours
    **b.**   Microbes
    **c.**   Nitrates
    **d.**   Clay particles

**Q2.166** You are told that a molecule contains 2.67 g of carbon, 0.22 g of hydrogen and 7.11 g of oxygen. Which of the following statements is true?

    1.   The empirical formula cannot be determined without further information.
    2.   The molecular formula cannot be determined without further information.
    3.   The empirical formula is $CHO_2$.

    **a.**   2
    **b.**   2 and 3
    **c.**   1 and 2
    **d.**   1
    **e.**   None of the above

**Q2.167** A compound contains 58.6% oxygen, 39% sulphur and 2.4% hydrogen by mass. Given the following relative atomic masses: H=1, O=16 and S=32, what is the empirical formula of this compound?

    **a.** HSO        **b.** $HSO_3$    **c.** $H_2SO_2$    **d.** $H_2SO_3$    **e.** $H_2SO_4$

**Q2.168** 0.8 litres of a 3-molar $H_2SO_4$ solution is to be made into a 1-molar solution. How many litres of distilled water must a person mix with the 0.8 litres of a 3-molar solution to create a 1-molar solution?

    **a.** 0.8 litres  **b.** 1.6 litres  **c.** 2.4 litres  d. 3.0 litres  **e.** 3.2 litres

**Q2.169** You are given a mixture of salt and coarse ground pepper. What is the correct sequence for obtaining pure salt from such a mixture?

    **a.**   Filter, add water, evaporate
    **b.**   Add water, evaporate
    **c.**   Add water, filter, evaporate
    **d.**   Add water, filter

**Q2.170** In a science experiment, a student measures a set amount of calcium carbonate with hydrochloric acid, producing carbon dioxide gas: $CaCO3(s) + 2HCl(aq) \rightarrow CaCl2(aq) + H2O(l) + CO2(g)$.

The rate of this reaction can be measured using the apparatus shown here.

Which additional piece of equipment is needed to find out the rate of reaction shown by the equation above?

    **a.**   A clock
    **b.**   A burette
    **c.**   A thermometer
    **d.**   A condensation funnel

**Q2.171** Zn and $Cu^{2+}$ undergo an equimolar redox reaction, whereby $Zn^{2+}$ is formed. After the reaction, what is the oxidation number of Cu?

    **a.** 1
    **b.** 0
    **c.** -1
    **d.** 2
    **e.** -2

**Q2.172** Which of the options represents the balanced version of the following redox equation in acidic aqueous conditions?
$MnO_4^- + Cl^- \rightarrow Cl_2 + Mn^{2+}$

    **a.**  $2MnO_4^- + 10\ Cl^- \rightarrow 2Mn^{2+} + 5\ Cl_2$
    **b.**  $MnO_4^- + 5\ Cl^- + 8\ H^+ \rightarrow Mn^{2+} + 2\ Cl_2 + 4\ H_2O$
    **c.**  $2MnO_4^- + 10\ Cl^- + 16\ H^+ \rightarrow Mn^{2+} + 5\ Cl_2 + 8\ H_2O$
    **d.**  $2MnO_4^- + 10\ Cl^- + 16\ H^+ \rightarrow 2Mn^{2+} + 5\ Cl_2 + 8\ H_2O$
    **e.**  None of the above

**Q2.173** Which of the options is true regarding the eventual oxidation state of the following reaction? $2Al_2O_3 + 3C \rightarrow 4Al + 3CO_2$

| | Aluminium | Carbon |
|---|---|---|
| **a.** | Reduced | Reduced |
| **b.** | Oxidised | Oxidised |
| **c.** | Reduced | Oxidised |
| **d.** | Oxidised | Reduced |

**Q2.174** What is the reducing agent in the following reaction?
$CH_4 + 2O_2 \rightarrow CO_2 + 2H_2O$

    **a.**  $CH_4$
    **b.**  $O_2$
    **c.**  $CO_2$
    **d.**  $H_2O$

**Q2.175** Which of the options is true regarding the eventual oxidation state of the following reaction: $HNO_3 + NaHCO_3 \rightarrow NaNO_3 + H_2CO_3$ ?

    **a.**  Nitrogen is reduced and oxygen is oxidised
    **b.**  Oxygen is reduced and carbon is oxidised
    **c.**  Hydrogen is reduced and sodium is oxidised
    **d.**  No oxidation or reduction takes place
    **e.**  None of the above

**Q2.176** Bromine consists of 2 isotypes: $^{79}_{35}Br$ and $^{81}_{35}Br$ in the ratio of 1:1. What is the relative atomic mass of bromine?

    **a.**  35
    **b.**  79.5
    **c.**  80
    **d.**  80.5
    **e.**  81

**Q2.177** Chlorine consists of 2 isotypes in the following ratios: 75% $^{35}_{17}Cl$ and 25% $^{37}_{17}Cl$.

What is the relative atomic mass of chlorine?

    **a.**  17
    **b.**  35.5
    **c.**  36
    **d.**  36.5
    **e.**  37

**Q2.178** Gallium is made up of 60% gallium-69 and 40% gallium-71. Calculate the $A_r$ of gallium.

    **a.**  68.9
    **b.**  69.0
    **c.**  69.5
    **d.**  69.8
    **e.**  70.2

**Q2.179** Tanium is made up of 20% Tanium-150 and 80% Tanium-X. This results in a relative atomic mass of 152. What is X?

    **a.** 150.5
    **b.** 151.5
    **c.** 152.5
    **d.** 153
    **e.** 154

**Q2.180** HCl gas and $NH_3$ gas form $NH_4Cl$ precipitate according to the following equation: $HCl(g) + NH_3(g) \rightarrow NH_4Cl(s)$.

When cotton balls that contain aqueous solutions of the gases are inserted at either end of a glass tube, the gases diffuse towards the middle of the glass tube to form the precipitate.

If a 20 cm glass tube is used, which of the following options denote the most likely distances X and Y? (Relative atomic masses: H = 1, N = 14, Cl = 35.5). Note: in this diagram, distances X and Y are not to scale.

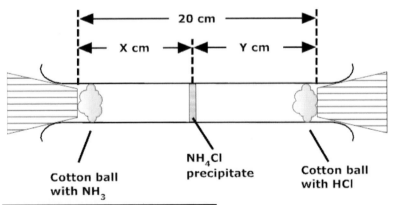

Cotton ball with $NH_3$      $NH_4Cl$ precipitate      Cotton ball with HCl

| | X (cm) | Y (cm) |
|---|---|---|
| **a.** | 12 | 8 |
| **b.** | 10 | 10 |
| **c.** | 8 | 12 |
| **d.** | 9 | 11 |

441

**Q2.181** Butane is completely combusted to produce carbon dioxide and water vapour. Determine the values of $a$ and $b$ to balance the following chemical equation representing this reaction.

$$a\ C_4H_{10} + 13O_2 \longrightarrow b\ CO_2 + 10H_2O$$

    **a.**   $a = 2, b = 6$
    **b.**   $a = 2, b = 8$
    **c.**   $a = 3, b = 12$
    **d.**   $a = 4, b = 10$
    **e.**   $a = 4, b = 16$

**Q2.182** When gaseous sulphur dioxide is oxidised in the presence of oxygen, sulphur trioxide is produced. What is the limiting reagent when 160 grams of sulphur dioxide forms 153 grams of sulphur trioxide in a reaction that runs to completion?

$2SO_2 + O_2 \rightarrow 2SO_3$ (Relative atomic masses: O=16, S = 32)

    **a.**   $SO_2$
    **b.**   $O_2$
    **c.**   $SO_3$
    **d.**   $SO_2$ and $O_2$
    **e.**   $O_2$ and $SO_3$

**Q2.183** If 1 mole of $C_4H_{12}$ is reacted with 3.5 moles of $O_2$, how many moles of $H_2O$ are produced?

    **a.**   1
    **b.**   2
    **c.**   2.5
    **d.**   3
    **e.**   3.5

**Q2.184** Given relative atomic masses Mg=24, O=16, H=1, Cl=35.5, how many grams of magnesium chloride are formed when 8g of magnesium oxide is dissolved in excess hydrochloric acid?

   **a.** 13
   **b.** 15
   **c.** 17
   **d.** 19
   **e.** 21

**Q2.185** Given relative atomic masses C=12, H=1, O=16, that the relative molecular mass for $Fe(C_5H_5)_2$ is 186, and that the relative molecular mass of $Fe(CN)_5NOH$ is 217, what is the relative atomic mass of N?

   **a.** 12
   **b.** 14
   **c.** 16
   **d.** 18
   **e.** 20

**Q2.186** Given the following relative atomic masses: H=1, N=14 and O=16, and that the relative formula mass of ammonium sulphate, $(NH_4)_2SO_4$, is 132, what is the relative atomic mass of S?

   **a.** 18
   **b.** 24
   **c.** 28
   **d.** 32
   **e.** 38

**Q2.187** When calcium carbonate is strongly heated, it undergoes thermal decomposition to form calcium oxide and carbon dioxide gas via the following equation: $CaCO_3 \rightarrow CaO + CO_2$ (relative atomic masses Ca=40, C=12, O=16). Calculate the tonnage of calcium carbonate decomposed if 28 tonnes of calcium oxide and 22 tonnes of carbon dioxide gas are produced with no additional products.

   **a.** 22
   **b.** 28
   **c.** 50
   **d.** 100
   **e.** 120

**Q2.188** Cyclohexane (C₆H₁₀) is drawn as follows:

**Q2.188a** Using this information, determine the total number of carbon atoms in the following molecule:

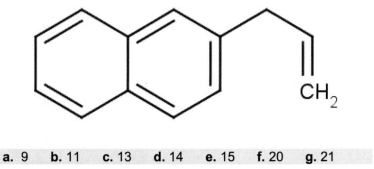

**a.** 9    **b.** 11    **c.** 13    **d.** 14    **e.** 15    **f.** 20    **g.** 21

**Q2.188b** Using this information, determine the total number of hydrogen atoms in the following molecule:

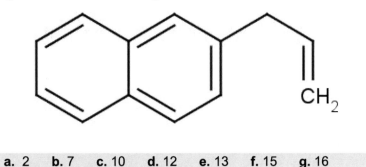

**a.** 2    **b.** 7    **c.** 10    **d.** 12    **e.** 13    **f.** 15    **g.** 16

**Q2.188c** Using this information, calculate the relative molecular mass of the following molecule [A$_r$ values: H = 1; C = 12]:

   **a.** 131    **b.** 156    **c.** 178    **d.** 180    **e.** 181    **f.** 191

**Q2.188d** Using this information, place the following molecules in increasing order of relative molecular masses [A$_r$ values: H = 1; C = 12]:

| | Smallest to largest |
|---|---|
| **a.** | A → B → C → D |
| **b.** | D → A → B → C |
| **c.** | C → D → A → B |
| **d.** | A → D → B → C |
| **e.** | B → A → D → C |
| **f.** | A → B → D → C |

445

**Q2.189** On complete combustion in air, a sample of an unknown hydrocarbon yielded 176 grams of $CO_2$ and 108 grams of $H_2O$ with no additional products. (Relative atomic masses: H = 1, C = 12, O = 16.) Which one of the following might be the formula of the hydrocarbon?

    a.   $CH_2$
    b.   $CH_3$
    c.   $CH_4$
    d.   $C_2H_4$
    e.   $C_2H_8$

**Q2.190** A gas X has no smell, is not poisonous, and reacts with hydrogen at high temperature and pressure. What is Gas X?

    a.   Carbon monoxide
    b.   Helium
    c.   Nitrogen
    d.   Chlorine
    e.   Bromine

**Q2.191** The presence of water leads to corrosion of iron bars. To prevent such corrosion, iron bars can be coated with an element such as zinc using electroplating, in a process called galvanisation.

Which of the following statements is correct?

    a.   During corrosion of an unplated iron bar, water is oxidised. During electroplating, iron acts as anode

    b.   During corrosion of an unplated iron bar, oxygen is reduced; during electroplating, zinc acts as cathode

    c.   During corrosion of an unplated iron bar, iron is oxidised; during electroplating, zinc is deposited on the anode

    d.   During corrosion of an unplated iron bar, iron is reduced; during electroplating, zinc is deposited on the cathode

**Q2.192** The following reaction $C_2H_4(g) + H_2(g) \rightarrow C2H6(g)$ is governed by the rate equation: rate = k $[C_2H_4]$ $[H_2]$.

At a fixed temperature and in a closed system, the reaction mixture is compressed to four times the original pressure. Which of the following is the factor by which the rate of reaction changes?

    **a.**   4
    **b.**   8
    **c.**   12
    **d.**   16
    **e.**   32

**Q2.193** There is an equimolar mixture of He, $N_2$, $CO_2$ and Ar gases in container A. Container B is in a state of vacuum. The two containers are separated by a pipe initially blocked by a closed valve.

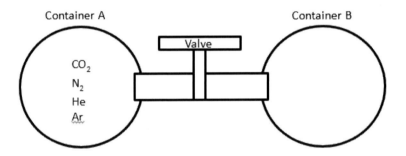

When the valve is opened, what will be the relationship between the number of moles of each gas in Container B before equilibrium is reached? (The relative molar mass of the gases are $N_2$ = 28, $CO_2$ = 44, Ar = 40 and He = 4.)

    **a.**   He > $N_2$ > Ar > $CO_2$
    **b.**   Ar > He > $N_2$ > $CO_2$
    **c.**   He > Ar > $CO_2$ > $N_2$
    **d.**   $CO_2$ > $N_2$ > He > Ar

**Q2.194** TLC (thin layer chromatography) is used to separate a mixture of several compounds (placed on to spot A) based on the different polarities of that compound. This is done by dipping a plate, onto which the mixture has been placed, into Solvent H for 90 minutes.

Solvent H moves up the plate by capillary action. The plate is then dried, rotated 90 degrees and then put into a different solvent, L, where capillary action is, again, allowed to happen.

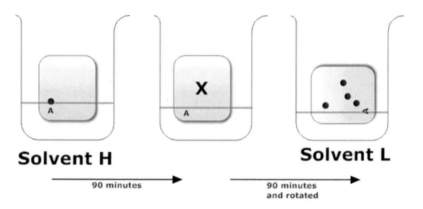

**Solvent H**          **Solvent L**

90 minutes

90 minutes
and rotated

Which of the following plates 1–4 is most likely be the one marked as plate X in the diagram above?

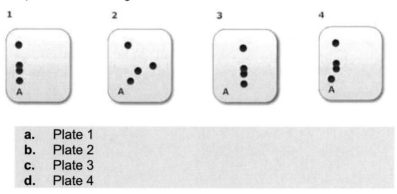

| | |
|---|---|
| **a.** | Plate 1 |
| **b.** | Plate 2 |
| **c.** | Plate 3 |
| **d.** | Plate 4 |

**Q2.195** Hydrogen and nitrogen react to form ammonia.

$N_2(g) + 3H_2(g) \leftrightarrow 2NH_3 (g)$ $\Delta H = -92kJ/mol$

Which statement is correct?

a. Ammonia is made in industry by the Contact process.
b. Ammonia is used in industry to make hydrogen and nitrogen.
c. Hydrogen is obtained from natural gas.
d. High pressures favour the reverse reaction

**Q2.196** How does an isotope of an element differ from the standard element?

a. Different numbers of protons and neutrons
b. Different number of electrons only
c. Different numbers of neutrons and electrons
d. Different numbers of protons and electrons
e. Different number of protons only
f. Different number of neutrons only

**Q2.197** Which three of the following statements below are accurate reasons for the fact that the yield from industrial chemical processes is not normally 100% efficient?

1. Mass is lost as energy.
2. Some reactants react to form waste products.
3. Background radiation spoils some of the reactants.
4. Reactants are not 100% pure.
5. Some reactions are reversible.

a. 1, 2 and 3
b. 1, 4 and 5
c. 2, 3 and 4
d. 2, 4 and 5
e. 3, 4 and 5

**Q2.198** Why would lithium be stored under oil?

    **a.** It can poison the air around it
    **b.** To prevent contact with water vapour
    **c.** Because of its terrible odour
    **d.** To avoid crystallisation
    **e.** To prevent it from rusting

**Q2.199** For which three of the following factors would an increase be associated with a faster rate of reaction?

    1. Activation energy.
    2. Bond length.
    3. Concentration.
    4. Surface area
    5. Temperature.

    **a.** 1, 2 and 3
    **b.** 1, 4 and 5
    **c.** 2, 3 and 4
    **d.** 2, 4 and 5
    **e.** 3, 4 and 5

**Q2.200** Which of the following statements is always true for an exothermic reaction?

    **a.** It is faster than an endothermic reaction
    **b.** It reduces the entropy of the universe
    **c.** It is the result of bond formation
    **d.** It releases energy in the form of heat
    **e.** All of the above

**Q2.201** Which of the following options shows the types of bonds found within and between chemical species in order of increasing strength?

    **a.** Covalent < Ionic < Hydrogen < Van der Waals
    **b.** Hydrogen < Covalent < Ionic < Van der Waals
    **c.** Van der Waals < Hydrogen < Ionic < Covalent
    **d.** Hydrogen < Van der Waals < Ionic < Covalent

# 2E Scientific Knowledge and Applications Mathematics – 86 questions

## Answers from page 541

**Q2.202** Richard buys 5 bags of crisps from his local shop. He gives the cashier a £5 note and receives £0.75 of change back. Richard notices that the cashier has given him too much change, and he gives £0.25 back to the cashier. What is the price of one bag of crisp?

    **a.** £ 0.80
    **b.** £ 0.85
    **c.** £ 0.90
    **d.** £ 0.95
    **e.** £ 1.00

**Q2.203** A car travelling at an average speed of 50 miles per hour (mph) made a trip in 5 hours. If it had travelled at an average of 65 mph, how many minutes shorter would the trip have been?

    **a.** 23 minutes
    **b.** 47 minutes
    **c.** 69 minutes
    **d.** 115 minutes
    **e.** 231 minutes

**Q2.204** A field has a surface of 2000 acres. The owner is dividing the field between his 3 sons. The second son gets a portion 4 times the size of the first son's and the third son gets a portion 5 times the size of the second son's.

What is the surface of the first son's portion?

    **a.** 80 acres
    **b.** 200 acres
    **c.** 320 acres
    **d.** 800 acres
    **e.** 1600 acres

**Q2.205** When 2 is subtracted from 5x, the result is half of the sum of 10 and 3x. What is the value of x?

    **a.**  - 4.5
    **b.**  0
    **c.**  2
    **d.**  4
    **e.**  6

**Q2.206** Richard bought oranges at a cost of 6 for £0.42, and then sold them on at a price of 8 for £0.72. If, having sold all his oranges, Richard made a £4.80 profit, how many oranges did he sell?

    **a.**  16
    **b.**  24
    **c.**  160
    **d.**  240
    **e.**  480

**Q2.207** An amount of £10,000 pounds was deposited into a savings account. If the savings account earns interest at a rate of 6 percent compounded annually, which of the following represents the value, in pounds, of the savings at the end of 2 years?

    **a.**  $10,000 \times (1 + 2 \times 0.06)$
    **b.**  $10,000 \times (0.06)^2$
    **c.**  $10,600 \times 1.06$
    **d.**  $10,000 \times 1.12$
    **e.**  $2 \times 10,000 \times 1.06$

**Q2.208** £5,000 pounds were deposited into a savings account. The annual interest rate is 7% compounded quarterly. What is the value of the savings at the end of 3 years?

    **a.**  $5,000 \times (1.0175)^{12}$
    **b.**  $5,000 \times (1.07)^3$
    **c.**  $5,000 \times (1.07)^{21}$
    **d.**  $5,000 \times (1.07)^{12}$
    **e.**  $5,000 \times (1.0233)^3$

**Q2.209** The average height of 3 members of a five-a-side football team is 175cm. What does the average height in centimetres of the other 2 players have to be if the average height of the entire team equals 178cm?

    **a.**   178cm
    **b.**   181cm
    **c.**   182.5cm
    **d.**   183.5cm
    **e.**   184cm

**Q2.210** A light-year is approximately $6 \times 10^{12}$ miles. Approximately how many miles from Earth is a galaxy that is $2 \times 10^{6}$ light-years away?

    **a.**   $1.2 \times 10^{17}$
    **b.**   $1.2 \times 10^{18}$
    **c.**   $1.2 \times 10^{19}$
    **d.**   $3.0 \times 10^{6}$
    **e.**   $1.2 \times 10^{73}$

**Q2.211** If the sum of two positive integers is 24 and the difference of their squares is 48, what is the product of the two integers?

    **a.**   108
    **b.**   119
    **c.**   128
    **d.**   135
    **e.**   143

**Q2.212** Evaluate: $\dfrac{3 \times 10^{-2}}{\sqrt{3.6 \times 10^{3}}} \times (2 \times 10^{2})^{3} \times \sqrt{6.4 \times 10^{7}}$

    **a.**   $3.2$
    **b.**   $3.2 \times 10^{2}$
    **c.**   $3.2 \times 10^{4}$
    **d.**   $3.2 \times 10^{7}$
    **e.**   $3.2 \times 10^{-2}$

**Q2.213** If X Braeburn apples cost 20 pence each and Y Golden Delicious apples cost 9 pence each, what is the average (arithmetic mean) cost, in pence, per apple?

a. $\dfrac{X+Y}{2}$

b. $\dfrac{29(X+Y)}{2}$

c. $\dfrac{20X+9Y}{29}$

d. $\dfrac{20X+9Y}{X+Y}$

e. $\dfrac{29}{X+Y}$

**Q2.214** If the cost of one apple is X/2 and the cost of a pear is Y/3, what is the average (arithmetic mean) cost for A units of apples and B units of pears?

a. $\dfrac{3AX+2BY}{6(A+B)}$

b. $\dfrac{3A+2B}{12}$

c. $\dfrac{3AX+2BY}{6}$

d. $\dfrac{3AX+2BY}{A+B}$

**Q2.215** If the average (arithmetic mean) of X, Y, and Z is 50, what is the arithmetic mean of (3X -10), (3Y + 20), and (3Z + 50)?

    **a.**   70
    **b.**   120
    **c.**   130
    **d.**   150
    **e.**   170

**Q2.216** What is the average (arithmetic mean) of 8 numbers if the average of 5 of the numbers is 24 and the sum of the remaining 3 numbers is 40?

    **a.**   8
    **b.**   20
    **c.**   29
    **d.**   37.33
    **e.**   45

**Q2.217** In a hospital, a senior registrar's annual salary is £50,400 greater than the annual salary of each of the two junior doctors, who both earn X pounds each per year. What is the average (arithmetic mean) of the 3 annual salaries?

    **a.**   2X
    **b.**   £10,800 + X
    **c.**   £12,600 + X
    **d.**   £16,800 + X
    **e.**   £16,800 + 2X/3

**Q2.218** If the average (arithmetic mean) of A and B is 60 and the average (arithmetic mean) of B and C is 80, what is the value of C - A?

    **a.**   10
    **b.**   20
    **c.**   30
    **d.**   40
    **e.**   50

**Q2.219** For the month of June, the average (arithmetic mean) of the daily high temperatures recorded with a thermometer was X degrees.

If the average for the first 13 days of the month was (X-10) degrees, what was the average, in degrees, for the remaining 17 days of the month?

    a.   X + 10

    b.   $\dfrac{17X+130}{2}$

    c.   $\dfrac{130X+17}{X}$

    d.   $\dfrac{17X+10}{17}$

    e.   $\dfrac{17X+130}{17}$

**Q2.220** The cost of a private plane flight to Barcelona from London is £500 per person. Meals are extra and cost £12 per person.

The number of people who paid for a meal was 100 less than the number who did not pay for a meal. The total income generated was £151,200.

How many people paid just for the flight and no food on this trip?

    a.   100
    b.   110
    c.   120
    d.   150
    e.   200

**Q2.221** A student on a gap year is planning a long road trip of 5,000 to 8,000 miles. The cost of petrol will be £1.10 to £1.50 per litre, and his car will average 30 to 50 miles per gallon.

What is the maximum possible cost of petrol he could incur for the trip? (Use 1 gallon = 4.5 litres)

    **a.**   £ 675
    **b.**   £ 1,080
    **c.**   £ 1,125
    **d.**   £ 1,320
    **e.**   £ 1,800

**Q2.222** If x and y are inversely proportional; and x = 10 and y = 5, what is y when x is 25?

    **a.**   1
    **b.**   1.5
    **c.**   2
    **d.**   4
    **e.**   5

**Q2.223** What is the median of the following fractions?

$$\frac{17}{36} \quad ; \quad \frac{1}{2} \quad ; \quad \frac{2}{8} \quad ; \quad \frac{13}{18} \quad ; \quad \frac{9}{27}$$

    **a.**   17/36
    **b.**   1/2
    **c.**   2/8
    **d.**   13/18
    **e.**   9/27

**Q2.224** What is the median of the following numbers?

$$\frac{17}{24} \quad ; \quad 0.5 \quad ; \quad \frac{3}{8} \quad ; \quad 0.75 \quad ; \quad \frac{2}{16} \quad ; \quad 0.25 \quad ; \quad \frac{6}{6}$$

a. 17/24
b. 0.5
c. 3/8
d. 0.75
e. 2/16
f. 0.25
g. 6/6

**Q2.225** In which interval does the following sum fall: $\frac{7}{8} + \frac{1}{10}$?

a. Between $\frac{1}{2}$ and $\frac{3}{4}$

b. Between $\frac{6}{7} + \frac{1}{14}$ and 1

c. Between 1 and $1\frac{1}{10}$

d. Between $1\frac{1}{10}$ and 1.5

e. None of the above

**Q2.226** Evaluate: $(25^2 - 15^2) + (32^2 - 18^2)$

a. 350
b. 500
c. 710
d. 1100
e. 1210

**Q2.227** When Y is multiplied by 4/7, it results in 6/7. What is Y?

    **a.** 2/7
    **b.** 2/3
    **c.** 3/2
    **d.** 24/7
    **e.** 7/2

**Q2.228** Which of the following is equivalent to 114/2000?

    **a.** $\dfrac{5}{10}+\dfrac{7}{10}$

    **b.** $\dfrac{5}{10}+\dfrac{7}{100}$

    **c.** $\dfrac{5}{100}+\dfrac{7}{100}$

    **d.** $\dfrac{5}{100}+\dfrac{7}{1000}$

    **e.** $\dfrac{5}{1000}+\dfrac{7}{1000}$

**Q2.229** Which of the following is the closest estimate for $\dfrac{50.2 \times 0.49}{199.8}$ ?

    **a.** 1/10
    **b.** 1/8
    **c.** 1/4
    **d.** 5/4
    **e.** 25/2

**Q2.230** Which of the following is the closest estimate to $\dfrac{61.25 \times (0.998)^2}{\sqrt{404}}$ ?

   a.  1
   b.  2
   c.  3
   d.  4
   e.  5

**Q2.231** If $d = \dfrac{a+b}{1 + \dfrac{ab}{c^2}}$ , $a = \dfrac{c}{2}$ , $b = \dfrac{3c}{4}$ , what is the value of d in terms of c?

   a.  10c / 11
   b.  5c / 2
   c.  10c / 3
   d.  10 / (11c)
   e.  5 / (2c)

**Q2.232** If x>5000, which of the following is the value closest to x / (2x + 1)?

   a.  1/6
   b.  1/3
   c.  10/21
   d.  1/2
   e.  3/2

**Q2.233** 95 percent of the revenue of a company came from the sale of computers. The remaining revenue, totalling £450,000, came from selling DVDs. What was the total revenue of the company?

   a.  £ 1,500,000
   b.  £ 2,500,000
   c.  £ 4,500,000
   d.  £ 9,000,000
   e.  £10,000,000

**Q2.234** If, in the formula $X=\dfrac{1}{(2r)^3}$, r is halved, by which factor is X multiplied?

    **a.**   1
    **b.**   8
    **c.**   64
    **d.**   1/8
    **e.**   1/16

**Q2.235** Richard and Max made 450 cakes altogether. If Richard made 3.5 times as many cakes as Max made, how many cakes did Max make?

    **a.**   100
    **b.**   150
    **c.**   250
    **d.**   350
    **e.**   400

**Q2.236** A chocolate cake mixture is made from flour, sugar and chocolate powder. If 1/4 of the mass of mixture is chocolate powder, and 1/5 is sugar, and the remainder is 990 g of flour, what is the total mass of the cake mixture?

    **a.**   1200 g
    **b.**   1500 g
    **c.**   1800 g
    **d.**   2000 g
    **e.**   4950 g

**Q2.237** An industrial colour printer can print 4 pages per second. How many minutes will it take to print 6,000 pages?

    **a.**   20
    **b.**   25
    **c.**   38
    **d.**   40
    **e.**   44

**Q2.238** What is the set of values for which $3 - x^3 < 11$ and $2x - 3 < 3$ ?

    **a.**    $2 < x < 3$
    **b.**    $x < 3$
    **c.**    $-2 < x < 3$
    **d.**    $x > 2$
    **e.**    $x > -2$

**Q2.239** A mouse fed with a high fat diet (HFD) feed weighs 450 grams, and a mouse fed with control feed pellets weighs 250 grams.

What percentage of the weight of the control mouse does the weight of the HFD mice represent?

    **a.**    55%
    **b.**    80%
    **c.**    155%
    **d.**    180%
    **e.**    230%

**Q2.240** A disk has an area equal to $25\,\pi$. What is its radius?

    **a.**    6
    **b.**    5
    **c.**    $2\sqrt{3}$
    **d.**    $4\sqrt{2}$
    **e.**    $5\sqrt{2}$

**Q2.241** What is the area of a rectangle with length $3X+1$ and width $X-3$?

    **a.**    $2X^2 + 8X - 3$
    **b.**    $X^2 - 8X - 3$
    **c.**    $3X^2 + 8X - 3$
    **d.**    $3X^2 - 8x + 3$
    **e.**    $3X^2 - 8X - 3$

**Q2.242** The supply of coffee beans is given by the following formula:

$$S = 3X^2 + X - 10$$

The demand for coffee beans is given by the following formula:

$$D = 2X^2 + 4X$$

where X is the price of coffee beans in pounds. At which of the following values of X (expressed in pounds) will the supply of coffee beans equal demand?

  a.  6
  b.  5
  c.  4
  d.  3
  e.  2

**Q2.243** A man starts at point A and walks 30m east, and then another 40m north to point B. What is the distance between A and B when measured as a straight line?

  a.  20 m
  b.  35 m
  c.  50 m
  d.  120 m
  e.  2500 m

**Q2.244** A runner and a walker leave at the same time from the intersection of two roads. The runner jogs due north at a constant rate of 6 miles per hour while the walker walks due west at a constant rate that is 3.5 miles per hour slower than the runner's rate. How far apart, to the nearest mile, will they be after 2 hours?

  a.  4 miles
  b.  11 miles
  c.  12 miles
  d.  13 miles
  e.  15 miles

463

**Q2.245** In the figure below, the square ABCD and the triangular region ACE each have area 36.

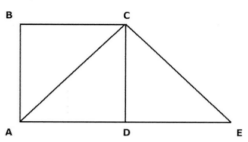

What is the perimeter of the triangle ACD?

  a.   12
  b.   $12 + 6\sqrt{2}$
  c.   18
  d.   $18 + \sqrt{72}$
  e.   24

**Q2.246** In this figure above, ABDE is a square and the length BC is equivalent to CD. Which of the following statements is not true?

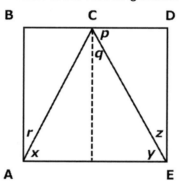

  a.   AC = CE
  b.   Angle r = angle z
  c.   Angle x = angle y
  d.   Angle p = angle z
  e.   The areas of triangles ABC and CDE are equal

**Q2.247** The number of admissions to hospital is represented by a circle graph (pie chart). 43% of admissions are emergency admissions, 18% are from the surgical department, 12% are from the oncology department, 7% are from out-patients and the rest are related to chronic diseases. How many degrees of the circle are used to represent admissions due to chronic diseases?

    **a.**   20
    **b.**   36
    **c.**   40
    **d.**   72
    **e.**   90

**Q2.248** A rigid ladder is leaning against a wall that is perpendicular to level ground. The top of the ladder touches the wall at 4m above the floor. The bottom of the ladder is 3 metres from the base of the wall. If the top of the ladder slips down 1 metre, how many metres will the bottom of the ladder slip along the ground?

    **a.**   1
    **b.**   $4 - 4\sqrt{3}$
    **c.**   $4\sqrt{3} - 3$
    **d.**   4
    **e.**   5

**Q2.249** For which of the following equations is it true that the value of the expression is the same when X = - 456 as it is when X = 456?

        1) $50 - 2X$
        2) $50 - 2X^2$
        3) $(50 - 2X^3)^2$

    **a.**   1
    **b.**   2
    **c.**   3
    **d.**   2 and 3
    **e.**   1, 2 and 3

**Q2.250** For all integers a, b, c, and d:

*(a, b, c, d) is defined as: $(a - c)^2 + (2d - b)^3$.

What is the value of *(1, 2, 3, 4)?

    a.   9
    b.   38
    c.   40
    d.   212
    e.   220

**Q2.251** The operation @ is defined by the following equation:

$$x @ y = \frac{x - y}{2x - y}$$

Which of the following equals 0?

    a.   -2@2
    b.   2@-2
    c.   2@2
    d.   2@1
    e.   1@2

**Q2.252** If a sequence of 8 consecutive odd integers with increasing values has 9 as its 7th term, what is the sum of the terms of the sequence?

    a.   22
    b.   32
    c.   36
    d.   40
    e.   44

**Q2.253** In a sequence of 10 numbers which has 1 as the first number, each successive number is 1 greater than the reciprocal of the number that immediately precedes it. What is the third term of this sequence?

    **a.**   0.5
    **b.**   1
    **c.**   1.5
    **d.**   2
    **e.**   2.5

**Q2.254** If $(X - 3)(Y - 1) = 0$ which of the following must be true?

    I.  $X = 3$ and $Y = 1$
    II.  If $X \neq 3$ then $Y = 1$
    III.  If $X = 3$ then $Y \neq 1$

    **a.**   I only
    **b.**   II only
    **c.**   III only
    **d.**   II and III only

**Q2.255** If $(-3, C)$ is a point on the graph of $y = 3x^2 - 2x + 3$, then C is:

    **a.**   12
    **b.**   15
    **c.**   24
    **d.**   -36
    **e.**   None of the above

**Q2.256** Consider a graph representing $y = (x - 5)^3 + 2(x+2)^2 + (x-3) + 7$ and a point P $(7,176)$. Unit = centimetre. Point P is:

    **a.**   More than 10cm below the curve
    **b.**   Less than 10 cm below the curve
    **c.**   On the curve
    **d.**   Less than 10cm above the curve
    **e.**   More than 10 cm above the curve

**Q2.257** Consider two graphs:

Graph A: $y = 4x$

Graph B: $y = \dfrac{9}{x} + 16$

At what values of x do they meet?

    **a.**   x = - 0.5 and x = + 0.5
    **b.**   x = + 4.5 and x = - 4.5
    **c.**   x = + 0.5 and x = - 4.5
    **d.**   x = - 0.5 and x = + 4.5
    **e.**   They don't meet

**Q2.258** The product of 2 positive integers A and B is four times the sum of A and B. If A = 12, what is the value of B?

    **a.**   2
    **b.**   4
    **c.**   6
    **d.**   8
    **e.**   12

**Q2.259** An author has a monthly salary determined by the formula: Salary = £2500 + X/10, where X is the retail value of the books sold, expressed in pounds per month.

In July his salary was £4,000 and in August, it was 20% greater. What was the value of the books sold in August?

    **a.**   £2 900
    **b.**   £2,980
    **c.**   £10,000
    **d.**   £15,000
    **e.**   £23,000

**Q2.260** In a certain hospital, there are 5 times as many nurses as there are doctors, and 1/3 as many doctors as there are healthcare assistants. If 5Z is the number of healthcare assistants, how many nurses are there in the hospital?

    **a.**   3Z/5
    **b.**   5Z/3
    **c.**   3Z
    **d.**   25Z/3
    **e.**   None of the above

**Q2.261** Calculate the following equation:

$$\frac{8^4-1}{3(8^2+1)}$$

    **a.**   11
    **b.**   21
    **c.**   25
    **d.**   35
    **e.**   43

**Q2.262** Which of the following sums is the greatest?

$$I. \quad \frac{1}{\sqrt{2}} + \frac{1}{\sqrt{3}} + \frac{1}{\sqrt{4}} + \frac{1}{\sqrt{5}}$$

$$II. \quad \frac{1}{2^2} + \frac{1}{3^2} + \frac{1}{4^2} + \frac{1}{5^2}$$

$$III. \quad \frac{1}{2^2} + \frac{1}{2^3} + \frac{1}{2^4} + \frac{1}{2^5}$$

$$IV. \quad \frac{1}{2} + \frac{1}{3} + \frac{1}{4} + \frac{1}{5}$$

    **a.**   I
    **b.**   II
    **c.**   III
    **d.**   IV

**Q2.263** If x = 0.02 and n = 10000, then calculate the following equation:

$$\sqrt{\frac{x(0.1-x)}{n}}$$

   a.   0.4
   b.   0.04
   c.   0.004
   d.   0.0004
   e.   0.00004

**Q2.264** Calculate the following:

$$(\sqrt{7} - 2)(\sqrt{7} + 2)$$

   a.  $\sqrt{14} - 4$
   b.  $\sqrt{7} - 4$
   c.  3
   d.  5
   e.  7

**Q2.265** Calculate the following equation: $\sqrt{5} - \sqrt{125}$

   a.   $-\sqrt{120}$
   b.   $-2\sqrt{5}$
   c.   $-4\sqrt{5}$
   d.   $-2.5$
   e.   $-0.00004$

**Q2.266** If $167^2$ = 27,889 what does 167 x 501 equal to?

   a.   $(27,889)^3$
   b.   167 x 4
   c.   27,889 x 3
   d.   27,889 + 3
   e.   $(27,889)^2$

**Q2.267** Consider the following diagram:

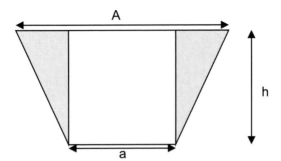

What is the combined area of the two grey triangles?

    **a.**  $(A + a) / (2h)$
    **b.**  $2Ah$
    **c.**  $h (A + a) / 2$
    **d.**  $h (A - a) / 2$
    **e.**  $ah / 2$

**Q2.268** The sides of an equilateral triangle measure X.

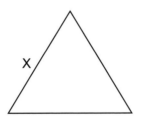

What is the formula for the triangle's area?

    **a.**  $X^2 / 2$
    **b.**  $X^2 \sqrt{3} / 4$
    **c.**  $X^2 \sqrt{4 / 3}$
    **d.**  $X^2 \sqrt{2}$
    **e.**  $X^2 \sqrt{2} / 3$

**Q2.269** Consider the following regular octagon, in which all sides measure X:

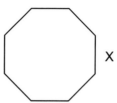

X

What is the area of the octagon?

a. $2(1+\sqrt{2})X^2$
b. $2(1-\sqrt{2})X^2$
c. $\sqrt{3}(1+\sqrt{2})X^2$
d. $7X^2$
e. $2X^2/(1+\sqrt{2})$

**Q2.270** Consider the following graph in which lines AB and CD are parallel, with AD and BC intersection at a point X.

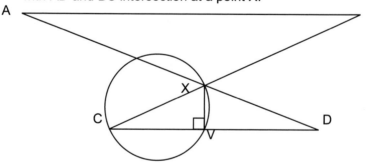

We know that (drawing not to scale): the triangle CVX is a rectangular triangle, AX = 6, DX = 2 and BC = 12

What is the radius of the circle?

a. 0.5
b. 1
c. 1.5
d. 2
e. 2.5

**Q2.271** A quarter of a circle with radius R fits within a right isosceles triangle as follows:

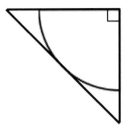

What is the following expressions provides the area of the section of the triangle which lies outside of the quarter circle?

    **a.**   $(R^2 + \pi/4) R^2$
    **b.**   $(1 - \pi/4) R^2$
    **c.**   $(2/3 + \pi/4) R^2$
    **d.**   $(4 - \pi) R^2$
    **e.**   $R^2 - \pi R^2$

**Q2.272** Felicity is hosting a dinner party and plans to make a large apple and pear tart. In the shop, pears and apples are priced individually and sold at a fixed price per item (i.e. not by weight).

There are no labels showing the prices of apples and pears; however the customer in front of her in the queue bought a bag of 6 apples and 8 pears for £4.10. The customer before that bought a bag of 8 apples and 2 pears for £2.

To make her tart she needs to use of apples to pears of 4:1. She can only spend £12 in total on fruits. In view of her budget, how many apples will she be able to use to make her tart?

    **a.**   12
    **b.**   24
    **c.**   36
    **d.**   48
    **e.**   60

**Q2.273** A company has patented an electric scented wax melter which uses small cubes of wax of various sizes. The energy required to melt a cube of wax is directly proportionate to the mass of the cube. An experiment has shown that it takes exactly 35 minutes to melt a 3-gramme cube of wax with a smaller 2W heater. How long does it take to melt a 7.5-gramme cube of wax with a 10W heater?

    **a.**   7 minutes
    **b.**   14 minutes
    **c.**   17.5 minutes
    **d.**   22.5 minutes
    **e.**   35 minutes

**Q2.274** A chocolate factory is famous for making chocolates in the shape of equilateral triangular pyramids, with edible glaze on all sides. The company is trying to make smaller versions of those chocolates, such that they look the same but each triangle has a base and height which is half of that of the original chocolate. How much less glaze is needed to make the new chocolate compared to the old chocolate?

    **a.**   2
    **b.**   3
    **c.**   4
    **d.**   8
    **e.**   16

**Q2.275** An airline pilot is unsure of the exact number of passengers he has allowed on board his plane. He thinks there are 25 people in total but that there could be as many as 3 more of 3 fewer people. Each person weighs between 60kg and 80kg. When flying without passengers (i.e. a pilot alone) the plane requires 100 litres. For each 100 kg of additional weight, the pilot needs to allow for an additional 2-4 litres of jet fuel, depending on the weather and the route he expects to follow. What is the range for the fuel he needs in total?

    **a.**   26.4 – 89.6
    **b.**   52.8 – 105.3
    **c.**   126.4 – 189.6
    **d.**   152.8 – 205.3
    **e.**   189.6 – 205.3

**Q2.276** A drone enthusiast has programmed a hover drone to trace out a regular polygonal shape. The drone flies along its programmed path. The drone's first bearing is 135° and its third bearing is 225°.

What shape is the drone tracing?

    **a.**   Triangle
    **b.**   Pentagon
    **c.**   Hexagon
    **d.**   Octogon
    **e.**   Nonagon
    **f.**   Decagon

**Q2.277** An engineer has taken a square piece of metal and cut a half-circle out of it, as shown in the diagram below. The area of the remaining part is 16 cm².

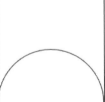

Which of the following expressions gives the length of the side of the square?

    **a.**   $8\sqrt{\dfrac{2}{8-\pi}}$

    **b.**   $4\sqrt{\dfrac{2}{4-\pi}}$

    **c.**   $8\sqrt{\dfrac{2}{4-\pi}}$

    **d.**   $4\sqrt{\dfrac{2}{4+\pi}}$

    **e.**   $8\sqrt{\dfrac{2}{8+\pi}}$

**Q2.278** A British firm wishes to purchase a length of a ship's anchor from a French retailer. The retail price is calculated as a one-off charge of €2160 plus €720 per metre. The Euro (€) to Pound (£) exchange rate is £1 = €1.2.

Which of the following expressions gives the length of the anchor chain L, given its price X, where X is expressed in Pounds?

    **a.**  L = 600(X – 3)
    **b.**  L = X/600 - 3
    **c.**  L = X/720 - 3
    **d.**  L = (X-2160)/720
    **e.**  L = (X-1800)/720

**Q2.279** If $\sqrt{3-2x} = \sqrt{2x}+1$, what is the value of $4x^2$ ?

    **a.**  2
    **b.**  4
    **c.**  $6x - 1$
    **d.**  $3x + 2$
    **e.**  $4x + 1$

**Q2.280** If the radius of a cylinder is increased by 30%, by how much is the cylinder's volume increasing?

    **a.**  30%
    **b.**  33%
    **c.**  60%
    **d.**  69%
    **e.**  90%

**Q2.281** Which of the following is a simplified form of $\sqrt{27}.\sqrt{144} + \sqrt{108}$ ?

    **a.**  $30\sqrt{3}$
    **b.**  $42\sqrt{3}$
    **c.**  $18\sqrt{6}$
    **d.**  $36\sqrt{3} + 3\sqrt{12}$
    **e.**  $12\sqrt{3} + 3\sqrt{12}$

**Q2.282** Take two positive integers A and B, with the following relationships:
- B% of A equals 100
- 50% of 50% of A equals B

What is the value of A?

    **a.**   25
    **b.**   50
    **c.**   100
    **d.**   200
    **e.**   1000

**Q2.283** A man runs from his house to work at a speed of R mph. On his way back, he walks from his workplace to home at a speed of W mph, using the same route as he used in the morning. The total return journey takes a time T. Which of the following expressions calculates the distance between his home and his workplace?

    **a.**   (R + W) / T
    **b.**   RT/W
    **c.**   RWT / (R+W)
    **d.**   (R + W) / RWT
    **e.**   RW / (R+W)

**Q2.284** In the past 10 years, Stock Market Index A has doubled in value from its low of 3,500 whilst Index B has declined by 80% from its high of 40,000. From now on, Index B is expected to grow by 5% every year, and Index A is expected to grow at twice that rate. Readings of the index at taken once a year. In how many years is Index A expected to exceed Index B?

    **a.**   1
    **b.**   2
    **c.**   3
    **d.**   4
    **e.**   5

**Q2.285** If $\sqrt{17+\sqrt{264}}$ can be written in the form $\sqrt{a}+\sqrt{b}$, where a and b are integers, and b<a, what is the value of a-b ?

    **a.** 1
    **b.** 2
    **c.** 3
    **d.** 4
    **e.** 5

**Q2.286** Evaluate $(15^2 - 5^2) + (27^2 - 23^2) + (14^2 - 6^2) + (57^2 - 43^2)$

    **a.** 1900
    **b.** 1920
    **c.** 1940
    **d.** 1960
    **e.** 1980

**Q2.287** For which values do both of the following relationships hold true?

$$17 - x^2 > 8$$

and

$$3x + 2 \geq 11$$

    **a.** $-3 < x < 3$
    **b.** $0 < x < 3$
    **c.** $0 < x \leq 3$
    **d.** $0 \leq x < 3$
    **e.** $1 < x \leq 3$
    **f.** No possible value

# Scientific Knowledge and Applications Biology – Answers

### Q2.1a – a: Autosomal dominant
The pattern of inheritance is dominant since all 3 generations have the disease. Recessive traits usually skip a generation (i.e. carriers only). Only 1 allele is required in this case for the disease to be passed on. Males have only one X chromosome, and thus cannot be carriers for X-linked conditions. If the inheritance was X-linked, then, since this disease is dominant, parents A and B would produce sons who have no disease (X comes from the normal mother and Y from the father), whereas they should produce daughters who do (X from the father is dominant). Here, this is not the case; thus this disease is autosomal dominant.

### Q2.1b – a: A and D
Modelling RR as homozygous diseased allele and rr as normal allele:

- We know that the disease process is autosomal dominant. So D, G, H should be Rr (because they have an unaffected (rr) parent).
- A is also Rr because if A was RR then all progeny would be Rr, which is not the case since E is unaffected.

### Q2.2a – b: 25%
If we define allele $X^C$ as colour blind, and X as the normal allele, we can model this scenario by drawing a Punnett square as follows:

|  |  | Father colour blind | |
|---|---|---|---|
|  |  | $X^C$ | Y |
| Mother carrier | $X^C$ | $X^C X^C$ | $X^C Y$ |
|  | X | $X^C X$ | X Y |

XY are boys and XX are girls. Of all the boys that can be produced, we can see that 50% would be colour-blind ($X^C Y$). Since each birth is independent, the probability that both boys are colour-blind is calculated as 0.5 x 0.5 = 0.25, i.e. 25%.

## Q2.2b – b: 25%

XY are boys and XX are girls. Of all the girls that can be produced, we can see that 50% would be colour-blind ($X^C X^C$) whereas 50% would be $X^C X$ (carriers) and not colour-blind. Since each birth is independent (we are told they are 3 and 5 years old meaning they cannot be twins), the probability that both girls are colour-blind is calculated as 0.5 x 0.5 = 0.25, i.e. 25%.

## Q2.3 – a: 0%

Taking "s" as the gene for sickle cell anaemia, and "S" as the normal allele, we can model the scenario with the following Punnett square:

| | | Father diseased | |
| --- | --- | --- | --- |
| | | s | s |
| Mother | S | Ss | Ss |
| carrier | s | ss | ss |

Because this is autosomal recessive, the sex of the children does not matter. From the Punnett square, we see that all the children in this scenario would contain the allele for sickle cell anaemia (50% carriers, 50% sickle cell patients).

## Q2.4 – a: $X^H X^h$

Since this is an X-linked recessive disease, A must be $X^H Y$ (normal) and B is $X^h X^h$ (diseased). Therefore D, who is a female, would inherit $X^H$ from parent A (the father) and $X^h$ from parent B (the mother).

## Q2.5 – a: The genetic code is degenerate

The genetic code has five key properties:

1.  It is universal: the same code is used across all known species.

2.  It is composed of nucleotide triplets.

3.  It is unambiguous: the same codon (nucleotide triplet) will always encode for one amino acid, "Start transcription", or "Stop transcription". Example: ACG only encodes for threonine, and no other amino acid.

4.   It is non-overlapping: each nucleotide is part of only one codon; there are no overlapping codons.

5.   It is degenerate, meaning that several codons can encode for the same amino acid. This is sometimes also called "redundant".

## Q2.6 – d: RrTt

The white and small-thorned rose has the recessive genotype rrtt and can therefore only produce gametes of one class: rt. The first generation (F1) offspring's phenotypic ratio is 1:1:1:1. Since both the recessive (white petals, small thorns) and dominant (red petals, large thorns) traits are present in the offspring, the unknown parental genotype must contain both recessive alleles (r and t) and both dominant alleles (R and T) to give its offspring's phenotypes. The unknown parental genotype must therefore be RrTt, and produces the following gametes: RT, Rt, rT, rt. Combined with the gamete "rt", this  gives RrTt, Rrtt, rrTt and rrtt, all with equal probability of 25%.

## Q2.7 – b: 3 genotypes and 2 phenotypes

When an allele is dominant, any genotype that has the dominant allele will have the same phenotype as the homozygous dominant. This means that the genotypes PP and Pp will have the same phenotype.

If we look at the Punnett square below, we see that there are 3 possible genotypes (PP, Pp, pp) but only 2 possible phenotypes (large peas, small peas).

|   | P | p |
|---|---|---|
| **P** | PP (25%, large peas) | Pp (25%, large peas) |
| **p** | Pp (25%, large peas) | pp (25%, small peas) |

## Q2.8 – a: Only male infants will die from the disorder

Sex-linked recessive genes are carried on the X chromosome. Because men only have one X chromosome and therefore do not have a compensating dominant allele, all male children who carry the diseased X chromosome-linked gene will be affected by the disease. Since the disease in question is lethal in infancy, all males with the diseased X chromosome-linked gene will die before they can have children and therefore Option d cannot be true.

Since men cannot be viable carriers, any daughters they may have will have at least one X chromosome that does not contain the fatal allele. Because the gene is recessive, we can conclude that females can be carriers but cannot die from the fatal disease. Thus, Option a is true and Options b and c are false.

Option e is false because a male child born of a mother who is a carrier has a 50% chance of inheriting the "healthy" X chromosome and therefore only 50% of male infants born from carriers will die.

Note that the text of the question states we should ignore the possibility of mutations that arise spontaneously. This is because, although this would be really rare, a mutation could lead to the defective (carrier) allele arising in a female, resulting in infant death.

### Q2.9 – e: Mitochondrial
This disease is transmitted only through mothers, so this is a mitochondrial inheritance disease. Nuclear DNA has two copies: one from the mother and one from the father. However, mitochondrial DNA is only inherited from the mother. It is not X-linked dominant because daughters of affected males aren't affected. It is not X-linked recessive because daughters of a normal father and affected mother are affected. It is not autosomal dominant because all the children of affected females are affected, and none of the children of affected males are affected. An example of mitochondrial disease is Leber's hereditary optic neuropathy.

### Q2.10 – a: Switching to vegetarianism would help support a greater number of people
Energy decreases as it moves up trophic levels, due to losses of waste and metabolic heat when organisms from one trophic level are consumed by organisms from the next level. Indeed, it is often said that a food chain can sustain no more than six energy transfers before all energy is used up. Net production efficiency (NPE) measures how efficiently each level uses and incorporates the energy from its food into biomass. Animals have low NPEs whereas vegetables have high NPEs.

For example, edible kilocalories produced from kilocalories of energy required for cultivation are 18% for chicken, 7% for grass-fed beef, 6% for farmed salmon and 1% for shrimp. In contrast, potatoes yield 123%, corn produces 250% and soy results in 415% of input calories converted to calories able to be utilised by humans. This disparity in efficiency reflects the reduction in production from moving up trophic levels. Thus, it is more energetically efficient to form a diet from lower trophic levels (e.g. vegetables) than higher trophic levels (e.g. animals).

Option b is controversial and does not actually belong to the argument in the question. Even if it were shown to be correct, it merely addresses the fact that vegetarianism may be healthier and not how it could support an expanding population.

Option c is incorrect: strict vegans and vegetarians often have mineral/iron deficiencies. We know from the syllabus that humans are omnivores and produce various enzymes such as proteases to digest proteins, thus we know that humans cannot subsist on plants alone without deficiencies of various minerals and vitamins that can be obtained from an animal-based diet. The rationale for converting to vegetarianism is to increase efficiency.

Option d: Biodiversity is irrelevant and, in any case, a move towards universal vegetarianism may actually negatively impact on biodiversity if an increasing number of crops are grown for consumption by humans rather than by animals.

**Q2.11 – a: (1) dsDNA   (2) ssDNA   (3) dsRNA   (4) ssRNA**
Only RNA uses U bases and only DNA uses T bases. Therefore Specimen 1 and Specimen 2 are DNA, and Specimen 3 and Specimen 4 are both RNA. Option a and Option c are the only two possibilities. Specimen 1 binds A with T and C with G, therefore it is double stranded. Hence the answer is Option a, since Option c has Specimen 1 as single stranded.

**Q2.12 – a: Sherpas have greater vital capacity and enlarged thoracic cavity**
People living at high altitude are expected to have greater respiratory vital capacity. The partial pressure of oxygen in the atmosphere is much lower at high altitude than at sea level (the air is thinner), so the Sherpas will have to inhale a greater volume of air than people living at sea level to extract

the same level of oxygen. Mountain dwellers generally have an enlarged thoracic cavity so that they can inhale and exhale a larger volume of air per breath. Hence Option a is correct and Options b and c are incorrect.

Option d is incorrect because red blood cells help carry oxygen, and so Sherpas would be expected to have a higher concentration of red blood cells, if anything. If they had a lower concentration of red blood cells, they would be anaemic and would likely feel short of breath as their oxygen-carrying capacity would be reduced.

### Q2.13 – d: T U V S
We are given that U to V = 7 and that S to V (or V to S) = 10. Since we also know that U to V = 17 (i.e. 10+7), then it means that U, V and S appear either in the order UVS or SVU. Similarly, we are told that S to U = 17 and U to T = 8; and since S to T = 25 (i.e. 17+8) then S, U and T appear either in the order SUT or TUS. If we combine the two conclusions above, we can see that the T must be next to the U at the end of the chain. Hence the answer is TUVS.

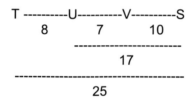

### Q2.14 – e: 1, 2 and 4 only
The celery plant cells placed in water would initially swell. Normally the rigid cell wall would keep the cell rigid and limit its expansion. However, the cellulase added to the water destroys the cell walls, as a result of which the cells will lose their structural attachments to each other and their rigid shape. Once the cell wall is dissolved, plant cells act in a similar way to animal cells. Osmosis/diffusion occurs, water moves from high to low water potential and gets drawn into the cells, causing the cells to swell and burst.

### Q2.15 – c: 2, 3 and 6 only
Only bacterial cells contain chromosomal (free) DNA and flagella. All animal, plant and bacterial cells contain a cell membrane. But only plant cells have cell walls, chloroplasts and a vacuole.

**Q2.16 – c: 9**
To calculate this, we need to know the mutation rate, the number of base pairs that could potentially mutate, and the time taken to divide (i.e. the actual number of base pairs after division has taken place). The number of mutations is calculated as Mutation rate x Number of base pairs x Number of cell divisions. So it is $1 \times 10^{-6} \times 3{,}000{,}000 \times 3 = 9$.

**Q2.17 – b: Pregnancy test**
Human chorionic gonadotropin hormone is released by pregnant women's growing placenta. Its role is to promote the maintenance of the corpus luteum during the beginning of pregnancy. However, you do not have to know this to be able to answer the question.

Antibodies are produced by the mouse's white blood cells. Those antibodies can bind to the hCG. The antibodies are very unlikely to be useful to treat infertility since they would bind to hCG, which is released upon pregnancy and therefore, by definition, in those who are fertile. The antibodies are also very unlikely to prevent fertilisation (i.e. the joining of the sperm with the egg) as hCG is released in pregnancy and so post-fertilisation.

Paternity testing would require DNA testing as opposed to hormones.

However, since hCG is released in pregnant women and antibodies are bound to hCG, then it is not inconceivable that the antibodies can be used to detect the presence of hCG and thus provide a signal that a woman is pregnant (which is exactly what pregnancy tests are used for).

**Q2.18 – c: Embryonic stem cells can potentially replace damaged nerve cells in the spinal cord**
Stem cells are unspecialised cells capable of renewing themselves through cell division and, under certain conditions, they can be induced to become tissue or organ specific cells with special functions. In some organs, such as bone marrow, stem cells regularly divide to repair and replace damaged tissue but in other organs, such as the heart, they only divide under special conditions (e.g. they require the correct surrounding environment and right stimuli).

Embryonic stem cells can give rise to each of the different cell types of the adult body. Adult stem cells (somatic) are stem cells that repair the tissue in which they are found (e.g. bone marrow). Both embryonic and adult stem cells have the potential to replace damaged nerve cells of the spinal cord. However, not <u>all</u> injuries can be corrected by adult stem cells (Option a) and embryonic stem cells only have the <u>potential</u> (not guaranteed) ability to repair damaged nerve cells.

## Q2.19 – d: Both a and c could be correct
The disease is autosomal dominant; therefore an infected individual inherits one copy of the gene from an affected parent. In this type of inheritance pattern, each offspring of an affected individual has a 50% risk of inheriting the mutant chromosome and thus being affected with the disorder. This means that both parents can be heterozygous for the disorder (and thus both affected), or only one parent is affected and the other not affected. Therefore both a and c could be correct. Option b is not correct because, if both alleles were affected, then all the children would be affected.

## Q2.20 – c.
In the stomach: pepsin, released in the stomach, breaks the bonds of the peptide on the amine side ($NH_2$) of Phe and Tyr amino acids. This results in the following breaks:

$NH_2$ – Gly – Lys – Met – Thr –|– Phe –|– Tyr – Arg – Pro – COOH

This results in the following amino acids/peptides:
Gly – Lys – Met – Thr
Phe
Tyr – Arg – Pro

In the small intestines: trypsin, released by the pancreas, breaks down the carboxyl group of Lys and Arg amino acids resulting in the following breaks:

Gly – Lys –|– Met – Thr
Phe
Tyr – Arg –|– Pro
This results in the following amino acids/peptides:
- Gly – Lys
- Met – Thr
- Phe
- Tyr – Arg
- Pro

**Q2.21 – b: Leg veins > inferior vena cava > right atrium > right ventricle > left ventricle > carotid artery > pituitary**

The oestrogen gets into the skin capillaries then goes to the leg veins, which drain into the inferior vena cava (the superior vena cava drains the veins of the head and upper body). The inferior vena cava drains into the heart at the right atrium > right ventricle > pulmonary artery > pulmonary veins > left atrium > left ventricle, before being pumped into the aorta and into the brain (via the carotid artery) where the oestrogen acts by inhibiting FSH release from the pituitary to have its contraceptive effects. Remember that oestrogen is released from the ovaries normally.

**Q2.22 – b: Hydrochloric acid**

Amylase is an enzyme which breaks down starch into smaller carbohydrates molecules. In the saliva, it converts it into maltose. The other type, pancreatic amylase, breaks maltose down into glucose in the small intestines. Proteases are enzymes which break down proteins into amino acids. Lipase is an enzyme which break down fat so that the intestines can absorb it. Hydrochloric acid is not an enzyme but is secreted by the stomach, and activates enzymes. A trick is to spot the suffix "-ase".

**Q2.23 – c:10%**

Adenine (A) and thymine (T) always pair up, and so do cytosine (C) and guanine (G). This is called complementary base pairing. If 30% of the bases are adenine, then 30% of the bases will be thymines, which leaves 40% for both cytosine and guanine. So, 40/2= 20% of the bases will be either C or G. And the difference of base pairs between A and G will be 30 – 20 = 10%.

**Q2.24a – f: F**

Urea is freely filtered from the glomerulus, and 40% will be found in urine; it means that 60% is reabsorbed along the lengths. The ascending limb loop of Henle and terminal collecting ducts are permeable to urea. There are urea transporters at the collecting ducts transporting urea into the medulla, which then diffuses into the ascending loop of Henle. This results in a "recycling" of urea. In the presence of ADH, urea concentration in the collecting tubules becomes very high because water is removed via open water channels. ADH further increases the permeability of the inner medullary collecting tubules to urea, allowing more urea to diffuse into the medullary interstitium.

**Q2.24b – b: B**
The proximal convoluted tubule absorbs around two-thirds of salt and water isotonically (the osmotic potential of the fluid leaving the proximal tubule is the same as that of the initial glomerular filtrate). This means that salt is absorbed and water is free to move across the membrane to balance the osmotic gradient.

**Q2.24c – b: B**
The proximal convoluted tubule normally absorbs 100% of all the glucose filtered via the presence of the co-transporters on the microvilli.

**Q2.25 – d: Glucose influx into the filtrate is occurring faster than it can be reabsorbed**
Glucose is normally completely reabsorbed from the glomerular filtrate into the proximal convoluted tubule via co-transporters (along with amino acids and inorganic phosphate) and thus does not appear in the urine. When glucose does appear in the urine, it means that the glucose transporters in the proximal convoluted tubule are saturated and are unable to reabsorb all the glucose from the filtrate. This can occur in diabetes when the patient has a higher blood glucose level than normal, thus saturating the transporters.

**Q2.26 – b: 1, 3 and 4 only**
The liver is a major body organ with many functions. It breaks down hormones and removes glucose from the blood through the action of the hormone insulin. Cholesterol is an organic molecule synthesised in the liver that plays an important part in the stability of cell membranes. The kidneys (and not the liver) filter the blood, remove urea and excrete it in urine (though urea is made in the liver from protein waste products before being released into the blood stream).

**Q2.27 – a: Oxygen carriage in the bloodstream**
The kidneys are a critical organ, hence the relationship between mortality and renal failure. When kidneys fail, they stop producing erythropoietin, which in turn limits haematopoiesis (red blood cell production). Patients then become anaemic (low red blood cell counts), and their ability to carry oxygen to tissues/organs falls. Many patients with end-stage renal failure are given erythropoietin supplementation for this reason. The kidneys also

affect blood pressure via the renin-angiotensin system, aldosterone secretion and electrolyte management. However, there is no direct effect on pulmonary gas exchange, cognition or myocardial contractility.

## Q2.28 – e: All of the above

Without regular water intake, our plasma osmolarity increases as the amount of available water goes down (high solute concentration = high osmolarity), i.e. osmolarity of blood increases with dehydration and decreases with overhydration. In circumstances of high osmolarity, osmoreceptors in the hypothalamus signal the pituitary to release ADH in response to elevated plasma osmolarity. ADH acts on the collecting ducts in the kidneys to increase passive water absorption along the increasing osmotic gradient, resulting in concentrated urine in the tubule and a less concentrated blood plasma. Collectively, these processes form a part of the endocrine response to dehydration. This is endocrine because hormones from a distant organ (the pituitary) travel through the bloodstream to affect the kidneys.

## Q2.29 – c: Allowing urea to diffuse into the filtrate under filtration pressure

The Bowman's capsule is a capillary-dense sac at the beginning of the nephron. The sac contains the glomerulus. Blood flows into the capillaries via the afferent arteriole and leaves via the efferent arteriole. The high blood pressure forces small molecules such as urea, sodium chloride, glucose, water and amino acids across the filter from the blood in a process called ultrafiltration.

## Q2.30 – b: Increase the surface area available for absorption

The luminal surface of the proximal convoluted tubule has a brush border (composed of densely packed microvilli) to increase the surface area available to reabsorb solutes from the filtrate. Since the brush border is made from microvilli, not cilia, it has little or no bearing on the direction or rate of fluid movement.

## Q2.31 – c: Collecting duct → Ureter → Urinary bladder → Urethra

**Q2.32 – d: 5 → 6 → 4 → 7 → 2 → 3 → 1**
The blood comes from the inferior vena cava (5), goes to the right atrium (6), the right ventricle (4), the pulmonary arteries (7), the left atrium (2), the left ventricle (3) and finally out to the aorta (1). Remember that, unless stated, hearts are presented in the anatomical position that you will see as medical students and as doctors, i.e. the heart is positioned so that the heart's right-hand side is placed on the viewer's left side, i.e. as if you were facing the patient.

**Q2.33 – d: The left atrium and the left ventricle**
Oxygenated blood returning from the lungs goes back into the heart at the left atrium via the pulmonary veins. From there, it flows into the left ventricle, which pumps it to the systemic circulation. The right atrium and the right ventricle pump deoxygenated blood to the lungs via the pulmonary artery.

**Q2.34 – e: 7 → 8 → 2 → 1**
The blood from the stomach passes via the portal vein (7) to the liver and then through the inferior vena cava (8) into the heart It then passes through the pulmonary artery (2) to the lungs and leaves the heart via the aorta (1).

**Q2.35 – a: The aorta**
The blood pressure is greatest in the aorta as the blood has just been ejected from the left ventricle.

**Q2.36 – d: In the capillaries only**
The capillaries are one cell thick and blood flows slowly to allow for efficient and complete oxygen exchange.

**Q2.37 – a: Equal, or increased, oxygen concentration in the blood that reaches the systemic tissues**
Don't be put off by the scary-sounding name of an unknown medical condition; all the information you need is there. Just think back to basics.

Blood passing through the aorta is headed for the systemic circulation. This is at a higher pressure than blood passing through the pulmonary artery to the pulmonary circulation. If there is a connection between the two vessels, oxygenated blood will be "shunted" from the aorta to the lower pressure pulmonary arteries; so less oxygenated blood will reach the rest of the body.

The pulmonary artery will carry blood that is more oxygenated than normal to the lungs (since highly oxygenated blood from the aorta is mixing with deoxygenated blood on its way to the lungs). The changes in pressure and flow will put greater demand on the left side of the heart to maintain systemic perfusion as well as the right side of the heart in pushing against the blood flows coming via this "left to right shunt". So Option a is the only one that is NOT true.

## Q2.38 – e: Right atrium > right ventricle > left atrium > left ventricle
The vena cava brings deoxygenated blood to the right atrium. From there, the blood flows to the right ventricle, which pumps it to the pulmonary circulation via the pulmonary artery. Reoxygenated blood returns to the left atrium, travels to the left ventricle and is pumped to the systemic circulation via the aorta.

## Q2.39 – c: Precipitous drop of blood pressure
By the time the blood has reached the capillaries, the blood pressure would have largely dissipated. There is a large number of capillaries and, in total, their cross-sectional area is extremely large. This enables slow flow of blood through the capillaries to allow efficient diffusion of nutrient and waste into and out of the circulation system.

## Q2.40 – e: Pulmonary veins
The oxygen-haemoglobin dissociation curve is a sigmoid-shaped curve.

On the x-axis is the partial pressure of oxygen in the local environment. On the y-axis is the % saturation of the haemoglobin molecule (i.e. the percentage loading of haemoglobin with oxygen).

This curve tells us that, when the local oxygen concentration is low (low partial pressure of oxygen), haemoglobin releases oxygen molecules (i.e. haemoglobin saturation falls). In other words, haemoglobin binds oxygen least avidly when the local oxygen concentration is low and binds most avidly in an oxygen-rich environment. The most oxygen-rich environment from the options given is the pulmonary veins, which carry blood that has just been oxygenated in the alveolar capillaries of the lungs.

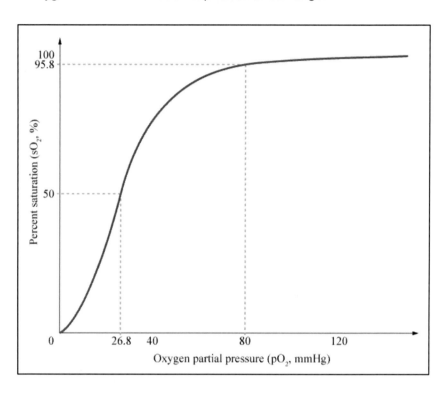

### Q2.41 – e: Saphenous vein
Atherogenesis takes place in the wall of the blood vessels due to increased shear forces. In veins, where blood pressure is much lower than in the arteries, the shear forces on the walls are much lower; therefore atherosclerotic plaques are much less likely to form.

### Q2.42 – a: Lack of lipid emulsification
The liver secretes bile into the duodenum, which emulsifies fats in the digested chyme. Emulsification serves to vastly increase the available surface area of the ingested fats. This allows lipases to break down the fats efficiently. In situations where bile production is insufficient, as described in the question stem, the lipid droplets are not properly emulsified and simply pass through to the faecal matter.

**Q2.43 – a: 2 only**
Negative feedback ensures that, in any control system, changes are reversed and returned to the set level. It plays a major part in homoeostasis. For option 1, when blood glucose levels are high, beta cells in the pancreas releases insulin, which converts glucose into glycogen. This lowers the blood glucose levels back to normal. Glucagon, on the other hand, is released by alpha cells and converts glycogen into glucose, causing blood glucose levels to increase. For option 2, when water concentration in the blood is low, receptors detect the change and ADHs are released, letting water be reabsorbed from kidney tubules. Water concentration in the blood then rises back to normal. For option 3, when body temperature is low, blood vessels near the skin constrict (vasoconstriction). This raises body temperature, and prevents heat loss from the body.

**Q2.44 – b: 3.6 dm³**
The volume of each breath is 600 cm³. In 2 minutes, the patient has 30 breaths i.e. a total volume of 30 x 600 = 18000 cm³.

20% of that air is oxygen i.e.18000 x 0.20 = 3600 cm³ = 3.6 dm³

**Q2.45a – e: E (i.e. the small intestine)**
Most chemical digestion occurs in the small intestines, where brush borders (microvilli) increase the surface area for digestive enzymes to work from.

**Q2.45b – c: C & E (i.e. stomach & small intestine)**
The stomach is where protein digestion first begins, as a result of the hydrolysis of the peptide bonds that bind the individual amino acids in the polypeptide chain. Protein digestion continues in the small intestine as trypsin, chymotrypsin, carboxypeptidase, and many other enzymes hydrolyse specific parts of peptides.

**Q2.46 – e: Ileum**
The large intestine is the major site of water and salt absorption, and can be divided into the caecum, with attached appendix, the ascending colon, transverse colon, descending colon, sigmoid colon and rectum. The ileum is the terminal portion of the small intestine.

## Q2.47 – e: None of the above

The large intestine absorbs the majority of the water. The caecum, rectum, and all of the colon are all parts of the large intestine.

## Q2.48 – e: Kidney excretion

The equation for cellular respiration is glucose (sugar) + oxygen = carbon dioxide + water + energy (as ATP). Therefore respiration adds carbon dioxide to the atmosphere in both plants and animals. Combustion (complete) produces carbon dioxide and water from an organic molecule. Decomposition is the breakdown of organic matter into its simplest components: carbon dioxide, water and nutrients. Excretion from kidneys releases urea, salts and water but not carbon dioxide.

## Q2.49 – d: 1, 2 and 3

Bile is produced by the liver and is stored in the gallbladder. It aids in the digestion of lipids in the small intestines as well as the neutralisation of the stomach acid that enters the small intestine. Branches of the hepatic artery, hepatic portal vein and bile duct connect to form sinusoids. The liver receives oxygenated blood from the heart through the hepatic artery and blood rich in digested nutrients from the intestines through the hepatic portal vein.

## Q2.50 – c: 1000

A cross between two heterozygous would produce SS, Ss and sS (all three purple) and ss (white). Therefore, you would expect 75% purple and 25% white.

$0.75 \times 2000 = 1500$
$0.25 \times 2000 = 500$
$1500 - 500 = 1000$

## Q2.51a – e: X, Y, W, V

The sensory neurone is the neurone that detects the pinprick, which would be X. The electrical impulses travel down the sensory neurone until they reach the relay neurone at Y in the spinal cord. The electrical impulses then travel along the motor neurone (also known as the effector neurone) out of the arc (W) to innervate the effector itself (finger muscles – V) to make a movement. All of this is done without any involvement of higher thinking processes.

### Q2.51b – c: Chemical, Chemical, Chemical
The information passes from the sensory neurone to the relay neurone via neurotransmitters, which are chemicals present in the synapse. Similarly, the relay neurone passes information to the motor neurone via neurotransmitters. The effector (muscle) is stimulated by chemicals (acetylcholine) to cause a contraction by the motor neurone. In the past, curare was used on poison-tipped arrows to block those chemical receptors in the muscle, causing relaxation of the muscle. The information is passed along the sensory neurone, the relay neurone, the motor neurone and along the muscle fibres via electrical impulses; however, at the junctions between the sensory neurone and relay neurone, the relay neurone to motor neurone and the motor neurone to the muscle itself, information transmission is via chemical neurotransmitters.

### Q2.52 – c: Same, Increase, Increase
The text states that a chemical in grapefruit inhibits the liver enzyme CYP3A4. This makes the enzyme less effective at its function, but doesn't destroy it – which means that the concentration of the enzyme is the same. The concentration of the <u>active</u> CYP3A4 is decreased however. With less CYP3A4 to degrade warfarin, we can expect a higher level of warfarin in the blood. This would cause blood to clot less easily, leading to a high INR.

### Q2.53 – e: 3 would be lower
Homeostasis is the property of a system that regulates its internal environment and tends to maintain a stable, constant condition of properties such as temperature or pH. With an impaired homeostatic (i.e. temperature) response, the volunteer is likely to have a greater drop in temperature in the ice bath (steeper 2 with a lower point 3, and reaching 3 earlier), and a less steep 4 as the body struggles to return to normal body temperature in time.

### Q2.54a – e: Decreases, Contracts, Contracts
The pressure at X is the pressure inside the lungs (intrathoracic pressure), Y represents the intercostal muscles and Z represents the diaphragm. Contraction of the diaphragm increases the volume of the lungs, decreasing the

pressure inside, which creates a partial vacuum. The intercostal muscles connected to the rib cage, when contracted, lift the rib cage, thus aiding in increasing the thoracic volume. Environmental air then follows its pressure gradient down to fill the lungs.


### Q2.54b – b: Increases, Relaxes, Relaxes
Relaxation of the diaphragm compresses the lungs, decreasing their volume while increasing the pressure inside them. The intercostal muscles simultaneously relax, further decreasing the volume of the lungs. With the pathway to the mouth clear, this increased pressure forces air out of the lungs.


### Q2.55 – c: Peripheral nervous system and central nervous system
The spinal cord is part of the central nervous system, but the spinal nerves, which are formed from axons leaving the spinal cord, are part of the peripheral nervous system. The basal ganglia are a part of the brain within the central nervous system. Cortical just refers to anything on the outside portion of an organ, e.g. cerebral cortex or adrenal cortex.


### Q2.56 – d: Decreased carboxyhaemoglobin
During exercise, due to the increased demands of oxygen by the muscles, the blood would have decreased oxygen, increased carbon dioxide, increased lactic acid (from the exercising muscles) thus a lowered pH, and increased temperature (from the heat dissipated from the muscles during contraction).


### Q2.57 – d: 5 and 7
You are given limited choices to try and prove that solution X is an enzyme. Taking each possibility, in turn:

- Option a: adding acid to the cube of beef does not yield a lot of amino acids. Nor does adding direct solution X – thus this does not prove (or disprove) that solution X is an enzyme.

- Option b: does not add any further information, since heat can destroy enzymes, but we do not have conclusive evidence with those two tubes to say that solution X is an enzyme.

- Option c: does not suggest that X is an enzyme since some enzymes get denatured by alkali environments.

- Option d: from tube 5 we see that solution X + acid gives large amounts of amino acids; but from tube 7 we see that if a boiled solution X is used instead, there are only traces of amino acids. This suggests that there is something in solution X that cuts up the protein into amino acids, and which is destroyed by heat. This is consistent with an enzyme (though it is not absolute proof, hence the wording "is likely to be" in the text of the question).

## Q2.58 – b: Exhalation – intercostal muscles relax
The muscles involved in breathing are the diaphragm and the intercostal muscles of the rib cage.

During exhalation, both the diaphragm and the intercostal muscles relax, causing a decrease in the size of the thoracic cavity.

During inhalation, the diaphragm contracts and flattens, while the intercostal muscles contract, pushing the rib cage up and out. These actions cause an overall increase in the size of the thoracic cavity and decrease the pressure in the lungs.

## Q2.59 – b: Pharynx → Larynx → Trachea → Bronchi → Alveoli
Air molecules enter the respiratory tract either through the nostrils or the mouth before reaching the pharynx. From the pharynx, air moves through the larynx onwards to the trachea, which eventually divides into the two main bronchi, one for each lung. The bronchi branch into smaller and smaller divisions, the terminal branches of which are called the bronchioles. The bronchioles then lead to clusters of alveoli.

## Q2.60 – e: D < B < C < A
A hummingbird would be expected to have a high surface area per unit volume of body (as its surface area is small compared to its mass). An elephant, on the other hand, has a large volume of body but a relatively small surface area. As a general rule, the greater the mass of an organism, the higher that organism's metabolic rate (in absolute values of calories needed to sustain life); this is also known as Kleiber's law, which is the observation

that, for the vast majority of animals, an animal's metabolic rate scales to the ¾ power of the animal's mass.

However, metabolic rate is higher <u>per unit of body mass</u> in small animals compared to larger ones. This is because the higher metabolic rate of small animals requires a greater delivery of oxygen to tissues around the body. Thus this is linked to the respiratory rate, i.e. animals with a higher respiratory rate would be the smaller ones (and thus having the largest relative surface area:mass ratio).

## 2G  Scientific Knowledge and Applications
## Physics – Answers

**Q2.61 – c: 8.5 m/s**
The speed of sound in air obeys the following wave formula: $v = f\lambda$, where:
- $v$ = speed of sound (m/s)
- $f$ = frequency (Hz)
- $\lambda$ = wavelength (m)

We know that the runner experiences the frequency of sound at 97.5% of normal; therefore if we define $v'$ as the speed of sound that the runner experiences, we have: $v' = 0.975f \times \lambda$

We therefore have $\lambda = \dfrac{v}{f}$  and  $\lambda = \dfrac{v'}{0.975f}$

We know that: $v' = v - v_{runner}$.

Therefore: $\dfrac{v}{f} = \dfrac{v - v_{runner}}{0.975f}$

Which gives: $v\,(0.975f) = f\,(v - v_{runner})$.

Cancelling $f$ on both sides gives $0.975\,v = v - v_{runner}$

And therefore $v_{runner} = (1 - 0.975)\,v$
$= 0.025 \times 340$
$= 8.5\,m/s$.

**Q2.62 – d: The frequency of the second note is double**
We are told that the wavelength of the second note is half the wavelength of the first. Since $v$ (speed of sound) $= f\lambda$ is a constant, if the wavelength halves, then the frequency must double. The amplitude of a sound wave is the same thing as loudness and is essentially the maximum displacement of the sound wave; it is independent from its wavelength. The intensity of a wave is proportional to the amplitude squared and is therefore also independent from the wavelength.

**Q2.63 – a: 1,565 m**
The distance travelled can be calculated with the following equation: distance = speed x time. This gives d = (1490 m/s) x (2.1 s) = 3129 m. However, this represents the distance to the bottom and back; therefore the distance to the ocean floor is half of that number, i.e. 1,565 m.

Bearing in mind that on the day of the BMAT exam you will not be allowed to use a calculator, even though the question asks you to take the speed of sound as 1,490 m/s, you would benefit from working out the answer using approximate numbers. For example, in this case, rounding it to 1,500 m/s and rounding 2.1 seconds to 2 seconds would give 3,000 m. Try doing this whenever the answers are sufficiently distant.


**Q2.64 – c: More than 400 Hz**
This question is about the Doppler Effect, which describes the difference between the perceived frequency of a sound and its actual frequency when the source of the sound and its actual frequency are moving relative to each other.

When the source of the waves is moving towards the observer, each successive wave crest is emitted from a position closer to the observer than the previous wave. Therefore each wave takes slightly less time to reach the observer than the previous wave and the time between the arrival of successive wave crests at the observer is reduced, causing an increase in the frequency.

While they are travelling, the distance between successive wave fronts is reduced; so the waves "bunch together". Conversely, if the source of the waves is moving away from the observer, each wave is emitted from a position further from the observer than the previous wave; therefore the arrival time between successive waves is increased, reducing the frequency. The distance between successive wave fronts is increased, so the waves "spread out".

Since the frequency of the sound gradually increases towards 400 Hz as the ambulance approaches, it means that the frequency perceived by the bystander has a frequency lower than 400 Hz.

**Q2.65 – f. Beam: Same – Spring: Decreased at equator**
You don't need to know about different gravitational forces between poles and the equator in detail; you simply need to apply analysis of the measuring equipment to basic GCSE gravity knowledge. You can see that object X balances with the mass on the beam balance, and this should be the same no matter where you go (South Pole or Equator) since the gravitational forces exerted on the mass and on object X are the same. However, with a spring balance, the gravitational effects work on object X differently: the mass will show as lower at the equator than at the South Pole because of the lower gravitational field.

**Q2.66 – a: 2 m/s**
The period of a wave is the time taken for it to make one complete cycle, which is defined here by the wave hitting the side of the swimming pool. The period of this wave is 5 seconds. The frequency is calculated as the inverse of the period, so the frequency is 0.2 Hz. The wavelength is given as 10 metres. Using the wave formula $v = f\lambda$, we can substitute the figures given and we see that the velocity is 2 m/s.

**Q2.67 – b: Longitudinal waves because the medium moves parallel to the propagation of the wave**
The fact that sound waves are longitudinal is something that you either know or not. This directs you to Options a or b. By definition, longitudinal waves are waves that have the same direction of displacement of particles as their direction of travel; therefore Option b is the correct answer (Option a is contradictory).

**Q2.68 – e: Decrease, Decrease, No change**
The relationship between frequency and period, and between frequency and wavelength is an inverse one: $f = 1/T$ and $f = v/\lambda$. An increase in frequency will therefore result in a decrease in both the period and the wavelength. There is no change in the amplitude.

**Q2.69 – e: Speed and wavelength**
Waves change speed when they pass across the boundary between two substances with different densities, such as air and water (causing refraction). However frequency does not change.

If frequency does not change but speed does, then wavelength must change, since speed = frequency x wavelength.

## Q2.70 – b: Work done is the same, the final momentum is greater

The amount of work done, force and distance are related by the formula:

$$\underset{\text{(joule, J)}}{\text{work done (WD)}} = \underset{\text{(newton, N)}}{\text{force applied (F)}} \times \underset{\text{(metre, m)}}{\text{distance moved (d)}}$$

The force being worked against is gravity, so d is always equal to the height change of the object which is the same whether a ramp is being used or not. Here, the same amount of force is applied (i.e. force "X"). So, in this case, work done is the same since both F and d are the same.

Force, change in momentum and time taken for the change are related by the following formula:

$$\underset{\text{(newton, N)}}{\text{force required to move object}} = \frac{\text{change in momentum (kg(m/s))}}{\text{time taken for the change (second, s)}}$$

The force required to move the object is reduced with a ramp compared to without. This is because the force of gravity that the person has to push the object against is no longer completely vertical. There would also be a component of the force that is parallel to the ramp. The reduction in the force required is a constant, however the distance at which you have to push the object in the direction of the force is now increased by a similar constant. So, even though the work done overall is the same, you would require a smaller force, but across a greater distance.

The question says that the same force X is used up a ramp and without a ramp. By using the same force, you would reach a greater final velocity at the top of the ramp. From the equation: momentum = mass x velocity, we see that the momentum of the object at the end of the ramp would thus be increased as well.

## Q2.71 – a: Triple the force and halve the block's mass

Here we are looking for the combination that increases acceleration the most. Force, mass and acceleration are related by the following formula:

$$\underset{\text{(newton, N)}}{\text{force (F)}} = \underset{\text{(kilogram, kg)}}{\text{mass (m)}} \times \underset{\text{(metre/second}^2\text{, m/s}^2)}{\text{acceleration (a)}}$$

Evaluating the different answers for acceleration, we find that acceleration can be expressed as a= F/m.

Therefore to get the greatest acceleration, we require the largest force possible over the smallest mass possible. This points to Option a (6 times the initial acceleration).

### Q2.72 – c: 12 m/s
Use the equation F = ma. The mass of the shuttle is 5000kg, and the acceleration is unknown. However, we know that a =Δv / Δt. Therefore:

$$\frac{F}{m} = \frac{\Delta v}{\Delta t}$$

Substituting in the figures known (m = 5000, F = 10000N, Δt = 6 seconds) we get: Δv=(10000 / 5000) × 6 = 12 m/s.

### Q2.73 – b: The density of hot air is lower than that of the air surrounding the balloon
Gas molecules bounce around against each other and the balloon container walls. As the air inside the balloon is heated, the air molecules have a greater vibrational energy due to the higher temperatures. When the balloon is full of hot air, if the air continues to heat up, it expands and flows out of the hole in the bottom of the balloon. The density of the air decreases as the hotter gas takes up more volume. The decreased density means that there is less mass and therefore less weight of the balloon than the surrounding air, allowing the balloon to rise. (Note: Although the hole at the bottom is essential, it is not what causes the balloon to rise.)

### Q2.74 – a: 5000J, 0J
Use the formula F = ma to calculate the force required to move the mass: F = 250 x 10 = 2500N. The work done in lifting the barbell to a height of 2 m can be calculated with the formula: Work Done (J) = Force (N) x Distance Moved (m), which gives: Work Done = 2500 x 2 = 5000J. Using the same equation, it follows that the work done to hold the barbell in place is: Work Done = 2500 x 0 (since the barbell is still) = 0J.

**Q2.75 – a: As the electric potential difference between two points de-creases, the electrical power decreases**
Electrical power is equal to the amount of charge passing a point per unit time (current) multiplied by the electric potential difference between the two points (voltage). Power, potential difference and current are related by the following equation:

$$\text{Power (P)} = \text{Current (I)} \times \text{Potential difference (V)}$$
$$\text{(Watt, W)} \quad \text{(Ampere, A)} \quad \text{(Volt, V)}$$

Therefore, as potential increases, so does power. Similarly, as current (or charge per unit time) increases or decreases, so does the power (respectively).

**Q2.76 – c: Same length of wire + halving the diameter of the wire**
The equation for resistance is given by:

$$\frac{\text{resistance (R)}}{\text{(Ohm, }\Omega\text{)}} = \frac{\rho\ (\text{resistivity, }\Omega m) \times l\ (\text{length, m})}{A\ (\text{cross-sectional area, m}^2)}$$

For a cylindrical wire, resistance changes by an inverse factor of the square of the change in radius (1/2 diameter) and is directly proportional to the change in length of the wire. Therefore, halving the diameter of the wire (which is equivalent to halving the radius) will quadruple the resistance, whereas doubling the length would only double it.

**Q2.77 – a: Painting surface A silver**
Remember we are trying to reduce radiation, not conduction (which would be reduced by creating a vacuum). Dark matt surfaces absorb heat radiation falling on them better than silver (thus option C or D would result in greater heat radiation loss).

Silvered surfaces reflect nearly all heat radiation falling on them, and emit much less heat radiation (at any given temperature) – thus if surface A (or B, or C) were to be painted silver it would reduce heat radiation.

**Q2.78 – d: 6**
Because resistors in parallel and in series would give a different resistance, we can see that we can arrange the four resistors into different configurations of circuits to get six functionally different circuits.

See diagrams below:

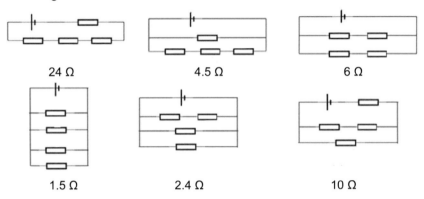

| 24 Ω | 4.5 Ω | 6 Ω |
| 1.5 Ω | 2.4 Ω | 10 Ω |

**Q2.79 – a: A**
In circuit B, there are 2 light bulbs in series. In a series circuit, total resistance is the sum of all the resistances of the individual light bulbs. Since the battery is the same 12V battery, the current would be shared between the 2 bulbs, thus less light would be produced in each bulb.

In circuit C, bulb X is in a sub-circuit along with another light bulb in series. There is a short circuit across the two bulbs (including bulb X) so no current passes through bulb X or its series neighbour; thus neither will glow under any circumstances. Bulbs in a parallel circuit will all glow at full power and with the same brightness if they have the same resistance.

In circuit A, there is only one bulb, which will glow at full power.

**Q2.80 – d: Increase fourfold**
For circuits in parallel, the equation is: $\dfrac{1}{R_{total}} = \dfrac{1}{\Omega_1} + \dfrac{1}{\Omega_2} = \dfrac{1}{6} + \dfrac{1}{6} = \dfrac{1}{3}$
Thus $R_{total} = 3\,\Omega$.

For circuits in series, total resistance of the circuit is added. So with two 6Ω resistors, the total resistance is 12Ω. The overall resistance would thus increase fourfold from 3Ω to 12Ω.

## Q2.81 – d: 2Ω

The potential drop across the external resistor is given by Ohm's law: $V = I \times R = 0.5 \times 10 = 5V$. This means that the potential on the other side of the resistor is 1V, thus the potential difference across the internal resistor (i.e. the battery itself) is 1V. Ohm's law would then give us the resistance of the internal resistor: $R = \frac{V}{I} = \frac{1V}{0.5A} = 2\Omega$

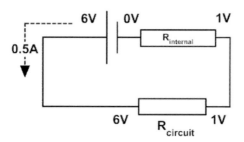

## Q2.82 – d: The power produced by the battery will be increased

Switching on switch P effectively adds a resistor in parallel to the whole circuit. Since resistance in parallel is added reciprocally, the total resistance of the circuit will decrease. This will, in turn, increase the current and the power. The voltage of the battery will not change.

## Q2.83 – d: There is no magnetic force acting on the particle

Stationary and moving charges generate an *electric* field, but only moving particles generate a *magnetic* field. A magnetic field radiates concentrically outwards from a source. A charged particle sitting still in a magnetic field experiences no force. A moving charge will experience a force only if the movement has an aspect of perpendicular vector to the magnetic field. In that case, the force would be perpendicular to the magnetic field and to the charge's path.

## Q2.84 – d: All of the above

As the magnetic field increases, a current is generated in the wire loop. The magnitude of this current will be directly proportional to the rate of increase of the magnetic field. Since the current is increased steadily (i.e. at a constant rate), the current through the wire will be constant. Since a current is induced, a second magnetic field is generated in a direction consistent with the right-hand rule for the direction of current flow. This new magnetic field will be in the opposite direction to the increasing magnetic field.

**Q2.85 – a: I only**
All magnets are dipolar, meaning that they *all* have a north and a south pole. For a magnetic field to be produced, there must be a flow of charge, or current. Ferromagnetism means that the materials can retain magnetisation and become magnets. Magnetic rods can also be made of other paramagnetic and diamagnetic material.

**Q2.86 – e: Violet**
The behaviour of electromagnetic radiation depends on its wavelength. Higher frequencies have shorter wavelengths, and lower frequencies have longer wavelengths. Violet has the shortest wavelength and thus the highest frequency. Correspondingly, red would have the longest wavelength and the lowest frequency in EM radiation.

**Q2.87 – d: Energetic free electrons move from the hotter end to the cooler end**
In a solid substance, when an object is heated the particles vibrate about their positions. Each copper molecule has delocalised (free) electrons and it is those free electrons that conduct both heat and electricity.

**Q2.88 – b: B**
In lens B, light is going in the wrong direction. The lens is a divergent (bi-concave) lens, and therefore the beam of light should diverge (spread) more than when it penetrates the lens.

**Q2.89 – e: V, IV, I, III, II**
The relationship between wavelength and frequency is inverse (a longer wavelength should have a lower frequency), so make sure you have read the question properly (it asks for wavelength).

Looking at the order of the electromagnetic spectrum (ROYGBIV), the frequencies increase in that order (and therefore wavelengths decrease in that order). Therefore Orange light has a higher wavelength than Indigo. Ultraviolet light will fall beyond Violet and thus has a smaller wavelength. Infrared will fall before Red and therefore have a higher wavelength. X-rays are very high energy waves, which have high frequency and low wavelength. Their wavelength is lower than that of ultraviolet. The order of these waves, from lowest to highest wavelength, is therefore X-rays, Ultraviolet, Indigo, Orange, Infrared, i.e. V, IV, I, III, II, which is Option e.


**Q2.90 – d: large, warm**
The larger the surface area the easier it is for the liquid to evaporate from the surface, since fast moving particles at the surface of the liquid will overcome the forces of attraction from other particles and will escape. The warmer the starting liquid, the quicker the particles move, hence warmer liquids evaporate quicker than colder ones.


**Q2.91 – b: 2 seconds**
We know the initial velocity (u = 0 because it is at rest), the acceleration due to gravity (a = 9.8m/s$^2$), and the distance that the object travelled (s = 19.6). We can find out the time taken (t) by using the following equation:

$$s = ut + \frac{1}{2}at^2$$

This gives:

$$19.6 = \frac{1}{2}\,9.8\,t^2$$

Solving for t, we get t$^2$ = 4 and therefore t = 2 seconds.


**Q2.92 – e: None of the above**
The density of a solid is the mass per unit of volume. Therefore density would only change if the volume and/or the mass changed without cancelling each other out. Taking a solid to the Moon or immersing it in a swimming pool will not alter its mass and its volume will be negligibly affected by the lack of gravity and water pressure. Since the question asks for a substantial change in density, neither Option a nor Option b is suitable. Doubling both the mass and the volume of the solid will not affect the mass:volume ratio and therefore the density will remain the same.


**Q2.93 – a: A perfect sphere**
Water has both cohesive and adhesive forces acting on it at all times. In space, there is no other force (e.g. gravity) acting on water; therefore, when it is put into space, it has nothing to have adhesive interactions with. Water's

cohesive force is greater than the adhesive force in space. Without gravity, this phenomenon occurs in all directions and the water forms a sphere. If the adhesive forces between water and space were greater than the cohesive forces then water would act to maximise its surface area (increase the amount of adhesive force) thereby flattening out into a very thin sheet that expands in all directions. However, in space there is no adhesive force, so water has to minimise its surface area.

We can see the effect of adhesive forces on Earth each time it rains. Water free-falls from clouds as drops, each held in its own "bag" created by surface tension. The tear-shaped raindrops would be round spheres, were it not for the drag of the air they fall through.

**Q2.94 – e: C, A, B**
We know that the block floats on A but sinks in B, thus the initial order for density would be A > block > B. Given that substance C is denser than A, the order of densities is therefore C > A > block > B. Since the denser material sinks to the bottom, C would be at the bottom and B at the top, with A in between.

**Q2.95 – c: Both are the same**
No matter which direction (upwards/downwards) the object is thrown, the acceleration is downwards in each case. On the way up the object is slowing down, thus it must be accelerating in the downward direction. On the way down the object is speeding up and it is accelerating in the downwards direction too.

**Q2.96 – d: 2.25 m**
At the instant the cannonball reaches the maximum height, the vertical velocity is zero (v). Taking "up" as positive and the initial velocity (u) as 5m/s, we can solve for the height (s) using the equation: $v^2 = u^2 + 2as$.
This gives $0 = 5^2 + 2 \times (-10) \times s$, and therefore $s = 25 / 20 = 1.25$ m.

Since we are told to measure the distance from the ground, we must add the height at which the cannon is positioned (i.e. 1 m), which gives a total of 2.25 m.

**Q2.97 – b: The bullet will reach the ground first**
The cannonball must rise higher than the bullet since it is shot upwards, and the bullet is shot horizontally. When the cannonball reaches the top of its flight upwards it will then be falling freely. The bullet on the other hand is in free fall from the outset when it leaves the muzzle, as it flies horizontally. Since they both start from the same height and since, at the point in time when the cannonball starts falling freely, the bullet has already begun doing so, the bullet will reach the ground before the cannonball. Mass has nothing to do with the time required to reach the ground.

**Q2.98 – a: 2**
If we call s the height from which the tennis ball was first launched then we have the following equation: $v_1^2 = u_1^2 + 2as$.

Since we are increasing the initial height of the other object by 4, then we can model the second ball as: $v_2^2 = u_2^2 + 2a(4s)$.

Since both balls start with no initial velocity then $u_1 = u_2 = 0$, and taking $a = 10$ m/s$^2$, we can simplify both equations as $v_1^2 = 20s$ for the lower ball and $v_2^2 = 80s$ for the higher ball.

Solving for v, we get that $v_1 = \sqrt{20} \times \sqrt{s}$ for the lower ball and $v_2 = \sqrt{80} \times \sqrt{s}$ for the higher ball. The ratio of velocities is therefore $\sqrt{80} / \sqrt{20} = \sqrt{4} = 2$. So quadrupling the height only doubles the final velocity as it hits the floor.

**Q2.99 – b: 1 → 4 → 3 → 2**
Chemical energy from the muscle (via the oxidation of glucose stores) is used to move the axe, resulting in a mechanical potential energy (as the axe is moved up against gravity to a height, in readiness to swing down). The axe is then brought down and the gravitational potential energy is turned into kinetic energy as the axe is moved downwards and gathers speed. Once the axe makes contact with the wood, it breaks the chemical bonds of the wood resulting in splintering the wood into chunks, releasing sound, heat and kinetic energy of wood fragments splintering.

**Q2.100 – d: The Earth would move in a straight line tangential to its previous orbit**
The disappearance of the sun would remove the force keeping the Earth in an elliptical orbit. Orbital mechanics is quite a complicated branch of mathematics, but the solution to this question is entirely based in Newton's First law; in the absence of the force of the sun's gravitational pull, the Earth's speed would remain constant but the direction would no longer change, resulting in a continuous motion along a straight line into space.

Imagine a rock on the end of a string. If you were to swing it in circles about one's head and then release it, it would fly off in a straight line.

**Q2.101a – d: The car is reversing from t=10s and t=15s**
The area under the graph is (15+5) x 10 / 2 = 100, meaning that the car has travelled 100 m. The car has a constant acceleration from 0 to 5 seconds (steady increase in velocity showing as a straight line). The car has a constant velocity from 5 to 10 seconds (flat line). The car is then decelerating from 10 to 15 seconds (shown as a declining straight line). For the car to be reversing, the velocity graph would need to be below 0.

**Q2.101b – c: C**
The car initially speeds up then drives at constant speed, before slowing down. Graph A represents a car accelerating throughout. Graph D represents a car travelling at constant velocity without slowing down. Graph B makes no sense; it implies that the car is instantly teleported back and forth from one place to another.

**Q2.101c – b: B**
For the first 5 seconds, the acceleration of the car is constant, thus the acceleration/time graph should show a constant line. Then since velocity becomes constant from 10 to 15 seconds, the acceleration would be 0 and we are therefore expecting a flat line along the x-axis. Then as the car slows down smoothly the acceleration graph should go into the negative y-axis.

**Q2.102 – d: A rounders ball thrown by the pitcher and hit by a batter**
This graph shows an object at constant velocity with a sudden change in direction. Option a would show a gradual acceleration change. Earth would

have a constantly changing velocity, and a pendulum would have a gradual change in velocity. The closest thing would be a rounders ball that was thrown in one direction then hit suddenly to the opposite direction. A standing golf ball would initially have no velocity.

Note that, in reality, the ball would experience a small slowdown instead of a constant speed, but the question is asking for the most probable. Option d is the closest of all options.

**Q2.103 – b: The force of the floor is the same as the force of gravity against his feet**
Since the individual is travelling at constant velocity, the net force acting on him is zero. This means that the force of gravity and the force of the floor are balanced.

**Q2.104 – d: 45,000 km/hr$^2$**
Acceleration is calculated using the following formula:

$$acceleration = \frac{change\ in\ speed}{time}$$

The change in speed is 45 km/h since the car went from 45 km/h down to complete rest. The time taken is 3.6 seconds. Since there are 3600 seconds in one hour, this can also be expressed as 3.6 / 3600 = $1\times10^{-3}$ hours.

Therefore: acceleration = $\dfrac{45}{1\times10^{-3}}$ = 45,000km/h$^2$

**Q2.105 – d: 17.5 m/s**
The circumference of a circle is $2\pi r$, so we can estimate the track's perimeter to be approximately 6,300 m. The car can drive this in 6 minutes (or 360 seconds). The ratio is 6300 / 360 seconds = 17.5 m/s.

**Q2.106 – e: 40m**
Use the following kinematic equation: $v^2 = u^2 + 2as$.
This gives: $0 = 20^2 + 2(-5)s$. Therefore s = 40m.

**Q2.107 – b: Velocity positive, acceleration negative**
The car is still moving forwards so the velocity is positive. The acceleration must be negative as it is slowing down.

**Q2.108 – Graph B**
Velocity is denoted as a slope in a displacement over time graph. Constant velocity would be represented as a straight line on a distance vs time graph. Graph A shows a displacement changing exponentially with time, i.e. an acceleration. Graph C shows a constant acceleration and therefore an increasing velocity. Graph D shows an increasing acceleration and therefore an exponentially increasing velocity. Graph B shows a constant displacement throughout time, meaning that the car is stationary, i.e. has a constant velocity of 0.

**Q2.109 – e: 1000 m**
Use the equation $v^2 = u^2 + 2as$. We know that the final speed is 0 (as the car comes to a stop). Also the acceleration would be negative (since the car is decelerating), so we can simplify the equation to be $u^2 = 2as$. We can see that, by increasing the speed by a factor of 10, we get a $10^2$ increase in distance. Thus the distance would be 1000 m.

**Q2.110 – d: 100 m**
From $t = 0$ to $t = 5$ the car moves forward as its velocity is positive. The area under the graph up to that point represents the distance moved by the car whilst going forward. That area is calculated as (20 x 5) / 2 = 50 m. From t = 5 to t = 10, the car is reversing. The magnitude of distance moved is also (20 x 5) / 2 = 50 m. In total the car has therefore travelled 100 m.

**Q2.111 – e: 17,800 m**
Substituting the figures given in the equation: $s = ut + \frac{1}{2}at^2$ gives:
$s = (40)(400) + \frac{1}{2}(0.02)(400)^2 = 17,600$ m.
Therefore, in 400 seconds with an acceleration of 0.02 m/s$^2$, the truck would travel 17,600 m. Add this to the original 200 m marker; the truck would therefore pass the 17,800 m marker.

**Q2.112 – b: -10,000 J**
The kinetic energy of a body can be found using the following equation:

$$\underset{\text{(joule, J)}}{\text{kinetic energy (E)}} = \frac{1}{2} \times \underset{\text{(kilogram, kg)}}{\text{mass (m)}} \times \underset{((\text{metre/second})^2, (\text{m/s})^2)}{\text{speed}^2 (v^2)}$$

The original mass of the car is unknown but we can find out by how much the kinetic energy changes when 2 people jump out.

$$\underset{\text{(newton, N)}}{\text{force (F)}} = \underset{\text{(kilogram, kg)}}{\text{mass (m)}} \times \underset{(\text{metre/second}^2, \text{m/s}^2)}{\text{acceleration (a)}}$$

Therefore, the change in mass is - 980 N x (2 / 9.8 m/s$^2$) = - 200 kg. Substituting this into the equation for kinetic energy we get:

$$\Delta E = \frac{1}{2} \times -200 \times 10^2 = -10{,}000 \text{ J}$$

**Q2.113 – e: All of the above**
All of the statements are true. Friction opposes the direction of motion. As frictional forces act, kinetic energy is converted into heat, which dissipates into the environment. Frictional forces, therefore, fall into the category of non-conservative forces (as the heat cannot be stored/trapped and re-converted back into kinetic energy). Another example of non-conservative forces is air resistance.

**Q2.114 – d: 48 revolutions/second**
The circumference of a circle is $2\pi$ r. We know that the radius of the toy tyre is 40 mm. Thus the circumference can be estimated to be 250 mm. We know that the tyre was rolling at a speed of 12 m/s at the bottom of the ramp. Therefore the number of revolutions per second at the bottom of the ramp was: 12000/250 = 48.

**Q2.115 – e: A thin, flat disc of black metal**
Factors affecting an object's ability to emit thermal radiation are its colour and its surface area. Dark objects are both good emitters and absorbers of thermal radiation, whereas white objects are poor emitters and absorbers.

The greater the surface area, the greater the ability to emit thermal radiation. Any object that has a volume will be wasting surface area because it is wasting metal in filling its shape instead of a surface area. However, the disk will have most of its metal on the surface and will therefore optimise radiation.

**Q2.116 – d: A conducting coil rotating in a magnetic field**
A conventional generator works by causing a coil to rotate in a magnetic field and thus generating an electric current by electromagnetic induction.

**Q2.117 – e: 12 m/s**
The sum of the momentums before the collision is equal to the sum of the momentum after the collision (since friction is ignored) and we need to use the conservation of momentum equation to determine the speed of the truck after the impact: m = mass and u = velocity.

$m_{car} u_{(car)initial} + m_{truck} u_{(truck)initial} = m_{car} u_{(car)final} + m_{truck} u_{(truck)final}$
$(2000 \times 30) + (5000 \times 0) = (2000 \times 0) + (5000 \times u_{(truck)final})$
$u_{(truck)final} = 60{,}000/5{,}000 = 12$ m/s

**Q2.118 – e: 60N**
When the lift is at rest, the cannonball has a mass of 10kg, and a force of 100N (using g = 10 m/s$^2$) acting upwards to balance it. When the lift is accelerating downwards at 4 m/s$^2$ we can use the following equations to model its behaviour:

F = ma (i.e. the net force acting on the cannonball)
F = mg – T (i.e. the difference between the weight of the cannonball and the force projected upwards by the floor)

Since the acceleration of the lift and gravity point in the same direction, we can combine both equations together to get: ma = mg – T. Substituting in the figures given we get: (10 x 4) = (10 x 10) – T i.e. T = 60N

**Q2.119 – e: 5 s**
We can use the following kinematic equation to solve this question: v – u = at, where v is the final velocity (in this case, 0 m/s as the ball comes

to rest), and u = 0.5 m/s (given). Using a = 0.1 m/s² (given) we get: 0 – 0.5 = (-0.1) t. Solving for t gives 5 seconds.


## Q2.120 – a: Equal to X
The lift is moving at constant speed, therefore no net force is experienced, and so no acceleration is present. The tension in the cable must therefore match the weight of the lift.


## Q2.121 – d: The lead ball does not reach terminal velocity
When an object is falling, two forces act upon it: the weight of the object (force acting downwards caused by gravity) and the air resistance (frictional force acting in the opposite direction to the direction of travel).

According to Newton's laws, an object will accelerate if the forces acting upon it are unbalanced (in this case, the force of gravity is greater than the air resistance). The amount of acceleration is directly proportional to the magnitude of the unbalanced forces acting upon it. Eventually, the air resistance balances the force of gravity, there is no more acceleration and the object reaches a steady speed (called terminal velocity).

Since the lead ball weighs more than the Styrofoam ball, it will experience a greater force of gravity (and, correspondingly, a greater force of air resistance when it reaches terminal velocity). The lead ball will thus accelerate much more before the air resistance can balance the force of gravity. As the much lighter Styrofoam ball falls, the air resistance soon increases until it balances the weight of the Styrofoam ball, which thus reaches terminal velocity. The lead ball, however, never reaches terminal velocity and thus it continues to accelerate as it falls.


## Q2.122 – b: The horizontal force of the road on the wheels
The force that propels the car forward must be a force of some angle acting on the car or the wheels. That narrows the answer to Options a, b or c. The acceleration of the car is horizontal, therefore the net force must be horizontal; hence Option b is correct. The car exerts a force on the road so that, via Newton's third law, the road exerts a force on the car.

**Q2.123 – b: The net force acting on the car is backwards**
Since the Formula 1 car is undergoing non-uniform motion (it is slowing down), it has a net force acting upon it. The net force points in the direction opposite to the car's direction as a result of friction between the wheels and the road and air resistance.

**Q2.124 – a: The reading has an amplitude of 50 mmHg**
Wavelengths can be calculated from any point of the wavelength to the same point in the cycle. Therefore, there are 5 complete wavelengths shown in the tracing. The reading ranges between 80 mmHg and 130 mmHg so the amplitude is 50 mmHg. Though the object is in periodic motion (repeating itself over time), it is not in simple harmonic motion because it cannot be described with a simple trigonometric function (due to the pressure notch on the downswing).

**Q2.125 – d: 72 m**
The distance that the player will have run in 12 seconds is given by the speed-distance equation: $s = \frac{1}{2}(u + v)\,t = \frac{1}{2}(0 + 12)\,12 = 72$ m.

**Q2.126 – c: 100 N**
The force is given by the equation $F = ma$. Acceleration thus needs to be worked out first. Acceleration = change in speed over time taken, thus:

$$\text{acceleration} = \frac{12 - 0}{12} = 1 \text{ m/s}^2$$

Thus $F = 100 \times 1 = 100$ N.

**Q2.127 – d: D**
The heat transfer between 2 mediums (i.e. the heating element of the kettle and the water) is directly proportional to the temperature difference between the 2 sides. As the 2 sides get closer in temperature, less heat will be transferred per unit time, as the water is already at a hotter temperature.

**Q2.128 – c: The frequency with which the earthquake was shaking was at the natural frequency of the statue**
Much like a soprano breaking a crystal glass with her voice, a statue when oscillated at its natural frequency will be demolished. The natural frequency is a frequency such that, when matched by an external oscillator (such as an earthquake or a voice), the object's oscillations will continue to add up. This is known as resonance. The statue collapsed because the earthquake happened to be at just the right frequency and it began to resonate with the structure.

**Q2.129 – a: A**
The half-life is the amount of time it takes for half the isotopes to decay. Therefore the graph should show that, for each movement in the X axis (time), the Y axis (amount of $^{201}$Hg) decreases by half each time. We would thus expect a curve following the equation $y = 1/2^x$. Option A is the only suitable option.

**Q2.130 – e: 1200 years**
Since substance B is not normally found on an asteroid, we assume that all the substance B present comes from the decay of substance A. The total amount of substance A must therefore be 44% + 6% = 50% at the start. A half-life is the amount of time that it takes for a substance to decay to exactly half of its initial amount/percentage. The quickest way in the BMAT exam is to quickly jot down what each half-life corresponds to, and rounding down to make sums easier.

| Half-life | 0 | 1 | 2 | 3 |
|---|---|---|---|---|
| Substance A | 50% | 25% | 12.5% | 6.25% |
| Substance B | 0% | 25% | 37.5% | 43.75% |

Thus, we see that it takes around 3 half-lives before it can get to the corresponding amounts of substance A & B found in the samples. Since each half-life is 400 years, we thus calculate that 400 x 3 = 1200 years.

**Q2.131 – f: C&F**
The equation for mass and density is governed by $density = \frac{mass}{volume}$.

Thus an object can have the same mass if it is double the density and half the volume of another object, or half the density and double the volume. Thus we can see that instrument C has double the density and half the volume of instrument F.

### Q2.132 – i: Technetium 99
A tracer in the human body is normally a gamma radiation source. Alpha radiation would not escape the body as it would be blocked by the skin alone. High energy beta radiation may penetrate the body, but would cause great injury to the body (same with alpha radiation courses), via interaction with cells. Gamma radiation sources can travel through dense materials and would travel through the body with ease. A short acting gamma radio-active source is the most ideal.

### Q2.133 – f: 4 counts/second, Gamma, 240 minutes
The half-life can be derived from the table by looking at the times between which the count has halved. We can see that at time=6, the count (83) is approximately half that of time=2 (count = 164). Similarly, at time=10, the count (41) is approximately half that of time=6 (count=83). The half life is therefore 4 hours (6 – 2, or 10 – 6), i.e. 240 minutes.

The count rate at 0 can therefore be calculated by doubling the count at time = 4 hours i.e. 120 x 2 = 240 counts/minute, which is also equal to 4 counts/second.

So far, we can see that both Option b and Option f would satisfy those re-quirements. However, we know that Alpha radiation sources cannot pene-trate more than a few centimetres of air (the detector is 30 cm away from the source); therefore only Option f is suitable.

### Q2.134 – e: 2, 3 and 5
Liquids become less dense at higher temperatures as the space in the atom expands (just as a conducting hot metal rod is bigger than a cold rod). Some objects, therefore, will float in a cold liquid, which is denser, but will sink in the less dense hot liquid.

Hot air rises because it is less dense than the cooler air.

The volume of a cup of hot liquid is not constant. When the liquid is first poured into the cup, it is hot and therefore occupies a greater volume. A ring is formed on the sides of the cup at the surface of the liquid formed from dried coffee, marking its highest extent, which eventually is lowered as the cooling coffee contracts.

### Q1.135 – Figure D

When the metal disc is heated up, the disc expands outwards, thus we can rule out Figure A (which shows the outside of the disc remaining the same).

We now need to establish what happens to the inner diameter. Since the metal disc is uniform, the hole will expand in the same ratio as the metal, hence the disc should look in the same proportions but just bigger in size. Indeed, as the disc is heated up, the distance between the atoms increases everywhere. Since the distance between the atoms at the edge of the hole increases, and the number of atoms does not change, the circumference of the hole will increase. Hence Figure D is the answer. (Pushing the atoms inwards to make a smaller hole would rather crowd them together and would not be thermodynamically favoured.)

For a real life example – think of a barrel hoop. A metal band is heated and then put over the barrel staves to hold them together. Once the barrel band cools down, it starts to compress the barrel together.

### Q2.136 – Figure C

Unstable nuclei disintegrate spontaneously and at random. The more un-decayed nuclei there are, the more frequently disintegrations are likely to occur.

As X decays into Y exponentially, you would expect to see an exponential decrease of X nuclei (similar to figure A); this corresponds to an exponential increase of Y as well. But since Y is also unstable and will also decay, it will undergo an exponential decay too. Thus we see figure C is the answer. Initially when X decays into Y, Y increases, but when there is more and more Y, there is also a component of Y decay into Z (which is stable). Thus Y decreases exponentially.

**Q2.137 – g. weight decreases, mass unchanged.**
The mass of an object is a measure of the amount of matter it contains; measured in kilograms. The weight of an object is a measure of the force exerted on the object by gravity (measured in newtons). The pull of gravity on the earth gives an object a downward acceleration of about 9.8 m/s2 on Earth's surface, but less as it moves away from Earth. Thus, whilst weight decreases, the mass remains the same.

**Q2.138 – b: As miscibility of two fluids increases, emulsion formation increases**
Liquids are a condensed phase resulting from molecular interactions. Their short intermolecular distances make it extremely difficult to compress them further. In contrast to the solid phase, the liquid phase is still relatively disordered. Miscibility refers to the ability of two liquids to mix to form solutions. If two liquids are unable to mix, they are called immiscible and are thus more likely to form emulsions (e.g. a mixture of oil and vinegar).

**Q2.139 – e: None of the above**
The y-axis is pressure and the x-axis is temperature. Temperature and pressure are the two factors which directly affect the phase of a substance and conventionally the y-axis is used for pressure and the x-axis for temperature.

**Q2.140 – b: Ball A has greater air resistance**
Since both balls are at terminal velocity (constant velocity), there is no acceleration. The air resistance (drag) counters the weight of both balls.

Ball A experiences a greater force of gravity due to its greater weight and therefore requires greater air resistance than ball B to balance that greater force of gravity.

**Scientific Knowledge and Applications Chemistry – Answers**

## Q2.141 – d: Carbon-11 has the same atomic number as Carbon-12

The atomic number (also known as the proton number) is the number of protons found in the nucleus of an atom. Isotopes of a particular element have the same number of protons but a different number of neutrons and hence different atomic weights. Here, Carbon-11 has 11 nuclear particles whereas Carbon-12 has 12 particles. The difference is in the number of neutrons, NOT protons. Therefore, Carbon-11 and Carbon-12 have the same atomic number but Carbon-11 has a smaller atomic weight. Conversely, Boron-11 is produced from the decay of one proton from Carbon-11. Therefore, Boron has a smaller atomic number than Carbon-11.

## Q2.142 – c.

A very dilute amino acid solution means that there are many water molecules (high water concentration), and few amino acid molecules (low amino acid concentration). Both amino acid or water molecules move in random movements, and diffuse throughout the solution. Each molecule undergoes Brownian motion (the random collision with other molecules), and so all the molecules are randomly moving (thus we can exclude options a, b and e). We know that it is a very dilute (but fully mixed) solution of amino acids, so the amino acid molecules are far away from each other (option c), and the water molecules are close together.

## Q2.143 – a: I and II only

Ethanols are flammable; they burn in air to product carbon dioxide and water. For example: $2CH_3OH + 3O_2 \rightarrow 2CO_2 + 4H_2O$. Ethanoic acid can be made by oxidising ethanol (ethanol + oxygen → ethanoic acid + water). Fermentation of glucose results in the production of ethanol and carbon dioxide, this reaction allows bread to be fluffy and full of air, and the ethanol evaporates in the hot oven.

## Q2.144 – b: Bromine molecules and the molecules in the air are always moving around.

Bromine liquid is a very volatile (i.e. easily evaporated) halogen (group 17). Fast moving bromine particles at the surface of the bromine liquid will overcome the forces of attraction from the other particles and escape. This is evaporation. Bromine molecules are larger and denser than air molecules (which consists mostly of nitrogen and oxygen), but both are in a state of constant motion colliding with other molecules causing them to gradually diffuse and spread in all directions filling the gas jar. Because bromine is denser and larger, it moves slower than air molecules, hence the slow spread.

### Q2.145 – c: 0.5
The number of moles contained in a sample of 100% $^{150}$Tanium is:

$$\text{moles} = \frac{\text{mass of sample}}{\text{molecular weight}} = \frac{78}{150} \text{ i.e. just over 0.5.}$$

Therefore, in a sample containing 96%, the number would be 0.5 (no need to calculate the exact figure as the options given are sufficiently spaced).

### Q2.146a – a: A
The top left number is the Atomic Mass, which is the sum of protons and neutrons. The bottom left number is the Atomic Number, which is the number of protons (also equivalent to the number of electrons). The number of protons is thus the Atomic Mass number minus the Atomic Number. Carbon-12 thus has 6 protons (Atomic Number), 6 electrons and 6 neutrons.

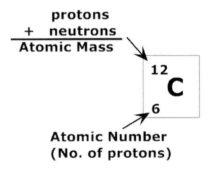

protons
+ neutrons
Atomic Mass

12
C
6

Atomic Number
(No. of protons)

### Q2.146b – d: D
Boron-11 has 5 protons (thus 5 electrons) and 6 neutrons.

### Q2.147 – c: The concentration of the solvent is at a minimum
The concentration of the solvent is at a minimum when the concentration of the solute is at its maximum.

### Q2.148 – c: Both solutions will have the same boiling point
The boiling point of a liquid depends on the number of particles in the solution, and not on their specific properties. Both NaCl and KCl dissociate into 2 particles each, so they will have the same effect on the boiling point of water.

## Q2.149 – d: Saturated fats

Fats (especially saturated fats) can store over twice as much energy (about 9 kcal/g) as carbohydrates and proteins (about 4 kcal/g) can. The more saturated the fat is, the more bonds there are to break, resulting in greater energy storage potential.


## Q2.150 – a: $C_2H_4$

This question tests the knowledge that carbon always forms four covalent bonds, nitrogen three, oxygen two, hydrogen one, chlorine one. Some elements form covalent bonds by sharing electrons with other atoms in the outer shell. Each covalent bond provides one extra pair of shared electron for each atom (so each covalent bond is a shared pair of electrons). Thus $C_2H_4$ would share 8 pairs of electrons and $CH_3OH$ would share 5 pairs.


## Q2.151 – c: Compound A = $C_4H_{10}$ – Compound B = $C_3H_8$

Alkanes have the general formula $C_nH_{2n+2}$ (e.g. if an alkane has 6 carbons it has to have $(2\times6)+2 = 14$ hydrogens. Alkanes have a higher boiling point when the molecule is larger. Thus option c fulfils the criteria. In options a and b, compound B would boil before Compound A.

Be careful not to confuse alkanes with alkenes $C_nH_{2n}$. In option d, compound B is an alkene and thus does not fulfil the criteria.


## Q2.152 – B

A first order reaction has a constant half-life. In the first 10 minutes, 15 molecules of compound X are transformed into compound Y. This represents 1 half-life. In the following 10 minutes, half of the remaining 15 molecules of compound X should turn into compound Y, giving a 7:23 split.


## Q2.153 – c: Decreases, Increases

As a reaction progresses, the reactants are used up. Since the rate of reaction is proportional to the concentration of reactants, the forward reaction gradually slows down. As more products are formed, the rate of reverse reaction increases. Equilibrium is reached when the rates of forward and reverse reaction are equal.

**Q2.154 – e: Beaker 2 contains a mixture of $CaCO_3$ and CaO**
Option a and Option b are false since, in an equilibrium, the forward and reverse reaction would be equal. So there would be CaO and $CaCO_3$ in both beakers. Option c and Option d are false because the equilibrium system contain solids (both CaO and $CaCO_3$); therefore, once the system is in equilibrium, calcium ions do not have a way of leaving their respective beakers. When CaO is combined with $CO_2$ in Beaker 2, $CaCO_3$ is formed.

**Q2.155 – d: Propane molecules have a smaller mass than butane molecules.**
Propane contains 3 carbon and 8 hydrogen atoms, whereas butane contains 4 carbon and 10 hydrogen atoms. This is in the BMAT specification, and you should know common alkanes' molecular formulas (methane is $CH_4$, ethane is $C_2H_6$). The greater the length of hydrocarbons, the higher the boiling point. If something has a higher boiling point, then it will be liquid as opposed to gas, and thus will take longer to reach the naked flames as it first needs to evaporate. Thus even if you do not know the exact formulae, you can work out that a smaller molecule (option d) have a lower boiling point and would result in faster diffusion across space to reach flames.

**Q2.156 – c: The catalysed reaction pathway has a lower energy of activation than the uncatalysed reaction pathway**
A catalyst provides an alternative route for the reaction with lower activation energy; so the catalysed reaction will have lower activation energy than the uncatalysed reaction. The catalyst will drive the forward and back reactions equally (i.e. does not affect the equilibrium). Since a catalyst is not part of the net reaction, it cannot be a limiting reagent. The level of catalyst present may, however, dictate the rate of the reaction.

**Q2.157 – a: Cl**
A catalyst is neither produced nor consumed in a reaction, and should not appear in the net reaction: $O_3 + O \rightarrow 2O_2$. The catalyst Cl does not appear. ClO does not appear either, but it is produced then consumed in the intermediate reaction, so it is classified as an intermediate.

**Q2.158a – b: B**
Particles can only react when they collide. If you heat a substance, the particles move faster and so collide more frequently, resulting in a faster

rate of reaction and therefore a shorter completion time. There is, however, no change in the activation energy of the reaction. If the question asked about a biological catalyst mediated reaction, then increasing the temperature may denature (destroy) the biological catalyst and slow the reaction down instead.


## Q2.158b – a: A
When a catalyst is introduced into a system, the rate of reaction increases as it provides a lower energy alternative route for the reaction. This results in a lower total reaction time.


## Q2.159 – e: I, II, III and IV
When the temperature of a system is increased, the rate of reaction also increases as particles move faster and collide more often. An increased concentration of reactant also increases the probability of collision and therefore increases the rate of reaction. Increasing the concentration of catalyst or the surface area of a catalyst provides more active sites and therefore also increases the rate of the reaction.


## Q2.160 – d: Oxygen
Oxygen has a lone pair of electrons and is usually a strong negative charged dipole which allows it to act as hydrogen bond acceptor.


## Q2.161 – a: In a strong acid, the ions completely separate, while only a fraction of them separate in a weak acid.
Weak acids dissociate partially, donating only a partial amount of protons into the solution. Weak bases are less protonated than stronger bases. The pH is a measure of acidity. The pH of pure water is 7.0. Solutions with a pH lower than 7 are acidic. Solutions with a pH greater than 7 are alkaline. Thus, strong acids should always have a <u>lower</u> pH than weak acids.


## Q2.162 – a: Acts as a base (Reaction 1); Acts as an acid (Reaction 2)
In reaction 1, water acts as a Bronsted–Lowry base as it accepts a proton, forming $H_3O^+$. In reaction 2, water donates a proton, thus acting as a Bronsted–Lowry acid.

## Q2.163 – d. Equilibrium moves to the left - Rate increases

In exothermic reactions the ΔH is negative. The products are at a lower energy than the reactants, and the reaction gives out energy. On the other hand, in endothermic reactions the ΔH is positive. This is part of the BMAT Chemistry: Bond Energies syllabus. When equilibrium is on the right, there will be a lot of products and not many reactants. If it lies to the left, the concentration of reactants will be greater than that of products. If in equilibrium there is an exothermic reaction to the right, then there will be a reverse endothermic reaction to the left. If in an exothermic reaction you raise the temperature, the equilibrium tries to move to decrease it (i.e. move in the endothermic direction – to the left). In this case, when raising the temperature, the equilibrium moves to the left, and the rate of the reaction is quicker (since the direction is endothermic – to the left, and thus heating the reaction up will result in a quicker reaction).

## Q2.164 – b: 2

1 mole of gas under standard conditions for temperature and pressure is always 22.4 litres.

## Q2.165 – c: Nitrates

The filters can remove impurities such as clay particles through the physical nature of smaller and smaller filters to which impurities will get attached (i.e. gravel to carbon filters). Odours in impure waters can be removed by carbon filter, and microbes can be killed by chlorine gas. However nitrates will not be filtered out nor react with chlorine, and thus will still be ingested by the drinker.

## Q2.166 – b: 2 and 3

We are given the relative amounts of each of the atoms within a molecule; therefore the empirical formula can be determined. First, you must determine the molar ratio of each of these atoms by dividing the mass by the atomic weights of each of the atoms. We have:

- Carbon: 2.67 / 12 = 0.22
- Hydrogen: 0.22 / 1 = 0.22
- Oxygen: 7.11 / 16 = 0.44

Therefore the C:H:O ratio is 1:1:2, giving the empirical formula $C_1H_1O_2$ (or more simply, $CHO_2$). The molecular formula cannot be determined without further information. Specifically, we need to know the molecular weight.

**Q2.167 – d: $H_2SO_3$**

To keep the calculation simple, assume that the compound weighs 100 grams in total. Thus the percentage composition of the compound can be converted straight into grams.

From the formula moles = mass / molecular weight, we can calculate the individual moles for each component of the compound:

- Oxygen: 58.6 / 16 = 3.6
- Sulphur: 39 / 32 = 1.2
- Hydrogen: 2.4 / 1 = 2.4

The O:S:H ratio is therefore 3:1:2, which can be written as $H_2SO_3$.

**Q2.168 – b: 1.6 litres**

A 3-molar solution is a solution with 3 moles per litre. Thus in 0.8 litres of a 3-molar solution, there are 2.4 moles (0.8 x 3 = 2.4). In order to obtain a 1-molar solution, the total volume of the solution containing those 2.4 moles would need to be in 2.4 l of distilled water. Since the current volume of the solution is 0.8 l, we require an additional 1.6 litres to get 2.4 l.

**Q2.169 – c: Add water, filter, evaporate**

A mixture of salt and pepper can be mixed with water. The salt will dissolve whereas the pepper will not. We can then filter the pepper out. Then, to get pure salt, we can evaporate the remaining salty liquid.

**Q2.170 – a: A clock**

A clock is needed to work out the rate of reaction i.e. how fast a reaction occurs. This can be calculated when the reaction is fully completed and no further reduction in weight is seen on the scale (as the equation is only in one direction). A burette is a graduated glass tube with a tap at one end used for delivering known volumes of a liquid, especially in titrations; as such it would add any value. We do not need to know the temperature, nor are we collecting the carbon dioxide product; hence neither the thermometer nor the condensation funnel are relevant.

**Q2.171 – b: 0**

In this equimolar redox (reduction-oxidation) reaction, 2 electrons are traded between these two metals. Since zinc loses 2 electrons, that must mean that $Cu^{2+}$ gains 2 electrons in the reaction and forms an uncharged

Cu atom. The oxidation number of a monoatomic species is equal to its net charge (zero in this case).

**Q2.172 – d: $2MnO_4^- + 10\ Cl^- + 16\ H^+ \rightarrow 2Mn^{2+} + 5\ Cl_2 + 8\ H_2O$**
Redox reactions take a long time to work out. Whenever a question looks like it may take a disproportionate amount of time, it is worth thinking of other ways of getting to the answer. In this case, only Option d actually balances; the others do not. Therefore Option d has to be the answer. For those who are keen to check the longer approach, the process is as follows:

Step 1: Identify the species being oxidised and reduced:
$Cl^-$ (Oxidation number = - 1) is oxidised to $Cl_2$ (Oxidation number = 0).
Mn is reduced (Oxidation number decreases from 7+ to 2+).

Step 2: Write half-equations:
$Cl^- \rightarrow Cl_2$
$MnO_4^- \rightarrow Mn^{2+}$

Step 3: Balance the two half-reactions with respect to mass, then with respect to charge:
$Cl^- \rightarrow Cl_2$

Multiply the left side by 2 so that the number of chlorine atoms is equal on both sides: $2\ Cl^- \rightarrow Cl_2$

The atoms are now balanced, but you still need to add electrons to balance charge: $2\ Cl^- \rightarrow Cl_2 + 2e^-$. This half-equation is now balanced.

Now, move on to Mn. We have $MnO_4^- \rightarrow Mn^{2+}$

Add $H_2O$ and $H^+$ as needed to balance the equation with respect to atoms first:

$MnO_4^- \rightarrow Mn^{2+} + 4\ H_2O$
$MnO_4^- + 8\ H^+ \rightarrow Mn^{2+} + 4\ H_2O$

Now that the atoms are balanced, you need to add electrons to balance the charge on both sides of this half-reaction. There are 7+ charges on the left side and only 2+ charges on the right side.

Thus, we need to add 5 electrons to the left side to balance charges:

$MnO_4^- + 8\,H^+ + 5e^- \rightarrow Mn^{2+} + 4\,H_2O$

The half-equation is now balanced with regard to mass and charge.
<u>Step 4: Combine the two half-reactions and cancel out terms</u>:
First, you must make sure the electrons in the two half-reactions are equal. Right now, there are 5 e$^-$ in the Mn half-reaction and only 2 e$^-$ in the Cl$^-$ half-reaction. So, multiply the Mn half-reaction by 2 and the Cl$^-$ half-reaction by 5.

$2\,Cl^- \rightarrow Cl_2 + 2e^-$
Multiply the whole half-reaction by 5.
$10\,Cl^- \rightarrow 5\,Cl_2 + 10e^-$

$MnO_4^- + 8\,H^+ + 5e^- \rightarrow Mn^{2+} + 4\,H_2O$
Multiply the whole Mn half-reaction by 2.
$2MnO_4^- + 16\,H^+ + 10e^- \rightarrow 2Mn^{2+} + 8\,H_2O$

Now combine these two half-reactions.
$2MnO_4^- + 10\,Cl^- + 16\,H^+ + 10e^- \rightarrow 2Mn^{2+} + 5\,Cl_2 + 10e^- + 8\,H_2O$

Simplify: $2MnO_4^- + 10\,Cl^- + 16\,H^+ \rightarrow 2Mn^{2+} + 5\,Cl_2 + 8\,H_2O$

**Q2.173 – c: Aluminium is reduced; Carbon is oxidised**
To calculate the oxidation states, you have to memorise the states of certain atoms. For the BMAT, you will most likely only need to know the states in the table below to solve the questions asked.

| Oxidation State | Atom |
| --- | --- |
| 0 | Atoms in elemental form |
| +1 | Hydrogen (except when bound to a metal: then -1) |
| -2 | Oxygen (except when it is in a peroxide like $H_2O_2$) |

The fundamental principle is that the sum of the oxidation states of all atoms in a neutral molecule must be zero, while in ions the sum of the oxidation states of the constituent atoms must be equal to the charge on the ion. For example, the oxidation state of sulfur in $H_2S$ is -2 (because the oxidation state of $H_2$ is 2 x 1 = +2). Similarly the oxidation state of sulfur in $H_2SO_4$ is calculated as: $-(2 \times 1 + 4 \times -2) = +6$.

In this question's redox reaction, aluminium's oxidation state begins as +3 (calculated as: $-[3 \times -2]\,/\,2$) and ends as 0 (i.e. becomes reduced – gains electrons), while carbon begins as 0 (i.e. it is in its elemental form) and ends as +4 (i.e. becomes oxidised – loses electrons).

**Q2.174 – a: CH₄**
In that reaction, carbon's oxidation state begins as -4 and becomes +4 (oxidised – lost electrons). Oxygen's oxidation state goes from 0 to -2 (reduced – gained electrons). Since a reducing agent is the compound containing the atom being oxidised, then methane is the reducing agent (reductant), whereas the dioxygen is the oxidising agent.

**Q2.175 – d: No oxidation or reduction takes place**
In this acid-base neutralisation reaction, no oxidation states are changed, so no redox reaction takes place.

**Q2.176 – c: 80**

$$\text{Relative atomic mass } (A_r) = \frac{[(50 \times 79) + (50 \times 81)]}{100} = 80$$

**Q2.177 – b: 35.5**

$$\text{Relative atomic mass } (A_r) = \frac{[(75 \times 35) + (25 \times 37)]}{100} = 35.5$$

**Q2.178 – d: 69.8**

$$\text{Relative atomic mass } (A_r) = \frac{[(60 \times 69) + (40 \times 71)]}{100} = 69.8$$

**Q2.179 – c: 152.5**

$$(A_r)152 = \frac{[(20 \times 150) + (80 \times X)]}{100} \text{, which gives X=152.5}$$

**Q2.180 – a: X=12cm and Y=8cm**
$NH_3$ has a molecular mass of 17. HCl has a molecular mass of 36.5. Molecules with lower mass are able to diffuse faster along the tube, so $NH_3$ is able to move further along the tube, meaning that distance X would be greater than distance Y.

**Q2.181 – b: a=2 ; b=8**
$aC_4H_{10} + 13O_2 \rightarrow bCO_2 + 10H_2O$

To calculate $a$ and $b$, it is easier to work out everything in its simplest format. We see that there are 20H on the right-hand side, thus we require 20H on the left-hand side.

So we put a 2 in front of $C_4H_{10}$: $2C_4H_{10} + 13O_2 \rightarrow bCO_2 + 10H_2O$

To balance the carbons now we require 8C on the right, thus we put an 8 in front of $CO_2$: $2C_4H_{10} + 13O_2 \rightarrow 8CO_2 + 10H_2O$

A final check to see that all the items in the equation are balanced (C, H and O) and it's done.


**Q2.182 – b: $O_2$**
The relative atomic mass for $SO_2$ is 64 grams, $O_2$ is 32 grams and $SO_3$ is 80 grams.

Normally 2 moles of $SO_2$ (128 grams) can make 2 moles of $SO_3$ (mass of 160g) with the addition of oxygen.

Here only 153 grams are produced; thus the limiting factor has to be oxygen.


**Q2.183 – d: 3**
Firstly work out the reaction when $C_4H_{12}$ is completely combusted with $O_2$. $C_4H_{12} + X\ O_2 \rightarrow 4CO_2 + 6H_2O$, where **X** is the unknown amount of $O_2$ used.

By balancing the equation, we get $C_4H_{12} + 7O_2 \rightarrow 4CO_2 + 6H_2O$. Thus normally combusting $C_4H_{12}$ we would use 7 moles of $O_2$, forming 4 moles of $CO_2$ and 6 moles of $H_2O$.

With a limited amount of $O_2$ (3.5 moles), only half the amount of $H_2O$ would be produced, so only 3 moles.

$$\textbf{0.5}\ C_4H_{12} + \textbf{3.5}O_2 \rightarrow 2CO_2 + 3H_2O$$

**Q2.184 – d: 19**
First, write the balanced equation for the reaction between magnesium oxide and hydrochloric acid:

$$MgO + 2HCl \rightarrow MgCl_2 + H_2O$$

The relative molecular mass of MgO is 24 + 16 = 40g. Therefore 8g represents 8 / 40 = 0.2 moles.

We know from the equation that 0.2 moles of MgO will produce the same quantity of $MgCl_2$, i.e. 0.2 moles.

One mole of $MgCl_2$ has a molecular mass of $24 + 2 \times 35.5 = 95$. Therefore the reaction will produce $0.2 \times 95 = 19g$ of $MgCl_2$.


**Q2.185 – b: 14**
We first need to calculate the unknown relative atomic mass of Fe. We know that $Fe + 2 \times (5 \times 12 + 5 \times 1) = 186$, therefore $Fe = 56$.

We can therefore calculate the relative atomic mass of N as follows:
$56 + 5(12+N) + N + 16 + 1 = 217$, i.e. $6N + 133 = 217$, i.e. $N = 14$.


**Q2.186 – d: 32**
We are given that O=16, H=1 and N=14 and that the formula is $(NH_4)_2SO_4$ (relative formula mass = 132).

This means that there are 2N, 8H, 1S and 4O in the compound. The relative atomic mass equation is therefore $2 \times 14 + 8 \times 1 + 4 \times 16 + S = 132$.
Thus $S = 132 - 100 = 32$.


**Q2.187 – c: 50**
$CaCO_3 \rightarrow CaO + CO_2$
$(40 + 12 + 3 \times 16) \rightarrow (40 + 16) + (12 + 2 \times 16)$
$100 \rightarrow 56 + 44$
We are told that only 28 tonnes of CaO and 22 tonnes of $CO_2$ were produced (i.e. half the amount in the equation). It means that 50 tonnes of $CaCO_3$ were decomposed (i.e. half of 100).

**Q2.188a – c: 13**
Questions relating to molecular structure diagrams occur regularly at the BMAT and are often asked in that format i.e. you are given the molecular structure diagram for a relatively simple molecule and are asked to use the information given to answer other questions. Note that, practically speaking, the information provided is pretty much pointless if you already know how molecular structure diagrams work; however, at the BMAT, the information is always provided in order to enable candidates who have not learnt it in their course to deduce the relevant information and use it to solve other questions.

In the molecular structure diagram for Cyclohexane ($C_6H_{10}$), each vertex of the hexagon represents a carbon atom, two of which are linked by a double bond, hence why there are 10 hydrogen atoms instead of 12. It follows from it that the number of carbon atoms in the molecule represented in this question equals 13, as there are 13 vertices (see diagram below for individual numbering).

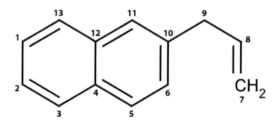

**Q2.188b – d: 12**
Each vertex represents a carbon atom, each of which can form 4 bonds. Since a carbon atom is represented by a vertex on the diagram, and the number of lines coming out of each vertex represents a bond to another carbon atom (with double lines representing double bonds), the number of missing bonds to make it up to 4 will represent the number of hydrogen atoms. Therefore:

At vertex 1: Number of bonds shown = 3, hence Number of H atoms = 1
At vertex 2: Number of bonds shown = 3, hence Number of H atoms = 1
At vertex 3: Number of bonds shown = 3, hence Number of H atoms = 1
At vertex 4: Number of bonds shown = 4, hence Number of H atoms = 0
At vertex 5: Number of bonds shown = 3, hence Number of H atoms = 1

At vertex 6: Number of bonds shown = 3, hence Number of H atoms = 1
At vertex 7: Number of bonds shown = 2, hence Number of H atoms = 2
Note that the 2 H atoms in question are those contained in CH2.
At vertex 8: Number of bonds shown = 3, hence Number of H atoms = 1
At vertex 9: Number of bonds shown = 2, hence Number of H atoms = 2
At vertex 10: Number of bonds shown = 4, hence Number of H atoms = 0
At vertex 11: Number of bonds shown = 3, hence Number of H atoms = 1
At vertex 12: Number of bonds shown = 4, hence Number of H atoms = 0
At vertex 13: Number of bonds shown = 3, hence Number of H atoms = 1
Total number of hydrogen atoms: 12


## Q2.188c – d: 180

To calculate the mass, you need to work out both the number of carbon atoms and the number of hydrogen atoms. The number of carbon atoms is equal to the number of vertices: in this case, 13. The number of hydrogen atoms can be counted using the method shown in the answer to the previous question. Alternatively, you could draw the hydrogen atoms on the graph, ensuring that each carbon atom has 4 bonds, and count them:

This gives 24 hydrogen atoms.
The relative molecular mass is therefore 13 x 12 + 24 x 1 = 180.


## Q2.188d – d: A → D → B → C

The easiest and safest (though not the quickest) way to go about ordering the molecules in increasing order of relative molecular masses is to calculate each mass individually using the same method as in the previous question.

This gives the following:

A = 10 C + 8 H = 128
B = 12 C + 16 H = 160
C = 14 C + 24 H = 192
D = 11 C + 16 H = 148

In increasing order: A → D → B → C.

Note that this is also the order of the number of carbon atoms within each molecule. Since carbon atoms have a far greater mass than hydrogen atoms, this will usually be the case. Although not an exact calculation, this may help you in "guessing" the answer should you run out of time at the exam.

**Q2.189 – b: CH$_3$**
Consider the reaction: $C_xH_y + O_2 \rightarrow A \times CO_2 + B \times H_2O$.
The total atomic mass of the end product is $A(12+32) + B(2+16)$.

We know that: $176 = A(12 + 32)$ and that $108 = B(2 + 16)$.
Therefore A = 4 and B = 6. Thus $C_xH_y + O_2 \rightarrow 4\ CO_2 + 6\ H_2O$.
There are 4C and 12H on the left-hand side. So the ratio of C:H is 1:3; thus $CH_3$ is the most plausible compound combusted.

**Q2.190 – c: Nitrogen**
Carbon dioxide and chlorine are both poisonous and thus can be discounted. Chlorine and bromine have a smell. Nitrogen is non-poisonous, has no smell and also reacts with hydrogen in the Haber process.

**Q2.191 – b: During corrosion of an unplated iron bar, oxygen is reduced; during electroplating, zinc acts as cathode**
During corrosion, metals react with oxygen. The metal atoms lose electrons when they form the rust (called metal oxide), i.e. the metal is oxidised and oxygen is reduced.

The equation can be written as: $2Fe + O_2 \rightarrow 2FeO$. This can be split up into the separate equations:

- Oxidation reaction (lose electron): $2Fe \rightarrow 2Fe^{2+} + 4e^-$, where Fe is oxidised and Fe is the reducing agent.
- Reduction reaction (gain electron): $O_2 + 4e^- \rightarrow 2O^{2-}$; where O2 is reduced and O2 is the oxidising agent

During the galvanisation process, the zinc coating, being less noble than iron, tends to corrode selectively. Dissolution of this sacrificial coating leaves behind electrons, which concentrate in the iron, making it cathodic and thus inhibiting its dissolution.

**Q2.192 – d: 16**
In a closed system, then formula $P.V = n.R.T$ will apply. If the temperature is constant, then increasing the pressure of the gaseous reaction mixture by 4 times will increase the concentrations of $C_2H_4$ and $H_2$ by 4 times each. Using the given equation rate, we can see that this will lead to an increase by a factor of $4 \times 4 = 16$.

**Q2.193 – a: He > $N_2$ > Ar > $CO_2$**
According to Graham's Law, the rates of effusion of different gases are inversely proportional to the square roots of their molar masses. Thus, if the molecular weight of one gas is four times that of another, it would diffuse through a small valve in a vessel at half the rate of the other gas.

Put more simply: heavier gases diffuse more slowly. Thus after a time, but before equilibrium is reached, there will be more of the lighter gases in container B than heavier ones.

**Q2.194 – a: Plate 1**
To obtain the correct plate, one simply needs to reverse the capillarity process. So we need to project the dots on the final plate onto the horizontal line marking the level of Solvent L and then rotate the place 90 degrees to the right. This gives Plate 1.

**Q2.195 – c: Hydrogen is obtained from natural gas.**
Ammonia is made by the Haber process from hydrogen and nitrogen and is used for fertilisers. The Contact process produces sulfuric acid in high concentrations needed for industrial processes. The nitrogen comes from the air (78% nitrogen), and the hydrogen comes from natural gas (or oil cracking). High pressures favour the forward reaction since there are 4 molecules of gas on the left-hand side and only 2 on the right-hand side.

**Q2.196 – f: Different number of neutrons only**
An isotope is a variation in the number of neutrons, which affects the mass and nuclear stability of an element. A variation in protons would change the element to a different element in the decay series, whereas a variation of electrons merely produces an ion.

**Q2.197 – d: 2, 4 and 5**
Industrial processes are never 100% efficient as a return on their material investment because losses are inevitable. The reactants can evaporate out of a containment vessel, can react along undesirable pathways (including reversible reactions back into the original reactants or by-products) and the reactants themselves are never 100% pure.

**Q2.198 – b: To prevent contact with water vapour**
Alkali metals, including lithium, are highly reactive. They must be stored under oil in order to prevent their violent reaction with water vapour.

**Q2.199 – e: 3, 4 and 5**
An increase in concentration increases the likelihood that two reactant particles will meet and react. An increase in temperature increases the fraction of particles that have a sufficient energy to undergo a successful reaction in the reacting mix. An increase in surface area (i.e. using smaller particle

size such as finely ground powder instead of a large lump) ensures greater contact with the reactants and thus increases the rate of reaction.

### Q2.200 – d: It releases energy in the form of heat

Endothermic reactions absorb heat while exothermic reactions give off heat. While exothermic reactions are often favourable, they are not exclusively so.

The overall entropy of the universe, as dictated by the Second Law of Thermodynamics, is what ultimately drives reactions. Energy is always released when bonds are formed; however, the overall reaction is only exothermic if the energy released in forming new bonds is greater than the energy required to break the original ones.

### Q2.201 – c: Van der Waals < Hydrogen < Ionic < Covalent

Van der Waals forces and hydrogen bonds are relatively weak intermolecular forces that hold molecules together. Van der Waals forces are all the electric forces that attract neutral molecules to one another in gases, in liquefied and solidified gases, and in almost all organic liquids and solids.

Solids that are held together by van der Waals forces characteristically have lower melting points and are softer than those held together by the stronger ionic, covalent and metallic bonds.

A hydrogen bond is a stronger, more intermolecular interaction specific to molecules containing an oxygen, nitrogen or fluorine atom that is attached to a hydrogen atom.

Ionic and covalent bonds are very strong intramolecular forces that hold atoms/ions together within molecules. In an ionic bond, the atoms are bound by attraction of opposite ions, whereas, in a covalent bond, atoms are bound by sharing electrons.

# 21 Scientific Knowledge and Applications Mathematics – Answers

### Q2.202 – c: £0.90
Richard gives £5.00 for the 5 bags of crisps, and receives £0.75 back. Therefore, at that point, he has paid £5.00 – £0.75 = £4.25. He then gives £0.25 back to the cashier, making his total spend £4.50 i.e. £0.90 per bag.

### Q2.203 – c: 69 minutes
The distance travelled by the car is 5 x 50 = 250 miles. If the car had been going at 65mph, it would have driven the distance in 250 / 65 = 3.85 hours. The time difference is therefore 1.15 hours i.e. (x 60) = 69 minutes.

### Q2.204 – a: 80 acres
If we call X the portion given to the first son, then the portion given to the second son is 4X and the portion given to the third son is 5 x (4X) = 20X. This gives (20 + 4 + 1) X = 2000 i.e. 25X = 2000 and therefore X = 80.

### Q2.205 – c: 2
The equation is: $5x – 2 = 0.5 (10 + 3x)$.
This gives $10x – 4 = 10 + 3x$.
Hence $7x = 14$ and therefore $x = 2$.

### Q2.206 – d: 240
The unit purchase price is 0.42 / 6 = 7p
The unit selling price is 0.72 / 8 = 9p
The profit per orange is therefore 9p – 7p = 2p
The number of oranges sold to make a profit of £4.80 is 4.80/0.02 = 240

### Q2.207 – c: 10,600 x 1.06
The amount available in the savings account at the end of year 2 will be: $10,000 \times 1.06^2$, which is equivalent to 10,000 x 1.06 x 1.06 i.e. 10,600 x 1.06.

Option a is the formula for the amount of money available to the investor over 2 years if he withdrew the interest paid at the end of year 1 and then left the original 10,000 invested, essentially getting £600 of interest every year and spending it. It is the same as option d.

Option b corresponds to the interest paid at the end of year 2 on the interest paid at the end of year 1. Option e is the amount that would be obtained by investing two lots of £10,000 for one year.

**Q2.208 – a: 5,000 x $(1.0175)^{12}$**
Compound interest is calculated by using the formula:

$$\text{Final amount} = I\left(1+\frac{R}{n}\right)^{nt}$$

where I is the initial deposit, and R is the interest rate (expressed as decimals), n is the number of times the interest is compounded per year and t is the number of years. In this case, we have R=0.07, n=4 and t=3. Therefore R/n = 0.175 and nt=12.

**Q2.209 – c: 182.5cm**
The sum of the heights of the 3 members is 3 x 175 = 525cm.

If the average across the whole team of 5 members is 178cm then the sum of their heights is 5 x 178 = 890.

So, the sum of the heights of the remaining 2 players is: 890-525=365cm and, consequently, their average height is 365/2 = 182.5cm.

**Q2.210 – c: 1.2 x $10^{19}$**
1 light year is 6 x $10^{12}$ miles and we are asked to find the distance in miles corresponding to 2 x $10^6$ light-years.

This is calculated as: (6 x $10^{12}$) x (2 x $10^6$) = 12 x $10^{18}$ = 1.2 x $10^{19}$

**Q2.211 – e: 143**
Let the numbers be X and Y. The sum of the integers is 24 thus it can be written as X + Y = 24. The difference between their squares is 24, thus it can be written as $X^2 - Y^2 = 48$, but also (X + Y) (X - Y) = 48.

We know that X + Y = 24, therefore 24(X – Y) = 48 i.e. X – Y = 2.

Combining it with X + Y = 24 gives X = 13 and Y = 11; thus their product is 143.

**Q2.212 – c: $3.2 \times 10^7$**
To find the solution it is best to deal with each component separately.
We can spot that the two numbers 3.6 and 6.4 sitting inside the square root signs would make perfect squares 36 and 64 if we could adjust the powers of 10 sitting next to them. So:

$$\sqrt{3.6 \times 10^3} = \sqrt{36 \times 10^2} = 6 \times 10 = 60$$
$$\sqrt{6.4 \times 10^7} = \sqrt{64 \times 10^6} = 8 \times 10^3$$

Also $(2 \times 10^2)^3 = 2^3 \times 10^{2 \times 3} = 8 \times 10^6$

So the equation now becomes:

$$= \frac{3 \times 10^{-2}}{60} \times 8 \times 10^6 \times 8 \times 10^3$$

$$= 10^{-2+6+3} \times \frac{3 \times 8 \times 8}{60}$$

$$= 10^7 \times \frac{8 \times 8}{20}$$

$$= 3.2 \times 10^7$$

**Q2.213 – d:** $\dfrac{20X + 9Y}{X+Y}$

The arithmetic mean is the total cost of all apples divided by the number of apples.

**Q2.214 – a:** $\dfrac{3AX + 2BY}{6(A+B)}$

We have A units of apples costing X/2 each, and B units of pears costing Y/3 each. The arithmetic mean is therefore calculated as follows:

$$\frac{A\left(\frac{X}{2}\right) + B\left(\frac{Y}{3}\right)}{A+B} = \frac{3AX + 2BY}{6(A+B)}$$

**Q2.215 – e: 170**

The arithmetic mean we need to calculate is

$$\frac{(3X-10) + (3Y+20) + (3Z+50)}{3}$$

This can be rewritten as:

$$\frac{3(X+Y+Z) + 60}{3} \quad \text{or} \quad X+Y+Z+20$$

The arithmetic mean of X, Y and Z is 50; therefore X+Y+Z = 3 x 50 = 150. Therefore the mean we needed to calculate is 150+20=170.

**Q2.216 – b: 20**

The average of 5 of the numbers is 24; therefore their sum is 5x24=120. The sum of the remaining 3 numbers is 40; therefore the sum of all 8 numbers is 120 + 40 = 160. The overall average is therefore:160/8 = 20.

**Q2.217 – d: 16,800 + X**

The total of all 3 salaries is (50,400 + X) + X + X i.e. 50,400 + 3X. The average is 1/3 of that amount i.e. 16,800 + X.

**Q2.218 – d: 40**
We know that (A+B)/2 = 60; therefore A+B = 120.
We know that (B+C)/2 = 80; therefore B+C = 160
C-A = (B+C) – (A+B); therefore C-A = 160 – 120 = 40.

**Q2.219 – e:** $\dfrac{17X+130}{17}$

If we call Y the average temperature over the remaining 17 days of the month, then we can write the following equation:

$$X= \frac{13\,(X-10)+17Y}{30}$$

This gives: 30X = 13(X-10) + 17Y
Then: 30X = 13X – 130 + 17Y

And therefore: $Y = \dfrac{17X+130}{17}$

**Q2.220 – e: 200**
Let X be the number of people who did not have a meal on the plane. Thus X – 100 would be the number of people who had a meal.

We know that people who paid for flight only spent £500 each, and that those who paid for flight + meal paid £512. Therefore we can write:
512(X – 100) + 500 X = 151,200.

Therefore 1012X = 151,200 + 51,200 = 202,400 i.e. X = 200

**Q2.221 – e: £1,800**
To get the highest cost, he would have to travel the longest distance (8,000 miles), with the most expensive fuel estimate (£1.50/litre) and the least fuel efficient estimate (30 miles per gallon). This would consume 8000/30 x 4.5 = 1200 litres and would cost 1200 x 1.5 = £1,800.

**Q2.222 – c: 2**
We know that x goes from 10 to 25 i.e. is 2.5 times greater.

Since x and y are inversely proportional, this means that y must be 2.5 times lower. This gives 5 / 2.5 = 2.

**Q2.223 – a: 17/36**
Firstly, arrange all the fractions into common denominators. The common denominator is 36.

$$\frac{17}{36} \; , \quad \frac{1}{2}=\frac{18}{36} \; , \quad \frac{2}{8}=\frac{1}{4}=\frac{9}{36} \; , \quad \frac{13}{18}=\frac{26}{36} \; , \quad \frac{9}{27}=\frac{1}{3}=\frac{12}{36}$$

Ordering the numerators gives: 26, 18, 17, 12, 9.
Thus the answer is 17/36.

**Q2.224 – b: 0.5**
All fractions can be expressed with a common denominator of 24.

$$\frac{17}{24} \; ; 0.5=\frac{12}{24} \; ; \; \frac{3}{8}=\frac{9}{24} \; ; \; 0.75=\frac{18}{24} \; ; \; \frac{2}{16}=\frac{3}{24} \; ; 0.25=\frac{6}{24} \; ; \; \frac{6}{6}=\frac{24}{24}$$

Ordering the numerators gives: 24, 18, 17, **12**, 9, 6, 3. Thus the answer is 12/24 i.e. 0.5.

**Q2.225 – b: Between $\frac{6}{7} + \frac{1}{14}$ and 1**

We can calculate the sum using 40 as common denominator. This gives: 35/40 + 4/40 = 39/40 i.e. just under 1, which eliminates options c and d. This is also greater than 3/4, thus eliminating option a.

We now need to calculate 6/7 + 1/14 (the lower end of Option b). This is equal to (12+1)/14 = 13/14 = 39/42. Since 39/42 is lower than 39/40 then we can conclude that the sum is within the interval given in option b.

**Q2.226 – d: 1100**
Using $(a^2 - b^2) = (a+b)\,(a-b)$, we get:
$(25^2 - 15^2) + (32^2 - 18^2) = (25-15)(25+15) + (32-18)(32+18)$
$= (10 \times 40) + (14 \times 50) = 400 + 700 = 1100$

**Q2.227 – c: 3/2**
Since the denominator remains at 7, all that is required here is to multiply 4 by Y in order to give 6. Therefore Y = 6/4 = 3/2.

**Q2.228 – d:** $\dfrac{5}{100} + \dfrac{7}{1000}$

The fraction 114/2000 is equivalent to 57/1000 or 0.057, which is 5/100 + 7/1000.

**Q2.229 – b: 1/8**
The fraction can be approximated as 50x0.5/200 = 25/200 = 0.125 i.e. 1/8.

**Q2.230 – c: 3**

The fraction can be approximated as $\dfrac{60 \times (1)^2}{\sqrt{400}}$ i.e. 3.

**Q2.231 – a.** $\dfrac{10c}{11}$
In working out the equation we have to substitute the values for a and b.

$$d = \frac{a+b}{1+ \dfrac{ab}{c^2}} = \frac{\dfrac{c}{2} + \dfrac{3c}{4}}{1+ \dfrac{(\dfrac{c}{2})(\dfrac{3c}{4})}{c^2}} = \frac{\dfrac{5c}{4}}{1+ \dfrac{3}{8}} = \frac{\dfrac{5c}{4}}{(\dfrac{11}{8})} = \frac{40c}{44} = \frac{10c}{11}$$

**Q2.232 – d: 1/2**
x / (2x+1) can be rewritten as 1 / (2 + 1/x).
As x becomes larger, the 1/x becomes very small, leaving just 1/2

**Q2.233 – d: 9,000,000**
We know that £450,000 represents 5% of sales. Thus total sales are 20 x 450,000 = 9,000,000.

**Q2.234 – b: 8**
If r is halved, the denominator is increased by $(1/2)^3 = 1/8$.
This makes X increase by a factor of 8.

**Q2.235 – a: 100**
Calling X the number of cakes made by Max, the total number of cakes made is defined as $X + 3.5X = 4.5X$. Therefore $4.5X = 450$; thus $X = 100$.

**Q2.236 – c: 1800g**
The chocolate and sugar account for 25% and 20% respectively, a total of 45%. Therefore, the flour must account for the remaining 55%. The total weight is therefore $990 / 0.55 = 1800g$.

**Q2.237 – b: 25**
6,000 pages divided by 4 pages/second = 1500 seconds. This is equivalent to $1500/60 = 25$ minutes.

**Q2.238 – c: -2 < x < 3**
We know that: $3 - x^3 < 11$ therefore by subtracting 3 on each side we get:
$3 - x^3 - 3 < 11 - 3$ i.e. $- x^3 < 8$. This gives us $- x < 2$ and therefore $x > - 2$

We also know that $2x - 3 < 3$. Therefore, adding 3 on both sides we get:
$2x - 3 + 3 < 3 + 3$  i.e. $2x < 6$
Dividing by 2 on each side gives $x < 3$.

Hence $-2 < x < 3$

**Q2.239 – d: 180%**
The key is to ensure you get the percentages the right way round. We are asked for the weight of the HFD mouse as a percentage of the weight of the control mouse. This is calculated as $450/250 = 1.8$ i.e. 180%.

**Q2.240 – b: 5**
The area is calculated as $\pi r^2$, which we know from the question to equal $25\pi$. Therefore $r^2 = 25$ and thus $r = 5$.

**Q2.241 – e: 3X² – 8X – 3**
The area is calculated as (3X+1)(X-3) and expands as $3X^2 - 9X + X - 3$ i.e. $3X^2 - 8X - 3$.

**Q2.242 – b: 5**
Supply = Demand when $3X^2 + X - 10 = 2X^2 + 4X$.
This gives: $X^2 - 3X - 10 = 0$.

At that point you can try the options one after the other to see which one works (sometimes it is the fastest way of getting the right answer).

Alternatively, you can write the equation as (X-5)(X+2) = 0 and see that this gives X = 5 or X = -2. Since X has to be positive then the answer is X = 5.

**Q2.243 – c: 50 m**
Since the man first walks east and then north, his journey will follow the shape of a right angle.

Using the Pythagorean theorem, we can calculate the magnitude of his displacement X from point A to point B as $X^2 = 30^2 + 40^2$
Therefore, $X = \sqrt{2500} = 50m$.

**Q2.244 – d: 13 miles**
In 2 hours, the runner will have travelled 12 miles towards the north. During that time, the walker, whose speed is 6 – 3.5 = 2.5 mph, will have travelled 5 miles towards the west. Using the Pythagorean theorem again (since they are travelling on paths which form a right angle and started from the same point at the same time) we have: $X^2 = 12^2 + 5^2 = 169$. Therefore X = 13.

**Q2.245 – b: 12 + 6√2**
Since the area of square ABCD is 36, we deduce that each side of the square measures $\sqrt{36} = 6$. We therefore now know that AD = CD = 6.

The distance AC is calculated using the Pythagorean theorem and is equal to $\sqrt{36 + 36}$ i.e. $\sqrt{72}$ or $6\sqrt{2}$.

Thus the perimeter of the triangle ACD is $6+6+6\sqrt{2} = 12 + 6\sqrt{2}$.
Note that the information given about ACE is not needed to solve this question.

### Q2.246 – d: Angle p = angle z

Since point C is exactly midway between BC and CD, the length of line AC would be equal to the length of line CE, and the angles r and z would be equal (and so angles x and y would be same as well).

However, angle p would not equal angle z (it would equal angle y). The only way that p could equal z would be if we had CD = DE, but this would not be possible in a square.

### Q2.247 – d: 72

The total percentage of admissions is 43 + 18 + 12 + 7 = 80%. So the rest is 20%. The pie chart represents 360 degrees. 20% is therefore equivalent to 72 degrees.

### Q2.248 – a: 1

You can represent the problem as follows:

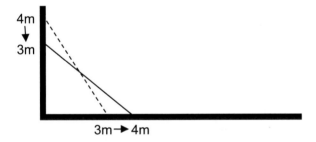

In essence this is a right angled triangle (4m by 3m by X, where X is the length of the ladder). So we can use the Pythagoras theorem to find the length of the ladder X: $X^2 = 4^2 + 3^2$. Therefore the ladder measures X=5m.

If the ladder slips 1 m from the top of the ladder, since the ladder is a rigid body, it will still be 5 m long. The distance from the top of the ladder to the floor will be 3m, the length of the ladder with be 5m; therefore the distance to the wall will be 4m. You can work this out by using Pythogoras again, but more cleverly by noticing that we have simply swapped the height and the distance to the wall in the equation. The increase is therefore 1m (from 3m to 4m).

**Q2.249 – b: 2**

To save time, remember that you do not have to work out the exact values of the equation given. All you have to do is to say whether the equations are equivalent when X is either 456 and when -456.

The only time the result will be the same is when X is <u>directly</u> elevated to the power of an even number e.g. $X^2$, $X^4$ etc. This is the case for option b.

In option 1, the result will clearly be different. In option 3, if the formula is developed it will contain some $X^6$, which will remain the same regardless of the sign borne by X, but also some $X^3$, which will switch sign depending on the value of X.

**Q2.250 – e: 220**

This is a simple matter of substituting letters for value. The calculation gives: $(1 – 3)^2 + (2 \times 4 – 2)^3 = 4 + 216 = 220$

**Q2.251 – c: 2@2**

The only way in which x@y can equal 0 is if x=y so that the top half of the formula equals 0. Option c is the only option satisfying that condition.

**Q2.252 – b: 32**

First, write out the sequence. We know that the $7^{th}$ number is 9.

| Term | 1 | 2 | 3 | 4 | 5 | 6 | **7** | 8 |
|------|-----|-----|-----|-----|-----|-----|-------|-----|
| Pattern | -3 | -1 | 1 | 3 | 5 | 7 | **9** | 11 |

The sum of this sequence is -3 + -1 + 1 + 3 + 5 + 7 + 9 + 11 = 32

**Q2.253 – c: 1.5**

Firstly write out the sequence, we know that the $1^{st}$ number is 1.

So the second term would be 1 plus the reciprocal of the first term ($\frac{1}{1}$) thus would be 2. The third term would be 1 plus the reciprocal of 2 which would be ($\frac{1}{2}$), so the third term would be 1.5

**Q2.254 – b: II only**
For option I: only one of the two terms has to equal 0, not necessarily both.
For option II: if X is not equal to 3 then Y must be 1 to balance the equation.
For option III, if X is 3 then Y can be any number (including 1) since the product is 0 regardless.

Hence only option II is correct, which is option b.


**Q2.255 – e: None of the above**
For the equation $y = 3x^2 - 2x + 3$ when the x value is -3, we get the following result: $y = 3(9) - 2(-3) + 3$, $y = 27 + 6 + 3 = 36$, which is not on the option list.

**Q2.256 – b: Less than 10cm below the curve.**
The relative position of the point to the curve is determined by the relative value of y using x = 7 compared to 176.

We have $y = (7-5)^3 + 2(7+2)^2 + (7-3) + 7 = 8 + 162 + 4 + 7 = 181$. The graph therefore uses the point (7, 181). Thus Point P (7,176) is 5 cm below the curve and option b is therefore the correct answer.


**Q2.257 – d: x = - 0.5 and x = + 4.5**
When the graphs meet, we have

$$4x = \frac{9}{x} + 16$$

This gives: $4x^2 = 16x + 9$ i.e. $4x^2 - 16x - 9 = 0$.

This can be written as: $(2x - 4)^2 - 25 = 0$
i.e. $2x - 4 = 5$ (which gives x = + 4.5)
or $2x - 4 = - 5$ (which gives x = - 0.5)


**Q2.258 – c: 6**
We know that AB = 4 (A+B).
If A = 12 then 12B = 4B + 48 and therefore 8B = 48 and B = 6.

**Q2.259 – e: £23,000**
In August, the author's salary was 4,000 x 1.2 = £4,800.
We therefore have 4800 = 2500 + X/10 and therefore X = £23,000.


**Q2.260 – d: 25Z/3**
We also know that the number of doctors is 1/3 of the number of healthcare
assistants (which is 5Z); so the number of doctors is 5Z/3. We also know
that the number of nurses is 5 times the number of doctors. Therefore there
are 5 x 5Z/3 = 25 x Z/3 nurses.


**Q2.261 – b: 21**
There are 3 ways of getting to the answer. The long way is to do the actual
calculation, which may take a little time without a calculator.

A shorter way is to use the relationship: $(a^2 - b^2) = (a - b)(a + b)$

$$\frac{8^4-1}{3(8^2+1)} = \frac{(8^2-1)(8^2+1)}{3(8^2+1)} = \frac{(8^2-1)}{3} = \frac{63}{3} = 21$$

In addition, you can use an approximate method by saying that the equation
is roughly $8^4 / (3 \times 8^2) = 8^2 / 3 = 64/3 = 21.3$. This method works fine if the
options are not too close together. If 22 was an option, it would prove a risky
gamble.


**Q2.262 – a: I**
You could work out each of the sums in turn, however some of the options
can be excluded straight away. From the equations we can see that option
I and IV are rather large. However option II and III are reciprocal squares,
this means that the bottom number will be exceedingly large, meaning that
the whole fraction itself will be very small. So we can immediately exclude
option II and III. In option I we see that are reciprocal root of the numbers.
This means that the numbers in the denominator will be smaller compared
to same order in option IV and thus the whole fraction would be larger. So
option I would give the largest sum.

**Q2.263 – d: 0.0004**
Writing the equation out we get:

$$\sqrt{\frac{x(0.1 - x)}{n}} = \sqrt{\frac{0.02(0.1 - 0.02)}{10000}} = \frac{\sqrt{0.0016}}{\sqrt{10000}} = \frac{0.04}{100} = 0.0004$$

**Q2.264 – c: 3**
We know that $(a - b)(a + b) = a^2 - b^2$. So the formula is equivalent to:
$\sqrt{7}^2 - 2^2 = 7 - 4 = 3$

**Q2.265 – c: - 4√5**
Solving the equation we get:
$$\sqrt{5} - \sqrt{125} = \sqrt{5} - \sqrt{5^2 \times 5} = \sqrt{5} - 5\sqrt{5} = -4\sqrt{5}$$

**Q2.266 – c: 27,889 x 3**
The key here is to recognise that $501 = 3 \times 167$.
Hence $167 \times 501 = 3 \times 167^2$ i.e. $3 \times 27,889$.

**Q2.267 – d: h (A – a) / 2**

The area of the trapezium can be calculated as: $\dfrac{(A+a)h}{2}$

The area of the white square is ah.

Therefore the area of the two triangles can be calculated as $\dfrac{(A+a)h}{2}$ - ah

which can also be written as $\dfrac{(A+a)h - 2ah}{2}$ i.e. $\dfrac{(A - a)h}{2}$

**Q2.268 – b: X² √3 / 4**

The triangle's sides measure X. If we call H the height of the triangle and draw a vertical line from the top vertex to the bottom side, we obtain 2 rectangular triangles, with one side measuring X/2.

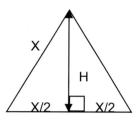

Using Pythagoras, we can write: $(X/2)^2 + H^2 = X^2$.

From this we deduce: $H^2 = X^2 - (X/2)^2 = X^2 - X^2/4 = 3X^2/4$

Therefore: $H = \dfrac{X\sqrt{3}}{2}$

The area of the triangle is calculated as HX/2, which is therefore equal to:

$$H = \frac{X\sqrt{3}}{2} \frac{X}{2} = \frac{X^2\sqrt{3}}{4}$$

**Q2.269 – a: 2 (1+√2) X²**

The octagon can be split into the following pattern: 4 triangles, 4 rectangles and one square.

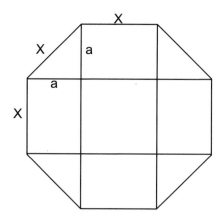

We know that the area of the square is $X^2$, but in order to calculate the areas of the triangles and rectangles we need to know a. From Pythagoras we have: $X^2 = a^2 + a^2 = 2a^2$ ;and therefore a= $X/\sqrt{2}$.

We can now calculate the total area as:
- Area of the central square = $X^2$
- + 4 x area of rectangle = $4(Xa) = 4\,X^2 / \sqrt{2}$
- + 4 x area of triangle = $4(a^2)/2 = 2a^2 = 2\,X^2 / 2 = X^2$

i.e. $X^2 + 4X^2/\sqrt{2} + X^2 = 2X^2 + 4X^2/\sqrt{2} = 2X^2\,(1 + 2/\sqrt{2}) = 2X^2\,(1 + \sqrt{2})$

## Q2.270 – c: 1.5
If CVX is a rectangular triangle then CX must be the diameter of the circle.

Since AB and CD are parallel, we also know that DX/DA = CX/CB. This gives: $2/(6+2) = CX/12$ and therefore CX = 3.

Therefore the radius is 1.5.

## Q2.271 - b: (1 - π/4) R²
If the radius of the quarter circle is R then the length of the side opposite the right angle is 2R. The easiest way to find the answer to this problem is to imagine that we complete the square and circle as follows:

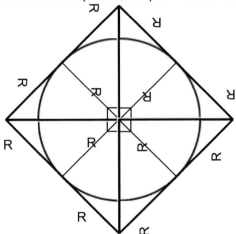

The area of the full square is $(2R)^2$.
The area of the full circle is $\pi R^2$.

Therefore the area of the square outside the circle is: $4R^2 - \pi R^2$.
To get the answer we must then take a quarter of that i.e.
$(4R^2 - \pi R^2)/4 = (1 - \pi/4) R^2$.


### Q2.272 – d: 48
If we call A the price of an apple and P the price of a pear, we can write the following equations:

$6A + 8P = 4.10$ (Equation 1)
$8A + 2P = 2.00$, which is also equivalent to $32A + 8P = 8.00$ (Equation 2)

Equation (2) – Equation (1) gives:
$(32-6) A = 8 - 4.1$ i.e. $A = 3.9 / 26 = 0.15$
Therefore $P = (2 - 0.15 \times 8)/2 = 0.80/2 = 0.40$

If we use a 4:1 ratio of apples to pears then each portion of 5 mixed fruit containing 4 apples + 1 pear will cost $4 \times 0.15 + 0.40 = £1.00$.

Hence, with £12, Felicity will be able to purchase 12 portions of 5 fruits, i.e. $4 \times 12 = 48$ apples.


### Q2.273 – c: 17.5 minutes
Using a 10W heater should decrease the melting time by 5 times. However the cube is $7.5 / 3 = 2.5$ times larger. Hence the total melting time will only be decreased by 2 times. The answer is therefore $35/2 = 17.5$ minutes.


### Q2.274 – c: 4
Each side of the chocolate has an area of $H \times B /2$, where H is the height and B is the base. If both H and B are halved, then the surface of each side becomes a quarter of what it was before and so the total area of the choc-olate becomes a quarter of the total area of the old chocolate.

**Q2.275 – c: 126.4 – 189.6**
The lowest amount of fuel will be for 25 – 3 = 22 people weighing 60kg each, requiring 2 litres of fuel per 100kg.

This gives: 22 x 60 / 100 x 2 = 26.4 litres

The highest amount of fuel with be for 25+3 = 28 people weighing 80 kg each, requiring 4 litres of fuel.

This gives: 28 x 80 / 100 x 4 = 89.6 litres

We need to add 100 to both numbers to find the range.


**Q2.276 – d: Octogon**
Bearings are always measured from the north line in a clockwise direction. If the first bearing is 135° and the third bearing is 225° then the exterior angle between each move is (225 – 135) / 2 = 45°. Since the sum of a polygon's external angles is always 360° and this polygon is regular (meaning that each exterior angle is 45°), then the number of sides is equal to: 360 / 45 = 8. Hence it is an octagon.

**Q2.277 – a:** $8\sqrt{\dfrac{2}{8-\pi}}$

If we call X the side of the square then the square's area is $X^2$.
The half circle cut out will have radius X/2 and therefore its area is: $\frac{1}{2}.\pi.(X/2)^2$.

Hence we can write: $X^2 - \frac{1}{2}.\pi.(X/2)^2 = 16$.

This can also be written as: $X^2\left(1 - \dfrac{\pi}{8}\right) = 16$

Or $X = 4\sqrt{\dfrac{1}{1-\dfrac{\pi}{8}}} = 4\sqrt{\dfrac{8}{8-\pi}} = 8\sqrt{\dfrac{2}{8-\pi}}$


**Q2.278 – b: L = X/600 – 3**
Converting all prices in Pounds:
2160 / 1.2 = £1800
£720 / 1.2 = £600

Thus we can write: X = 1800 + 600L
Thus (X-1800)/600 = L
Hence L = X/600 − 3

## Q2.279 – c: $6x - 1$

We are given the following: $\sqrt{3 - 2x} = \sqrt{2x} + 1$

Squaring both sides, we obtain: $3 - 2x = 2x + 2\sqrt{2x} + 1$

This is equivalent to: $2 - 4x = 2\sqrt{2x}$

Dividing by 2, we obtain: $1 - 2x = \sqrt{2x}$

Squaring both sides gives: $1 - 4x + 4x^2 = 2x$

Hence $4x^2 = 6x - 1$

## Q2.280 – d: 69%

The volume of a cylinder is calculated as: $\pi.R^2.h$, therefore multiplying R by 1.3 will multiply the volume by $1.3^2$ = 1.69, representing an increase of 69%

## Q2.281 – b: $42\sqrt{3}$

We can rewrite $\sqrt{27} \times \sqrt{144} + \sqrt{108}$ as follows:

$= \sqrt{3 \times 9} \times 12 + \sqrt{36 \times 3}$

Taking squares out of the square roots gives:
$3\sqrt{3} \times 12 + 6\sqrt{3} = (3 \times 12 + 6)\sqrt{3} = 42\sqrt{3}$

## Q2.282 – d: 200

The two relationships can be expressed as follows:
- A x B / 100 = 100 i.e. A x B = 10000
- 0.5 x 0.5 A = B i.e. 0.25 x A = B

Substituting B = 0.25 x A into the first equation gives:
0.25 x A x A = 10000 i.e. $A^2$ = 40000; hence A = 200.

**Q2.283 – c: RWT / (R+W)**

Let's call D the distance between his home and his workplace and J the amount of time he is running to get to work (and hence the amount of time he is walking back from work will be T-J). We can write:

D = R.J for the way to work
and
D = W (T-J) for the way back from work.

This gives RJ = W (T-J)
i.e. RJ = WT – JW
i.e. RJ + JW = WT
i.e. J (R + W) = WT
Hence J = WT / (R+W)

We know that D = RJ. Hence D = RWT / (R+W)


**Q2.284 – c: 3**

The indices' current values are:
- Index A: 3500 x 2 = 7000
- Index B: 40000 x 0.2 = 8000

The indices will increase as follows:

|   | Current | Year 1 | Year 2 | Year 3 |
|---|---------|--------|--------|--------|
| A | 7000 | x 1.10 = 7700 | x 1.10 = 8470 | x 1.10 = 9317 |
| B | 8000 | x 1.05 = 8400 | x 1.05 = 8820 | x 1.05 = 9261 |

Note: The easiest way to calculate a 5% is to calculate 10 % and halve it. Hence at Year 3, Index A exceeds Index B


**Q2.285 – e: 5**

$\sqrt{17 + \sqrt{264}} = \sqrt{a} + \sqrt{b}$

If we square on both sides, we obtain: $17 + \sqrt{264} = (\sqrt{a} + \sqrt{b})^2$
i.e. $17 + \sqrt{264} = a + 2\sqrt{ab} + b$
i.e. $17 + 2\sqrt{66} = (a + b) + 2\sqrt{ab}$
Hence we can take $(a + b) = 17$ and $ab = 66$.

There are only four possible pairs of integers whose product can be 66: 1 x 66, 2 x 33, 3 x 22 and 6 x 11. The only pair which satisfies the relationship $(a + b) = 17$ is $a = 11$ and $b = 6$. Hence $a - b = 5$

**Q2.286 – d: 1960**
The easiest and fastest way to the answer is to use the relationship: $(a - b) \times (a + b) = a^2 - b^2$. This gives:

$(15^2 - 5^2) + (27^2 - 23^2) + (14^2 - 6^2) + (57^2 - 43^2)$
$= (15-5) \times (15+5) + (27-23) \times (27+23) + (14-6) \times (14+6) + (57-43) \times (57+43)$
$= (10 \times 20) + (4 \times 50) + (8 \times 20) + (14 \times 100)$
$= 200 + 200 + 160 + 1400$
$= 1960$

**Q2.287 – f: No possible value**
The relationship $17 - x^2 > 8$ gives $17 - 8 > x^2$ i.e. $x^2 < 9$.
Therefore $-3 < x < 3$

The relationship $3x + 2 \geq 11$ gives $3x \geq 9$ i.e. $x \geq 3$. Since we cannot have simultaneously $x < 3$ and $x \geq 3$, then no value is possible.

# Section 3

# Writing Task

## 34 Essays

# 3A Writing Task Introduction & Advice

## Format and importance of Section 3 of the BMAT

Section 3 of the BMAT is a writing task lasting 30 minutes. In that time, candidates must select one topic amongst four proposed topics and must then write an essay that fits within the space allowed on the answer sheet, which consists of approximately 30 lines on an A4 sheet.

As a doctor or a vet, you will be faced with many conflicting pieces of information, and it is important that you can write a well-reasoned and coherent piece of work. The writing task allows examiners to judge the candidates' ability to reason, argue and counterargue.

Unlike other sections of the BMAT, the essay that you write as part of Section 3 will be communicated to the medical schools to which you have applied, and it may therefore be used as part of the interview process. For example, it is not uncommon for candidates to be asked at interview to critique their own essay and to explain how, with hindsight, they would organise their thoughts differently.

## How your essay will be marked

In 2010, the BMAT marking scheme moved from a 15-point scale to a 5-point scale. Essays are marked by two examiners, each of whom gives a score between 1 and 5 for the quality of the content.

Scores are based on an overall impression of your essay, which means that minor errors will not penalise your essay. In addition, your essay is also marked for use of English on a scale of A, C and E. The use of the English scale is primarily designed to help admission advisors understand whether an essay is deficient because of problems with the English itself or whether it was poorly argued.

The marks given by the two examiners are compared. If the two marks for quality of content and use of English are the same, or occupy adjacent positions on the scale, the average of the two marks will be reported. So, for example, if a candidate is marked 3 by Examiner X and 4 by Examiner Y, his/her mark will be 3.5. Similarly, if a student obtains mark A from Examiner X for his/her English and mark C from Examiner Y, he/she will be allocated a final mark of B.

If there is a larger discrepancy in the marks, the essays are marked for a third time for standardisation, and the final mark awarded is checked by the Senior Assessment Manager.

**Scoring scale – Quality of Content**

0: Trivial, irrelevant or absent response.

1: Answer that has some relevance to the question, but which does not address the question in the way demanded. The essay lacks logic, has little focus or has serious errors that render it confusing or incoherent.

2: Essay fulfils most of the requirements of the question, but may misinterpret an important aspect of the question. The points are set out in a relatively logical manner but the candidate has misinterpreted some aspects of the question, has failed to consider counterarguments or, when present, those counterarguments are weak.

3: The essay addresses all aspects of the question, presenting both a reasonable argument and counterargument. The argument is rational, but lacks sophistication and scope. The candidate may have missed parts of the argument.

4: A good essay addressing all aspects of the question with clear and balanced arguments and counterarguments. Few weaknesses are present.

5: An excellent essay with virtually no weaknesses. All aspects of the question are addressed. The writing is clear and compelling with effective structure and logic. The arguments are sophisticated and presented with a breadth of knowledge.

**Scoring scale – Quality of English**

A. Good use of English, with fluency, wide range of vocabulary, sound sentence structure, grammar, spelling and punctuation. Very few errors.

C. Reasonable use of English, with reasonable fluency, simple sentence structures, range of vocabulary, acceptable grammar with some errors.

E. Weak use of English, hesitant, with a structure that is difficult to follow. Flawed sentence structure, limited vocabulary range and frequent errors.

X. Anything deemed below Level E.

Don't worry too much about crossing out part(s) of your essay or inserting new information. The essay will be marked only on the resulting quality of English (so crossed out text will be ignored).

Nevertheless, we would recommend that you plan your essay sufficiently in advance in order to avoid crossing any text out or adding any text in retrospect. Although your English score may not suffer, too many deletions or additions could make the text hard to read; this would, in turn, make it difficult for examiners to fully grasp the arguments that you are developing and may therefore impact, consciously or subconsciously, on your Quality of Content score.

# What the examiners are looking for

### 1) A full answer

All essay topics will consist of several parts. For example, you may be given a statement or quote and be asked to explain the statement, identify a counterargument and then debate.

The starting point in the marking scheme is whether the candidate has answered all parts of the question. A candidate who has missed one part out will never score more than 2, regardless of the quality of his/her writing on the areas that were dealt with.

Read the topic carefully and ensure that everything is dealt with.

## 2) A logical presentation

Answering what could amount to four sub-questions in a few hundred words is challenging. A lack of planning could lead to a dishevelled answer, which is hard to read and understand. Good planning will, however, result in a clear answer in which the key points can be found easily by the reader.

Do not rush to put pen to paper. Spend some time planning your work. Make sure also that the structure of your answer is apparent. This can be achieved through the use of paragraphs. It is also possible to use bullet points or numbered lists to set out important information.

## 3) Pertinent points

You will be assessed on your ability to communicate your ideas concisely. Get to the point, argue each point with examples that are directly relevant, and do not digress. A paragraph of 125–150 words represents only 4 or 5 sentences. If you over-elaborate, you will use space that should be used for other parts of the question; that will have serious consequences for your score.

In addition, you need to be able to argue from different viewpoints, comparing and evaluating different perspectives, before coming to a conclusion. Do not just give your own views! The essay should also have specific examples and evidence to provide support for those viewpoints.

## 4) A good writing style

It is important that the essay reads well and offers sophistication in vocabulary and sentence structure. Features that contribute to giving a bad impression include:

- Arguments being presented in a partisan manner ("I personally think that…").

- Repetition of words (e.g. "Also").
- Poor punctuation and inappropriate use of apostrophes.

- Faulty agreements (e.g. "The media was biased").

- Fragmented sentences ("Most people would consider such argument inappropriate. Given that it is not borne out in practice."). Make sure that each sentence is complete.

- Run-on sentences ("Homecare has been expanding tremendously over the past decade partly due to technological advances that enable treatments to be a part of the home setting, which at one time could only be performed within the hospital environment."). Split into shorter sentences whenever you can.

- Overuse of the passive tense ("It is through this legislative action that the proposed benefits of a smoking ban may be implemented."). The passive tense is fine when used in small doses. Try to construct active sentences whenever you can.

- Faulty parallelism ("<u>Eating</u> too much, <u>snacking</u> between meals and too little <u>exercise</u> can lead to obesity."). Be consistent. If you can, use verbs or nouns throughout a list, but not both.

- Use of vague pronouns ("In this report, <u>they</u> suggest that nothing can be done"). Use "the authors" or name the authors.

- Inappropriate links ("When not going to school, my hobbies involve cycling"). This implies the hobbies go to school!

- Misplaced words ("I could see my mother coming through the window"). That must have hurt!

- Wordiness, i.e. phrases that considerably elongate a sentence without adding much value ("It is important to realise that", "It is evident that this term is associated with much ambiguity. Many concepts and ideas come to mind upon first hearing this phrase; however, a true grasp of its meaning is quite difficult to establish."). Try to convey your ideas in fewer words and scrap any waffle.

- Incorrect comparisons ("The level of anger that the smoking ban generates is higher in the north compared to the south"). Use "than" instead of "compared to".

Double constructions ("The reason for the failure was <u>due to the fact that</u> money was short in supply", or "The new system is unpopular both with doctors as well as nurses"). A reason can't be "due to". This example could be worded as "The failure was due to a lack of money". You can't have the word "both" with "as well as"; this should be "both with doctors and nurses" or "with doctors as well as nurses".

# How to prepare for the Section 3 written task

### Building a general awareness
Some of the essays deal with general society issues such as:

- Whether it is right that rich people should be able to gain better treatment than poorer people.
- Whether people with self-inflicted injuries should be entitled to NHS treatment.
- Whether it is right that pet owners can take the decision to have their pet euthanised.

Other topics deal with the analysis of a concept. For example:

- The meaning and usefulness of ambition.
- The purpose of science.
- The meaning of honesty and integrity.

You should therefore place yourself in situations where you can learn to form opinions and share ideas. This could be, for example, by:

- Reading newspaper articles on topical issues or ethical dilemmas.
- Reading accessible medical journals.
- Watching television programmes and discussing with family.
- Debating on internet forums.

This will help you build a mental database of ideas and examples upon which you can draw to write your essay.

### Learning to argue and structure
Before you can write an essay at full speed, try to write short essays without the pressure of time. Pick a topic and map out your arguments for the essay using bullet points and brief notes. Once you have developed a skeleton answer, take your time to develop each paragraph properly and revisit it

until you are perfectly happy. Read each passage several times to see if you can reword it more succinctly and/or more meaningfully.

**Practising under timed conditions**
Work through mock essay titles under timed conditions. See how many words you can write under timed conditions and how fast you can think of ideas. This will make you much better prepared than the majority of your competitors. Try your hand at different styles of topics to see which suit you best. That will save you much grief on the day of the exam.

# How to write a BMAT essay

Every candidate will have their own method to approach the exercise: with, at one end of the spectrum, those who will start writing their essay straight away and, at the other end, those who will do so much thinking that they will have barely any time left to write their essay.

Having analysed the experience of many candidates, the least stressful approach and the one we would recommend is as follows:

| | | |
|---|---|---|
| 1. | **Choose the question** | **2 minutes** |
| 2. | **Brainstorm ideas** | **3 – 5 minutes** |
| 3. | **Draft an outline** | **5 – 8 minutes** |
| 4. | **Write the essay** | **15 – 20 minutes** |

The suggested times are only approximate. If you find that you move rapidly through the brainstorming steps, then you will have more time to write the essay. Once your essay has been written on the answer sheet, there is no going back, so make sure that you plan accordingly.

## 1. Choose the question

When you turn the page and see the list of four questions, your heart might sink. Don't panic; take a deep breath and examine the topics in detail. When making your choice, the main questions you should ask are:

- Do you find the topic interesting? There is no point in choosing a topic that is not something you would enjoy writing about because this will translate into a wooden essay.

- Do some ideas come to mind straight away? If nothing comes to mind at all, or if you only get vague ideas when you read the topic, you are likely to spend the bulk of your 30-minute time allocation thinking about the topic instead of writing the essay. You may also never end up with a complete set of ideas.

- Are you confident that you can address all the components of the question? This is an important criterion if you want to score more than 2 out of 5.

Most candidates choose a practical topic rather than one of the esoteric essay titles, but you don't have to follow the trend. Conversely, don't feel that you have to choose one of the more philosophical titles simply because you want to be different. Go with a topic with which you feel comfortable.

Because the exam is for both medicine and veterinary science entry, the topics are chosen to span a range of interests. It is perfectly acceptable for a medical school applicant to choose a topic relating to veterinary science (e.g. on pet euthanasia) and vice versa. The exam is testing your ability to balance and express arguments and, if the topic seems particularly attractive, don't hesitate. You may then be asked to justify your choice at the interview later on; but provided you can argue your case successfully, this will not be a problem. It is better to score well on a seemingly unrelated topic than poorly on a directly relevant topic.

Finally, remember that you need to address all parts of the question. Underline the question parts to make sure that you answer them all as you brainstorm them.

2. **Brainstorm ideas**

Jot down key phrases and words that relate to the essay title. Make a list of arguments for and against, and identify ideas or examples that you can use to bring both together before coming to a conclusion.

On the day of the exam, you can use the actual Section 3 question paper as a rough work area. Do not use the lined paper provided for your rough work and drafts, as your essay is limited to one side of the answer sheet. Therefore, although any rough work present on that page will not be taken into account, it will considerably reduce the space that you can use to write the final essay.

You might find at this stage that you don't have as many arguments as you would wish. Don't be afraid to start again from scratch from step 1 and choose a different essay title.

3. **Draft an outline**

Unless you have been allowed to use a word processor (which won't apply to most candidates) then you will need to write your essay by hand. That means that once you have committed it to paper, it is subsequently difficult to change anything other than a small selection of words. The drafting stage will help you put your ideas together and form a roadmap for the essay, making it easier to write the text linearly when you get to it.

List the different parts of the question and, under each heading, write an outline of your arguments and examples in bullet point fashion. At that stage, you are not trying to write the essay in a nice way; your aim should be to ensure that your arguments and counterarguments are complete and that the progression is logical.

Address each point in the order set out in the question. Not only is it likely to be the most logical structure but it will also make it easier for the examiners to identify that you have addressed all the points.

At that stage you should also calculate a rough allocation of words for each section. Those using a word processor will be allowed 550 words. The others (i.e. most candidates) are only allowed 30 lines of text which, at a rate of 10/12 words per line, means that they will only be able to fit 300–360 words within the space allowed.

## 4. Write the essay

Once you have been through a successful planning phase, writing the essay should be a lot easier. In writing your essay, you should pay particular attention to the following:

- **Plan the space**

  Before you write your essay in the answer box, make sure that you plan for space properly. It would be a shame to write a good introduction, which takes half the space allowed because your handwriting is too big, only to find out that you need to develop four ideas and conclude within the remaining half. Give yourself some mental boundaries (e.g. "I have to write the introduction in 4 lines maximum. Then paragraph 1 should take 10 lines, paragraph 2 should take 8 lines, etc.").

- **Keep it concise**

  Most candidates tend to write essays of between 200 and 350 words. Though you have to be careful to make it all fit within the box, do not feel obliged to fill the space for the sake of it. A concise well-argued essay will score more highly than a waffly essay.

- **Use paragraphs**

  The examiners will often sit and mark hundreds of essays a day. Make their job easier by using neat handwriting so that your arguments can be easily understood. You can also make their job easier by having clearly defined paragraphs. If you are not pushed for space, you could leave a blank line between paragraphs. However, if space is a problem, start a new paragraph on the next line, but indent the first line.

- **Don't over-explain**

  When you want to illustrate a point, you only need to mention one example. Marks won't be awarded to a point if it has already been given credit before. As such, using multiple examples to address one issue will not lead to a better mark; it will only leave you with less space to discuss other valid points.

- **Make sure you have strong introductions and conclusions**

  Your essay must stand out from the crowd.

# Useful words to help structure your essay

**Giving examples**
- For example
- For instance
- To illustrate
- Specifically
- E.g. (but do not overuse)

**Supporting argument**
- Furthermore
- In addition
- Similarly
- Just as
- Also
- Moreover

**Indicating consequence**
- Consequently
- As a result
- Thus
- Hence

**Stress importance**
- Clearly
- In fact
- Most importantly
- Surely
- Truly

**Weakening arguments**
- However
- Although
- Whilst
- Rather
- Instead
- Yet
- On the other hand
- Conversely
- On the contrary

**Deciding against**
- One cannot deny that
- It could be argued that
- Granted
- Admittedly

**Concluding remarks**
- In summary
- In conclusion
- Ultimately
- In closing

# Guide to a perfect 5A BMAT essay structure
# Advice from an examiner

Here is an account from a BMAT examiner on how they would tackle a perfect 5A essay for the following essay title:

**The best way that local councils can stop landfill sites being filled up by consumer-generated waste is to impose strict limits on the amount of rubbish they will accept from each household.**

**Explain the reasoning behind the statement. Argue to the contrary that councils should impose rubbish collection limits. To what extent do you agree that there should be limits set?**

### Segment 1 – Introduce with a general statement
"I would always introduce the essay with a restatement of the general situation. This gives a smooth start to the debate and sets candidates apart from weaker test takers who jump straight into either agreeing or disagreeing with the claim."

*Landfill sites are increasingly castigated for their environmental impact and the stain they make on landscapes; consequently, waste management and disposal is an issue that has grown in importance in recent years. The debate usually opposes those who believe that waste disposal should be better managed at landfill sites and those who assert that councils should aim to reduce the amount of waste produced in the first place (for example by imposing limits) and encourage recycling.*

### Segment 2 – Set out an argument or counterargument to the claim
"Candidates should use the next few paragraphs to either agree or disagree with the premises of the claim, giving appropriate examples to illustrate their points."

*Limiting the amount of waste that is collected from households may cause issues which are difficult to avoid or counter, such as fly-tipping, i.e. the illegal dumping of waste either in someone else's garden, on the street or in woodlands. As well as creating bigger eyesores than landfills, it also creates a feeling of dirtiness and, possibly, insecurity; it also increases council tax as councils need to pay contractors to dispose of the rubbish thrown in*

573

*public places. Such policy could therefore prove very counterproductive. Limiting the amount of waste collected from each household could also prove logistically difficult to implement. Indeed, it would favour households with low occupancy and cause issues for large families.*

## Segment 3 – Set out the counterargument
"Candidates should set out clearly the opposite view, again using a few examples."

*On the other hand, it is worth considering that most households are composed of people who would behave in the way that the council expects they might. Limiting the level of rubbish collections would likely encourage many households to cut down on waste: for example, by consuming less or choosing goods with less packaging or more ecofriendly wrappers. This may also encourage households to reuse, donate or resell items that are no longer necessary and which they would otherwise have thrown away. Such policy, if coupled with enhanced recycling facilities, could also encourage people to recycle goods, thus limiting the amount of rubbish that makes its way to landfill sites.*

## Segment 4 – Conclusion
"Having a proper conclusion is essential as it brings the arguments together and ensures a clean end to the essay. Candidates should ensure that they have addressed all parts of the question; indeed, some questions ask for a personal opinion instead of a simple debate. When giving an opinion, candidates should avoid sitting on the fence and should make an effort to demonstrate that they are able to take a stance even when there are ambiguities or unknowns in the information presented. This is, after all, what they will be asked to do as doctors. I also particularly value candidates who try to broaden the debate by bringing other related issues into the mix."

*In view of the arguments, I agree with the policy to introduce limits on the amount of waste collected from households, which could prove effective in reducing the amount of waste being sent to landfill sites. However, this can only be introduced if it is backed up by other policies, which encourage more recycling, and a tough stance being taken in respect of fly-tipping. Careful consideration should be given on how such policy should be introduced so that the allowance granted to each household reflects the needs of that household and does not disadvantage larger families.*

# Pearls of wisdom from BMAT examiners

During the course of writing this book, we have talked to many official BMAT examiners who have kindly shared their thoughts with us. You will undoubtedly find the following statements of value during your preparation for the written task:

- "The markers for Section 3 do not actually have a set mark scheme for the essay titles. We normally sit down and write the essays ourselves and thus have a good idea of the time and space constraints that the candidates face. As a result, we are extremely flexible when it comes to awarding marks. Any reasonable attempt at a question would get a decent mark. A very good attempt that uses an approach and examples which are different to the other candidates' would get the best mark."

- "Since 2010, candidates have been given four essay choices instead of just three. There is no difference in the marking; choosing a difficult topic does not mean that you will be marked more leniently for trying. Each essay is marked on its own merit; so choose a topic with which you are comfortable."

- "If you miss out a part of the question, no matter how good the rest of the essay is, it will score a maximum of 2 points."

- "Many candidates forget the first part of the question, which is often to define the argument. Instead they jump straight into the arguments for and against, leading to an automatic score of 2. Be systematic and, as much as you can, address the points in the order requested by the question."

- "If a student addresses all the points asked in the question, they can't get fewer than 3 marks for quality, even if their arguments are basic."

- "The A4 lined sheet provided for the essay is actually smaller than a standard A4 sheet. The top is taken up by a header, which is for the candidate's details and exam centre details. Don't worry; the examiners don't get to see the headers (they are guillotined off). However, it is important to know that this means that there is less space to write your essay than you may realise."

575

- "I have seen 500 words of waffle which got a score of 2 and I have seen 200 words of well-reasoned arguments which scored the maximum mark. The majority of the essays that I mark normally fill the page."

- "If you are doing the essay on computer in your exam centre because you have got permission to do so, then you are at a slight advantage due to the fact that you can type a maximum of 550 words. If you hand-write this, you would struggle to fit this into the 1 A4 page provided. But don't be cheeky and write 600 words. Trust me; the examiners will count every single word to ensure that it meets the exam criteria. I caught 2 candidates out this year alone!"

- "All the information that you write will be checked if it is outside the knowledge of the examiners. Unlike many other exam boards, examiners are paid by the hour, and so have the luxury of spending a long time over an essay."

- "Don't make up information as any facts quoted by candidates will be verified. If an examiner feels that you have made up a piece of information, senior examiners will be involved and you might be penalised heavily. Common mistakes include made up statistics, made up quotes or completely incorrect assumptions presented as facts. I have seen many quotes from supposed genuine societies or charities which turned out to be fake."

- "Don't rely overly on stock phrases or clichés. Phrases such as "It's horses for courses" or "It's a matter of the glass being half empty or half full" can give a sloppy feel to the essay. If you do insist on using such phrases, make sure you use them in the correct context and with the correct wording. 'Wheel reinvention' does not read quite the same as 'Reinventing the wheel'."

- "Any comments which may raise issues of fitness to practise as a doctor will be raised with the senior assessment manager."

- "Don't over-worry about the spelling and grammar. As long as the mistakes are sparse, the examiners will be lenient if the content of the essay more than makes up for it."

- "Religious arguments have to be appropriate to the context. It is appropriate to relate the views that some religious groups may hold in the context of a well-balanced argument. It is not appropriate to use the essay as a platform to promote one's views."

- "Inappropriate use and lack of general knowledge is a major problem (e.g. vets don't take the Hippocratic Oath!)"

- "On the answer sheet, there is a space for initials. This is the students' initials (not school initials; you'd be surprised how many people make that mistake!)"

- "The whole written answer must fit within the boxed area. Some students write PTO (Please Turn Over) and continue in the other side; anything appearing outside the answer box will not be marked at all."

- "Some candidates use bullet points or numbered points to address their issues. In some cases, this can be highly effective to present a point of view concisely."

- "Don't feel obliged to define every scientific term you use. Use your judgement. For example, writing 'A placebo (i.e. a harmless pill, medicine, or procedure prescribed more for the psychological benefit than its physiological effect)' may be useful but it will waste a lot words and space for no particular benefit."

- "I often have to mark the same essay title day after day. I soon get a feel for the quality of the arguments. To get the top mark, your essay must stand out. You can achieve that through a strong introduction and by setting out your points in different paragraphs. Some of my colleagues are positively influenced by the use of a quote as an attention-grabber, though I personally dislike them. Most quotes are also inaccurate, which does not help…"

- "Stick to balancing the arguments and try not to make your own views too obvious (they do not matter to an examiner). For example, a sentence such as 'the author's views are a real breath of fresh air in such a negative world' would be inappropriate."

# 3B Writing Task
## 16 Critiqued Essays

In this section we present a range of essay topics, which we illustrate with different types of answers which candidates may have given, representing a total of 16 critiqued essays. Each of the example essays shown is marked so that you can get an idea of the level required to achieve different scores.

## Essay 1

**People who smoke should not be treated by a publicly funded health service.**

Explain the reasoning behind this statement. Suggest arguments against this statement. To what extent, if any, does the statement justify a change in public attitude to smoking?

### Essay 1 – Example 1: Score 4A

The essence of this statement is that those who make lifestyle choices that have a detrimental effect on their health, and indeed spend a significant amount of money in doing so, should not be entitled to healthcare which is ultimately financed by the general public.

Smokers, however, would argue that they contribute financially to the health service to the same extent as non-smokers; it therefore seems reasonable that they should be able to use it for their needs, whatever these might be. Smokers would consider it unfair for them to have to contribute to a service they cannot use.

Fundamentally, the argument for this statement is equally applicable to other lifestyle choices, such as drinking alcohol, the effects of which are just as costly to public health and yet less frowned upon. For example, many people consciously decide not to take part in regular exercise or eat healthily, with a similarly poor effect on health. It is hard to draw the line and make a clear distinction between cases when care should be provided and when it should not.

Another perspective to consider is whether smoking is actually a choice that many smokers make, and whether they actually have any control over it. One might argue that some people took up smoking through peer pressure, or simply because they have not been educated well enough by the state about its dangers. Consequently, if the state is to share some of the blame, it should also share some of the costs.

The public attitude to smoking is an ever-changing opinion, constantly evolving with better education and scientific research. Still, for the non-smoking taxpayer, it seems unfair that their money should be spent on those who knowingly damage their health, especially when it could be perhaps spent more fairly on others.

## Examiner's comment:

Although this essay is short (299 words), the candidate writes clearly and the arguments are sound.

The initial paragraph sets out not only the proposition but also explains why smokers should not be treated by a publicly funded health service.

The second and third paragraphs explore counterarguments, and the fourth one explores an interesting take on this side of the argument.

The conclusion summarises the author's position. However, the candidate did not address the issue of changes in public perception with enough quality to warrant full marks. Too much space is allocated to counterarguments and not enough to public attitude towards smoking.

## <u>Essay 1 – Example 2: Score 5A</u>

In any nation with a publicly funded health service, dissent on the topic of smokers' entitlement is common. Proponents of refusing healthcare to smokers argue that these people are taking unnecessary medical risks, the consequences of which fall on the general public in the form of increased costs. While it initially seems a reasonably popular idea, this suggestion has fundamental flaws that make it an unrealistic policy.

The first problem with this argument is that not all health issues can be attributed to smoking. A blanket ban on receiving publicly funded healthcare would be discriminatory in situations where smoking did not contribute to the medical issue and in cases where current non-smokers develop problems related to having smoked earlier in life. Any attempt to identify precisely which issues are caused or exacerbated by smoking – in the interest of prohibiting their treatment with public funds – would become hopelessly snarled in the complexities of the effects of smoking on different individuals.

In addition, it would not be fair to limit the level of healthcare available to smokers without similarly penalising those who engage in other risky behaviours. Drinking alcohol, driving quickly, eating unhealthy foods, and many other common activities could all be considered "unnecessary medical risks". Excluding people from the public health service for taking part in these would remove the majority of the very population that is funding the system in the first place.

The prominence of this controversy shows that emotions run high amongst the general public, with a disproportionate bias due to publicity and politicisation. This attitude does not extend to, say, alcohol consumption, because that is viewed as more of a social norm. Other "risk factors" face even less prejudice; for example, few people would seriously consider denying *healthcare to athletes, though they are much more likely to suffer serious physical injuries than the general public.*

*When considering issues of healthcare policy, it is therefore important to consider smoking realistically in relation to other risk factors. A fair system cannot exclude people on the basis of their behaviour without understanding both the exact nature and the scope of the risk, without extending the ban to similar risks and without establishing clear boundaries.*

## Examiner's comment:

This 364-word essay scores highly both because of its structure and the strengths of its arguments.

The first paragraph sets out the argument for the proposition. The second and third paragraphs show a very good grasp of the fundamentals of the arguments against this issue.

More importantly, the candidate has addressed the public perception changes in the fourth paragraph and has come to a convincing synthesis of opinions in the conclusion.

There are obviously many ways in which the essay could be improved. Though the author touched on the issue of people who were previously smokers and had stopped, more could have been made about the situation with regard to passive smoking. For example, an individual who goes to smoky bars every day may suffer more ill-health than someone who smokes occasionally.

However, bearing in mind that space and time are limited, the aim is not to write a book providing the complete picture. What matters is that the arguments answer the questions posed in a well-balanced and well-developed manner, which the essay does successfully.

# Essay 2

**The needs of society outweigh the needs of an individual.**

Write a unified essay in which you address the following:

Briefly outline what you think the above statement means. Explain an argument in support of and in opposition to this statement. Discuss, giving examples, what factors influence the rights of the individual over that of the group?

## Essay 2 – Example 1: Score 2A

This statement suggests that some individuals might have to suffer "for the greater good". This general concept is known as utilitarianism, an ethical doctrine which states that, when considering different courses of action, that which creates the greatest "utility" is the best option. Utility, a measure of the pleasure or "good" resulting from an action, depends on several factors such as the duration and intensity of the pleasure and, most importantly, the number of people it affects. While at first glance it may appear to be an egalitarian concept, utilitarianism is often criticised for its sometimes ruthless applications, which disregard the effects on, and especially the rights of, the individual. In essence, if the net effect of an action outweighs the bad, then the action is considered morally justified.

It has been suggested that utilitarianism is a deep-rooted concept in humans, thought to extend back to our primitive ancestors, who may have had to make group decisions in order to survive. For example, helping a wounded individual would have clearly been of benefit to that individual; however, it may have made the group more vulnerable, for example, to predation. Thus, it is likely that the benefit to the group would have outweighed that of the individual and that the individual may have been left to die.

*The concept can be extended to bioethics: for example to the distribution of drugs and other medical resources such as carers or medication. While such a utilitarian approach might lead to overall greater happiness or "produc-tivity", couldn't this lead to the dismissal of the rights of elderly or disabled patients, whose future happiness is considered by utilitarians as less im-portant or worthy than that of others? For these reasons, the principles of utilitarianism, especially in the context of medical ethics, continue to be the source of much controversy.*

## Examiner's comment

This student has a good command of English and clearly understands the principles of utilitarianism that the essay is testing. Utilitarianism, put simply, is the "greatest happiness" principle, i.e. an action leading to a net benefit. An example in medicine would be vaccination resulting in herd immunity despite the pain of the individual injections.

However, he has not answered the question. Despite being well written and having outlined the statement, the essay has a paucity of specific examples when describing support or opposition to the statement.

The essay also does not mention much on the role of autonomy (rights of individuals) over that of the group.

Remember that if the essay, no matter how well written, does not cover ALL parts of the question, it will not achieve a score above 2.

## Essay 2 – Example 2: Score 4.5A

*The statement begs the question "Is it ever right to let one person bear a cost for the good of the group?" From my personal perspective, the factors influencing this depend on the "cost" and the "benefit" involved. Is this "cost" taxation or suffering? Is saving the lives of others a benefit, or merely a more convenient outcome? Depending on the circumstances, can this be justified? There are two main viewpoints for this question.*

Utilitarianism takes the stance that what is best for the group as a whole should outweigh the cost to the individual. From Kant's perspective, this is extended to the duty of the individual to the society, which is an act in itself as opposed to the outcome of the utilitarian system. Soldiers must defend their nation for the good of the population as a whole.

On the other hand, human rights are individualistic rather than communitarian. Your right to life cannot be sacrificed for anyone else's, no matter how big the group may be; it is only through protesting individual rights that a peaceful democratic society can be established. The rights of the individual must always be prioritised over the benefits of the group, as is obvious from extreme examples, such as slavery and the sex trade.

Torture provides a particularly interesting example. An individual's right of freedom from torture still stands, according to the human rights approach, even if their information could save the lives of millions of other innocent people. Most people here would take the utilitarian stance, even though they may not necessarily agree with the theory. But what if the lines between "right" and "wrong" were more blurred? Would our opinions change if the group incurred a cost for the benefit of the care of a disabled individual? And what if that disability was self-inflicted? These are complex questions made more complex by the fact that most people's opinions in principle will vary widely to what they may feel if they were the individual who had to lose out for the greater good. Ask the guy who is being tortured!

## Examiner's comment

This 348-word essay begins with a brief rewording of the original statement in a rhetorical question. This highly effective use of style in an essay instantly catches the attention of the examiner. The candidate uses multiple examples both for supporting the statement in paragraphs two and three, whilst also flipping the argument against itself and subsequently arguing for individual rights (autonomy). Although the candidate does not address the final sub-question as well as they addressed the others, it is nonetheless an impressive essay.

# Essay 3

**"Mapping the human genome has been compared with putting a man on the moon" Michael Dexter**

What do you understand by the statement above? Explain why the study of genetics could be helpful in medicine. Discuss the extent to which reliance on genetics may be dangerous?

## Essay 3 – Example 1: Score 2A

This achievement made a last-minute appearance in the 20th century, perhaps as a culmination of decades of rapid scientific advances. In itself, it is not an astounding technological breakthrough, as it was built on the back of many important successes in the fields of genetic analysis, molecular biology and biochemistry, such as the elucidation of the structure of DNA and, indeed, the invention of genetic mapping. These building blocks could perhaps be considered more important because of what they have now facilitated. However, the mapping of the genome is a crucial milestone and is of some significance.

Similarly, as of yet, sequencing of the human genome has allowed no major advances or benefits in the same way as other discoveries and inventions. For example, the 20th century has given us antibiotics, the use of insulin, the contraceptive pill, antiretroviral drugs, numerous imaging techniques and much more, which between them have saved and vastly improved many lives.

The extensive knowledge of the human genome so far only has potential, albeit enormous. As well as being the end of an era of improvement, it is also the beginning of possibly the biggest leap in medicine and understanding of ourselves in our history. This remains to be seen as more information is added to the map: linking diseases to genes, risks of diseases and thus unveiling a revolution in gene therapy, genetic counselling and even perhaps human genetic engineering as time progresses. Crucially, as ethics change in the next century, the applications of such genetic knowledge may reach new limits in its application, such as aesthetic use and the pursuit of longevity (as Dr Aubrey de Grey is initiating now).

Overall, then, the sequencing of the human genome is a triumph of a century of science but, perhaps more so, a starting point for centuries of progress.

## Examiner's comment

This 304-word essay is written eloquently but, unfortunately, it does not fully address the questions asked.

The first two paragraphs try to play down the achievement (which is not directly relevant to the questions asked). In fact, the candidate did not address why mapping the human genome was such a breakthrough until halfway through the third paragraph; and, when he does, it is not done clearly.

The student has trouble writing a coherent argument. In addition, he did not address the last part of the question at all, leading to an automatic 2 despite a strong ending sentence.

The essay above is a good example of an essay that could score highly if the question were asked slightly differently, but which does not satisfy the criteria for a high score for this particular set of questions.

## Essay 3 – Example 2: Score 4.5A

The completion of the human genome project meant that scientists today have access to the sequences of all 25,000 genes that make up the human genome. The medical consequences are vast, encompassing detection, diagnosis and treatment of disease.

Many diseases are hereditary. The famous example of haemophilia in the British Royal Family illustrates the clear transmission of disease-causing alleles through the generations. The human genome project has the potential to enable screening for these alleles to identify the carriers of the recessive allele, enabling those affected to make an informed choice about whether to risk having children.

In addition, some diseases, such as Huntington's chorea, do not display symptoms until later in life. The human genome project has allowed scientists to determine the exact base sequence that causes Huntington's chorea. It has been shown that simply exceeding the normal range of CAG repeats at a particular locus subjects the sufferer to a sudden and rapid degeneration of motor function. Screening could help prepare a person for their genetic fate, just as well as it could relieve the worry of a person at risk of having inherited this disease.

The human genome project could lead to earlier diagnosis of disease through screening, and ultimately a higher chance of survival. Scientists studying diseases may be able to focus on one particular gene and fully understand the resultant disease-causing pathway. Comprehensive understanding of the origin of the disease will inevitably lead to better treatments. Gene therapy, a new treatment method involving correcting defective genes, has been revolutionised by the publishing of the human genome. Finally, treatments can be tailored to the individual and will consequently have a much greater success rate.

The dangers of the human genome project lie in overreliance on genetic information in finding cures. The human genome has been available for over a decade, and it has not yet led to a cure of cancer as many hoped it would. There is also a danger that diseases we badly understand may be dismissed as "something genetic". A good example of this is stomach ulcers, which most people thought to be linked to personality types and therefore genetics, and which we now understand to be largely connected to a bacterial strain. Although now easily cured by a course of antibiotics, many people in the past suffered for years due to scientific misunderstanding and complacency.

## Examiner's comment

This 395-word essay addresses all the separate parts of the questions in turn.

The first paragraph summarises why human genome mapping is such advancement. The second, third and fourth paragraphs address the potential and current uses of human genome for medicine, and the arguments are linked and logical.

The final paragraph provides room to address the dangers of genome mapping by overreliance. Genetic mapping has led to certain therapeutics to treat cancer although it is not expected that a pre-undergraduate student would know this.

The reason why the essay was marked 4.5 (i.e. 4 by one examiner and 5 by another one) is that there does not seem to be a proper conclusion.

The examiner who marked 4 felt that the paragraph on the dangers of relying on genetics did address the question but was incomplete. In particular, it ignored the obvious, i.e. the issue of "designer babies" (foetal selection based on genetics) and the slippery slope of having to define boundaries of what would be acceptable or not, which is a major issue of concern for the general public.

The difference in the marks by the two examiners illustrates well the subjectivity of the marking, but also the fact that it is important to have a complete argument. It is, of course, good to have arguments that are slightly different to what other candidates might come up with, but not at the expense of the obvious.

# Essay 4

**Medicine – Art or Science?**

Write a unified essay in which you address the following:

Briefly define "science" and "art". Discuss, giving examples, in what ways could medicine be considered an art form, and in which ways could it be considered a scientific discipline?

## Essay 4 – Example: Score 5A

An art can be defined as a creative medium through which a person expresses an "idea", which may be an emotion or political ideology or even simply beauty. Conventional art forms would include art, music or drama, for example. In contrast to this, a scientific discipline is a discipline in which experimental rigour is applied to test hypotheses, the results of which are expressed in a theoretical framework.

Medical research is very much a scientific discipline insofar as a true understanding of the body and how it works can only be achieved through experiment and observation. The treatment of pathology and synthesis of drugs, however, may allow for a degree of creativity: a medical scientist must be innovative in thinking about how to treat symptoms when applying their understanding of the body, and a chemist or chemical engineer may be creative when designing a synthesis pathway. Although this all lends itself to creativity, the purpose of it is not expressive so it is not a true art form.

As for the human body itself, many would perceive it as beautiful and for centuries it has been a subject for artists. Leonardo da Vinci even expressed the mathematical anatomy of the body as a work of art in his famous Vitruvian Man. This can be misleading, though, since, although the human body may be perceived as a beautiful work of art itself, it was not "designed" for this purpose. The human body evolved to be the way it is as a means of survival and we artificially confer any beauty thereafter perceived onto it.

A doctor may be passionate about what he or she does— maybe even as passionate as an artist would be about their work — but this is not sufficient for medicine itself to constitute an art form. Similarly a surgeon may require the same dexterity and skill as an artist and may even need to be creative in how they approach a procedure. There is no question that medicine has intent and in extreme examples, such as reconstructive surgery, the intent may even be to create something that is aesthetically attractive. This is the point at which the boundary between medicine as a scientific discipline and an art form becomes the least distinct, as the surgeon may need to be creative in his or her application of the science of the body to reconstruct a part of the anatomy that is both functional and tasteful. In truth, much art has little other purpose than to look nice, i.e. an expression of beauty.

Although there are parallels between art and medicine, such as the need for the doctor or artist to be skilled, creative or dexterous, they are not the same thing and medicine is, in all circumstances, primarily a scientific discipline or the application of one. If the human body is to be perceived as a work of art then perhaps medicine plays the role of the critic in dissecting every brushstroke and the restorer in putting it back in again.

**Examiner's comment**
This 505-word essay clearly shows logical progression from argument to argument. The two definition paragraphs demonstrate clear well-thought-out examples illustrating the points made, with beautiful inter-weaving arguments. The final concluding paragraph succinctly sums up the argument in a well-balanced manner.

# Essay 5

**"Learning is the discovery that something is possible" – Fritz Perls**

Write a unified essay in which you address the following:

What do you understand by the word "effective" in the context of education? Explain how it might be argued that being taught is more effective than learning through discovery.

## Essay 5 – Example: Score 3.5A

Finding out information on your own is less effective than it being instilled into you by a more experienced individual. Effectiveness in this situation can be very ambiguous. How can one truly measure the effectiveness of a learning method, especially when the human mind is so unique to the individual and therefore different methods will work for some people and not for others? When discussing the effectiveness of learning, by what means are we deeming something to be effective? Is a way of learning effective if it produces successful examination results? Or is it deemed effective when those who are being taught fully understand the concepts, ideas and practicality of the subject in such a way they can apply it to every situation? Is a learning method effective if it is quick? So in this way is the effectiveness classified? To produce a logical argument to this statement, we must agree on what effective is. My interpretation is the mixture of timing and commitment to memory, instilling the ability to reuse the information learnt.

With this in mind one can argue that the most time-efficient method of learning is through being taught. When a teacher explains the complex details, greater amounts of information can be absorbed in a shorter period of time. In science subjects, there is a heavy amount of lecturing and small group classes. In these situations a professional on the topic will teach the students. We are not expected to learn how the body works, or how electrons are situated within an atom, without any assistance. Why is this? Because these pieces of information have already been discovered by scientists who had to spend years upon years and wait for advances in technology to confirm their ideas and prove them as fact. In this way learning through being taught is more effective than discovery.

To discover things like scientific fact, once the fact has been proven, surely many methods of individual discovery can fall into the category of being taught. However, another concept that can be missed out when discussing these methods is what it is that we are learning. I have mentioned that factual, scientific knowledge can be taught at a faster rate than it can be discovered but what about life lessons? Senses of morality, right and wrong? It is true to some extent that these are attitudes that are passed on to us from our parents, i.e. we are taught them, and for certain this is a very effective method of learning. Can we argue that learning through discovery is more effective? Or is it simply more common? After all we are taught that a knife is sharp- we can learn this through discovery of the pain it causes when we cut ourselves but perhaps it is more effective to be taught this and know then to avoid sticking the knife into flesh.

With the definition of effective that I have stated I would have to agree that it is. Through the efficient use of time and resources, the best way to learn is by being taught. Of course this can still be open to interpretation and vary wildly for individuals; but as a general rule teaching is simply the best!

### Examiner's comment

This essay (536 words) has an interesting take on the question and addresses all parts of the question. The use of rhetorical questions was effective at the beginning; however, it soon becomes tiring. The points made are interesting but the style can be confusing and lets the essay down. This is reflected by the split marking, giving a 3.5 average.

# Essay 6

**Using modern medicine today, are we hindering the evolution of the human species?**

Write a unified essay in which you address the following:

What do you understand by the statement above? Can you suggest examples where natural selection still applies and examples where it does not? What factors affect whether natural selection applies to humans?

## Essay 6 – Example 1: Score 5A

All organisms have a unique phenotype determined, to a large extent, by their genotype. Some phenotypes will allow an organism to survive to reproductive age and pass their genetic material on to future generations. In this way, genes that contribute to the phenotypes of organisms that survive and reproduce will propagate themselves through the gene pool. Genes that, in any way, hinder their own propagation will tend not to be inherited. This is natural selection.

To say that natural selection no longer applies to a species is to say that either genetic material no longer influences the phenotype of the organism it finds itself in – and hence that phenotypical characteristics are not inherited genetically – or that the genotype that contributes to the phenotype is not significant in determining whether an organism will reproduce or not: or a combination of these two factors.

Modern science has given rise to a range of means whereby humans can cheat death. It is true that advances in medicine, such as the development of vaccines, antibiotics and surgery, have improved the chances of survival in many people who would otherwise die before reproducing and that this may equilibrate survival chances between individuals who, in the past, would have responded differently to survival pressures.

There are, however, still strong selection pressures against lethal genetic defects that cannot yet be treated. Furthermore, medical care is not evenly distributed throughout the world and, in many parts, natural selection probably has more control over deaths from infectious diseases than it would elsewhere.

A greater threat to conventional natural selection is not necessarily modern science directly influencing the body but human intelligence, culture and ideas using science to overcome it. A professional woman might choose her career over a family, and with oral contraceptive pills she would even be able to copulate without ever reproducing.

The evolution of human society is closely linked to the evolution of intelligence and culture, which has been extremely rapid when viewed in the context of evolutionary history. Cultural ideas are passed down the generations and can be modified over time: a new unit of inheritance that could potentially be acted on by selection pressures. Perhaps through these ideas that exist in the human mind, a new form of natural selection will have the last word on shaping the future of the human race.

### Examiner's comment

In this 389-word essay, the two definitional paragraphs succinctly argue that natural selection can be affected by two factors. The third paragraph describes how modern medicine is able to overcome natural selection, whilst the fourth paragraph briefly covers how natural selection might still play a part in certain diseases. The fifth paragraph earns this essay a 5A score due to its unique take on the question of how intelligence and human control of their reproductive cycle can overcome natural reproduction and thus natural selection.

The concluding paragraph is strong and, moreover, raises a new idea that the evolution of the human species is not only down to phenotypical features but exists as ideas as well.

## Essay 6 – Example 2: Score 4.5A

Humans have experienced remarkable change since their lowly caveman beginnings. Life expectancy has soared from somewhere in the twenties to over eighty in the western world, for a variety of reasons. Something as simple as a cut, which could previously have been fatal through infection, is now utterly trivial thanks to our understanding of the necessity for basic hygiene. With the leaping development of modern medicine, patients with previously devastating diseases and conditions can be restored to good health and, crucially, go on to have children. So is natural selection still at all relevant for *Homo sapiens*, or have we escaped the constraining clutch of Mother Nature?

Natural selection is the increase in frequency, over successive generations, of genes that convey an advantage to an organism in its environment. Natural selection only applies if it comes into effect before the organism becomes sexually active. If you are genetically predisposed to have breast cancer from around the age of sixty, this will not be subject to natural selection. This is because, although the genes involved are detrimental, they will only come into effect after the menopause, by which time you have already had children and successfully passed on your genes. It is only your own life that is in jeopardy, not those of your offspring.

For humans, however, medical developments make it seem as though natural selection no longer applies. People with conditions such as asthma can be equipped with an inhaler to prevent their suffocation; blood transfusions save the lives of those involved in serious accidents; and simply improving diet and home comforts can ensure the rapid recovery of children from influenza and chicken pox. Furthermore, people with fertility problems who would never be able to reproduce can have a baby in a test tube. It would therefore seem that natural selection no longer applies.

Yet there are still many cases where natural selection is very evident for humans. There are diseases for which modern medicine has yet to find a cure, such as cystic fibrosis, which hugely reduce the fertility of a sufferer, reduce life expectancy and demonstrate natural selection in action. The deleterious genes will reduce in frequency in the gene pool.

Despite this, is natural selection really relevant in today's society? If you had asthma in the Stone Age, then you would be more likely to be caught and eaten by a lion or bear or other sharp-toothed predator, and therefore not pass on your genes. But there are no lions in society today. Again, genetic conditions such as red-green colour blindness meant that you may have been poisoned to death by toxic berries but, nowadays, as long as you know the relative position of the circles at traffic lights, the worst that may happen is that you end up purchasing the wrong kind of milk.

Fundamentally, the habitat that we have created for ourselves in the majority of the western world, with air conditioning, cars and fridges, means that our environment is no longer dynamic. Unless you are unfortunate to be one of the few people with a terrible genetic disease, the chances are that you will experience no serious problems until you reach past your reproductive prime. There is nothing to adapt to.

## Examiner's comment

This 538-word essay beautifully summarises this complex essay title. The proposition argues that modern medicine today is weakening our species as humans, because those of us who are not fit (bad health) are still able to survive and breed due to modern medicine. In comparison, if we allowed natural selection to kill off the weaker amongst us, the human species as a whole would benefit because only the fittest would survive and be able to breed.

The candidate begins by defining the various phrases used and argues strongly that natural selection does not apply to humans in the modern age due to medicine. He does not present as many high-quality arguments for natural selection pressures in humans. However, he concludes with a humorous point, and with a neat summation of the proposition. Overall it is a good essay, which some examiners may see as very good and others as good, hence the average of 4.5.

## Essay 7

**"A little bit of pain is good for you" – Pamela Anderson**

Write a unified essay in which you address the following:

What do you understand of the statement above? Give examples that illustrate how pain can be useful and others that illustrate the opposite.

### Essay 7 – Example 1: Score 3.5A

The above statement implies that the negative sensation is outweighed by the positive effects. The idea that pain could be a beneficial feeling is a notion most people, whilst experiencing the sensation, would find difficult to agree with. But in the long term, evolutionarily, and in the immediate term, for one individual, it often makes perfect sense.

Pain is beneficial in that it teaches the sufferer to not repeat whatever action has caused them the pain, and therefore the damage. For example, if an animal eats a poison, the poison will most likely induce a stomach ache. The animal, should it survive, will then link the pain with the item it ate and so, in the future, will avoid it and therefore increase its chances of surviving to reproduce. Another way in which pain can be seen to "help" is in the prevention of further damage to tissues. If an animal feels pain because of an action, it will rapidly stop doing it. This minimises the damage caused. For example, if an animal steps on something sharp, it will lift its foot and stop standing on it, thus reducing the damage done.

However, there are some situations in which pain can be seen to do more harm than good. Pain disorders can cause an individual to suffer extensively for no reason. They are not able to learn anything as there is no apparent cause, and they cannot do anything to stop the pain and minimise damage that is not there. This is clearly not helpful to an individual and, instead, greatly reduces their quality of life. When pain is particularly intense, an individual is likely to end up unconscious or be rendered immobile by it.

Overall, there seem to be two main functions of pain. Firstly, the short-term function "tells" an animal something is wrong and allows them to take action to stop the damage. This allows the animal to survive the isolated incident. Secondly, in the long term, pain provides a learning experience that will help the animal avoid a damaging and potentially fatal or fitness-reducing event. Therefore it can clearly be seen how pain is selected for in evolution. I think that the statement is right in most cases; overall pain does benefit the individual. However, at its extreme level, pain is highly detrimental and acts only to harm. Therefore it is context that determines the accuracy of this statement.

### Examiner's comment

The essay is 400 words long and begins by covering the benefits of pain in the first paragraph. It is a strong start and sets the tone for the rest of the essay. It lets the examiner know exactly where the overall argument structure for the essay lies. Some candidates try to argue for a stance, argue against a stance and then come to a conclusion. This student has gone for a more direct approach. Both work well.

The second paragraph continues supporting that pain is good, but the arguments used are fairly conventional and would have been seen by the examiners hundreds of times before. Slightly different arguments may make the essay stand out more; perhaps something on the fact that preparing for the BMAT can be a painful process but that more painful would be the pain of regret after scoring badly. This may add some humour to the otherwise rather dull day of an examiner.

The third paragraph covers a negative aspect of pain using one example only. The student should make an attempt to argue from a different perspective. The concluding paragraph summarises the prior arguments with a strong concluding statement. Overall the essay is slightly above average. The lack of good examples weakens the essay to a 3.5A. More examples would have pushed this to a 4A.

## Essay 7 – Example 2: Score 4A

Mrs Anderson suggests that, although unpleasant to experience, pain is a useful tool to enable us to recognise when a particular activity is dangerous, to allow damaged body tissues to heal, and to warn us against repeating such activities, which ultimately increases our chances of survival.

In the past, the sensation of pain would have been much more important and under greater selective pressure. For example, stomach pains caused by eating poisonous fruit would have served to warn early humans of the threat posed by such an activity. Gradually, recognition of dangerous activities would have become either instinctive or easily learned by mimicking parents; without pain, these instincts would not have arisen and humans would be at a constant risk of doing themselves serious harm. However, in the modern age, where medicine is able to cure a huge array of diseases and injuries, how relevant is the sensation of pain?

Although sustained pain has little use nowadays – when we have broken a leg, we know to rest it – pain is still important as a warning, especially in cases where there are no stimuli that are otherwise detectable. For example, when the level of $CO_2$ in an air mixture reaches dangerous levels, it triggers the brain, which alerts us to the fact that we are endangering our health. Were it not for this warning pain, we would be unaware of the danger we face.

However, pain is not always helpful and, in some cases, is completely useless. For example, patients diagnosed with neuralgia suffer sensations of burning pain, although there is no actual stimulus for the pain and the individual concerned is not in any particular danger. Furthermore, pain can often be-come more of a hindrance than a help. For example, if a patient suffers from an illness that gives them a sore throat, they may stop eating properly as a result of the pain. If this continues for long enough, this may eventually lead to malnutrition.

On balance, I would argue that pain carries out too important a function, i.e. as a warning against repetition of a harmful activity, to be considered as doing more harm than good, and still has importance in modern life.

### Examiner's comment

This 365-word essay covers the definition of the quote in the first paragraph, as well as some of the reasons as to why pain is beneficial.

The third paragraph contains a slight scientific simplification. When the levels of $CO_2$ rise in the inspired air, it triggers chemoreceptors in the body to fire more rapidly. This results in an increase in respiration rate. This also signals an uncomfortable feeling of suffocation but not, strictly speaking, pain in the scientific sense.

Remember that the examiners have the ability to check facts with specialists as required. The examiners do not expect the student to know university level respiratory physiology, and this simplification is an easy one to make. In fact, the examiner would be impressed at the level of scientific knowledge already exhibited. As such, it is likely that this sentence will simply be ignored for the purpose of marking. If a fact (or even a quote) were to be completely made up, then more severe penalties would be imposed.

Despite this, the student recovers by outlining the negative aspects of pain in the fourth paragraph. The final paragraph is a good attempt at summarising the issues but feels slightly odd in that it almost presents pain as an option that we could choose to discard if it had lost its importance.

Overall this is a good and well-structured essay but the scientific simplification and the average conclusion let it down.

## Essay 8

**Animal research is a social evil because if it advances human knowledge, it does so at the expense of human character.**

Briefly outline what the above statement means. Explain why it is unethical to experiment on animals. Discuss, giving examples, why it might be seen as acceptable to experiment on animals.

### Essay 8 – Example: Score 4A

Animal research played a vital role in many medical and scientific advances of that past century. Animals however do not have the ability to value life for its own sake; and so are vulnerable to exploitation. Animal research can be said to be a social evil due to the risk to the animal of unnecessary suffering, exploitation and abuse.

Humans cannot assume an automatic superiority or right to make decisions on behalf of animals; instead we should because of their vulnerable nature act as guardians to prevent their sufferings. Our social ethics do not allow us to use humans invasively to advance our knowledge or cure human disease. Animals are sentient creatures that can also experience and suffer pain, and if we cannot tolerate such treatment for humans, how are we supposed to tolerate such treatments for animals?

On the other hand, we have no good alternatives to animal research for some scientific research such as for testing the complex pharmaceutical responses to new medicines. Indeed, all drugs are usually screened in animal models for toxicity, side effects and efficacy that might kill a human test subject.

The suffering of animals whilst being tested can be minimised. In the UK the implementation of the Animals (Scientific Procedures) Act 1986 as well as the local Ethics Review Process gives protection for animals used in scientific purposes, by weighing up the potential benefits and to minimise suffering of animals.

Society at large already relies in a cost-benefit analysis of animal research. It accepts the use of animals in biomedical research; however, it does not tolerate their use in cosmetics testing. In my view, we should adopt a pragmatic attitude that allows animal testing if it causes minimal pain to the animals involved and if all other possible methods have been explored.

### Examiner's comment

The essay clearly addresses all three tasks. In a good presentation, the candidate explains the meaning of the statement, describes the situation of animal research and discusses the justifications and ramifications of such laws.

The candidate uses a subtle style in the second paragraph to develop the central idea that animals are sentient beings that should be protected.

The essay is organised and focused. The use of transitional devices (On the other hand...) allows the marker to flow from one argument to the next.

Occasionally the student draws attention to an issue by the use of rhetorical questions. The conclusion is solid and based on the synthesis of previous arguments.

Overall this is a good essay, though let down by the fact that paragraph 2 is not as developed as it could be. In addition, the candidate could have done more of the fact that tests carried out on animals cannot always be translated to humans. For example, we know that parsley is a poison to parrots and that morphine excites cats. As such, experimentation on animals needs to be shown to be valid and clear boundaries established.

The essay is good, though perhaps slightly run-of-the-mill, hence the score of 4.

## Essay 9

**People should not have private healthcare. It creates a two-tier healthcare system.**

Explain the argument behind this statement. Argue to the contrary, that patients are entitled to spend money on better healthcare if they choose to do so.

### Essay 9 – Example: Score 4.5A

The argument behind this statement is that allowing people to have private healthcare would result in a difference in treatment between those who can afford paying for their own care and those who have no option but to use the NHS. The statement also implies that the NHS provides a lower standard of care than the private sector.

The concept behind the NHS is that everyone should have access to free healthcare. However, the limiting factor is resources, the lack of which results in waiting lists and delays to treatment. As it stands, the NHS is free at point of use, and is paid for by general taxation. The private healthcare system is run separately, and is significantly more expensive, primarily because each individual must pay the actual costs of the services being provided, without any form of subsidy.

By only having the NHS system, free healthcare would be available to all; it would be nationally regulated (thus safer) and would follow guidelines set by the Department of Health. However, it can be argued that people should be allowed to use a private healthcare system if it exists. If people can afford better care than the NHS provides, why should they not be allowed to obtain it at their own expense? One might argue that, by denying them that opportunity, the State infringes on their human rights. In addition, individuals choosing to be treated privately benefit those who stay on the NHS in two ways:

(i) they continue to pay taxes but do not actually use the service that their taxes finance; and

(ii) they free up space within the NHS that can then be utilised by those who need access to NHS services, thereby reducing waiting time.

The current system allows all sections of society to obtain care at a level which is both satisfactory and sustainable. Should individuals who choose private healthcare be allowed to opt out of paying taxes destined to fund the NHS, the situation would be very different. But as long as they are required to finance the care of those who cannot afford private care then the only argument that remains against private healthcare is a moral argument. A good way forward would be to ensure that the NHS can provide a higher standard level of care, and NOT to dumb down the service that the luckier members of society can receive by paying a bit more.

## Examiner's comment

This 403-word essay addresses both tasks thoroughly and substantially.

The essay begins with a discussion of the statement. This first paragraph is characterised by the logical assumptive statement that is required to decode the statement. Many students forget to do this, and thus fail to explain the argument behind the statement. Each paragraph reflects a development of an idea that reflects one of the tasks set. The structure is focused and coherent. The conclusion also offers an interesting perspective, which led one examiner to allocate full mark.

A second examiner only marked the essay 4 because she felt that the student could have explored the meaning of the word healthcare a bit further. A parallel with the situation in dentistry or opticians would have been most appropriate to discuss the concept of fairness.

# Essay 10

**Science is concerned with what is true. Morality is concerned with what is right.**

Explain what the statement means. Argue to the contrary that science helps us to judge what is right. To what extent can decisions about what is right and wrong be informed by science?

## Essay 10 – Example 1: Score 0/1B

Science is about the study of nature: the finding out of scientific truths. Morality is concerned about right and wrong. In summary, this statement is asking whether certain scientific endeavours should be carried out ethically.

The British Scientific Society has released a news release, which stated that "scientific endeavours should always be concerned with its social impact and not just about its scientific impact". Even scientists acknowledge that their research should be within societal limitations.

This can be seen succinctly with the arrest of a Professor Hwang in South Korea who claimed success in stem cell research. It turned out that the eggs that he was experimenting on were from lab researchers, and there was little oversight into his research process, which led to fabrication of data. Such studies will not easily happen again since South Korea has subsequently implemented a ban on such research.

It is always hard to balance the scientific need with the societal acceptance of such research. Such arguments include the cost-benefit model. Nazi doctors experimented on concentration camp prisoners and, despite advancements in medical research that may benefit the rest of society, such invasive research would not be acceptable to society.

This argument can be extended to subtler conflicts such as animal testing, where the benefit of drug testing is balanced with the humane treatment of animals.

In summary, the scientific needs should be balanced with the morality of such research to come to a social acceptance.

---

**Examiner's comment**

Unlike GCSE or A-level markers who are paid by the number of scripts marked, BMAT examiners are paid at an hourly rate. This means that they have the luxury of checking and double-checking all facts presented in a submitted essay. The examiners have access to resources to check statements to ensure that they are not made up. The motto is "if in doubt, check it out", whether they are quotes, statements or scientific arguments. When a suspected falsification is found, the senior examiner will be notified and a penalty is levied. The severity depends on whether this is a scientific fact that is incorrect because a candidate has remembered it wrong or whether the candidate is making things up as in this case with the fictional "British Scientific Society". A completely made-up fact/quote impairs the rest of the essay and is often scored either a 0 or 1. Several cases are caught every year, and examiners are trained to spot such cases.

In any case, the essay does not really address all parts of the question, hence the poor score.

---

## Sample Essay 10 – Example 2: Score 4.5A

Science is an inquiry into the natural, and, fundamentally, a philosophy in the pursuit of truth about how the world works. Morality is a study of our priorities and our rights and is about our duties.

In America, with the Tuskegee Syphilis study, a group of African-Americans were deliberately not given penicillin to treat their syphilis to satisfy the scientific enquiry of the long-term effects of syphilis on the human body.

Such pure dedication to the "scientific truth" has conflicts with the autonomy of the individual. In many such cases the scientific question turns more on "*should* we be doing this study?", rather than the traditional "*can* we do this study?" Science often raises issues that force us to ask ourselves moral questions.

Alan Colman, in a speech, recounted his experience of making "Dolly the sheep". He described his ongoing scientific dilemma: on the one hand his job is to address unmet medical needs but on the other he is against human cloning and thinks it wholly unethical. Such conflicts are not unusual; we, on one hand, have a medical need, but we are also conflicted with the ethical constraints of society. Science does therefore help raise important issues, and helps us think about how we function both physically and morally. It is that very reflective process which enables us to make decisions that balance the need to know the truth with the need to retain a degree of morality.

There is an important cross-talk between the sciences and the arts regarding this very issue of morality and science. Sir David King (previously the UK's chief scientific advisor) has outlined core principles and responsibilities that a researcher should have; in order to consider the impact that their work would have on the society as a whole. With such clearer guidelines on ethical responsibilities of a scientist, experiments such as the Tuskegee Syphilis study would be a thing of the past.

**Examiner's comment**

The student clearly demonstrates an ability to discuss the topic. The organisation of the essay is coherent, though the questions are not clearly addressed in the order in which they were asked, which may cause some confusion (hence the score of 4.5).

The writer uses good examples throughout to back up their argument (Sir David King, Alan Colman) which showcases their general knowledge and analysis of science within society.

# 3C   Writing Task
# 18 Practice Essays

To help you practise writing essays, we have provided 18 further essay titles. In Chapter 3D on page 612, you will find a number of points related to each of the topics given, which may help you approach the essays constructively.

**Q3.1 Doctors should always maintain patient confidentiality and act with probity.** Explain what is meant by the above statement. Why might probity be important in a good doctor? Under what circumstances might an honest doctor be justified in revealing patient details in the course of their professional practice?

**Q3.2 Doctors should always tell the truth and be honest in their dealings.** Explain what is meant by the above statement. Why might telling the truth be important in a good doctor? Under what circumstances might an honest doctor be justified in being less than perfectly truthful in the course of his or her professional practice?

**Q3.3 Developed nations have an obligation to provide aid to the underdeveloped nations of the world.** Explain what you think the above statement means. Describe a specific situation in which a developed nation might not be obligated to provide aid to an underdeveloped nation. Discuss what you think should determine when developed nations have an obligation to provide aid to underdeveloped nations.

**Q3.4 The public's right to information should override the government's need for security.** Explain what you think the above statement means. Describe a specific situation in which the public's right to information might justifiably not override the government's need for security. Discuss what you think determines when the public's right to information should take precedence over the government's need for security.

**Q3.5 In a modern society, individuals should be allowed to do whatever they want.** Explain what the above statement means. Give an example of a situation in which individuals should not be allowed to do as they want. Decide whether or not individuals should be allowed to do as they want in a free society.

**Q3.6 People are getting older and, with the advancement of medicine, they are becoming more expensive to treat. Old people should not be treated on the NHS.** Explain the argument behind this statement. What assumptions does it make? Argue to the contrary that older patients are entitled to be treated on the NHS.

**Q3.7 I have never been ill a day in my life. Why should I pay for someone else's treatment?** Explain the argument behind this statement. What assumptions does it make? Argue to the contrary that people should pay taxes to support the NHS.

**Q3.8 We must not say every mistake is a foolish one – Cicero (106BC – 43BC).** Explain the reasoning behind the statement. Describe a specific situation in which someone might be educated more by positive experience than by mistakes. Discuss what you think determines whether or not one learns more from mistakes.

**Q3.9 Instead of allowing each university to set its own curriculum, a country should require all its medical students to study the same national curriculum until they graduate to become a doctor.** Explain the reasoning behind the statement. Argue to the contrary that countries should not impose a national medical curriculum. To what extent do you agree with the statement?

**Q3.10 Governments should focus on solving the immediate problems of today rather than on trying to solve the anticipated problems of the future.** What do you think is meant by this statement? Argue to the contrary. To what extent do you agree that governments should limit their involvement in trying to solve future anticipated problems?

**Q3.11 University students should base their field of study on the country's need for jobs in that field and not their own interests.** Explain what is meant by this statement. Argue to the contrary. To what extent do you agree that countries should direct a student's future career?

**Q3.12 Teachers' salaries should be based on their students' performance.** Explain what you think is meant by this statement. Argue to the contrary. To what extent do you agree that a student's performance should contribute to their teacher's salary?

**Q3.13 Nations should suspend government funding for the arts when a significant number of their citizens are hungry or unemployed.** Explain what is meant by this statement. Argue to the contrary. To what extent do you agree that it is inappropriate to use public funds to fund arts when people's basic needs are not being met?

**Q3.14 There should be a National Health Service for animals.** Explain the reasoning behind the statement. Argue to the contrary that people should not pay taxes to support an animal NHS. To what extent is an animal NHS required?

**Q3.15 Pets are not human beings. As such, veterinarian clinicians do not face the same ethical situation and, in particular, "convenience euthanasia" is justified.** Explain the reasoning behind the statement. Argue to the contrary that a vet should never agree to such a request. To what extent should pet owners influence the vet's decisions?

**Q3.16 It is acceptable for governments to ban dangerous breeds of dog and order that they should be put down.** Explain the argument behind the statement. Argue to the contrary and discuss possible alternatives to euthanasia. To what extent should governments dictate what we should and should not do?

**Q3.17** **The surest indicator of a great nation is represented not by the achievements of its leaders, artists or scientists, but by how its citizens treat their own animals.** Explain what is meant by this statement. Argue to the contrary. To what extent do you agree that greatness is measured in how humans treat their animals?

**Q3.18** **Society should make efforts to save endangered species only if the potential extinction of those species is the consequence of human activities.** Explain what is meant by this statement. Argue to the contrary that society should only limit their efforts to animals whose habitat is directly affected by human activities. To what extent do you agree with the original statement?

| 3D | Writing Task
Support for Practice Essays |

To help you with each of the essays, we have set out a numbers of points that you might wish to consider as part of your answer. The lists below are purely indicative and are by no means exhaustive.

### Q3.1: Confidentiality
- Doctors have had a duty of confidentiality to patients for centuries (outlined in the Hippocratic Oath).

- Probity is defined as integrity, honesty and decency.

- Confidentiality enables doctor-patient trust and is essential to allow patients to disclose and discuss potentially embarrassing problems.

- Patient confidentiality is a professional duty (according to the GMC).

- Public Health Regulations 1988: Certain notifiable diseases must be notified with local authorities (i.e. Tuberculosis). This is for public health purposes and to prevent further infections.

- Prevention of Terrorism Act 2000: doctors must report to the police any information that may prevent acts of terrorism

- Doctors may, in some cases, be allowed to release details about a patient if that patient poses a serious danger to others. The main issue is to determine how serious the risk needs to be. Should doctors notify the partner(s) of a patient who tested positive for HIV?

- A patient whose confidentiality is breached may stop attending clinics, which may endanger them and, in the case of transmissible illnesses, may be disastrous to public health.

- Discuss the need to balance trust and the protection of others.

## Q3.2: Truthfulness

- Definition of probity, GMC requirements of a doctor and doctor-patient relationships.

- Doctors are entrusted with the lives and health of patients and are accountable for their actions.

- Situations may arise when the doctor cannot be 100% open, e.g. when being honest with relatives would breach the confidentiality of a patient.

- Patients may not be able to cope with the truth. Clinical information if released to a patient may psychologically damage them (i.e. a diagnosis of terminal disease).

- If lying is dishonest, what about withholding information, i.e. lying by omission?

## Q3.3: Aid

- Humanitarianism and altruism are motivations for aid giving.

- Foreign goods flooding a local market may impair/destroy local farming and build dependence on handouts. Consider supporting by purchasing local goods instead.

- Previous involvement of donor country to aid recipient country (i.e. commonwealth country) results in greater political impetus to donate.

- Possible mismatch of aid (e.g. the recipient requires building equipment/financial help, not food)

- Giving aid as food may divert the aid recipient's own money away from food into supporting military budgets, which may then be misused.

- Link between aid and political influence. The recipient may feel obligated and indebted towards the donor.

- Aid may be better given in the form of technological assistance and training rather than through handouts.

## Q3.4: Freedom of information

- It is an extension of freedom of speech; a fundamental human right.

- Debate public interest versus national interest.

- Reasons why freedom of information should not override security include national security, medical confidential information on other people, ongoing police investigations.

- Should increase accountability of government (e.g. MPs' expenses).

- Use examples such as Wikileaks and the release of US diplomatic cables.


## Q3.5: Free will

- Free does not necessarily mean free of boundaries.

- Societies need rules to operate to avoid chaos and criminality.

- Doing what one wants means that others' status is not respected.

- Discuss the issue of freedom of speech or freedom of information in a context where there is no legal obligation or monitoring.

- Argue that too much control can also be counterproductive (e.g. over-regulation stifles creativity and therefore acts against the greater good).

- Conclude on the need to allow freedom but within clearly defined and agreed boundaries.


## Q3.6: The elderly

- Demographics are changing: smaller numbers of younger workforce paying taxes supporting a large elderly population. Older people are net receivers of state aid.

- People have increased longevity due to advances in public health and medicine in general.

- Assumes that medicines are expensive (some medicines will not be in patent any more); assumes that all old people require this expensive medical care; assumes private healthcare sector is large enough to be able to treat the elderly population, and that they have enough money to afford treatment.

- The NHS was founded with no age restrictions.

- Old people have paid taxes previously and contributed to society.

- Define the word "old". Who decides the cut-off point? Not all old people require expensive treatment if public awareness of keeping a healthy lifestyle is increased.

- Older people can contribute actively towards society until an advanced age (e.g. some of them are working beyond retirement age, doing volunteering work)

- If the care of the elderly is self-funded, many may not be able to afford it. Their conditions will deteriorate far more quickly than with publicly funded care. The burden will be carried by relatives and, if the state does eventually fund some of the care, it will cost it more.

## Q3.7: Taxation and healthcare

- The statement is based on a capitalist argument against the NHS. The individual would like to lower taxes so he does not have to fund other people's treatments on the NHS.

- Makes the assumption that rich people actually have cash (many own assets but have little cash) and that he himself will still be wealthy enough when he needs care.

- Discuss the US system where the rich get better treatment. Discuss also the principle of insurance, i.e. you pay a premium in case you need a benefit.

- Arguments in favour of supporting the NHS include:
  - Society needs to support its contributors. Those who generate wealth are not the richest but all the workers and employees who support economic activity.

- Parity between human beings and sense of collective responsibility.

- If people are put off seeking advice and care, they may only come into contact with the health system when they have no further options, meaning that they will be sicker than they might otherwise have been.

## Q3.8: Learning from mistakes

- Everyone makes mistakes in their lives; they are essential for self-improvement and development.

- It builds experience and is part of the learning process. Often life lessons are learnt this way. Mistakes can't be said to be stupid if there are positive lessons to take from them.

- Some mistakes may be considered foolish; for example, those that recur because no lesson was learnt from the first instance they occurred. Mistakes that originate from miscalculated risks or obvious flawed gambles might also be labelled by some as foolish. Often a mistake in scientific research can be costly as it might mean restarting the whole experiment again from scratch. The level of foolishness one might allocate to a mistake could be linked to how predictable and preventable that mistake was.

- Doctors often learn from seeing thousands of patients over the course of their careers, with surgeons learning from motor memory whilst operating. Many people learn simply by practising and through repetition, not just through mistakes. Though mistakes can be a good learning ground, they are not an essential requirement to all personal development.

- Recent research though shows that animals learn from their mistakes and remember it better than from just positive reinforcement.

- The amount of learning one gets from mistakes depends on how much personal reflection is undertaken, how the mistake was made and how it can be attenuated or eliminated the following time.

## Q3.9: Standard national curriculum

- Currently, each university is responsible for examining its medical students using its own syllabus throughout undergraduate training. Standards can then vary across the country. Developing the same national curriculum across the country would mean using a common syllabus and, possibly, common bank of exam questions to assess all medical students. This would reduce variation in standards in newly qualified doctors.

- A standardised system allows for progress to be monitored and assessments to be measurable and comparable on a national scale. Any student who is underperforming or who requires more help can be identified sooner, and measures can be taken as soon as possible.

- Standardisation limits freedom and creativity for both educators and students; the syllabus & assessments are less flexible and less personalised, which may not suit all students.

- A locally set curriculum allows students to choose which medical school suits them best (i.e. traditional vs. integrated courses), or schools that focus on areas of specific interest such as research.

- Standardisation increases pressure and breeds tendency for target-setting culture, which may be overwhelming for both students and educators; too much emphasis on league tables.

- Standards of newly qualified doctors can vary across the country. A national medical curriculum helps all medical students reach a common standard and ultimately improves patient safety. The teaching methods used by educators can be diverse, and each university should also set up its own "mock exams" at regular intervals to ensure standards are met.

## Q3.10: Current vs. future problems

- The purpose of a government is to look after its citizens. This would include both immediate problems (e.g. terrorism, natural disasters, inflation) and future problems (e.g. threats to stability).

- Governments have limited budgets and may need to prioritise current problems; e.g. in cases of natural disasters such as flooding, government resources should be used for damage control including rescuing those who are trapped in flooded areas, providing temporary shelter and food for those who have lost their homes, providing better ambulance service to help the injured, etc.

- Spending resources on problems that may or may not happen in the future may seem like a waste of time and money and citizens may find it difficult to understand why money is being spent on areas that do not require immediate attention. For example, is it sensible to spend money on a high-speed rail link, which may bring benefits years down the line, when there are immediate issues to sort out such as poverty or the need to recruit more people within the NHS?

- Prevention is better than cure. Taking flooding as an example (as above), better planning should take place to prevent future floods, e.g. build better drainage systems and dams. More money may be wasted later if proactive preventative action is not taken earlier.

- Conclusion: A government should be able to prioritise and multi-task as well as work efficiently to deal with both immediate (usually unexpected) problems and also problems that may occur in the future. A government should not limit its involvement in trying to solve future anticipated problems as prevention is a cheaper and more effective way to avoid chaos in a country. However, this needs to be accompanied by careful communication and management of expectations so that the population understands the purpose of the decisions that are being taken.

## Q3.11: Choosing study fields in line with national need

- Choosing a field of study is a delicate, difficult and potentially life-changing decision. Some students consider their own interests, talents and skills, while others base their choice on the employment opportunities in that field in the country, neglecting their own interests.

- Choosing a field of study based on national need will increase the prospects of getting a job and will also ensure that all needs are covered. Also studying for a university degree is expensive and most students have heavy debts (e.g. student loans) to pay off so job security and earning a decent wage are important.

- Choosing a field in which one is not particularly interested may lead to lack of motivation and lack of passion; this itself leads to poorer educational performance. It will also lead to a "what if" feeling, whereby students wonder whether they have made the right choice.

- Lack of interest can lead to lower retention rates, where students will switch to other fields of study, making them unlikely to graduate in 3 or 4 years with a standard degree and increasing the cost of their education.

- Availability of jobs changes all the time depending on many factors, e.g. economy, industry and politics; hence the job market can be unpredictable.

- Careful and thoughtful selection is key. An awareness of one's own capabilities is also important. The choice of field of study should not be solely based on interest or a country's need for jobs alone, but a combination of both factors, fulfilling material (job security, stable wage, ability to pay off debts) and spiritual (passion, interest, motivation, happier lifestyle) needs.

- Gaining transferable skills through studying a university degree (e.g. team working, leadership, problem solving, time management, critical thinking skills) may be more valuable than the actual degree itself. These allow students to apply for a wide range of jobs post-graduation.

## Q3.12 – Basing teacher's pay on student performance

- The idea of teachers' performance pay has been growing in interest for the past decade in countries such as the USA and UK, and has been implemented in certain schools. This model was actually used in the UK in the mid-1800s for more than 30 years, but abandoned due to public opposition, increased rates of cheating, etc.

- Teachers would be directly incentivised to improve students' grades; this should lead to students becoming better educated and therefore more successful as adults. It may also improve employment rates.

- It offers fair reward to teachers who invest more effort into making their students succeed.

- It may lead to unfair selection by schools. Selecting the more success-ful students and refusing access to those who struggle would lead to a very elitist system where only those with good potential receive educa-tion. This may make matters worse in areas where the population is already less educated.

- Performance would need to be defined precisely. It would require standardised testing/curriculum nationwide for fair comparison. There is also a danger that performance is purely defined in terms of measur-able targets and that students are merely taught to pass exams instead of acquiring other equally important interpersonal skills.

- Teachers would need more mentoring, support, supervision and train-ing in new techniques. Though this may improve results, it may also require a substantial investment in time and money.

- This approach may improve the overall standard in schools to an ex-tent, but may also cause teachers to work in isolation due to increased competition.

- Alternative methods to improve teacher effectiveness should be ex-plored such as reducing class size, providing teachers with more time to plan classes, and better mentoring scheme for teachers to help with their professional and personal development.

## Q3.13 – Funding of art in periods of greater need

- Arts play an important role in a country's culture and history; hence government provides funding to develop the arts, e.g. building museums, cinemas, theatres, historical sites. Art budgets are often limited in recognition of the fact that there are matters which may be regarded by the general public as more pressing.

- The government has the duty to enrich and preserve the culture and history of a country. It is important that people learn about their culture and history.

- Art also attracts tourism, bringing money into a country and boosting the economy. It also enhances people's quality of life.

- Art is often regarded as a luxury reserved for a certain elite. As such it may be seen to benefit only a small portion of the population. However, it can be counterargued that, in countries like the UK, much of the funding is actually spent on ensuring free access to museums.

- No country will ever be able to claim that it is fully providing for the basic needs of all its citizens. There will also be a degree of deprivation and unemployment everywhere, and waiting for total eradication of those issues before investing in projects deemed a luxury is impractical.

- Withholding funding from art will mean a depletion of the pool of artists residing in the country. This will make it difficult to invest and develop the arts when better times come. As such, there should be a degree of balance.

## Q3.14: Animal NHS

- We should look after animals, since they are bred for our companionship and control.

- Currently owners pay for the care needed for their pets. There are insurance schemes available but these can also be expensive. Extending insurance schemes to all owners would effectively act as an NHS for pets.

- Discuss the different types of people who own pets. They are on different places on the income spectrum. The current system means that poorer owners may struggle to pay vet bills, or may sacrifice some of their own lifestyle and health to pay for their pets' care.

- Discuss the difficulties in implementing such a system. Who should fund the NHS for pets? Pet owners only or everyone? How do you differentiate between those who own goldfish and those who own horses? How does one differentiate between owners who treat their pets well and those who don't?

- Argue whether the money spent on a pet NHS might be better spent on treating humans: for example some expensive chemotherapy treatments which are not currently approved for use by NICE due to their costs. In the third world the same amount of money could provide water and food for millions of people. Are the lives of dogs and cats equivalent to people's lives?

- Discuss the role of charities in caring for animals currently.

- Discuss the extent to which the existence of an animal NHS might influence behaviours. For example, owners may be less careful if they know that care is available for free at point of delivery. At the other end, it may also mean that animals that may have had to be put down or left to die because the owners could not afford their care may now be allowed to live.

## Q3.15: Convenience euthanasia

- Argue that the animal protection services euthanise hundreds of animals per year due to lack of space or for rehousing. Some animals are culled because they are too numerous or may harm, e.g. foxes, rats, badgers and rabbits in some countries.

- The argument rests on the fact that human life is superior to animal life.

- We exploit animals and make them dependent on humans for housing and food, thus we should be responsible for their care as well.

- Discuss what is a human? What about a comatose man on life support. A foetus? What would constitute humanness or life? Part of being human makes you inherently compassionate.

- Veterinarian clinicians have a duty of care to their patients, who, though not humans, expect their carers not to harm them.

- Humans may pay vets, but this should not give them the power to put down perfectly healthy animals for purely convenience reasons.

- Argue that if the customer's request is refused by a vet, they may go on to abuse the animal or kill it themselves in inhumane conditions.

- Some people may not be able to afford to keep a pet any longer. Forcing them to keep the pet may have negative consequences. Having said that, there may be alternatives, e.g. by getting the pets housed through charities instead.

## Q3.16: Dog ban and government interference

- Certain breeds of dogs are violent and pose a danger to other animals or humans.

- Governments have the priorities of public safety in mind. They provide policing and fire safety, and they are in the best position to judge whether an animal is safe or not. People are not allowed to keep lions for themselves as pets due to safety concerns, and dangerous dogs are no different.

- How do we define dangerous? Most would argue that some breeds are more predisposed to aggression than others but this is often evidenced through anecdotes only. Does the fact that two people are bitten by dogs of the same breed justify a ban and automatic euthanasia? What about situations where "standard" animals have become violent to-wards members of the public? Often the animal is put down but the breed as a whole is not put into question.

- How can we differentiate whether an animal is dangerous because of a trait inherent to the breed or because of the way they were trained by their owners?

- Is it right to put down a healthy animal who may be seen as dangerous through no fault of its own? After all, we protect dangerous animals such as lions. Is there not a case for simple ring-fencing dangerous animals in special places rather than simply killing them?

- Other than allowing those animals to live in reservations, alternatives could include imposing a licensing system and the wearing of a muzzle.

- The purpose of government is to establish boundaries within which we can operate as a society. Those boundaries are important but too many restrictions can impair personal freedom and choice, productivity and creativity, and can also build resentment. Having said that, when per-sonal freedom starts interfering with the safety and well-being of others, there may be a case for government intervention.

## Q3.17: Great nation

- People generally judge the greatness of a nation by the living conditions of the citizens, purchasing power and influence in the world. The achievements and success of certain citizens, e.g. artists and scientists, represent not the majority but only a minority of the population, and therefore cannot be used as a reliable indicator.

- Citizens who have animals and treat them well (e.g. providing animals with food, shelter, healthcare, beauty care, entertainment) tend to be educated, employed, self-sufficient and satisfied with life. Those who own animals and treat them well may be more caring individuals. On the other hand, some of them may also be more introverted individuals who are more interested in animal contact than human contact.

- Breakthroughs in science and technology (e.g. better medical treatment for diseases, reusable energy) can be used to improve the living conditions and general welfare of people, and in turn determine how great a nation is.

- The key to this argument is to define what the term "great nation" actually means. This will mean different things to different people and, as such, an ability to care for animals is as good a measure as anything. But it is just measuring one aspect of greatness.

## Q3.18: Endangered species

- Human activities have resulted in disturbance of the ecosystem and disruptions in food chains, resulting in widespread losses of species. Thus it makes sense that humans should take responsibility to ensure that such species are preserved.

- Human beings, being the smartest of all species, should work hard to protect endangered species and maintain environmental balance using advanced technology, which we are equipped with. Advanced technology developed by human beings can be used to detect diseases or mutations that wipe out certain species, or can breed species and provide artificial habitat to help them thrive and prevent their extinction.

- Human activity is not the only cause for extinction of certain species. Charles Darwin has offered the theory of "survival of the fittest". There are times when natural causes cause species to become extinct, e.g. competition for food and light. It is beyond society's responsibility to prevent such natural causes from taking place. To interfere with nature could throw our world out of balance.

- By definition, species that are endangered have little impact on the environment since there are few animals present. Spending limited resources on a few animals may be seen as a luxury, particularly if society has more pressing needs.

# MEDICAL SCHOOL INTERVIEWS
## ISBN: 978-1-905812-05-9

**AVAILABLE IN MOST BOOKSHOPS
AND AT WWW.ISCMEDICAL.CO.UK**